Recommended Reference Books
for Small and Medium-Sized Libraries and Media Centers

American Reference Books Annual
Advisory Board

RECOMMENDED REFERENCE BOOKS

for Small and Medium-Sized Libraries and Media Centers

Volume 37

2017 Edition

Juneal M. Chenoweth, Associate Editor

LIBRARIES
UNLIMITED™

An Imprint of ABC-CLIO, LLC

Santa Barbara, California • Denver, Colorado

LIBRARIES UNLIMITED
An Imprint of ABC-CLIO, LLC
130 Cremona Drive
P.O. Box 1911
Santa Barbara, California 93116-1911
www.abc-clio.com

Library of Congress Cataloging-in-Publication Data

Main entry under title:

Recommended reference books for small and medium-sized
libraries and media centers.

"Selected from the 2017 edition of American
reference books annual."
   Includes index.
   I. Reference books--Bibliography. 2. Reference
services (Library)--Handbooks, manuals, etc.
3. Instructional materials centers--Handbooks,
manuals, etc. I. Chenoweth, Juneal M.
II. American reference books annual.
Z1035.1.R435 011'.02 81-12394
ISBN 978-1-4408-5661-7
ISSN 0277-5948

Contents

Preface

Here is the interesting and challenging landscape for reference resources today. On the one hand, we clearly see the reference book diminished in the work of students, and the priorities of libraries. Going or gone are the vast collections of bound volumes in designated reference reading rooms. The disruptive element of course is technology: instantaneous access to online information. And reference seems to be the loser.

On the other hand, technology makes reference activity a winner too, but so seamlessly that the connection to old-fashioned reference work can be overlooked. All of us enjoy and use online tools to find airline ticket prices and flight schedules, weather forecasts and current conditions, currency exchange rates, stock prices, hotel and restaurant reviews, street maps, and foreign language translators. In the past we turned to print tools to meet these needs, with less convenience and less currency. Thanks to technology, we now have alternatives that match, and often surpass, yesterday's print reference works: timetables, weather almanacs, financial reports, tourist guidebooks, atlases, and bilingual dictionaries. So if reference is alive and well, but living under another name, where is the crisis? Which is to say, where is the change taking place?

Scholars have defined reference works in administrative, descriptive, and functional terms. The administration definition was something like this: "a reference book is a book located in a non-circulating reference collection." Today, we no longer focus on printed books (though we may work with their e-book descendants), and resource access is no longer confined to a specific place. The descriptive definition has been more durable: a reference work incorporates elements of organization and presentation that reflect and promote its intended use ... consultation as quickly and easily as possible. Hence subject indexes, alphabetical order for entries, or numerical coding, as well as newer features like cross-reference hot links. The functional definition perhaps has held up the best: while many sources can conceivably be used to answer a "reference question," a reference work is created for that purpose, and its form (those elements in the descriptive definition) follows that function. As long as readers seek information, that function has value.

Nor have the characteristics of "good" reference tools changed: when we want information, we want information that is accurate, objective, authoritative, current, and complete, as well as reliably accessible, clearly presented, and easily understood. Online reference sources meet these requirements just as thoroughly as do print-format classics like the *Oxford English Dictionary*, the *World Book*, the *National Geographic World Atlas*, or the *Statistical Abstract of the United States* (all of which have expanded to online versions).

One final element makes modern life tough for reference: the general discounting of authority. Reference tools rely on the notion that important information is stable and therefore can be discovered, described, and evaluated. Behind the pursuit of "facts" to answer a reference query is an assumption that "facts" exist, that one answer is true and "best," that the "right" answer is available to us, and that reasonable people will agree about the "correct" answer when they see it. We may expect to argue about the best 10 American novels, but we expect to agree about the melting temperature of copper. In a world of relativism, conspiracy theories and Heisenberg's uncertainty principle, not only are authorities in doubt, but even the facts themselves. And without the concept of correct facts, reference has no leg to stand on.

It is encouraging to see this aphorism widely quoted: "Everyone is entitled to his own opinion, but not to his own facts." When most of us can agree about facts, reference can thrive. Incidentally, this quotation itself illustrates the reference value of truth-seeking and fact-checking. Generally attributed to Daniel Patrick Moynihan, the *Dictionary of Modern Proverbs* (Yale, 2012) also documents similar statements extending back to Bernard Baruch in 1946.

If there are four participants in the ecology of reference—readers, authors, publishers, and librarians—then perhaps it is fair to say that two are leading and two are catching up. Readers still have plenty of questions to answer, and authors still eagerly turn out resources to meet that need. The challenges seem greatest for publishers and librarians, as value-added contributions shift from presentation in print to presentation in online form.

—Steven W. Sowards, Michigan State University Libraries

Introduction

We are pleased to provide you with volume 37 of *Recommended Reference Books for Small and Medium-Sized Libraries and Media Centers* (RRB), a far-reaching review service for reference books and electronic resources designed to assist smaller libraries in the systematic selection of suitable reference materials for their collections. As Steven Sowards points out in the preface, the reference landscape has changed considerably since the publication of RRB's first volume in 1981. Reference users no longer need to spend hours in a library consulting bound volumes, microfiche, or microfilm when much sought-after information is available online. As the preface also highlights, this easy accessibility does not eliminate the need for well-curated, professionally produced reference material and the guidance of trained librarians.

RRB reviews both subscription-based and free websites, as well as dictionaries, encyclopedias, indexes, directories, bibliographies, guides, concordances, atlases, gazetteers, and other types of ready-reference tools. Generally, encyclopedias that are updated annually, yearbooks, almanacs, indexing and abstracting services, and other annuals or serials are reviewed at editorially determined intervals. Reviews of updated publications attempt to point out changes in scope or editorial policy and comparisons to older editions.

This volume of RRB contains unabridged reviews chosen from the current edition of *American Reference Books Annual* (ARBA) and ARBAonline. These have been written by scholars, practitioners, and library educators in all subject specialties at libraries and universities throughout the United States and Canada. All titles in this volume are coded with letters that provide suggested selection guidance for smaller college libraries (C), public libraries (P), or school media centers (S). Although all titles in RRB are recommended acquisitions, critical comments have not been deleted. Reviewers are asked to examine books and electronic resources and provide well-documented critical comments, both positive and negative. Coverage usually includes the usefulness of a given work; organization, execution, and pertinence of contents; prose style; format; availability of supplementary materials (e.g., indexes, appendixes); and similarity to other works and previous editions.

RRB 2017 consists of 37 chapters, an Author/Title index, and a Subject Index. It is divided into four alphabetically arranged parts: "General Reference Works," "Social Sciences," "Humanities," and "Science and Technology." "General Reference Works" is subdivided by form: almanacs, bibliography, biography, and so on. Within the remaining three parts, chapters are organized by topic. Thus, under "Social Sciences" the reader will find chapters titled "Economics and Business," "Education," "History," "Law," "Sociology," and so on.

Each chapter is subdivided to reflect the arrangement strategy of the entire volume. There is a section on general works followed by a topical breakdown. For example, in the chapter titled "Literature," "General Works" is followed by "Children's and Young Adult Literature" and "National Literature." Subsections are based on the amount of material available on a given topic and vary from year to year.

Users should keep in mind that many materials may fall under several different chapter topics. The comprehensive Author/Title and Subject indexes found at the end of the volume will assist users in finding specific works that could fall under several different chapters. Additionally, readers seeking out reviews of digital resources can find these quickly using the Website and Database Review Locator.

   In closing, we wish to express our gratitude to the many talented contributors without whose support this volume of ARBA could not have been compiled. Many thanks also go out to our distinguished Advisory Board members whose contributions greatly enhance ARBA and ARBAonline. We would also like to thank the members of our staff who were instrumental in its preparation.

Contributors

Anthony J. Adam, Director, Institutional Assessment, Blinn College, Brenham, Tex.

January Adams, Asst. Director/Head of Adult Services, Franklin Township Public Library, Somerset, N.J.

Karen Alexander, Library Media Specialist, Lake Fenton High School, Linden, Mich.

Adrienne Antink, Medical Group Management Association, Lakewood, Colo.

Thomas E. Baker, Assoc. Professor, Department of Criminal Justice, Univ. of Scranton, Pa.

Augie E. Beasley, Retired Media Specialist, Charlotte, N.C.

Michael Francis Bemis, Asst. Librarian, Washington County Library, Woodbury, Minn.

Laura J. Bender, Librarian, Univ. of Arizona, Tucson.

Claire Berg, Information and Technology Literacy Specialist, Riverview Elementary School, Farmington, Minn.

Barbara M. Bibel, Reference Librarian, Science/Business/Sociology Dept., Main Library, Oakland Public Library, Calif.

Peg Billing, District Librarian, Tomahawk School District, Wisc.

Alicia Brillon, Reference Librarian, James E. Faust Law Library, Univ. of Utah.

Georgia Briscoe, Assoc. Director and Head of Technical Services, Law Library, Univ. of Colorado, Boulder.

Kim Brown, Library Media Specialist, North Reading High School, North Reading, Mass.

John R. Burch Jr., Dean of Distance Learning and Library Services, Campbellsville Univ., Ky.

Joanna M. Burkhardt, Head Librarian, College of Continuing Education Library, Univ. of Rhode Island, Providence.

Theresa Calcagno, IT & Engineering Librarian, George Mason Univ., Fairfax, Va.

Delilah R. Caldwell, Online Services Librarian and Adjunct Instructor, Southwestern College, Winfield, Kans.

Emily Cassady, Educational Reviewer, Dallas, Tex.

Bert Chapman, Government Publications Coordinator, Purdue Univ., West Lafayette, Ind.

Boyd Childress, Reference Librarian, Ralph B. Draughon Library, Auburn Univ., Ala.

Rosanne M. Cordell, (formerly) Head of Reference Services, Franklin D. Schurz Library, Indiana Univ., South Bend.

Gregory A. Crawford, Head of Public Services, Penn State Harrisburg, Middletown, Pa.

Gregory Curtis, Regional Federal Depository Librarian for Maine, New Hampshire, and Vermont, Fogler Library, Univ. of Maine, Presque Isle.

James D'annibale, Technology & Learning Commons Librarian, Wilson College, Chambersburg, Pa.

Linda DeVore, Media Center Director, Casa Grande (Arizona) Middle School.

Chris Dexter, 7th Grade English Teacher, East Valley Middle School, East Helena, Mont.

Scott R. DiMarco, Director of Library Services and Information Resources, Mansfield Univ., Mansfield, Pa.

Joe P. Dunn, Charles A. Dana Professor of History and Politics, Converse College, Spartanburg, S.C.

Bradford Lee Eden, Dean of Library Services, Valparaiso Univ., Valparaiso, Ind.

Sheri Edwards, Assistant University Librarian, Florida Atlantic Univ., Boca Raton.

Lorraine Evans, Social Science Research and Instruction Librarian, Univ. of Colorado, Denver.

Kay E. Evey, Retired Teacher-Librarian, Tukwila Elementary School, Tukwila, Wash.

Autumn Faulkner, Asst Head of Cataloging and Metadata Services, Michigan State Univ. Libraries, East Lansing.

Josh Eugene Finnell, Reference Librarian, Ohio.

Cynthia Foster, Librarian/Media Specialist, Chillicothe R-II High School, Chillicothe, Mo.

Brian T. Gallagher, Access Services Librarian, Head of Access Services, Univ. of Rhode Island, Kingston.

Kasey Garrison, Lecturer & Children's Specialization Coordinator, Charles Sturt Univ., Sydney, NSW, Australia.

Caroline L. Gilson, Coordinator, Prevo Science Library, DePauw Univ., Greencastle, Ind.

Christine Graves, Educational Reviewer, Downers Grove, Ill.

Deb Grove, Retired Library Media Specialist, Omaha, Neb.

Michael W. Handis, Assoc. Librarian for Collection Management, CUNY Graduate Center, N.Y.

Ralph Hartsock, Senior Music Catalog Librarian, Univ. of North Texas, Denton.

Muhammed Hassanali, Independent Consultant, Shaker Heights, Ohio.

Lucy Heckman, Reference Librarian (Business-Economics), St. John's Univ. Library, Jamaica, N.Y.

Mark Y. Herring, Dean of Library Services, Winthrop Univ., Dacus Library, Rock Hill, S.C.

Ladyjane Hickey, Reference Librarian, Austin College, Tex.

Jonathan F. Husband, Program Chair of the Library/Reader Services Librarian, Henry Whittemore Library, Framingham State College, Mass.

Kyla M. Johnson, NBCT Librarian, Farmington (New Mexico) High School.

Melissa M. Johnson, Reference Services, NOVA Southeastern Univ., Alvin Sherman Library, Ft. Lauderdale, Fla.

Bernadette Kearney, Teacher-Librarian, J.R. Masterman School, Philadelphia, Pa.

Donna J Kearns, Professor, Psychology Department, Univ. of Central Oklahoma, Edmond.

Craig Mury Keeney, Cataloging Librarian, South Caroliniana Library, Univ. of South Carolina.

Andrea C Kepsel, Health Sciences Educational Technology Librarian, Michigan State Univ. Libraries, East Lansing.

Amy Koehler, Support Services Librarian, Moody Bible Institute, Chicago, Ill.

Lori D. Kranz, Freelance Editor, Chambersburg, Pa.

Martha Lawler, Assoc. Librarian, Louisiana State Univ., Shreveport.

Shelly Lee, National Board Certified Library Media Specialist, Central Junior High, Moore, Okla.

Richard Nathan Leigh, Metadata & Digital Resources Developer, Ball State Univ. Libraries, Muncie, Ind.

Judyth Lessee, Head Librarian, Schutz American School, Alexandria, Egypt.

Robert M. Lindsey, Instruction and Reference Librarian, Pittsburg State Univ., Pittsburg, Kans.

Megan W. Lowe, Reference/Instruction Librarian, Univ. Library, Univ. of Louisiana at Monroe.

Tyler Manolovitz, Digital Resources Coordinator, Sam Houston State Univ.<197>Newton Gresham Library, Huntsville, Tex.

Kathleen McBroom, Coordinator, Compensatory Education and School Improvement, Dearborn (Michigan) Public Schools.

Peter H. McCracken, Library Technical Services, Cornell Univ.

Kevin McDonough, Reference and Electronic Resources Librarian, Northern Michigan Univ.<197>Olson Library, Marquette.

Jessica Crossfield McIntosh, Reference Services Coordinator, Asst. Professor, Otterbein Univ., Westerville, Ohio.

Susan C. McNair, NBPTS Librarian, Birchwood School, Columbia, S.C.

Lawrence Joseph Mello, Asst. Reference and Instruction Librarian, Florida Atlantic Univ., Boca Raton.

Christina Miller, High School Librarian, Instructor, York College (CUNY), Jamaica, N.Y.

Janis Minshull, Library Consultant, Phippsburg, Maine.

Sara Mofford, Youth Services Librarian, Catawba County Library System, Newton, N.C.

Lisa Morgan, Librarian I, Pasco County Library System, Zephyrhills, Fla.

Theresa Muraski, Associate Professor, Univ. of Wisconsin-Stevens Point, Stevens Point.

Madeleine Nash, Reference/Instruction Librarian, Molloy College, Rockville Center, N.Y.

Lawrence Olszewski, Director, OCLC Library and Information Center, Dublin, Ohio.

Amy B. Parsons, Metadata Librarian/Assoc. Professor, Courtright Memorial Library, Otterbein College, Westerville, Ohio.

Rares G. Piloiu, Information Literacy Librarian, Otterbein Univ., Westerville, Ohio.

Tina Qin, Chemistry Librarian, Michigan State Univ. Libraries, East Lansing.

Jack Ray, Asst. Director, Loyola/Notre Dame Library, Baltimore, Md.

Kali A. Rippel, Librarian, Las Positas College Library, Livermore, Calif.

Bruce Sarjeant, Reference, Documents & Maps Librarian, Northern Michigan Univ., Marquette.

Michaela Schied, Librarian, Indian River Middle School, Philadelphia, N.Y.

Mark Schumacher, Art and Humanities Librarian, Univ. of North Carolina, Greensboro.

Ralph Lee Scott, Professor, Assistant Head of Special Collections for Public Services, and Curator of Printed Books and Maps, East Carolina Univ. Library, Greenville, N.C.

William Shakalis, Assistant Librarian, Worcester State Univ., Worcester, Mass.

Ravindra Nath Sharma, Dean of Library, Monmouth Univ. Library, West Long Branch, N.J.

Stephen J. Shaw, Library Director, Antioch Univ. Midwest, Yellow Springs, Ohio.

Brian J. Sherman, Head of Access Services and Systems, Noel Memorial Library, Louisiana State Univ., Shreveport.

Breezy Silver, Collection Coordinator and Business Reference Librarian, Michigan State Univ. Libraries, East Lansing.

Todd Simpson, Assistant Professor/Catalog Librarian, York College, CUNY, Jamaica, N.Y.

Holly Skir, Librarian, York College, The City Univ. of New York..

Kay Stebbins Slattery, Coordinator Librarian, Louisiana State Univ., Shreveport.

Karen M. Smith, Head of Children's Services, Livonia Public Library, Livonia, Mich.

Mary Ellen Snodgrass, Freelance Writer, Charlotte, N.C.

Steven W. Sowards, Asst. Director for Collections, Michigan State Univ. Libraries, East Lansing.

John P. Stierman, Reference Librarian, Western Illinois Univ., Macomb.

Jianna Taylor, Teacher, Orchard Lake Middle School, West Bloomfield, Mich.

J. E. Weaver, Dept. of Economics, Drake Univ., Des Moines, Iowa.

Karen T. Wei, Head, Asian Library, Univ. of Illinois, Urbana.

W. Cole Williamson, Instruction Librarian, Sam Houston State Univ., Huntsville, Tex.

Angela Wojtecki, District Library Media Speicalist, Nordonia Hills City Schools, Macedonia, Ohio.

Julienne L. Wood, Head, Research Services, Noel Memorial Library, Louisiana State Univ., Shreveport.

Jessica Zubik, Youth & Teen Services Librarian, Chelsea District Library, Chelsea, Mich.

Website and Database Review Locator

Reference is to entry number.

Part I
GENERAL
REFERENCE
WORKS

1 General Reference Works

Almanacs

C, P, S

1. **The World Almanac and Book of Facts 2017.** New York, Infobase Publishing, 2017. 1008p. illus. index. $34.95. ISBN 13: 978-1-60057-206-7.

Now in its 150th year, *The World Almanac and Book of Facts* remains a core resource for libraries and for researchers. The 2017 edition continues the excellence of the series and is a compendium of statistics from the memorable year of 2016. Of special interest are the results of the 2016 U.S. elections, as presented in the year in review section. The editors have provided a good narrative of the presidential election while also giving a breakdown of the 2016 and 2012 votes by state and county. In addition, the results of senatorial, representative, and gubernatorial races are reported. The remainder of the year in review gives a chronology of events (from November 1, 2015 to October 31, 2016), obituaries of significant individuals who died during the year, key congressional activities, U.S. Supreme Court decisions, notable quotes, and historical anniversaries. The bulk of the work provides updated statistics from nine realms: economy, business, and energy; health and vital statistics; personalities, arts, and awards; science and technology; consumer information; U.S. history, government, and population; world history and culture; nations of the world; and sports. The sports section includes special information from the 2016 Summer Olympic Games held in Brazil. This is an indispensable ready reference tool and should be on the reference shelves of every school, public, and academic library.—**Gregory A. Crawford**

Dictionaries and Encyclopedias

S

2. **Britannica School Online. http://school.eb.com/.** [Website] Chicago, Encyclopaedia Britannica, 2015. Price negotiated by site. Date reviewed: 2016.

Britannica School Online gives students access to encyclopedia and magazine articles, images, videos, and websites. In addition to simple keyword search, the database offers interactive games, a virtual atlas, and research planning sheets. Teachers can find lesson plans and Common Core Standards. Labeled Elementary, Middle, and High School, the database can be adjusted to one of those three levels. It is fairly easy to navigate and has a breadth of topics. However, students will need to sift through results to find the most relevant. The Elementary and Middle options are preferred; the High School database fulfills the research needs of students with slightly higher-level reading skills, but does not challenge the student who requires articles from scholarly journals. It may be useful in high schools with struggling readers or special needs students. Even with these minor drawbacks, this is an excellent choice for school librarians looking for a comprehensive resource for differentiated instruction.—**Bernadette Kearney**

Directories

C, P, S

3.   **Find a Grave. www.findagrave.com/.** [Website] Free. Date reviewed: 2017.

    This site invites users to search for the burial places of millions of deceased, both the ordinary and the famous. There are no bells and whistles on this site, just a listing of a good variety of clickable search and browse possibilities, such as birth date or death date, location, cemetery, and more. Material on the site is included under five umbrella categories: Find Famous Graves, Find Graves, a new Transcribe Graves category, a recently updated Questions and Answers category, and Forums, Store, etc. Among other things, users can examine photos, add burial records, and leave virtual "flowers" should they find an entry for a loved one. Entries are user-created and so the information varies, but it may include cemetery location, birth date, death date, and photographs. Famous graves generally include biographies. Each entry has a Find A Grave memorial number for reference.

    It is important to note the presence of advertisements which also contain search fields that may direct users to completely different sites.

    With its vast database, this site would appeal to many users from the serious researcher to the casually curious browser.—**ARBA Staff Reviewer**

Websites and Databases

S

4.   **PBS Video Collection.** [Website] Alexandria, Va., Alexander Street Press, 2016. Price negotiated by site. Date reviewed: 2016.

    This is a selection of 245 videos of various lengths culled from PBS documentaries, weekly programs, and series. Disciplines range from art & design, diversity, and health sciences to history, literature and language, personal interest, science, and engineering. Through the advanced search feature users can narrow down videos by title, producer, running time, and year. Many of the videos are fairly recent, most from within the last five years. One helpful feature is the simultaneous display of a transcript for each video. A quick search of YouTube found none of these titles available for free. However, PBS is now offering "free" streaming access to many titles with a donation. I had trouble searching on my workstation, though the iPad interface worked better. I recommend requesting a trial to experience the database for yourself.—**Judyth Lessee**

C, P, S

5. **Pew Research Global Attitudes Project. http://www.pewglobal.org/.** [Website] Free. Date reviewed: 2017.

This page from the greater Pew Research Center site offers a global review of current events and driving issues gleaned from Pew's own rigorous data collection and analysis. The page combines a series of extensive reports with a selection of more condensed topical and/or interactive posts which enable users to study the information in a variety of ways.

Users can simply scroll through the posts to find their topics of interest, which cover religion, economy, government corruption, refugees, international relations, and much more. They can also conduct a basic keyword search or search poll questions. The substantial Survey Reports and Multi-Section Reports feature downloadable topic-focused and timely work complete with table of contents. The featured post, "What it Takes to Truly Be 'One of Us'" focuses on attitudes of nationalism. The Fact Tank hosts briefer blog posts analyzing individual data points extracted from Pew's research. Some recent posts describe such things as how global millennials feel about national identity or how international migrants move throughout the globe. Reports and posts are tagged for ease of reference.

All of the material is reflective of the data collected by Pew's wide-ranging Global Attitudes Study (2016) or separate targeted Pew queries. The site also organizes posts along Europe-specific research or media appearances of Pew research, and includes interactive maps, quizzes, and individual country surveys.

Applying its rigorous research capabilities toward some of the most compelling concerns across the globe today, and offering a number of ways to access and use the information, *Pew Global Attitudes and Trends* is a site with appeal across a number of disciplines.—**ARBA Staff Reviewer**

C, P, S

6. **Smithsonian Learning Lab. https://learninglab.si.edu/.** [Website] Free. Date reviewed: 2017.

This free site enables users to capitalize on the vast collections of the venerable Smithsonian Institute and use its resources in a variety of innovative ways. Simply structured, the site asks users to choose from three main tabs. Discover helps users explore the possibilities of over one million multimedia resources, such as videos, digital artifacts, blog posts, digital specimens, and artworks. Create allows users to make their own customized collection from these resources. Users can annotate their collection and upload their own resources as well. Share prompts users to adapt their collection for classroom work, disseminate it through social media, and more. A series of straightforward video tutorials guides users through each process. Users must register with the site in order to save and share their work. Supplementary features include Staff Picks, which highlight some of the more intriguing user-generated collections, and News Updates, providing general information about the Smithsonian Learning Lab, including awards and outreach projects. This site will thoroughly engage students across a broad age-range and greatly appeal to educators of numerous subjects.—**ARBA Staff Reviewer**

S

7.   **World Book Online.** [Website] Chicago, World Book, 2015. Price negotiated by site. Date reviewed: 2016.

World Book Online is a suite of digital tools that includes an encyclopedia, atlas, dictionary, digital learning tools, interactive activities, study aids, and curriculum guides. Information is offered on three levels: Kids, Student, and Advanced; each with grade-appropriate support and digital media that includes pictures, video, and maps, links to websites, and games. Kids presents interactive opportunities for learning and exploration geared to early and mid-elementary; Student focuses on middle-level learners with information organized into easy-to-locate areas. A well-defined research center guides students through the research process. Advanced features include primary sources, world newspapers, today in history, online book archive, and other tools. Pathfinders and research guides allow search and exploration to suit student needs. Searching is user-friendly and simplified for student success; illustrations and graphics within all levels are interactive. The range of materials offers easy integration into all learning environments and classroom activities, while engaging students through inquiry-based learning. Recommended.—**Peg Billing**

Part II
SOCIAL SCIENCES

2 Social Sciences in General

General Works

Handbooks and Yearbooks

C, P, S

8. Eastman, Cari Lee Skogberg. **Immigration: Examining the Facts.** Santa Barbara, Calif., ABC-CLIO, 2017. 281p. index. (Contemporary Debates). $63.00. ISBN 13: 978-1-4408-3534-6; 978-1-4408-3535-3 (e-book).

This is not an easy read, nor was it designed to be. It is written to dispel numerous myths and misconceptions about immigrants in this country by examining the truths behind controversial claims about immigrants made by both liberals and conservatives. There are eight topical chapters in this information-laden book, such as "Immigration and Children" and "Immigration and Crime/Public Safety." Each chapter has various questions related to its topic, each with an answer followed by a more in-depth answer called "The Facts." These sections address issues where conflicting data exists. Each question has a bibliography of vetted authoritative sources for the reader to locate more information about the topic. This book tries to give a balanced viewpoint on the contentious issue of immigration in this country. This resource would be a welcome addition to any high school, college, public, or special library that wants to have a wealth of information about this controversial topic in one volume.—**Augie E. Beasley**

P, S

9. **Exploring Issues. www.exploringissues.com.** [Website] San Diego, Calif., Reference Point Press, 2017. Price negotiated by site. Date reviewed: 2017.

This database of articles explores 21 timely and current political, social, and cultural issues at the national and international level, covering a wide range of topics from e-cigarettes and vaping to illegal immigration to climate change. The articles cover the multiple, diverse sides of these issues, showing both positives and negatives, which provide useful support for young people developing their own understandings and perspectives. The articles are written with advanced language, making the database most appropriate for upper secondary students, although the easy navigation, reference help, contextual examples, and useful infographics can support younger audiences. Sources are cited throughout and extra source notes include further references and contact information for organizations dealing with these issues. However, some topics lack depth and with so few issues covered, it may not be a feasible purchase in comparison to other databases that address more content.—**Kasey Garrison**

C, S

10.   **Issues: Understanding Controversy and Society. http://www.abc-clio.com/ABC-CLIOCorporate/product.aspx?pc=ISSUW.** [Website] Santa Barbara, Calif., ABC-CLIO, 2016. Price negotiated by site. Date reviewed: 2016.

ABC-CLIO's *Issues* database provides a useful resource for navigating the hot-button issues of our day. The database covers many important current events issues. The database is as diverse in the issues it covers as it is deep. One of the advantages of such a broad database of information is that the information may be updated quickly and efficiently. No longer do students and researchers have to longingly wait for a supplemental volume to discover the latest developments in information. Now, with the click of a mouse and several keystrokes, online databases can be quickly and accurately updated by publishers. In no area is this as important as CLIO's *Issues* database.

The *Issues* database covers many areas currently pertinent to our world including crime and business, economics and justice, education, environmental topics, family and youth, gender and sexuality, health and medicine, law and politics, race and ethnicity, religion and spirituality, society and culture, and war and conflict. As the student can gather, this is a database that is broad based and expansive. However, while the database is wide it is also deep and contains a wealth of information about each topic.

For example, when a user clicks on the "war and conflict" tab, a wealth of options is presented with an array of topics from the ethics of war, to refugees, to torture. When one further drills down into a topic, an overview of that topic is presented with several additional click-through options.

The ethics of war entry consists of a one-page introduction that provides context. The entry also contains links to further reading so that the student can explore the topic more deeply. Further, the entry contains a link to different "perspectives." In the ethics of war entry, for example, entries on the ethics of the crisis in Darfur, the debate over torture, dropping the atomic bombs at the end of World War II, and the genocide in Rwanda are considered. This is useful for students as it provides a way that the information at hand can be appropriately applied to controversial issues.

The database also includes a "news you can use" feature. This feature allows a way that users can track news that is relevant to the topics at hand in the database. This saves the user time, making the necessary information easily accessible.

The *Issues* database is very user friendly and is a valuable resource for researchers. Highly recommended for high school and academic libraries.—**Sara Mofford**

3 Area Studies

General Works

Handbooks and Yearbooks

P, S

11. **A to Z World Culture. http://www.atozworldculture.com/.** [Website] Petaluma, Calif., World Trade Press, 2017. Price negotiated by site. Date reviewed: 2017.

Available only to paid subscribers, *A to Z World Culture* is an online encyclopedia solely devoted to the countries of the world. Users simply select from 175 available countries to access a particular and extensive profile. A substantial list of specific topics is available in the left sidebar, such as Music, Religion, Education, Language, Holidays and Festivals, and Climate. There are several broader topics as well: the Overview provides a Cultural Overview, summarizing information regarding ethnicity, religion, folklore, and more; a Country Snapshot, discussing the land, people, and history; and Country Facts, offering a listing of quick facts, such as formal country name, capital, area, and currency. The Country Profile tab is also broken down into subtopics of Demographics, Economy and Trade, Geography, Government Leaders, and People. Tabs in the sidebar also link to helpful tools such as Language Glossaries, Maps, Teaching Tools, and Lesson Plans.

Information within the topic categories is presented either as statistics or via generous essays with easily digestible paragraphs. The abundant use of color photography throughout the site gives subscribers a good sense of the national costume, architecture, landscape, and the many other things that help bring a culture to life.

Certified teachers, administrators, or librarians considering subscribing to this site may enjoy a thirty-day free trial. Potential subscribers may also access a sample country profile as they consider a subscription. This digital encyclopedia offers a clean interface and would have broad appeal. Recommended.—**ARBA Staff Reviewer**

C, P, S

12 . **BBC Country Profiles. http://news.bbc.co.uk/2/hi/country_profiles/default.stm.** [Website] Free. Date reviewed: 2017.

This freely accessible page of the greater British Broadcasting Company news site offers a quick way to access a spectrum of information on countries and territories of the world. *BBC Country Profiles* lets users select countries and territories from eight regions (including International Organizations). Choosing one allows quick and free access to the particular profile. Each profile offers a succinct description of the country/territory and its place in the global milieu. Users may also scroll through further information, such as Facts, Leaders, and Media. The profile also includes a timeline of key dates in the country/territory's history and may include links to a selection of topical news stories. Each profile includes a map, a depiction of the country/territory flag, photographs, and archival audio/visual content if available. Coupled with the ease of navigation, the site's simply structured approach to its information would have a broad appeal to secondary students and educators.—**ARBA Staff Reviewer**

C, P, S

13.   **UN Data. http://data.un.org/.** [Website] Free. Date reviewed: 2017.

    This simply structured site allows free access to myriad statistics, estimates, and projections related to 20 general categories of current global topics such as tourism, crime, trade, human development, and finance. The material, gathered from 35 databases run through various United Nations agencies, is accessible via the Databases tab where users can scroll through the categories. Some categories offer access to more than one database. The Updates tab displays the UN Data Twitter feed noting database revisions as they happen in addition to other relevant news. The Country Data Services tab reroutes users to individual statistics center websites for nearly 150 countries and territories. Added features include an extensive glossary, information on the metadata or background on the various data collections, access to the Monthly Bulletin of Statistics and other data resources, and a listing of Popular Searches, such as Germany, population, and GDP. The abundant data would appeal to students, researchers, policy-makers, and many others. The site can also be accessed by the social media platforms Facebook and Twitter.—**ARBA Staff Reviewer**

United States

General Works

Handbooks and Yearbooks

C, P

14.   **Mountain West Digital Library. http://mwdl.org/.** [Website] Free. Date reviewed: 2017.

    This freely available archive database, supported by member repositories, the Utah Academic Library Consortium, the Digital Public Library of America, the National Endowment for the Humanities, the Bill and Melinda Gates Foundation, and more, gathers nearly 700,000 resources from museums, universities, historical societies, and other sources. Archives are representative of the western states of Utah, Montana, Nevada, Idaho, Arizona, and Hawaii. Users have access to diaries, correspondence, photographs, maps, newspaper clippings, birth records, census data, academic papers, and much more. Users can access the material in two main ways aside from conducting a general search. They can search thematic Digital Collections (e.g., American Westward Migration, the African American Experience, BYU Family Histories, etc.) or search via particular Digital

Library Partners, some of which include Brigham Young University, The Rocky Mountain Laboratories Library, and Life Story Library Foundation. In addition to the records and artifacts, the site includes a brief summary of each collection.

The site makes it easy to browse by broad topic, such as genealogy, events, or places; more focused topics like yearbooks, prohibition, or migration can also be searched. Clicking on the Collections tab at the top of the page will present an alphabetized directory. In some cases, if a resource is no longer hosted by the Mountain West Digital Library, there is a link to its current location. This site is home to items applicable to many fields. It will certainly interest historians, but will be just as useful for such disciplines as demography, genealogy, women's studies, or ethnic studies.—**ARBA Staff Reviewer**

Alabama

C, P, S

15. **Encyclopedia of Alabama.** http://www.encyclopediaofalabama.org/. [Website] Free. Date reviewed: 2016.

The *Encyclopedia of Alabama* is a free, online resource pertaining to Alabama's history, culture, geography, and natural environment. Auburn University, the Alabama State Department of Education, and the University of Alabama collaborate on this award-winning encyclopedia. The site aims to provide trustworthy and authoritative information, updated regularly. When possible, the site uses multimedia content.

Searchers can discover information under a variety of tabs: Category, Indexes, Features, Galleries, and Quick Facts. The 12 categories include sports and recreation, business and industry, history, and agriculture, among other topics. There are several indexes, including people, places, and events. The features section covers myriad facets of Alabama history and life from Alabama animals, to Alabama governors, to the Scottsboro Boys. Clicking on the Scottsboro Boys link, for example, brings users to a brief synopsis of the arrest and the trials. From there, users can click on a variety of links to related topics like segregation, hobo culture in Alabama, and the NAACP. Under Galleries, searchers can find collections of Alabama baseball players, flowers, fossils, poets laureate, folk pottery, and more. For those young students working their way through state reports, the Quick Facts section provides the necessaries—flag, coat of arms, state bird, high and low elevations, etc.

Overall, a fine resource for students of all ages. Highly recommended.—**ARBA Staff Reviewer**

New York

C, P

16. **Nonstop Metropolis: A New York City Atlas.** Rebecca Solnit and Joshua Jelly-Schapiro, eds. Oakland, Calif., University of California Press, 2016. 224p. illus. maps. $29.95pa. ISBN 13: 978-0-520-28595-8.

This volume is the last of a trilogy of atlases which focuses on three U.S. cities and how maps tell stories and highlight historical and cultural phenomenon that tend to get lost in modern-day society. Volume one is titled *Infinite City: A San Francisco Atlas*, and volume 2 is titled *Unfathomable City: A New Orleans Atlas*. This third volume is divided into 26 maps, all showcasing various historical and cultural dimensions of the city of New York. For instance "Singing the City" highlights the many songs and musicals that were composed in New York City, while "What is a Jew" explores the lost world of Jewish Flatbush. The book's dimensions will require some libraries to classify it as oversize or lay it sideways on the shelf, but the color maps and pictures throughout are unique and indicate that the publisher took great care in decisions regarding size and cost; the price is quite reasonable given the colorful maps and useful information. Whether purchased for a library's collection or as a conversation piece on one's tabletop, this book and its companion volumes are well worth the value.—**Bradford Lee Eden**

South Carolina

C, P, S

17.   **The South Carolina Encyclopedia. http://www.scencyclopedia.org/sce/.** [Website] Free. Date reviewed: 2017.

This freely accessible resource, under the editorship of Bob Ellis at South Carolina University (USC), builds on the 2006 print volume edited by Walter B. Edgar and is a joint project of South Carolina Humanities, the University of South Carolina Press, the USC Libraries, the USC Center for Digital Humanities, the USC College of Arts & Sciences, the USC Institute for Southern Studies, the South Carolina State Library, and many other organizations. The original 600 articles have been enhanced with photos, videos, documents, and audiotapes. There are plans to add more entries and to make necessary updates to older articles.

The database is easy to navigate using a basic search, an alphabetical search, or one of the many tabular options: Article Authors, Categories, Time Period, Regions, County, and Media. Users can select from such categories as African Americans, Agriculture, Education, or Women and from such time periods as Colonial Period (1670-1764) or Post-War America (1946-1954). Counties are listed in alphabetic order and regions include Midlands, Peedee, Upstate, and Lowcountry. Media has four sublinks, which are Images, Videos, Recordings, and Documents. There are approximately 1,100 images, 40 videos, and 150 documents. As of this review, there were three recordings. For each of these images, videos, or documents, there is a link to an associated entry. The videos vary in length from a 30-second one of Charleston civil rights activists getting released from jail to a nearly 30-minute video of an interview with civil rights activist Eugene A. R. Montgomery. The entries also vary in length depending on the subject at hand. Entries all have tabular links at the top to take users to related materials. In the case of the article on jazz, users can quickly jump to other related articles, click on images and video, and link to the Tin Pan Alley Sheet Music Collection at the University of South Carolina University Libraries. Valuably, entries also have bibliographic references that users can consult for further research.

Highly recommended.—**ARBA Staff Reviewer**

Middle East

General Works

Handbooks and Yearbooks

C

18. **Comparative Political and Economic Perspectives on the MENA Region.** M. Mustafa Erdoğdu and Bryan Christiansen, eds. Hershey, Pa., Information Science Reference/IGI Global, 2016. 386p. maps. index. (Advances in Electronic Government, Digital Divide, and Regional Development (AEGDDRD) Book Series). $205.00 (individual chapters available for purchase in electronic format). ISBN 13: 978-1-46669-601-3; 978-1-46669-602-0 (e-book).

MENA is an acronym for the Middle East and North Africa regions of the world. It is an important area of the world not only for its location, but for its regional politics and its natural resources. This book is a part of a series, whose mission is to use social media and mobile technologies to provide public services and foster economic development. The contributors are professors of economics and each of them presents the MENA regions' economic and development issues, especially since the Arab Spring of 2013.

Topics discussed include: the pros and cons of decentralization on national unity, the ascendance of the Islamic State on the area, globalization and the women's labor market, economic growth and its relation to happiness in this region, the state of health care and universal health care as a remedy for the poor health care being delivered, and the quality of education. The authors present the regions' cultural, social, and economic issues and offer solutions for the improvement for the citizens of this region.

I was very interested in reading the chapters because they give a glimpse of the MENA people, their cultures, their health care, their education, and their economies. The media does not cover these aspects of MENA, but this book provides a better understanding of these areas.—**Kay Stebbins Slattery**

C, P

19. **Penn's Holy Land Digital Images Collection. http://dla.library.upenn.edu/dla/ holyland/index.html.** [Website] Free. Date reviewed: 2017,

This page consolidates a number of the University of Pennsylvania's collections of Holy Land artifacts. The archives here are sizeable and include a variety of materials such as field reports, photographs, manuscripts, maps, and drawings. Users can conduct a basic search but should utilize the generous choice of filters listed on the right sidebar. Users can narrow their search via hundreds of categories from the general to the specific, with Stations of the Cross, Cartography, Ruins, Minarets, White Mosque, and Hiram's Tomb to name a few. Alternative searches can be made via more general terms, such as year, physical description (e.g., photograph, map, etc.), creator, and title. The artifact page will generally include year of origin, title, creator, category, notes, collection name, identification number, and geographical location. Users can also find links to items related to the artifact from this page. The left sidebar provides links to similar University of Pennsylvania collections and resources as well as links to further outside resources. This site would be extremely useful for those studying ancient civilizations, architecture, photography, archeology, and much more.—**ARBA Staff Reviewer**

4 Economics and Business

General Works

Dictionaries and Encyclopedias

C, P, S

20. Hanson, Janice. **The Social Media Revolution: An Economic Encyclopedia of Friending, Following, Texting, and Connecting.** Santa Barbara, Calif., Greenwood Press/ABC-CLIO, 2016. 441p. index. $89.00. ISBN 13: 978-1-61069-767-5; 978-1-61069-768-2 (e-book).

This volume is clearly aimed at a variety of readers, of all ages. The 166 entries range from eBay and Etsy to censorship and copyright, from privacy and piracy, to Flickr and Pinterest. Each item contains references for "Further Reading." "Social media" is viewed in a wide context, going far beyond the standard sites one thinks of as social media: Instagram, Facebook, Twitter, etc. With Web 2.0, change has accelerated incredibly, whether "socially, economically, technologically [or] culturally" (p. xxiv). A five-page timeline indicates the historical dimension of this work, presenting information on many topics (people, companies, and inventions) that predate the recent explosion of social media activity.

High schools, public libraries, and most college/university libraries will find this a useful introduction to the multidimensional shift taking place in web-based communication today. Given the subject of the work, perhaps the e-book option would be a reasonable choice.—**Mark Schumacher**

C, P

21. **The SAGE Encyclopedia of Economics and Society.** Frederick F. Wherry, general ed. and Juliet Schor, consulting ed. Thousand Oaks, Calif., Sage, 2015. 4v. index. $650.00/set. ISBN 13: 978-1-4522-2643-9.

Historical and ethnographic narratives documenting how economic issues impact our social universe comprise this four-volume encyclopedia. Articles are presented alphabetically. The diverse topics range from entertainment to traditional economic subjects such as Dodd-Frank. The economic spin on less traditional topics such as B Movies is not always obvious, but this does not detract from the resource in any way. The thread that connects society and economics is clearly evident throughout. The Reader's

Guide in volume one organizes the diverse list of articles into 15 broad categories. Such organization helps with navigation and can benefit those who enjoy browsing as a means of discovery. Articles are well constructed and clearly written. Most are a few pages in length and contain major subsections and a list of further readings. The tone throughout is very consistent, even with the diversity and range of topics. Volume four contains a glossary, a resource guide, and an index. *The SAGE Encyclopedia of Economics and Society* would be a good resource for academic libraries serving undergraduate students.—**Lorraine Evans**

Directories

C, P, S

22. **OpenCorporates. https://opencorporates.com/.** [Website] Free. Date reviewed: 2017.

This free-to-use site is home to the largest open database of companies and company data in the world. As of this review, the site had information for 126,063,092 companies. The aim of the site's founders is to make company information widely available for public benefit, especially in service of those who want to combat antisocial purposes such as corruption, money laundering, or organized crime. The site is able to provide open access to journalists, NGOs, academics, and others by charging proprietary data users for access to structured data. Under the About tab, users can learn about the team behind *OpenCorporates,* which was launched in 2010, and view a database timeline, founding principles, and more. Clicking on the Using Our Data tab offers further information about the philosophy of working for the public good, who uses the data, and the data used by *OpenCorporates.* Most visitors to the site will use the basic search function on the main page, which allows for searches by jurisdiction (country or U.S. states) or by company name or company officers. Once a basic search is completed, users can apply further filters using advanced options under the main search box. Results will give researchers a company number, status, incorporation date, company type, jurisdiction, registered address, previous names, directors/officers, registry page, company network and/or company grouping, the source or sources used, and the date data was last updated. There are different export options available.—**ARBA Staff Reviewer**

Handbooks and Yearbooks

C, P

23. **Handbook on the Economics of the Internet.** Johannes M. Bauer and Michael Latzer, eds. Northampton, Mass., Edward Elgar, 2016. 608p. $330.00. ISBN 13: 978-0-85793-984-5.

On a nearly daily basis, we hear that the Internet has turned our lives upside down. The interconnectedness of the Internet has provided access to information to members of society who never had access to this information before. Intellectually, we are aware that the Internet has had some sort of an impact on our economy, but we may not be able to adequately explain that impact.

In their *Handbook on the Economics of the Internet,* editors Johannes M. Bauer and Michael Latzer offer a wide range of essays on the effect that the Internet has had on our economy. Bauer, of Michigan State University, and Latzer, of Switzerland's University of Zurich, have compiled a diverse tapestry of essays that explain, detail challenges, and offer a prognosis for the future of an Internet economy.

The handbook does not shy away from controversial topics in the news. It includes an essay by Ian Brown on the economics of privacy, data, protection, and surveillance. In this essay Brown explores the "privacy paradox," in which individuals that claim to be concerned about privacy behave in a manner that contradicts this claim. Instead of a blanket analysis, Brown's essay is unafraid to dive into the weeds of the privacy paradox, analyzing the motivations, drawbacks, and external factors that make privacy such a controversial, diverse, and fascinating topic.

The handbook also includes an essay by Ryland Sherman and David Waterman that explores the economics of online video entertainment. Sherman and Waterman's essay traces the evolution of online video entertainment, which has been in existence since the mid 1990s, to the place it occupies in the market today. The essay explores the unique place that online video entertainment occupies in the marketplace today, and considers whether Internet distribution differs from online media, the programming available on Internet distribution platforms, and whether this online video distribution has been a net positive for consumers. Sherman and Waterman, by their own admission, agree that their research is nowhere near complete and remains in its infancy. However, this academic evaluation of streaming video is fascinating for academics, students, and consumers.

Bauer and Latzer have compiled an excellent primer about the economics of the Internet. While this book is useful, it may be most useful as a starting point for the academic to research further. Bauer and Latzer have attempted to answer the question "... but how does a person make money on the Internet?" By all accounts, they have succeeded at answering that question, with the caveat that the economics of the Internet is an ever-evolving science. Bauer and Latzer's book is a useful tool in navigating this new science, and will be a valuable resource to students and academics alike.

Recommended for academic and public libraries.—**Sara Mofford**

C, S

24.   Lind, Nancy S., Erik T. Rankin, and Joseph R. Blaney. **Today's Economic Issues: Democrats and Republicans.** Santa Barbara, Calif., ABC-CLIO, 2016. 387p. index. (Across the Aisle). $97.00. ISBN 13: 978-1-4408-3936-8; 978-1-4408-3937-5 (e-book).

This volume in the Across the Aisle series presents both Democratic and Republican economic philosophies and the effects they have on people in the United States, especially when power swings from one party to another.

This 408-page book begins with a standard introduction. The contents are not listed as numerical chapters, but are constructed in alphabetic format beginning with Bankruptcy and ending with Wall Street Bailout. This creates an ease of access for researchers seeking specific economic topics. Furthermore, the resources at the conclusion of the book, particularly the bibliography and index, are abundant with avenues for extended study.

Chapters represent financial philosophies, histories, and contemporary conversation within the Democratic and Republican parties, portraying both common ground and areas of disagreement. The text presents theories and histories and uses such tools as bulleted lists to convey mainstream Republican and Democrat positions. Text boxes highlight quotes from Supreme Court decisions, newspaper editorials, politicians, and party representatives. Each chapter/entry is level research from political theorists, economists, social workers, and social scientists. Topics discussed include but are not limited to financial industry regulation, health care, infrastructure, immigration, job creation, social security, and stimulus spending. With an intense political climate in the United States today, it's refreshing to read a book that does not rely on political rhetoric and strives for balance.

A resource tool, *Today's Economic Issues: Democrats and Republicans* is good for advanced placement high school and college-level students, researchers, and practitioners seeking information in the areas of economics, U.S. history, sociology, and political science.

Recommended.—**Janis Minshull**

C, P, S

25.   **National Bureau of Economic Research Publications. http://www.nber.org/ pubs.html.** [Website] Free. Date reviewed: 2017.

The National Bureau of Economic Research (NBER) has been long devoted to creating and providing the highest quality research on economic issues and policies covering topics like political economics, health care economics, international trade and investment, and much more. This site offers access to a variety of the NBER's publications. Users can search the publication database via a bibliographic or full text search, narrowed by category of Working Papers, Chapters, Books, and Digest/Reporter. Users can alternatively click on the individual entity graphic. The NBER Digest summarizes recent and topical Working Papers for a general audience. Users can examine the recent edition, published monthly, or browse the archives. The Reporter publishes quarterly and reviews broader NBER topics, conferences, and more. Users can view the recent Reporter and browse its archives as well. Selecting Books will provide links to sites where interested users can order NBER hardcover publications and read summaries of their contents. The bulk of the NBER's work is found via Working Papers, as nearly 1,000 are published each year. Interested users can pay a subscription fee to access the material online, or can pay a nominal fee per paper (hard copy subscriptions are also available and come with online access as well). The fee is determined by the type of subscription desired—full or topical, but is quite reasonable. A great deal of the material on the site is freely available. This will appeal to a great many students, educators, policy-makers, and others studying the economy across many categories—**ARBA Staff Reviewer**

C, P

26.   **SAGE Business Cases. https://us.sagepub.com/en-us/nam/sage-business-cases.** [Website] Thousand Oaks, Calif., Sage, 2016. Price negotiated by site. Date reviewed: 2016.

This database provides a convenient, well organized, and reputable wealth of business case studies. These case studies will prove useful to academic and student alike. The case studies are indexed into many diverse topics so that the researcher can quickly and accurately obtain the most useful takeaway from each case study.

Not only are these case studies plentiful in number, they are also from reputable sources. Institutions represented in the database include prestigious universities like

Northwestern University, Yale University, and Georgetown University. Further, the very well respected Society for Human Resource Management contributed several cases to the database. The database also contains an international flavor, as China's Tsinghua SEM and the United Kingdom's University of Cambridge contributed cases.

One interesting entry into the database is a case study on Starbucks. Most people know Starbucks as the ubiquitous coffee chain down the street and perhaps know their preferred order at Starbucks, but do not know the history of the company. The company started in a single location in an industrial area of Seattle, Washington, and grew to its size today with nearly 17,000 locations. The case explores the challenges that accompanied this growth, including a genuine controversy about Starbucks' decision to sell food. While it made intellectual sense for Starbucks to expand into the food market, it also caused great controversy for an interesting reason: the smell of the food was overpowering the smell of the coffee. Howard Schultz, Starbucks' charismatic founder, found this unanticipated sensual invader to be a great affront to Starbucks' brand. Starbucks, Shultz maintained, should always smell like coffee over anything else. Readers will enjoy reading about the way Starbucks and Schultz worked around this problem to create the hybrid coffee shop and restaurant that Starbucks has fashioned itself into today.

Another useful feature of the SAGE business cases are the teaching notes. Instructors can personalize the teaching notes to meet the needs of their students and ensure that students are getting the most out of the course. While instructors will likely not use the teaching notes wholesale, they do provide a good starting place.

Both instructors and students will find SAGE's business case database useful. Instructors will want to assign cases from *SAGE Business Cases,* and students will almost certainly find the wide depth and breadth of the database useful for research purposes.

Highly recommended for academic and public libraries.—**Sara Mofford**

C, P

27.   **SAGE Business Researcher. https://us.sagepub.com/en-us/nam/sage-business-researcher.** [Website] Thousand Oaks, Calif., Sage. Price negotiated by site. Date reviewed: 2016.

The development of this SAGE database, *SAGE Business Researcher,* provides readers with a very strong foundation in business research. Beginning in 2015, this annual subscription (or may be purchased with option for annual updates) will help develop student inquiry into how contemporary world events relate to business management.

Issues of the *SAGE Business Researcher* come out approximately twice a month and provide balanced, authentic information. The issue includes: Executive Summary, Overview, Background, Current Situation, Looking Ahead, Time Line, Resources for Further Study, Short Articles (relating to the topic), Data Download, and a Q & A with experts. Each section is clear and concise with the Resource collection offering more research options with books, articles, reports and studies, organizations, and additional notes. Excel color charts are downloadable, photographs are relevant to issue topics, and footnotes throughout the articles can be linked to documentation.

Navigation through this SAGE database is convenient. Subject matter entered into the search bar readily brings up relevant issues. A large sidebar promotes easy access to browsing by business category topics such as Ethics and Social Responsibility, International Business, or Marketing. Topics vary with the amount of issues—Entrepreneurship has 7 issues; Technology, 15 issues. Another search option is to browse by Content Type which will be extremely useful for those students seeking to modify their search to just reports, short articles, data, or expert views. The consistent organization of issues throughout the database affords the researcher with ease of structure.

Business article topics are very current and very relevant to management and practical for study or implementation. Meetings and Team Management, Big Data, or Behavioral Economics are examples of past issues. Recent issues are Electric Power Industry, The Worldwide Work Force, and Product Recalls. The sampling of business topics mentioned in this review portrays the database as one with a broad spectrum with multiple layers of documentation.

Extremely thorough in approach and with a precision in how the information is presented, article writers demonstrate an authoritative knowledge of their specific topic. Additional experts are included to give perspective. All issues are well documented, providing more than adequate resource options for further study. Issues are completely relevant to current business management themes, and this database also archives issues to provide historical prospective. *SAGE Business Researcher* is an excellent database for graduates, postgraduates, and those seeking to hone their business skills.

Highly recommended.—**Janis Minshull**

C, P

28.   **SAGE Business Stats. https://us.sagepub.com/en-us/nam/sage-business-stats.** [Website] Thousand Oaks, Calif., Sage. Price negotiated by site. Date reviewed: 2016.

SAGE Publications creates a succinct database on a platform with a multitude of options and ways to manipulate data with *SAGE Business Stats.* Data can be challenging to find and data with accurate citing, even more difficult. There is no need to look further with this easily accessible SAGE database. *Business Stats* is available for annual subscription or purchase.

The data here is current (up to 2014) and the options for ways to access the information is staggering. With 7,000 data series and over 300 million data points, the potential for students finding statistics for further analysis is great. This database includes 40 years of historical stats so students can gain previous perspective. Additionally, projections until 2050 can provide a student with a point of view on future trends.

Tabular options give access to topics: Detailed Age and Race Breakdowns, Earnings and Employment by Industry, Household Income Levels, New and Closed Businesses, Patent and Trademarks, Retail Sales by Industry, and Venture Capital Funding. Geographically, this data is accessible on a larger scale (by country), and incrementally filtered right down to a local zip code. Focusing on the Location tab, scholars can further filter data using a drop-down box with choices such as: Employment and Labor, Economy, or Social Welfare. Options for filtering are a significant advantage in this business database and place it high in standing.

The suggested data series listing can then be hyperlinked to the most relevant data which will be available in chart, map, and tables. Visualization of data is notable. Timeline dates can be modified for precision. Most valuable to this platform is the ability to "Compare" multiple data in one visual screen. Graphics allow for the exploration and analysis of more than one data set and find the composite or conflicting measures of that comparison. Related data for further study is gathered based on the research query. Thirdly, Sources provide the years of the data, notes, the original link, and additional documentation. Additionally, data that is pertinent can be managed with these options: Cite,

Share, Save, and Export. There is also a User Tips tab for information on manipulation of data suggestions. Students are able to download data (in Excel and CSV formats).

Gathering data no longer need be an arduous, time-demanding research process. With *SAGE Business Stats,* researchers are able to find numerous business data resources in one format. The ease with which one can find the data (because of the filters) and the ability to perform intricate comparisons of data elevates this database above others. This database is exceptionally useful to undergraduate and graduate students seeking ample selection of business data resources in a comparative format. This database will also be useful for those businesspeople and other researchers seeking demographic perspective.

Highly recommended.—**Janis Minshull**

P

29.   **U.S. Small Business Administration. www.sba.gov.** [Website] Free. Date reviewed: 2017.

This dynamic website offers a wealth of information targeting small business owners. It offers a variety of navigation tools to guide users to its generous content, and includes many interactive ways to learn about the Small Business Administration, including educational videos, newsletters and email update signups, "Learn More" boxes, and blog links. At the top of the home page users can click on six main headings: Starting & Managing, Loans & Grants, Contracting, Learning Center, Local Assistance, and About Us. Each heading leads to more specific and relevant topics. For example, clicking on Starting & Managing leads to topics such as Write Your Business Plan, Learn About Business Laws, Small Business Health Care, Cybersecurity, and much more. Visually, users will see bold, colorful tabs overlaying thematic photographs and illustrations which encourage users to click for more information. There is so much information that the Site Map is likely to come in handy. It is vital that an agency that serves so many communicates generously and clearly with its customers. This website easily meets that standard.—**ARBA Staff Reviewer**

Finance and Banking

Handbooks and Yearbooks

C, P, S

30.   **Current Value of Old Money. http://projects.exeter.ac.uk/RDavies/arian/ current/howmuch.html.** [Website] Free. Date reviewed: 2017.

This web page does not seek to directly answer questions, and specifically will not tell you the value of the leftover francs from your childhood trip to France. Instead, the page helps users access other online information regarding more general topics on a currency's purchasing power, worth, money supply, incomes, exchange rates, prices, and many other topics surrounding money. There are no frills to the site. Users simply scroll downward to find category links to Tools and Online Sources. Broad categories include regions of the world (the United Kingdom and Europe, Australia, the United States, Mexico, etc.), Prices in the Ancient World, Historical Exchange Rates, and Financial Costs of the World

Wars. Clicking on a specific link simply redirects to other sites; for example, clicking on Purchasing Power of Money in the U.S. from 1774-2007 takes users to MeasuringWorth. com and its value calculator. At the time of this review, some links led to expired pages. The site also lists a number of printed sources. While basic in design, the site does eventually lead to a vast amount of interesting monetary data which could be highly useful in many types of research.—**ARBA Staff Reviewer**

C, P, S

31. **MeasuringWorth.com. https://measuringworth.com/.** [Website] Free. Date reviewed: 2017.

This free site examines a variety of current and historical data for use in comparing a number of measures relative to the U.S. and U.K. economies (with some additional insight into Spain and Australia). Specifically, the site describes itself as "calculating relative worth over time." The crux of the site is its series of calculators. From the left sidebar, users can select from a list of Comparators, such as Relative Values, Stock Growth Rates, and Savings Growth. Users will find a text summary of comparator attributes and/or permutations alongside a specialized calculator designed to examine contemporary figures against historical ones. Users will generally supply the dates, values, amounts, etc. that they wish to compare. This section may be cross-referenced and contain helpful links to clarifying reports. Graphs display a listing of variables, such as population or long-term interest rates, from which users can choose to chart. The sidebar also contains a listing of 14 Data Sets examining such topics as the "U.S. Dollar-Pound Exchange Rate from 1791-Present," "The Price of Gold, 1257-Present," and more. U.S. data may go back to the founding of the nation (late eighteenth century) while data for the United Kingdom may reach back to the thirteenth century. As it deals with varying data and somewhat complex comparisons, the site goes to great lengths to convey its information clearly and in a well-organized fashion. Users can select from a number of tabs at the top of the page which link to excellent contextual information. Essays offers several takes on historical value comparisons, including a general piece on its intrinsic difficulty and a piece examining the economics of slavery. User Guides helps pinpoint type of economic information and also provides site tutorials. Additionally, there are links to a glossary and FAQs.—**ARBA Staff Reviewer**

P, S

32. **National Education Association: Resources for Teaching Financial Literacy. http://www.nea.org/tools/lessons/resources-for-teaching-financial-literacy.html.** [Website] Free. Date reviewed: 2017.

This page aims to provide K-12 educators with ideas to help ensure the financial literacy of their students. The page acts as a hub from which users can review different resources, investigate creative suggestions for teaching the concept of finance, and find ways to incorporate the idea of financial literacy into a range of lessons.

Users can scroll through a categorized listing of links to sites that offer a host of educational tools, tips, games, plans, and more across a variety of media (books, videos, etc.). Standards outline the basic financial knowledge students should ultimately possess and link to an online library of solid resources. Lesson Plans and Lesson Sets provide downloadable PDFs and links for K-12 plans matching a selection of financial topics.

Background Resources provide reports illustrating the importance of financial literacy and teacher preparedness; the Games link offers a variety of online activities designed to engage students of many grade levels in finance. Some of the more specific topics covered within the categories above include saving, spending, cost comparisons, credit, budgeting, and banking.

While particularly useful for teachers, parents and students would also find this site useful.—**ARBA Staff Reviewer**

Industry and Manufacturing

Handbooks and Yearbooks

S

33.   **U*X*L How Everyday Products are Made.** Thomas Riggs, ed. Stamford, Conn., Gale/Cengage Learning, 2016. 2v. illus. index. $182.00/set. ISBN 13: 978-0-7876-6547-0; 978-1-4144-0986-3 (e-book).

Do you have students interested in how different products are made and why? These two volumes will help them learn detailed facts about manufacturing processes and manufacturers. Each entry has 10 different bullets ranging from critical thinking questions, words to know, raw materials, safety, quality control, and more. There are many colored images and illustrations which contribute to increasing student understanding. These volumes would be good additions in a middle school reference section, and I could also see them as valuable additions for lower level high school students as well as reluctant readers. If you have extra monies available, these could be a useful asset for developing STEM activities. An index and a bibliography round out the work.—**Deb Grove**

P

34.   Wrenick, Frank E. **Automobile Manufacturers of Cleveland and Ohio, 1864-1942.** Jefferson, N.C., McFarland, 2016. 268p. index. $39.95pa. ISBN 13: 978-0-7864-7535-3; 978-1-4766-2356-6 (e-book).

Ohio is often forgotten in the shadow of Michigan as an early automotive manufacturing center, but, as this book shows, there was plenty of activity going on between 1864 and 1942.

The book has two sections, one on Cleveland and the other on the rest of the state. Each section has a narrative overview followed by alphabetical entries on each of the manufacturers. Entries range from one paragraph to six pages, depending on how long the companies were in business and how much information can be found about them. Some companies were created, but no car was ever produced. Sometimes a prototype was all that was ever seen. These venture companies are included. Companies such as Ford, which were based in other states but had a manufacturing plant in Ohio, are also included.

Four appendixes cover Cleveland Automobile Manufactures by Year; Cleveland Automobile Marques by Name and Address; Ohio Automobile Manufacturers by City; and Unusual Vehicle Names. A bibliography and index are also included. There are many black-and-white illustrations; most appear to be advertising, but some are old photographs.

Cleveland seems to be the focus of the book, and indeed 134 pages are devoted to that one city, while 92 pages cover the rest of the state. Every manufacturer in Cleveland has at least one footnote, and there are none in the rest of the Ohio section. One might think the book was written initially about Cleveland, and then the publisher or the author decided that wasn't enough so they expanded it. It is well written and very informative. Recommended for all collections where books on the history of automobiles or Ohio are in demand.—**Robert M. Lindsey**

Insurance

Directories

C, P

35. **Canadian Insurance Claims Directory, 2016.** 84th ed. Gwen Peroni, ed. Toronto, University of Toronto Press, 2016. 160p. maps. index. $55.00pa. ISBN 13: 978-1-4875-2020-4.

The *Canadian Insurance Claims Directory* includes listings of adjusters and insurance counsel in Alberta, British Columbia, Manitoba, New Brunswick, Newfoundland and Labrador, Nova Scotia, Ontario, Prince Edward Island, Quebec, and Saskatchewan. Each entry includes name, address, phone, fax, officers, association memberships, and, for larger organizations, a description and list of practice areas. Maps of each province are included. In addition, a directory of U.S. adjusters and insurance counsel is also provided. Associations are organized by state and each section is subdivided into cities; each entry includes name, address, phone, fax, email, website (where applicable), and officers. Additionally included are: directories (for Canada) of insurance associations and governing bodies, fire marshals and fire commissioners, superintendents of insurance by province and territories, and insurance companies. The directory also includes indexes of advertisers, insurance-related services, and insurance associations.

This resource is recommended for insurance practitioners, students and faculty, and researchers in insurance. It is especially important for academic libraries supporting a curriculum in insurance and also to special libraries.—**Lucy Heckman**

International Business

Handbooks and Yearbooks

C

36. **Corporate Espionage, Geopolitics, and Diplomacy Issues in International Business.** Bryan Christiansen and Fatmanur Kasarci, eds. Hershey, Pa., Information Science Reference/IGI Global, 2017. 373p. index. (Advances in Finance, Accounting, and

Economics (AFAE) Book Series). $210.00 (individual chapters available for purchase in electronic format). ISBN 13: 978-1-52251-031-4; 978-1-52251-032-1 (e-book).

This book focuses on the role of three factors in international business: geopolitics, corporate espionage, and diplomacy. The book is well organized. A table of contents is followed by a detailed table of contents. Chapters open with abstracts (identical to the chapter descriptions in the detailed table of contents) and end with references. There are black-and-white figures scattered throughout. The volume concludes with brief biographies of the contributors, a list of compiled references, and an index.

Under the editorship of Bryan Christiansen, from PryMarke, LLC, USA, and Fatmanur Kasarci, from the PryMarke Business Academy in Turkey, this volume covers a wide range of topics in 17 chapters. Topics include the influence of Japanese prime minister Shinzo Abe's economic policies on international business, the effects on international business of economic nationalism and patriotism, cybercrime (with a heavy emphasis on the United States, China, and Russia), the development of Korean pop music and the need for copyright regulations, the geopolitics of immigrant labor, and much more. The material is timely, particularly in light of the marked rise in nationalism in the twenty-first century and the simultaneous increase in cybercrime. This book is recommended to college libraries looking for a book on the effects of geopolitics, corporate espionage, and diplomacy on international business. College libraries can also buy electronic book chapters separately if the cost of the whole volume is prohibitive.—**ARBA Staff Reviewer**

Labor

Career Guides

P, S

37. **Careers in Manufacturing and Production.** Michael Shally-Jensen, ed. Hackensack, N.J., Salem Press, 2016. 347p. illus. index. $95.00. ISBN 13: 978-1-61925-894-5; 978-1-61925-895-2 (e-book).

One in a series on careers, this volume provides a compact resource for examining the wide variety of careers in manufacturing and production. The volume shares general information about this important and evolving employment sector, as well as more targeted information about individual jobs within the sector.

An introductory section provides useful background on U.S. manufacturing (the making of goods, parts, and materials), including a brief history, general statistics, and an overview of career options. Following this are alphabetically arranged chapters describing 27 different jobs, ranging from boilermaker to welder. Within each chapter, readers will find ample and varied information detailing specific duties, the expected work environment, occupation specialties (e.g., one can be an arc, gas, combination or production line welder), educational requirements, earnings and advancement potential, and much more. The use of such tools as bullet points, shaded sidebars, and tables make the material easy to navigate. Some special features include projected employment trends, "fun facts," the description of a typical day in the life on the job, a "snapshot" of the job, and a listing of applicable organizations readers can consult for more information. The

"Conversation With…" feature presents interviews with individuals in particular jobs and is insightful. The book also includes a list of selected schools which offer highly regarded programs in the particular field. An appendix explains the "Holland Code," which provides a useful tool to help potential employment seekers match their personalities with career possibilities. A bibliography and an index round out the work.

Clearly compiled, this book will appeal to those curious about the state of manufacturing and the many related jobs.—**ARBA Staff Reviewer**

P, S

38. **Careers in Sales, Insurance & Real Estate.** Michael Shally-Jensen, ed. Hackensack, N.J., Salem Press, 2016. 337p. illus. index. $95.00. ISBN 13: 978-1-61925-892-1; 978-1-61925-893-8 (e-book).

This volume provides an easily accessible resource for examining the wide variety of careers in sales, insurance, and real estate. The volume shares general information about the vast options of a sales career, and highlights two of the more prominent segments of sales. It also shares more targeted information about individual jobs within the sales sector.

An introductory section helps define what a sales career means in the United States today, including general statistics and an overview of career options. Following this are alphabetically arranged chapters describing 27 different jobs, ranging from actuary to wholesale sales representative. Within each chapter, readers will find ample and varied information detailing specific duties, the expected work environment, occupation specialties (e.g., an insurance underwriter can handle life, multiple line, automotive, pension and more, in regards to policies), educational requirements, earnings and advancement potential, and much more. Bullet points, shaded sidebars, tables, and other tools make the material easy to navigate. Some special features include projected employment trends, "fun facts," the description of a typical day in the life on the job, a "snapshot" of the job, and a listing of applicable organizations readers can consult for more information. Interviews with experienced professionals are sprinkled throughout the book in the "Conversation With…" feature. The book also includes a list of selected schools which offer highly regarded programs in the particular field, an appendix that explains the "Holland Code" which helps potential employment seekers match their personalities with career possibilities, a bibliography, and an index.

This book will appeal to those curious about the many careers in sales.—**ARBA Staff Reviewer**

P, S

39. **Careers: The Graphic Guide to Finding the Perfect Job for You.** New York, DK Publishing, 2015. 320p. index. $20.00pa. ISBN 13: 978-1-4654-2973-5.

Detailing information on over 400 careers, this volume starts with a very detailed careers chart, includes a more detailed table of contents, and ends with an extensive jobs index in the back. Included are familiar jobs, and many more a student might not have considered. Detailed information concerning job description, career paths, salary, industry profile, entry qualifications, skills guide, working hours, training, and related careers is presented in charts and tables that make it easy to find needed information. Any student wanting to do career research would be well advised to include this excellent resource in their search. Purchase this as a one-stop career must-have for high school libraries. Highly recommended.—**Cynthia Foster**

C, P

40. Clowes, Kat. **Put College To Work: How to Use College to the Fullest to Discover Your Strengths and Find a Job You Love before You Graduate.** Fresno, Calif., Quill Driver, 2015. 306p. index. $18.95pa. ISBN 13: 978-1-61035-253-6.

"What are you going to do with your college degree?" is a question many students dread. In the midst of midterms, papers, and socializing, it is difficult to remember that one's nonacademic future may only be a few semesters away. *Put College to Work* is full of empowering ideas and solid strategies that can help a college student gain focus and hone their ambitions so they can enter the rapidly changing job market with maximum preparedness.

The book funnels loads of useful information into four main parts which discuss self-analysis, school success, after-school success, and skill refinement. Within each part, brief chapters offer easily digestible segments brimming with personal anecdotes, useful research, action plans, timely tips, and more. Topics range from discovering passions and goals, to such things as time management, financial aid, alumni networking, interviewing, social media, and graduate school. The generous use of shaded text boxes (many of which reflect the author's "Tales from the Real World"), professional advice, "Tips and Tricks," and more help make the information extremely accessible and memorable.

A closing resources section is rich with exercises that can help readers assess their goals, skills, and passions. The section also includes resumé resources and an itemized four-year schedule useful for staying on track during the whirlwind of the college years.—**ARBA Staff Reviewer**

P

41. Hakala-Ausperk, Catherine. **Renew Yourself: A Six-Step Plan for More Meaningful Work.** Chicago, American Library Association, 2017. 130p. index. $50.00pa.; $45.00pa. (ALA members). ISBN 13: 978-0-8389-1499-1.

There is no better time than now to explore new career paths, plan that adventure you're dreaming about, or jump in to that degree work! *Renew Yourself: A Six-Step Plan for More Meaningful Work,* written by Catherine Hakala-Ausperk, encourages readers to contemplate what they value and how to find happiness in work and life.

With 129-pages, divided into six chapters with the typical who, what, when, where, why, and how questioning, Hakala-Ausperk gives a step-by-step approach to discovering passion and value in our work. She states "Contrary to what most people grow up thinking, work and life are not mutually exclusive. Finding meaning in one—or lack thereof—is going to impact the other" (p. xvii). Following the six steps is a personal plan template, a solid bibliography listing books and digital links for further research, and a serviceable index.

Each chapter defines one step in the process of renewing. Initially, the author creates exercises where readers will reflect on who they are, their history, and their options for redirection. "Since the purpose of this book is to help you get excited about your future, you need to pick a path and chart a course that truly matters and feel, finally, refreshed and renewed to follow it" (p. 25). As your intentionality presents itself, steps will aid in providing focus; the sections Find Your Sweet (Work) Spot, Try Being Appreciative, and Learn Something, Anything New remind us to build our confidence piece by piece. This book never suggests that change and renewal is easy, but provides a logical process, with exercises, for understanding our individual passions, setting personal goals, and implementing an action plan.

Renew Yourself: A Six-Step Plan for More Meaningful Work is a professional development tool that is useful to librarians, career and life coaches, social workers, and others seeking a pathway to meaningful occupations.

Recommended.—**Janis Minshull**

P

42.   Noer, David. **Keeping Your Career on Track: Avoiding Derailment, Enriching the Work Experience and Helping Your Organization.** Jefferson, N.C., McFarland, 2016. 205p. index. $25.00pa. ISBN 13: 978-1-4766-6448-4; 978-1-4766-2413-6 (e-book).

This efficient guidebook helps readers navigate a relatively novel concept in career management: derailment. Specifically, the book offers a significant number of ways in which to avoid career derailment at all levels of an organization.

In concise, well-organized sections, the book presents 99 real life examples (some personally witnessed by the author, some from popular history or current events) of "hazards" that can work to disrupt careers. Sections are organized by umbrella themes which include self-sabotage, incompatible needs, misdirected loyalties, dysfunctional traits, and more. Each section opens with a chapter summary charting "Derailment Risks and What to Do About Them."

The sections are then divided into chapters describing general types of career derailment, e.g., political quicksand, fantasy, functional fixedness, and irrelevance. Within these chapters then are the numbered hazards to avoid, such as "Unwillingness to Hear Feedback" (#13), "Making Undeliverable Promises" (#61), and "Building a Team by Demeaning Other Teams" (#81). The hazards are conveyed as tangible stories, which help hold readers' attention, and the author may provide insightful context within each story. Each chapter concludes with a brief but effective bulleted list of "Perspective and Advice."

Several appendixes provide further useful information for readers, and include an inventory of derailment risk assessment, a list of derailment risk categories, and derailment hazards. References and an index round out the work.—**ARBA Staff Reviewer**

Handbooks and Yearbooks

C, P

43.   **Handbook of U.S. Labor Statistics, 2016.** 19th ed. Mary Meaghan Ryan, ed. Lanham, Md., Bernan Press, 2016. 462p. index. $175.00. ISBN 13: 978-1-59888-824-9; 978-1-59888-825-6 (e-book).

The *Handbook of U.S. Labor Statistics* covers issues including "unemployment, employment projections for the future, income, the rapidly increasing costs of health care services, and the aging of the labor force." This reference source contains more than 225 tables and data and is compiled by the Bureau of Labor Statistics (BLS). The handbook is comprised of 14 chapters among which are: "Population, Labor Force, and Employment Status"; "Employment, Hours, and Earnings"; "Occupational Employment and Wages"; "Labor Force and Employment Projections by Industry and Occupation"; "Productivity and Costs"; "Prices"; "Consumer Expenditures"; and "American Time Use Survey." A new chapter for this edition is "Women in the Workforce," which includes statistics on wage and salary workers paid hourly rates with earnings at or below the prevailing federal minimum wage; contribution of wives' earnings to family income; and wives who earn more than their husbands. Each chapter includes highlights and specific trends of data; figures and tables of statistics; notes and definitions; and sources of additional information. The tables include data for a specific time period (e.g., Employment and Wages, by Occupation, May 2014) as well as historical data covering a range of years (e.g., Employment Status of the Civilian Noninstitutional Population, 1947-2014). The resource includes a subject index with cross-references; specific topics indexed include veterans, vacation leave, union workers, health care, commodities, air transportation, housing, and private sector. It also covers such very specific topics as: employment data for accountants and auditors; industries with the largest wage and salary employment growth and declines; hire levels and rates by industry per month from 2014-2015; and consumer expenditures on foods at home and away from home. *The Handbook of U.S. Labor Statistics* is highly recommended to academic and public libraries and provides a wealth of data and information.—**Lucy Heckman**

C, P, S
44.   **Occupational Outlook Handbook, 2016-2017.** U.S. Department of Labor and U. S. Bureau of Statistics, comps. Lanham, Md., Bernan Press, 2016. 1260p. index. $38.00. ISBN 13: 978-1-59888-814-0; 978-1-59888-815-7 (e-book).

The basic format of this biennial staple of public library reference collections has remained relatively unchanged over the years, and this edition is no exception. Focusing on the over 300 major occupations that provide the overwhelming majority of jobs in the United States, it describes each job with the same standard set of criteria: duties, work environment, education and training, median pay (as of 2014), and job outlook for the next decade. Occupations are listed alphabetically under 25 broad categories. The index is limited to major headings only; it provides no direct access to alternative job titles or to subcategories.

The updated one-page Projections Data lists the top 20 occupations in each of the following categories: fastest growing occupations, the number of new jobs, and highest paying occupations. It is probably no surprise that the majority of occupations in two of these categories come from medical-related fields.

The online version, freely available at www.bls.gov/ooh, contains the same information as the published version except that the median salaries are updated with 2015 data. The online site also allows direct linking to contacts for more information. As it has always been, the OOH is a valuable resource for students about to graduate from high school or college, recent graduates, individuals returning to the workforce after an absence, or anyone looking for a career change.—**Lawrence Olszewski**

Management

Handbooks and Yearbooks

C

45. Handbook on Corporate Governance in Financial Institutions. Christine A. Mallin, ed. Northampton, Mass., Edward Elgar, 2016. 296p. index. $175.00. ISBN 13: 978-1-78471-178-8.

As the world's economy begins to strengthen from the doldrums of the late 2000s and early 2010s, it is useful to reexamine mistakes from that period for lasting lessons. One of the most important lessons from that period is that intentional, well-defined corporate governance of financial institutions is an essential function of a healthy economy. In *Handbook on Corporate Governance in Financial Institutions,* edited by Christine A. Mallin of the University of East Anglia (Norwich, England), article authors provide an overview of selected topics in corporate governance. The book is organized by geographical location, and includes sections on Europe, the Americas, and the Asia-Pacific.

The book includes an article on American CEO pay, a topic that is frequently used to make political points. With the clear-eyed confidence that only empirical data can provide, the authors evaluate CEO pay in financial institutions and emerge with many interesting findings. One of the most interesting findings is that, despite popular conceptions, after 2008 (and the great recession), average CEO pay in financial firms is lower than average CEO pay in nonfinancial firms. The authors dedicate themselves to further study of this issue.

One of the most engaging chapters in the book is the seventh, which discusses corporate governance in China's city commercial banks. In this section, the authors pull back the curtain on the mysterious state-owned Chinese city commercial banking industry and paint a portrait of a Chinese banking industry in transition. At present, the Chinese banking industry is trying to root out corruption, keep up with emerging technology, and embrace mobile financial services.

Despite its title as a "handbook," the book could be more correctly classified as "selected topics" in corporate governance. It is a useful cross-cultural reference that could provide inspiration to businesses and policy-makers in other countries about best practices for corporate governance. The book is also readable, written in a reader-friendly engaging style.

Obviously a challenge in the area of corporate governance is the legal implications of corporate governance. What may be required of a publicly held company in France, for example, may not be required of a publicly held company in Nigeria. Readers should use caution, then, in assuming that every area of corporate governance is exportable to other countries. However, the book provides useful snippets on selected topics in corporate governance by country and will be a valuable resource for students, academics, and practitioners alike.

Recommended for academic libraries.—**Sara Mofford**

C, P

46. SAGE Video Business and Management Collection. http://sk.sagepub.com/video/business-management. [Website] Thousand Oaks, Calif., Sage. Price negotiated by site. Date reviewed: 2016.

The *SAGE Video Business and Management Collection* is a collection of hundreds of videos that can be viewed in both video and PDF format. SAGE Publications include many of their own productions in this extensive video collection.

Opening with Featured Videos, further examination of this database reveals typical business topics like Marketing with 191 videos, Entrepreneurship with 59 films, and Accounting with 6 titles. Lesser-known topics such as Information and Knowledge Management (1) and Other Management Specialties (27) also comprise the subject tool bar. Accessing subjects is easy via the standard search bar; also included is an advanced search option. A Content Type sidebar includes: Archival, Definition, In Practice, Interview, Key Note, Panel Discussion, Tutorial, and Video Case (which appears to be the SAGE publication name).

After a list of videos is retrieved, abstracts provide details about the specific films, a useful tool for further filtering. A click on a video title links users to the specific video page. Tabs for citations, adding to a personal list, or sharing are found on the right side of the screen. Options for viewing videos are standard with succinct, highlighted transcriptions scrolling in the right sidebar. The transcription is also available in downloadable PDF format. The video page has tabular options for Citations, Sharing, and saving to My List. Below the video is a one paragraph summary enabling researchers to evaluate the pertinence of the film to their area of study. Another practical feature for research is the Related Titles tab which includes relational information for continued study. Videos also can be viewed in chapters and segments that are part of a whole series.

This SAGE database gives students access to the world of business and offers a visual means for academic discourse. Topics cover a diverse array of subjects and run the gauntlet of business management. AMA-TV videos present contemporary news in business such as "Differentiating Products, Change, and QR Codes" which offers practical, constructive ideas. Some videos are more unique such as the BBC video "Birds" which gives eight examples of how bird habits in the wild relate to how one can run an effective business. Videos vary in duration from under five minutes to over an hour.

With good audio and visual components, the *SAGE Video Business and Management Collection* provides worthwhile film for business research. This database will be best used by students seeking both introductory and advanced information on business and management. This collection of films will also be useful to businesses seeking to enhance staff training.

Recommended.—**Janis Minshull**

Marketing and Trade

Handbooks and Yearbooks

C

47. **Analyzing the Strategic Role of Social Networking in Firm Growth and Productivity.** Vladlena Benson, Ronald Tuninga, and George Saridakis, eds. Hershey, Pa., Business Science Reference/IGI Global, 2017. 525p. index. (Advances in E-Business Research (AEBR) Book Series). $220.00 (individual chapters available for purchase in

electronic format). ISBN 13: 978-1-52250-559-4; 978-1-52250-560-0 (e-book).

Analyzing the Strategic Role of Social Networking in Firm Growth and Productivity is part of the series, Advances in E-Business Research; the series "provides multidisciplinary references for researchers and practitioners in this area" and covers "research on the concepts, issues, applications, and trends in the e-business field." This resource covers "the specific strategies for successful applications of social media for firm growth and expansion opportunities" and consists of chapters by specialists in the field. Topics covered include: the Irish radio industry's strategic appropriation of Facebook for commercial growth; the role of social media in marketing strategies in the airline industry; the use of social media in university career services; the use of social media as a learning tool; the management and performance of social media initial public offerings; and social media use in travel journalism. Authors of the chapters are from universities representing the United States, the United Kingdom, Australia, South Africa, the Czech Republic, Lithuania, Poland, Italy, Estonia, New Zealand, Spain, Germany, the Netherlands, Thailand, Turkey, and Singapore. Each chapter contains a list of references for further research and there is a compilation of references as a separate section in the book. A glossary of terms is provided at the end of each chapter. This resource is especially helpful in regard to case studies illustrating the use of Twitter and Facebook by specific companies; many chapters contain charts and statistics regarding use of social media. *Analyzing the Strategic Role of Social Networking in Firm Growth and Productivity* is highly recommended to libraries supporting programs especially in business, media and communications, and information technology. It is a valuable source for faculty, researchers, students, and practitioners.—**Lucy Heckman**

P

48.   Lemin, Daniel. **Manipurated: How Business Owners Can Fight Fraudulent Online Ratings and Reviews.** Fresno, Calif., Quill Driver, 2016. 151p. index. $14.95pa. ISBN 13: 978-1-61035-262-8.

"The customer is always right" is a longtime cliché that carries a new meaning in the age of the Internet. Specifically, customer reviews are no longer singular phone calls to store managers. Rather, a business' online presence allows, for better or worse, that singular phone call to be broadcast to everyone from the casual shopper to the longtime customer. This book helps readers address the specific concerns of the online ratings and reviews industry. Its clever title points to this industry's power to manipulate a business with devastating effect.

The chapters in part one show how cyberbullying, the rise of the SEO (search engine optimization) industry, the ease of fake reviews, and more have all contributed to the perilous online landscape. Chapters in this section also provide concise but helpful background on how the larger search engines (e.g., Google) work for a business, and gets to the nitty gritty about rating-and-review sites like Yelp or Angie's List. The chapters in part two offer "Tools and Tactics" by which business owners can develop strategies to fight against bad reviews, market the good reviews, detect fake reviews, and much more. For example, chapter ten instructs readers how to embed widgets from other sites onto their own website as part of a larger plan to broadcast good reviews, while chapter eleven discusses working with reputation management companies when technical expertise is required.

Charts, shaded text boxes, bullet points, key definitions, and more make for easy reference within both sections. With language and ideas that empower readers to take greater control of the online face of their business, *Manipurated* a is a fine and recommended business resource.—**ARBA Staff Reviewer**

C

49.   **Strategic Place Branding Methodologies and Theory for Tourist Attraction.** Ahmet Bayraktar and Can Uslay, eds. Hershey, Pa., Information Science Reference/IGI Global, 2017. 394p. index. (Advances in Hospitality, Tourism, and the Services Industry (AHTSI) Book Series). $205.00 (individual chapters available for purchase in electronic format). ISBN 13: 978-1-52250-579-2; 978-1-52250-580-8 (e-book).

This work examines one aspect of promoting tourism worldwide: branding, and in particular place branding. The 15 chapters explore topics such as region and city branding, branding techniques involving GIS mapping and "netnography," health tourism, street-level branding, and protecting urban "green infrastructure" through branding. Studies cover places around the world, from Barcelona, Spain and Portland, Oregon, to cities in India. The initial chapters define place branding, its importance to an area's economy, and methodologies to study it.

Scholars in urban studies, marketing, tourism, and several other fields will certainly find these studies of interest. This volume belongs in academic libraries of institutions where these subjects are studied. It should be noted that some of the chapters have copy-editing issues, which make the text more difficult to follow at times. Otherwise a most useful book in its field.—**Mark Schumacher**

5 Education

General Works

Dictionaries and Encyclopedias

C

50. **The SAGE Encyclopedia of Contemporary Early Childhood Education.** Couchenour, Donna and J. Kent Chrisman, eds. Thousand Oaks, Calif., Sage, 2016. 3v. $525.00/set. ISBN 13: 978-1-4833-4035-7; 978-1-4833-4033-3 (e-book).

Early childhood education transmutes as our culture, research, and implementation of services for the prenatal through kindergarten population guides us to improved learning options. SAGE has developed a beneficial three-volume print or online reference source that includes excellent contributions for introduction to a broad spectrum of education definitions, studies, programs, policies, and theories.

As the title states, this collection gives the most current explanations on a vast array of early childhood topics and is structured in encyclopedic form. Entries are arranged from "Abecedarian Project" through "Zero to Three."

Content of this compendium of early childhood education is meant to provide an inclusive and broad understanding of historical background, emerging curriculum, best practices, contemporary challenges, and solutions for this segment of our educational system. Developmental research is considered from topics of "Pre-Natal Mental Health" (Kingston et al, 2012) through kindergarten where the debate over skills learning or unstructured play continues. Optimal development is focal to entries with the end result of primary students (ages 6-8) being confident and successful learners.

Contemporary challenges in the form of autism, language, migrant families, multiracial classrooms, obesity, and work issues are addressed along with a plethora of others in this encyclopedia. There are ample entries defining early education programs like Early Headstart, HighScope, and Waldorf Education. Professional development is key to effective programs; "Master Teachers" and topics on assessment, coaching, mentoring, policies, and theories such as "Maturational Theory" and "Family Systems Theories" will enhance educators' knowledge.

Early childhood education has come a long way from the 1800s when it was first seen in the United States. Physical, cognitive, language, social, emotional, and aesthetic development ideas are found here along with best practices and what truly works for planning professionals.

As a starting point for research, *The SAGE Encyclopedia of Contemporary Early Childhood Education* is a robust resource for students and teachers in the field of early childhood education. Academic administrators and professionals in other areas of early childhood will benefit from having this available for staff.

Highly recommended.—**Janis Minshull**

C

51.   **The SAGE Encyclopedia of Online Education.** Steven L. Danver, ed. Thousand Oaks, Calif., Sage, 2016. 3v. index. $445.00/set. ISBN 13: 978-1-4833-1835-6.

This three-volume set explores the explosion of digital education with entries from scholars of interdisciplinary backgrounds which allows for broad coverage of this topic. Editor Steven L. Danver, of Walden University, has been involved with teaching in both traditional and online systems since the 1990s.

The first volume has the anticipated front matter resources, and each of the three volumes has similar introductory matter including a list of entries and reader's guide. Themes listed in the guide such as Instructional Practices and Pedagogy lead to subtopics such as Administrator Concerns and Laws and Regulations on both state and federal levels. Access to these more specific subtopics is easy because the encyclopedic entries are naturally alphabetic. Another streamlined approach for researchers who know their topic will be the extensive index found at the conclusion of volume three. The appendixes, also found in volume three, provide critical data on online education. The statistics and information in the appendixes strongly supplement the body of entries. Format of actual entries includes the body of information, the author, and options for extended study with *see also* references and further readings at the close of each submission.

Online education is a contemporary path to education where financial, geographical, socioeconomic, constraints of time, and discriminatory barriers are modified. However, web-based instruction has grown so rapidly that there are also adverse concerns about the quality of learning, substandard online institutions, and unethical recruitment. This encyclopedia includes history, technology, pedagogy, learning models, programs, regulations, and administrative aspects in both American educational systems and globally. Homeschool, K-12, college and university, remedial, adult, and at-risk students are some of the populations addressed. In these books, challenges and successes are thoroughly introduced with emphasis on improving academic rigor.

The introduction states that "by 2010, approximately 5.5 million students were participating in online courses…" (p. xxx). *The SAGE Encyclopedia of Online Education* is an excellent source for furthering the current role of the educational system in the digital form with overlays of traditional learning as well. This set will be most useful to students and potential students, faculty, and administrators searching for best practices in online, quality education.

Highly recommended.—**Janis Minshull**

C

52.   Spector, J. Michael. **The SAGE Encyclopedia of Educational Technology.** Thousand Oaks, Calif., Sage, 2015. 2v. index. $375.00/set. ISBN 13: 978-1-4522-5822-5.

The SAGE Encyclopedia of Educational Technology is a useful resource in the ever-changing world of educational technology. While technology in education is nothing new, the ever-expanding world of educational technology means that educational technology may become so vast that individuals have difficulty navigating this new and expansive landscape.

This encyclopedia contains 300-350 entries that are organized in A-to-Z fashion in two volumes. The encyclopedia is available in print and electronic format and contains a detailed index. The encyclopedia also contains a very useful reader's guide broken down into 29 topics for ease of use by the researcher. The researcher will enjoy this categorization of topics, as the reader's guide will save a significant amount of time.

The encyclopedia is not limited to traditional "in classroom" educational experiences. The encyclopedia also includes a significant amount of material on distance learning. The entry on Distance Learning for Professional Development is especially interesting. The article details the history of Distance Learning for Professional (nondegree) Development, including the original delivery method that included delivery by mail. The article also discusses the recent development of online professional development services, including an integration of professional development and social media and the much-trumpeted massive open online courses (MOOC) and the potential they offer for professional development. Finally, the entry includes an analysis and criticism of the methods for measuring the effectiveness of online distance learning professional development. The encyclopedia also includes an entry on Collaboration and Social Networking and the potential that educational technology offers to advance this new area. The entry includes an overview of social network sites, opportunities for collaboration through social network sites, and the implications of collaboration in social networking sites for learning. As online social networking is a fairly new technology, this is an evolving area and is subject to rapid advancement. However, this entry represents a valiant effort to detail this emerging technology and is a useful resource for researchers.

This volume will likely require updating in the future, not due to the fault of the authors and editors but because of the rapidly evolving nature of educational technology. As such, the electronic version of this encyclopedia may prove more useful to the researcher than the print version. However, either version of this encyclopedia will be a solid addition to the library of the researcher and academic alike.

Recommended for academic libraries.—**Sara Mofford**

Handbooks and Yearbooks

C

53.   **Adult Education and Vocational Training in the Digital Age.** Victor Wang, ed. Hershey, Pa., Information Science Reference/IGI Global, 2017. 295p. index. (Advances in Higher Education and Professional Development (AHEPD) Book Series). $190.00 (individual chapters available for purchase in electronic format). ISBN 13: 978-1-52250-929-5; 978-1-52250-930-1 (e-book).

This book provides a reference for the best ways to educate adults, often working adults who are seeking vocational skills. As formal educational institutions begin to adjust to offering more distance education programs to working adults, the method of instruction must adjust to this new student base. The adjustment to certificate programs is another reason that educational institutions must work to adjust their method of educational delivery to their new and nontraditional student base.

Victor Wang of Florida Atlantic University has used his extensive experience in adult education and vocational training to edit a wide-reaching anthology that includes 14 varied essays and case studies spread out over 294 pages. The essays are varied in scope and include the broad topics of critical thinking skills, gender considerations, instructional design, online learning, problem-based learning, school leadership, and serious games.

One of the hot topic essays, written by both Wang and Theresa Neimann of Oregon State University, is entitled "Deep Learning and Online Education as an Informal Learning Process: Is There a Relationship between Deep Learning and Online Education as an Informal Learning Process?" The essay considers two very different phenomena and the impact on adult education and vocational training. First, the essay explores informal learning, which is defined by the authors as a "universal current phenomenon of learning via participation, experience, or learning via student centered knowledge creation." This student-centered knowledge creation stands in stark contrast to more traditional learning methods which involve an instructor disseminating knowledge to students. While Wang and Neimann do not take a position that either method of instruction is superior to the other, they do make the point that the informal learning process may be more useful in an area like vocational education, where emphasis has traditionally been placed on peer-to-peer learning (i.e., the more experienced mentor providing "in the field" instruction to the new trainee). Further, the essay explores the impact that online education may have on these informal learning processes and the potential for online learning to strengthen or weaken this established method of learning.

Overall, the book is a very useful tool for those who are looking to explore online vocational learning and online adult learning. While the field is one that is constantly changing, the book provides a baseline for exploring current trends in an emerging field. This book is recommended for academic libraries.—**Sara Mofford**

C

54. Covili, Jared, and Nicholas Provenzano. **Classroom in the Cloud: Innovative Ideas for Higher Level Learning.** Thousand Oaks, Calif., Corwin Press, 2016. 200p. index. $31.95pa. ISBN 13: 978-1-4833-1980-3.

This book examines why educators need to expand their 1:1 device classrooms through cloud-based applications. The authors cover ways to store, communicate, collaborate, and create in the cloud—preferably for free. Also included are step-by-step instructions and anecdotes from teachers who are using these programs in their classrooms. Links are provided to these teachers' projects, but some links are private and require a login to access the materials. The book also touches on the digital divide that exists across this country and the budget cuts that have resulted in fewer people to provide professional development on the new technology. It should be noted that Google, which is promoted highly by the authors, has been accused of mining students' information when using their educational apps. If your students are going to use the GAFE products, be sure to have them log out of Google Drive so they can't access students' data. The authors do provide a list of apps for schools where the district filter will not allow access, but they are not detailed like the other resources. If a school is providing 1:1 devices and has no problems with the district filter, this book can be of use—keeping in mind the caveats listed above. Recommended.—**Linda DeVore**

C

55.   **Creating Teacher Immediacy in Online Learning Environments.** Steven D'Augustino, ed. Hershey, Pa., Information Science Reference/IGI Global, 2016. 356p. illus. index. (Advances in Educational Technologies and Instructional Design (AETID) Book Series). $185.00 (individual chapters available for purchase in electronic format). ISBN 13: 978-1-46669-995-3; 978-1-46669-996-0 (e-book).

This volume in IGI Global's Advances in Educational Technologies and Instructional Design (AETID) book series takes as its focus, as the title suggests, the concept of teaching immediacy in online learning environments. The book's 15 chapters tackle different aspects of this concept, with each chapter individually authored or co-authored, with Steven D'Augustino serving as the editor. Chapters one through seven concentrate on the issue of instructor presence in online courses, focusing on ways of improving or enhancing an instructor's immediacy in courses and addressing several different dimensions of the issue, such as vulnerability, cognitive functioning, and teaching. Chapter eight centers on tools for tackling synchronous and asynchronous teaching to foster instructor immediacy. Chapter nine examines social media, with a special focus on Facebook. Chapters 10 and 11 present strategies to enhance online courses and foster relationships between instructors and students. Chapters 12 and 13 concentrate on using media to enhance and facilitate effective, meaningful instruction. Chapter 14 tackles student perceptions of online instructors, and chapter 15 concludes the book with a case study of creating a game-like learning environment intended to enhance education. These chapters highlight current issues in online learning as well as anticipating trends and challenges, offering analysis and strategies which can help both online instructors and institutions looking to improve their online programs.

The book offers pretty decent geographical coverage, ostensibly providing an international perspective. However, it is rather United States-heavy. The chapter authors come from a variety of universities, though most of them are public institutions.

Format-wise, one questions the necessity of having the table of contents repeated three times. The book features a standard TOC which is then followed by a detailed TOC, which functionally offers brief abstracts of the chapters. This listing of contents with brief descriptions is essentially repeated in the preface. It would seem sufficient to have either a standard TOC or the detailed TOC. The inclusion of that same information in the preface seems questionable. Furthermore, each chapter features an abstract, so the detailed information is also repeated at least three times. The chapters are basically scholarly articles, so the structure of the chapters varies. Some chapters include brief "definitions of terms" while others do not. This is not necessarily a bad thing—just an observation. The illustrations are not great, which is surprising given IGI Global's usual insistence on high-definition images.

Despite these less-than-stellar observations, overall *Creating Teacher Immediacy in Online Learning Environments* is a well written and useful title, tackling critical issues of the online learning phenomenon and offering strategies which can help instructors and program developers alike. The price tag is a little steep for the title's length, but for those institutions looking to enhance their online programs and provide meaningful professional development resources to their online instructors, the price is worth the investment. Highly recommended for college/research libraries, particularly institutions with educational degree programs and eLearning programs.—**Megan W. Lowe**

P, S

56. **Digital Literacy Resource Platform.** **http://dlrp.berkman.harvard.edu/.** [Website] Free. Date reviewed: 2016.

Educators looking for quality resources addressing digital literacy will find something useful in this resource. This evolving collection focuses on copyright, online safety, privacy, creative expression, and information quality. Within each section the user will find a variety of resources, including lesson plans, infographics, videos, guides, research papers, and podcasts. The site is primarily designed as a resource for adults to use to find resources for classes and teaching, rather than a destination for students themselves. There are dozens of short videos on specific topics that will be useful to teachers in classroom settings. Some are created by high school or college students while some are professionally created. A unique feature is the Parent Collection, which provides items suitable for teachers to use in parent presentations or to send in weekly updates. Easy to search and packed with ideas, this is a resource that teachers can use over and over again. This will be on the agenda of new resources at our next staff meeting! Highly recommended.—**Claire Berg**

P, S

57. **Essential Lens: Analyzing Photographs across the Curriculum.** **http://www. learner.org/courses/lens/.** [Website] St. Louis, Mo., Annenberg Learner, 2016. Free. Date reviewed: 2016.

This online professional development resource provides educators with instructional materials for utilizing photographs in the classroom to enhance student understanding of varied concepts. Each of the cross-curricular collections contains a set of curated photographs along with suggestions for using the content in the classroom. Short videos provide effective methods for guiding students in examining and evaluating photographs. Teachers will also find key learning objectives, essential questions, discussion prompts, and activities incorporated into each collection. Correlations to national academic standards and Common Core State Standards are included where appropriate. Activities encourage students to closely examine photographs, helping them develop critical-thinking skills. Support resources include a short history of photography, a glossary of photographic terms, a guide to researching photographs, and links to additional sources for online photographic images. This resource should not be overlooked by teachers who are searching for ways to integrate visual literacy into their instruction. Recommended.—**Kim Brown**

P, S

58. Gliksman, Sam. **Creating Media for Learning.** Thousand Oaks, Calif., Corwin Press, 2016. 136p. index. $28.95pa. ISBN 13: 9781-4833-8543-3.

Students' digital interactions with their world outside of school can differ greatly from "text-on-paper" classroom assignments, making school seem irrelevant. This book is for the teacher who wants to bridge the gap and encourage student creativity by infusing technology into assignments. The author offers well-reasoned explanations as to why student-produced media products should be introduced into the curriculum, as well as hints on where to begin. From fairly simple photography, through audio and video projects, all the way to augmented reality, Gliksman explains the steps that students—and their teachers—need to learn to produce quality media. The author suggests programs, apps, and websites that can be used for different types of projects, and discusses the strengths and weaknesses of each. There is also a chapter on copyright and fair use with suggestions on how to ensure that students ethically use what they incorporate into their media productions. A companion website has project samples, additional resources, and a place for teachers to upload student projects which, over time, should give users even more ideas. Recommended.—**Christine Graves**

C

59. **Handbook of Research on Foreign Language Education in the Digital Age.** Congcong Wang and Lisa Winstead, eds. Hershey, Pa., Information Science Reference/IGI Global, 2016. 459p. illus. index. (Advances in Educational Technologies and Instructional Design (AETID) Book Series). $275.00 (individual chapters available for purchase in electronic format). ISBN 13: 978-1-52250-177-0; 978-1-52250-178-7 (e-book).

This volume is part of the ongoing IGI Global series Advances in Educational Technologies and Instructional Design which addresses topics on technology's integration with education and its effect on teaching practice. The *Handbook of Research on Foreign Language Education in the Digital Age* was managed by editors Congcong Wang and Lisa Winstead with contributions being reviewed at least twice and final contributions being decided by both reviewers and an advisory board.

Communication, language acquisition, and how to best teach the empowerment of such learning has been around for eons. In the twenty-first century, innovative technologies can advance pedagogy and student learning of languages. The collections of works here bring forth ideas, recognize challenges of teaching languages with technologies, and lay out the best approaches to using technology for the teaching and study of language.

This reference text explores current research, innovative pedagogy, trends, models, and approaches from multidisciplinary global perspectives. Case studies, such as chapter two which examines Massively Open Online Courses (MOOCs), examine the feasibility of intertwining language studies with technology. Content management systems, mobile devices, social media, website content builders, video, text documents, discussion boards, and audio can represent incredible opportunity for second language but can also represent barriers. The handbook also evaluates characterizing culture, heritage, and identity while using online sources. Chinese, Spanish, and Portuguese are more common languages discussed, and section four is devoted to marginalized languages resulting in a very broad usage potential

Usual front matter is enhanced with both a table of contents and a detailed table of contents where 17 chapters are represented with descriptions that will be useful to researchers unsure of what they need and also those who are seeking a specific vein of language and technology instruction. The five sections include: section one, Commentary; section two, Technologies across Continents; section three, Web Collaboration across Language; section four, Less Commonly Taught Languages; and section five, Teacher Education and Learning Strategies. Chapters are divided into efficient headings and also include, at times, practical information including glossary terms or pedagogical implications for teachers' classroom or virtual use. Information about the authors, a compilation of references, and an index round out the work.

Living in a global society, language acquisition is imperative for business people, leaders, and others with worldwide communication interests. The *Handbook of Research on Foreign Language Education in the Digital Age* is a very useful guide for the expansion of language education in the context of today's and future technologies and will be well loved by world language scholars and professors, as well as technology lovers seeking to understand how current digital devices and applications improve language studies and how this interplay will work in the future.

Highly recommended.—**Janis Minshull**

C

60.   **Handbook of Research on Professional Development for Quality Teaching and Learning.** Petty, Theresa, Amy Good, and S. Michael Putnam, eds. Hershey, Pa., Information Science Reference/IGI Global, 2016. 824p. index. (Advances in Higher Education and Professional Development (AHEPD) Book Series). $310.00 (individual chapters available for purchase in electronic format). ISBN 13: 978-1-52250-204-3; 978-1-52250-205-0 (e-book).

The *Handbook of Research on Professional Development for Quality Teaching and Learning* presents the latest research on a crucial question: what makes a quality teacher? In today's evolving world, the traditional educator path from college to classroom has been augmented. Teachers of today may enter the educational field in their mid-career after working in another job for years. There is no doubt that students benefit from instructors with diverse life experiences. However, there must be consistent standards that all teachers are held to in order to ensure that students are receiving a quality education. This question and others are answered in the handbook. Editors Petty, Good, and Putnam of the University of North Carolina at Charlotte have assembled a comprehensive handbook that is an indispensable resource for both researchers and education administrators. Each of the contributors to the handbook has exemplary academic credentials, adding further heft to their analysis. Further, the advisory board that Petty, Good, and Putnam assembled to review the contributions is equally as impressive.

Numbering 818 pages before the index, the book is as weighty as it is useful. The book contains 32 chapters broken up into four sections, including: Professional Development for Quality Teaching and Learning, Teacher Preparation and Professionalism, Preparing Teachers to Work with Diverse Populations, and Examining Outcomes of Teacher Preparation and Practice.

Chapter 22 is entitled "#UrbanLivesMatter: Empowering Learners through Transformative Teaching" and is especially salient. Inspired by the Black Lives Matter movement, authors Nicole Webster of Penn State, Heather Coffey, and Nathan Ash, both of UNC-Charlotte, explore the best ways to educate teachers on how to put into place "transformative teaching" in order to close the achievement gap between urban and nonurban students. The chapter discusses the urgent need for culturally responsive teaching, multicultural education, and critical literacy. The authors make the important point that the lives of their students do not exist in a vacuum. It is ineffective to teach civics to urban students who feel unrepresented in their government, for example, if those students are not presented with strategies to gain political power and implement changes in the government. The theoretical may not work with all students, and illustrating the practical effects of policies, both good and bad, on urban communities will bring the point home in a way that simply reading from a book would not.

This handbook is a useful resource and covers a tremendous amount of material. Highly recommended for academic libraries.—**Sara Mofford**

C

61. **Handbook of Research on Transforming Mathematics Teacher Education in the Digital Age.** Margaret Niess, Shannon Driskell, and Karen Hollebrands, eds. Hershey, Pa., Information Science Reference/IGI Global, 2016. 679p. index. (Advances in Higher Education and Professional Development (AHEPD) Book Series). $235.00 (individual chapters available for purchase in electronic format). ISBN 13: 978-1-52250-120-6; 978-1-52250-121-3 (e-book).

The editors have compiled a scholarly approach to surveying and reporting research about educating teachers in the use of technology to support mathematical learning among their students. The foreword explains the basis and assumptions in this approach to teacher preparation (called Technological Pedagogical Content Knowledge, or TPACK) from its introduction by Seymour Papert in 1993, and the preface gives further detail on the contents of each chapter. Each of the 22 chapters contains a list of its authors' affiliations, an introduction, background, conclusion, references, and key terms, with additional section headings specific to the chapter topic. The initial list of contributors is supplemented by a separate section about the contributors, and a simple table of contents is followed by a detailed TOC, with a short description of each chapter. A combined list of references and a general index complete the volume. The handbook is well designed, with such features as page numbers in the list of contributors, generous white space, and clear illustrations. One suggestion from this reviewer would be to add chapter numbers to the page headers. This well-researched and presented volume, aimed at teacher educators and K-12 administrators responsible for professional development, is highly recommended for all academic libraries supporting teacher education programs, graduate students, and faculty.—**Rosanne M. Cordell**

C

62. **Revolutionizing Education through Web-Based Instruction.** Raisinghani, Mahesh, ed. Hershey, Pa., IGI Global, 2016. 391p. index. (Advances in Educational Technologies and Instructional Design (AETID) Book Series). $185.00 (individual chapters available for purchase in electronic format). ISBN 13: 978-1-4666-9932-8; 978-1-4666-9933-5 (e-book).

On the surface, *Revolutionizing Education through Web-Based Instruction* is another good offering in IGI Global's Advances in Educational Technologies and Instructional Design (AETID) series. Chapters discussing the development of hypermedia systems and multimedia production, as well as how such technologies influence and potentially improve instructors' teaching practices reflect the title's main premise: how education can be revolutionized through web-based instruction. Additional topics like using digital and cross-platform storytelling, effective use of mobile technologies, learning styles, and best practices in web-based learning and teaching clearly support the title's premise and provide guidance in how instructors can make the most of web-based technologies and related concepts.

However, there are other chapters which do not seem to align so neatly (or at least obviously to this reviewer). The very first chapter looks at how educational approaches can help transform quantitative solutions with regard to climate change. The thrust of this chapter is more on climate change than anything, though it clearly addresses the application of educational approaches and other pertinent educational institutions and entities and their role in this process. However, for the most part, the educational aspect of the chapter feels tacked on, making the whole chapter seem significantly out of place. The second and third chapters take a similar approach: focusing on technology-related topics that legitimately connect to education, but not in the significant way one would expect from a title like this one. Chapters 4-17 are all far more aligned with the title and offer strategies and new ways of considering online education, offering case studies and practical applications of technology in the realm of education. But since those less-aligned chapters are first in the book, the book gets off to a potentially tangential start rather than a strong one that would hook readers looking for the theoretical and practical concepts that are suggested by the title.

If one ignores those first three chapters and focuses on 4-17, they will find a great many strategies and ideas that will support the online teacher and learner. Based on those chapters, this title is recommended, despite its price tag, particularly for academic libraries that support education degrees, especially those with instructional technology and online pedagogical features.—**Megan W. Lowe**

C

63. **The SAGE Handbook of Research in International Education.** 2d ed. Mary Hayden, Jack Levy, and Jeff Thompson, eds. Thousand Oaks, Calif., Sage, 2015. 633p. index. $160.00. ISBN 13: 978-1-4462-9844-2.

International education has become an important part of the academic world in the twenty-first century. Therefore, the book under review is very timely and a welcome addition to the education literature. This comprehensive book has 40 well-written chapters by educators and scholars from many countries. It is divided into four parts: Historical Roots, Definitions and Current Interpretations; Internationalism in the Context of Teaching and Learning; Leadership, Standards and Quality in Institutions and Systems of Education; and Promoting Internationalism and Globalization in National Systems: Case Studies. All chapters include references, tables, and figures. This edition will certainly help to improve education standards in many countries including Canada and the United States. Technology has linked all nations and this book will link all systems of higher education and research in the world for the benefit of all nations and students. Therefore, it is highly recommended for all academic libraries and major public libraries in all countries.— **Ravindra Nath Sharma**

C

64. **SAGE Video Education Collection.** http://sk.sagepub.com/video/education. [Website] Thousand Oaks, Calif., Sage. Price negotiated by site. Date reviewed: 2016.

SAGE Video has curated over 129 hours and over 450 videos that concentrate on education. Specifically this collection provides practical information on teaching settings and situations, guiding users in the application of educational theories to real-life situations. SAGE has divided these videos into 14 categories that range from Classroom Discipline and Organization to Working with Parents, Families and Communities. Within these categories SAGE has even more refined categories so the viewer can find specific topics that suit their interests and education needs. The viewer also has the ability to use the search bar in the collection to search for keywords tagged in each video. The viewer has the option of being able to follow along with the video by using the interactive transcripts of the video. A brief abstract accompanies every video in this collection along with publisher, publication year, content type, subjects, and keywords.

Viewers of this video collection are in for a unique interactive experience. Staying true to its purpose, all of these videos present practical information about implementing different theories and strategies. Even when videos are classified as definition- or lecture-style videos, such elements as graphics and pictures are added to keep the attention of the viewer and aid those who learn better with a hands-on approach. For example, Eric Jensen presents a lecture-style video on brain research. For some viewers, especially novice students of education, brain research can be an overwhelming topic. Jensen's creative instruction, however, presents meaningful pictures, videos, and graphs that enhance users' understanding of basic brain research and influence their planning and curriculum. Another beneficial video style in this collection is the tutorial videos. In the video titled *Parental Involvement vs. Parental Engagement in Education,* Ian Warwick describes many problems that educators have with parents. Not only does he describe these problems, he also provides plausible solutions for these problems along with stating research that supports his claims. This type of presentation and information will give educators knowledge and tools that they can use in their classrooms.

Highly recommended for academic libraries, public libraries, and professional development resources libraries in all levels of education.—**Sara Mofford**

Elementary and Secondary Education

Dictionaries and Encyclopedias

C

65.   The SAGE Encyclopedia of Classroom Management. W. George Scarlett, ed. Thousand Oaks, Calif., Sage, 2015. 2v. index. $375.00/set. ISBN 13: 978-1-4522-4139-5; 978-1-5063-1455-6 (e-book).

Working with an editorial board, W. George Scarlett has compiled 325 signed entries on classroom management in encyclopedic structure. Behavioral issues and breakdowns in discipline tarnish our world every day. Best teaching and learning environments form through effective classroom management. This collection offers future teachers options for developing their classroom style and offers those in the field with possibilities for change.

Articles are organized alphabetically; the electronic version has search boxes for specific queries. Another avenue for article access is the reader's guide which provides 16 thematic areas of content with some very hands-on categories such as Theories, Approaches, and Theoretical Constructs. The advantage of the guide will be a selection of choices under the same umbrella.

Submissions discuss general classroom management in terms of assessment, ethics, history, international classroom management models, and teacher education. Different leaders in classroom management are also introduced including: Jere Brophy, William Glasser, Marie Montessori, and Jean Piaget. Subset information on different populations provides additional teacher support; ADHD, English learners, deaf students, home school immigrant children, Muslim students, and special needs are some of the subjects with specific classroom management information.

Classroom management is essential to optimum learning for all students. Methodology samplings of Developmental Approaches, Responsive Classroom Approach, and Whole Class Methods along with many more provide intrinsic opportunities for student teachers and teachers to find systems that work with their classroom philosophy. Using the real-world strategies found in this collection will lead to classrooms where students thrive.

Back matter will be useful for extended research; two appendixes include a chronology and resource guide. Both will give scholars more resource options and necessary information to pull out specifics for more in-depth study.

Teachers can use this valuable guide to find a management style that works best, allowing them to elicit the best from all students. Evidence-based entries will support why such practices work and how to best establish them in a classroom scenario. While not definitive, this compilation will provide students who are pursuing a degree or position in the field of education with an excellent background in classroom management and point them in the direction for further study.

Highly Recommended.—**Janis Minshull**

Directories

C, P

66.   **The Comparative Guide to American Elementary & Secondary Schools.** 9th ed. Amenia, N.Y., Grey House Publishing, 2016. 1656p. index. $150.00pa. ISBN 13: 978-1-61925-931-7; 978-1-61925-932-4 (e-book).

This guide provides in-depth statistical data about 5,797 public schools with 1,500 or more students (except for single page state summaries which cover all public schools, regardless of student enrollment). The new edition includes district rankings by race and Hispanic origin, and new data tables highlighting test scores from the National Assessment of Educational Progress. The previous edition of this resource featured test scores in 4th- and 8th-grade reading, math, and sciences. The 9th edition has added "vocabulary, civics, geography, history, technology, and engineering literacy."

The format of the book is clear and easy to read despite the granularity of the data presented. There is a user guide that breaks down school district profiles and state and national educational profiles to facilitate comparative analysis. There are two main sections: State Chapters and National Chapters.

The State Chapter section is divided into four subsections. The first, the State Educational Profile, indicates the overall health of the state's schools, including student/teacher ratios, SAT/ACT test results, and graduation rates. The second subsection, State National Assessment of Educational Progress, presents 4th- and 8th-grade scores, broken down by gender, race, and ethnicity. School District Profiles are arranged alphabetically by county, then school district in the third subsection. The data provide numbers of librarians/media specialists, guidance counselors, enrollment, and finances. The fourth subsection, School District Rankings, covers 22 data points, including gender, student eligibility for discount or free lunches, and ethnicity.

The National Chapter section is divided into three subsections. The first, The National Educational Profile, indicates the overall health of all public schools in the nation, regardless of enrollment. It features many of the same data points as the State Educational

Profile. Second, national scores for the National Assessment of Educational Progress are provided, broken down by gender, race, and ethnicity. Lastly, National Rankings allow easy comparison, district by district. Data from the top and bottom 120 school districts are ranked.

A glossary of terms begins on page 1610, followed by two indexes: School District (an alphabetical listing of all districts in the guide) and City (an alphabetical listing of all cities including the page number of corresponding school district profiles).

A publisher's release from Grey House also stipulates that buyers of the print edition of the guide will receive "two years of free online access to GOLD, the Grey House Online Database." The latter contains more data points than the print version.

This valuable resource is highly recommended for school district, public, community college, and academic libraries supporting colleges of education.—**Laura J. Bender**

Handbooks and Yearbooks

C, S

67.   Kennett, Daron W., Kim Suzanne Rathke, and Kristin van Brunt. **The Game Plan: A Multi-Year Blueprint to Create a School Culture of Literacy and Data Analysis.** Lanham, Md., Rowman & Littlefield, 2016. 288p. index. $50.00pa; $49.99 (e-book). ISBN 13: 978-1-4758-1516-0; 978-1-4758-1517-7 (e-book).

The Game Plan: A Multi-Year Blueprint to Create a School Culture of Literacy and Data Analysis is a professional resource intended for instructional leaders to implement a six-year plan of action for implementing the Common Core Standards of literacy in the areas of social studies, science, and technical subjects. The book is divided into two sections: Developing the Culture and Building the Skill-Set. This resource begins with the basics including keys to choosing your literacy team. Also included are objectives to develop literacy and an assessment plan. The plan includes research-based professional development, semester-by-semester guidelines, strategies to keep all members of the team focused on the goal, instructional practices, and appendixes. The appendixes include literacy strategies, resources for leaders, and resources to extend beyond the school site. This step-by-step guide includes everything needed to develop a culture of literacy when implementing the Common Core Standards.

Recommended.—**Shelly Lee**

C, P, S

68.   **Khan Academy. www.khanacademy.org.** [Website] Free. Date reviewed: 2017.

Originally started by a hedge fund analyst helping his young cousins with their math homework, this is a free educational site open to any and all ages keen to learn about a gamut of topics with a strong focus on mathematics. Instructional videos and tutorials, often aligned to the Common Core Standards and also posted to YouTube, are created by content specialists from a range of backgrounds in education. Extra useful features include lessons supporting information literacy skills and strategies, help for standardized tests, assistive features for students with visual impairments, and availability in 10 languages. The ad-free site enlists users to create profiles to share and build a learning community. A reward system encourages motivated users to earn badges as they progress. Content pages also include interesting discussions with other members, including some of the content creators themselves. Other resources target parents and teachers, including a support community for asking and answering questions about using the site. Considering the no-cost price tag, easy to navigate site, useful support for important curriculum topics, and accessibility, this is a valuable resource worth checking out and sharing with your school. Recommended.—**Kasey Garrison**

S

69.   Mazeski, Diane, Becky McTague, and Margaret Mary Policastro. **Formative Assessment in the New Balanced Literacy Classroom.** North Mankato, Minn., Capstone Press, 2016. 168p. $24.95pa. ISBN 13: 978-1-4966-0295-4.

Aimed at those working with K-8 students, this title takes the reader through the process of implementing formative assessment in the balanced literacy classroom and school. The book begins by defining and discussing the purpose of both formative assessment and the balanced literacy classroom. Each section begins with Guided Questions to help readers internalize the information and focus on how to apply it to their own classrooms. Forms to assist in applying formative assessment in the following areas are included: Read-Alouds, Guided Reading, Language and Literacy Centers, Independent Reading and Writing, Teacher Surveys, and Sample Communications with Parents. A guide and suggested timeline for administrators to use is helpful in addition to an extensive reference list. Attractive layouts with diagrams, text boxes, and examples help clarify information. This is an excellent and easy-to-read presentation of text-dense materials that will serve teachers and administrators well. Highly recommended.—**Susan C. McNair**

C

70.   **Online Teaching in K-12: Models, Methods, and Best Practices for Teachers and Administrators.** Sarah Bryans-Bongey and Kevin J. Graziano, eds. Medford, N.J., Information Today, 2016. 324p. index. $65.00. ISBN 13: 978-1-57387-527-1.

This title is a collection of topics and case studies relating to online teaching and learning written by practitioners and professionals. The book is subdivided into three parts: foundations, supporting diverse learners, and implementation strategies. Each chapter includes an abstract, introduction, body, and conclusion. These are followed by references and, where appropriate, appendixes and/or a glossary. The entire book contains an appendix of abbreviations used. Individual chapters include subtopic headings in bold and black-and-white illustrations (charts, diagrams, etc.) where needed. The editors have maintained a consistency of style throughout in terms of presentation, but the multiple topics and individual author styles make some chapters easier to read than others. Recommended.—**Kyla M. Johnson**

C, S

71.   Prosser, Amy. **Tech Out Your Class: 6 Projects to Meet Common Core & ISTE Standards.** Eugene, Oreg., ISTE Publishing, 2016. 160p. $21.95pa. ISBN 13: 978-1-56484-379-1.

Step-by-step direction manuals are great, and this accessible guide to class technology projects that can be adapted for multiple grade levels certainly provides ample guidance. The resources provided support users no matter what levels of access or types of software

are available to them, and give seasoned techies ideas to expand and enhance existing projects. Readers are invited to browse through six chapters that address basic tasks: online research and collaboration; presentations; digital storytelling; spreadsheets and charts; screencasting; and blogging. Helpful tools include lists of corresponding Common Core and ISTE standards; subject-specific project ideas; planning charts; step-by-step directions including screenshots and flowcharts; and grading considerations, rubrics, and checklists. Each chapter ends with an overview, a "Big Picture" summary, a combination pep talk, and a reminder about how technology engages students and enhances learning. Information is presented in a straightforward and friendly fashion, with helpful hints scattered throughout. Readers will be inspired to try these technology innovations, and what's better, almost certainly be assured of success.

Recommended—**Kathleen McBroom**

C, P, S

72.   Rechtschaffen, Daniel. **The Mindful Education Workbook: Lessons for Teaching Mindfulness to Students.** New York, W. W. Norton, 2016. 274p. index. $24.95pa. ISBN 13: 978-0-393-71046-5.

A seemingly simple practice, mindfulness can have an extraordinary impact on our lives. Generally defined as being consciously aware of the present moment and one's place within it, mindfulness has been incorporated into therapies and education to great success. This book offers an interactive curriculum for educators wherein they can use mindfulness for themselves and for their classroom to great effect.

The material is divided into four sections which address creating mindfulness within oneself, making mindfulness accessible to the classroom, practicing mindfulness in accordance with learning objectives, and integrating mindfulness into the greater school environment. What might generally be perceived as profound concepts are nevertheless conveyed in easily digestible bits, with plenty of bold-faced paragraph headers, clear and affirming language, and proactive ideas for comprehending and enacting mindfulness.

Specifically, the material is presented as a workbook, meaning that it provides plenty of interactive lessons, worksheets, dialogue and journaling prompts, and more which help readers approach mindfulness practice and dissemination easily. For example, a section of the chapter on global literacy lessons walks educators through step-by-step instructions which build students' connection between the elements of the outside world and their senses. It offers dialogue questions, a journaling prompt to "draw a picture of yourself as your favorite element," and a plan to encourage students to seek out their "sit spot" in nature. Lessons are also designed to apply to students at various stages of their primary education. Bullet points, "inspiring quotes," highlighted learning objectives, and key vocabulary are additional tools used in this comprehensive and constructive workbook. Recommended for the libraries of schools of education and public libraries.—**ARBA Staff Reviewer**

C, P, S

73.   Wadham, Rachel L., and Terrell A. Young. **Integrating Children's Literature through the Common Core State Standards.** Santa Barbara, Calif., Libraries Unlimited/ ABC-CLIO, 2015. 179p. index. $45.00pa. ISBN 13: 978-1-61069-608-1; 978-1-61069-609-8 (e-book).

Integrating Children's Literature through the Common Core State Standards (Rachel L. Wadham is also the author, with Jonathan W. Ostenson, of *Integrating Young Adult Literature through the Common Core Standards* (see ARBA 2014, entry 506) begins with a brief introduction about the development, impact, and purpose of the Common Core State Standards (CCSS). The authors provide a short history of children's literature and research-backed examples about how integration of children's literature into the curriculum can help students achieve the "expectations" of the Core. For each of the Reading Standards (Reading Literature and Reading Informational Texts strands) for grades K-6, the authors suggest specific children's text options and activities teachers can use to implement the standards. An appendix contains activity templates related to each of the nine reading standards.

Readers of this book will learn a lot about children's literature; the CCSS; how children's literature (trade books, specifically) connects to the CCSS, and, in turn, how the CCSS can inform selection of texts; and how texts can be used "to engage students in their learning." The book contains a mind-boggling number of references to scholarly works and to children's texts (often with Internet links) and prolific examples of text analyses. This book is highly recommended for every K-6 teacher but will be especially valuable to those educators who want to maximize their students' achievement of Core standards.—**Christina Miller**

Higher Education

Directories

C, P, S

74.   **The College Blue Book.** 43d ed. New York, Macmillan Reference USA/Gale Group, 2015. 6v. $660.00/set. ISBN 13: 978-0-02-866299-2; 978-0-02-866313-5 (e-book).

This standard professional reference on higher education is an excellent place for high school counselors and undergraduate advisors to direct students and their parents. All the basic information is here in this six-volume set, and it identifies schools they may be interested in.

Narrative Descriptions lets you search geographically first and then by the schools listed. The descriptions for more than 4,500 colleges in the United States and Canada are listed. This includes entrance requirements, collegiate environment, and community environment in most cases. Costs per year are sometimes included. Once you have identified the schools you are interested in, the website address and school contact information is included. Occupational Education offers descriptions for 6,700 schools providing occupational or technical training. Descriptions include tuition costs, enrollment figures, and entrance requirements. In the Curricula and Areas of Instruction section users can search by subject area. Schools offering that subject are listed under each state. Scholarships, Fellowships, Grants, and Loans has more than 5,000 different sources of financial aid for students. Many of them are included in the general education area. Others are listed in eight broad subject areas. Other volumes offer different indexing, such as by subject, Degrees Offered by College and Subject, or by geographic area. Distance Learning

Programs has essays that pinpoint criteria and offer checklists for you to determine if this is a good fit for you. Tabular Data will be of interest to parents and guidance counselors advising students.

Highly recommended for high school guidance counselors and career centers, high school libraries, public libraries, undergraduate libraries, and career centers.—**Ladyjane Hickey**

Handbooks and Yearbooks

C

75. **Contemporary Approaches to Dissertation Development and Research Methods.** Valerie A. Storey and Kristina A. Hesbol, eds. Hershey, Pa., Information Science Reference/ IGI Global, 2016. 360p. index. (Advances in Knowledge Acquisition, Transfer, and Management (AKATM) Book Series). $195.00 (individual chapters available for purchase in electronic format). ISBN 13: 978-1-52250-445-0; 978-1-52250-446-7 (e-book).

The studies in this volume explore "the form, function and design of capstone projects of professional practice doctorate programs" (p. xviii), focusing on schools of education. The editors have brought together 19 studies, by 39 researchers, of various aspects of the topic, divided into three sections: "Nature of the Dissertation in Practice," "Innovative Approaches to the Professional Practice Doctorate," and "Impact of the Professional Doctorate on the Scholarly Practitioner." By examining the variety of programs available to current educational professionals—teachers, administrators, etc.—the authors explore the relationship between EdDs and PhDs, the potential research areas for practitioners, and the future of doctoral work in this field.

Any higher education institution, particularly those with colleges or schools of education, should consider this useful volume. Both students and faculty will benefit from the information presented here.—**Mark Schumacher**

C, P

76. **Developing Workforce Diversity Programs, Curriculum, and Degrees in Higher Education.** Chaunda Scott and Jeanetta Sims, eds. Hershey, Pa., Information Science Reference/IGI Global, 2016. 398p. index. (Advances in Higher Education and Professional Development (AHEPD) Book Series). $185.00 (individual chapters available for purchase in electronic format). ISBN 13: 978-1-52250-209-8; 978-1-52250-210-4 (e-book).

The editors of this volume have put together an important resource. Although there has been much discussion in higher education about the need for programs supporting workforce diversity career development, this reference work is one of the only sources emphasizing an interdisciplinary perspective toward development of these programs. The contributors to this book, 33 in addition to the editors, represent areas in human relations, marketing, management, counseling, medical education, and training, just to name a few. The target audience is broad, and goes beyond the boundaries of the academy. The focus in on both theory and practical applications that would appeal to researchers as well as business professionals, entrepreneurs, and college students.

The book consists of three sections containing a total of 17 chapters. Section one talks about a variety of existing workforce diversity programs that can either stand alone, or be integrated into other higher education initiatives. They include online courses, programs for black males, student-faculty mentorship, and education beyond the classroom, among others. Section two features strategies that can be inserted into existing curricula, such as team teaching, study abroad, counseling, and social justice/human relations programming. Section three highlights concepts that need to be incorporated into future development of workforce diversity degrees. Each chapter includes a list of references and suggestions for additional reading. There is a section about the contributors, as well as a comprehensive index beginning on page 396.

This work is highly readable. There are many personal anecdotes interleaved among the professional discussions. The writing provokes introspection in the reader. For example, in chapter six, where there is a discussion about racial dynamics, a light is shined on the darkness of learned racism in family, media, school, and day-to-day relationships. The reader is exposed to the ideology of white supremacy, repressive tolerance, and microaggressions. In short, this reference would be an important addition to corporate, public, community college, and university libraries.—**Laura J. Bender**

C

77. **Handbook of Research on Mobile Devices and Applications in Higher Education Settings.** Laura Briz-Ponce, Juan Antonio Juanes-Méndez, and Francisco José García-Peñalvo, eds. Hershey, Pa., Information Science Reference/IGI Global, 2016. 607p. index. (Advances in Mobile and Distance Learning (AMDL) Book Series). $300.00 (individual chapters available for purchase in electronic format). ISBN 13: 978-1-52250-256-2; 978-1-52250-257-9 (e-book).

The *Handbook of Research on Mobile Devices and Applications in Higher Education Settings* offers a broad overview of the state of mobile devices and applications (apps) in the higher education landscape. Organized into five sections, the book offers an introduction of mobile technology in higher education, examples of specific apps and how they can be implemented, perceptions of both students and teachers on how these apps are used, and case studies from teachers using apps and devices in their classrooms. Chapters are authored by scholars from all over the world, and while each can stand on its own, their presence as a collection allows the book to offer truly international coverage on the use of mobile technology in the academic setting. Especially helpful are the chapters that look at the use of devices or apps in specific educational settings, providing inspiration for the reader to apply them to their own instruction. A comprehensive reference list is included at the end of each chapter, guiding further reading for those that would like to dive deeper into a topic. This book is best suited for an academic library due to its focus on higher education but is well worth a look for anyone interested in using mobile technology in instruction.—**Andrea C Kepsel**

C, P

78. **Increasing Productivity and Efficiency in Online Teaching.** Patricia Dickenson and James Jaurez, eds. Hershey, Pa., Information Science Reference/IGI Global, 2016. 327p. index. (Advances in Educational Technologies and Instructional Design (AETID) Book Series). $185.00 (individual chapters available for purchase in electronic format). ISBN 13: 978-1-52250-347-7; 978-1-52250-348-4 (e-book).

The 29 contributors to this reference (including the editors) tackle head on the problems and concerns facing institutions and instructors offering online learning. They explore several possible solutions and ways to overcome challenges of student isolation and high dropout rates at a time when increased access to online courses is at an all-time high.

The book consists of four sections divided into 15 chapters. Section one highlights the design of content and courses including ways to design instruction for millennials, ideas to enhance courses using gaming and visualization techniques, the adaptation of existing classroom courses to the web, and a study of how grade appeals can improve course efficiency and quality. Section two discusses communication techniques essential to well-designed online courses. Some featured strategies include the use of social media, online collaboration, tools to connect with students such as online charts and calculation software, and discussion forums. Section three provides details about the critical areas of assessment and assignments using quizzes, discussion boards, self-directed learning projects, and the revised *Bloom's Taxonomy* to help students master the cognitive process. Section four builds on the previous three sections by emphasizing advanced frameworks for game design, cloud monitoring, simulations to increase student involvement, and advanced tools for online grading.

Each chapter includes a bibliography and a suggested reading list, and there is a compilation of references at the end of the volume. Chapters also include a listing of key terms and definitions. A comprehensive index begins on page 324.

Editors Dickenson and Jaurez have put together a valuable resource for teachers, researchers, and curriculum administrators who are tasked with improving and expanding quality and efficiency in online education. This reference is recommended for public, community college, and university libraries.—**Laura J. Bender**

C

79. Revolutionizing Modern Education through Meaningful E-Learning Implementation. Badrul Khan, ed. Hershey, Pa., Information Science Reference/IGI Global, 2016. 341p. index. (Advances in Educational Technologies and Instructional Design (AETID) Book Series). (individual chapters available for purchase in electronic format). ISBN 13: 978-1-52250-466-5; 978-1-52250-467-2 (e-book).

Revolutionizing Modern Education through Meaningful E-Learning Implementation is a resource aimed at gathering scholarly research to best educate and reach digital natives. The most commonly accepted definition of a digital native is a person born or brought up during the age of digital technology who has been familiar with computers and the Internet from an early age. Now, most school-age students are digital natives. As students change, so too must the method of delivery.

Revolutionizing Modern Education through Meaningful E-Learning Implementation as edited by Khan provides a series of essays on this very topic of E-Learning. The book is 339 pages long preindex, and discusses a wide range of topics, from Massive Online Open Courses (MOOCs), to Blended Learning, to reaching other cultures using Massive Online Open Courses, to faculty development in the e-learning environment.

One word in the book's title stands out: meaningful. While the accessibility of online education has certainly helped the masses access education in ways that they have not accessed education before, the quality and reliability of that education should be as close to face-to-face educational experiences as is possible. One of the fundamental problems in evaluating education, and especially online education, is assessing the effectiveness of the education from the perspective of the student. This assessment is especially rare but necessary in MOOCs, where students are only tangentially formally enrolled and have little, if any, opportunity to provide feedback to the course instructors. The essay "To MOOC or Not to MOOC, That is the Problem: A Learner's Perspective" begins to shed light on a quality chasm between MOOCs and face-to-face courses. The essay explores the explosion of MOOCs from the perspective of the student, and begins to cut through the hype behind MOOCs to evaluate the quality of said courses. The authors of the essay set out a methodology for evaluating these MOOCs based on dimensions such as institutional, management, technological, and interface design. The method of evaluation posed by the authors helps to provide a consistent framework across institutions, platforms, and courses so that students can begin to properly assess each course before they invest time and, in some cases, treasure, into enrolling in the course. Additionally, it will provide feedback to institutions so that they can improve their MOOC offerings.

Overall, *Revolutionizing Modern Education through Meaningful E-Learning Implementation* is a useful resource in a fluid world of changing online education. This book is recommended for academic libraries and professional development collections.—**Sara Mofford**

C, S
80.   William, K. Elliott, III, and Melinda K. Lewis. **Student Debt: A Reference Handbook.** Santa Barbara, Calif., ABC-CLIO, 2017. 303p. illus. index. (Contemporary World Issues). $60.00. ISBN 13: 978-1-4408-4487-4; 978-1-4408-4488-1 (e-book).

This title provides an overview to the challenges and potential solutions of exorbitant education costs in the United States. Beginning with a chapter providing background on student debt, the seven chapters provide research, essays (from contributing and relevant authors), data, documents, and more. Black-and-white photos and figures provide supplementary data such as "Total Student Loan Debt in Millions of (2014) Dollars." Chapters begin with a solid introduction and end with references for extended study.

This book explains the history of student loans beginning with the G.I. Bill in 1944 and comes full circle to policy, servicing student loans, bankruptcy laws, and the impacts of state and federal regulations on educational loans today. Documents like the "Student Loan Affordability Act" (2013) and the dialogue of those involved in legislation are included in this book. Layers unfold as various perspectives are presented. Loans create barriers and those who may benefit most from educational pursuits are often deterred by the potential debt to be accrued in pursuit of education. The book demonstrates that dramatic change is essential to reducing financial barriers to higher education; authors Elliott and Lewis inform readers that the national and state government, administrators, families, and students need to be the mechanism to ensure that change happens at all levels of the educational process.

Student Debt: A Reference Handbook is best suited for administrators of high school and college institutions seeking modification to financial aid programs. This guide will be particularly beneficial for parents and professionals in an advisory role working with students as they consider their education and career in the context of navigating financial aid.

Recommended.—**Janis Minshull**

C, P, S

81.　**World University Rankings and the Future of Higher Education.** Kevin Downing and Fraide A.Ganotice Jr., eds. Hershey, Pa., Information Science Reference/IGI Global, 2016. 532p. index. (Advances in Educational Marketing, Administration, and Leadership (AEMAL) Book Series). $190.00 (individual chapters available for purchase in electronic format). ISBN 13: 978-1-52250-819-9; 978-1-52251-820-5 (e-book).

This volume offers a detailed examination of world rankings of institutions of higher education: the process of creating the rankings and the groups that do so, rankings' impact on a country's standing in the educational realm, and activities undertaken by numerous institutions worldwide to enhance their standing. Some of the 22 chapters are quite technical, dissecting the process of creating the various ranking systems and proposing new statistical or analytical approaches for evaluating institutions of higher education, given the potential bias of some of the current tools.

This volume is clearly aimed at scholars studying higher education on a global scale. This will be most useful for academic libraries serving schools of education. Alas, as often is the case in books from this publisher, copyediting is not very good: words capitalized for no reason (four times in a five-line paragraph), errors of grammar, and incomplete citations in reference lists abound. Nevertheless, this information will be useful to those exploring these topics.—**Mark Schumacher**

Learning Disabilities

Directories

C, P

82.　**The Complete Learning Disabilities Directory, 2017.** 20th ed. Amenia, N.Y., Grey House Publishing, 2016. 537p. index. $165.00pa. ISBN 13: 978-1-61925-930-0.

The 20th edition of *The Complete Learning Disabilities Directory* begins with an introduction, a handy glossary, a user's guide, and a user's key. These are followed by 21 sections, such as Associations & Organizations, Government Agencies, Learning Centers, and Testing Resources. The book concludes with three indexes: "Geographic Index," "Entry & Publisher Name Index," and "Subject Index." The indexes refer to the entry numbers used throughout the book. There are guide words at the tops of pages, and each section is clearly subdivided to facilitate use. For example, in the section on ADHD, material is grouped by national programs, publications/videos, and websites. Within these groups, lists are alphabetic. The information provided for each entry varies, but all have basic contact information, the name of the director or key executive, and a brief description. This reliable and timely reference will save caregivers and professionals valuable time. It is recommended for public libraries and academic libraries serving schools of education. The title is also available at http://gold.greyhouse.com.—**ARBA Staff Reviewer**

Handbooks and Yearbooks

C, P

83.   Ingersoll, Irene. **College Success for Students with Disabilities: A Guide to Finding and Using Resources, with Real-World Stories.** Jefferson, N.C., McFarland, 2016. 238p. index. $29.95pa. ISBN 13: 978-1-4766-6288-6; 978-1-4766-2405-1 (e-book).

Beginning college is challenging enough, but for students with disabilities it poses many new issues that must receive prior planning if at all possible. Ms. Ingersoll was able to describe much of the information needed by students with disabilities in order to apply for college and to experience success while there. By pointing out the need to have current documentation of a disability and individual needs as a result of that disability, she has helped the reader to focus on getting ready right from the start. It is important to remind students (and their parents or teachers who might be helping them), that though some high school personnel may say they do not have to provide a current diagnosis (typically within the last three years), the student should use language to the effect that they are requesting the documentation to determine if they still have the disability and to what extent. They may not want to say they are seeking documentation in order to apply for services in college.

Entering college can be tricky, but one of the other first steps should be to identify which college is a good fit for this student. Some students want to attend a college they feel comfortable with and one that provides services, but they may find that college or university does not provide the degree option they are seeking. There is no need to request acceptance at a college of accommodations if the degree is not offered. It is important then, for students to learn advocacy skills prior to going to college and then to use the information presented in this book to continue to advocate once they apply to the appropriate colleges or universities.

Ingersoll has provided some excellent examples of students with various disabilities who sought supports on their campuses. These examples should be helpful for other students who might experience the same or similar needs on their own campuses. Ingersoll has also supplied information about some accommodations that might be made if the student needs physical accommodations (different desk size), or if the student might need accommodations with testing (extra time, etc.).

Reminding each student that he/she is responsible for their learning—including attendance and completion of assignments is imperative, and she stressed that early on in this book. By telling the reader the importance of meeting with each professor during their office hours, Ingersoll has also relayed some of the most important information for them to experience success. A description of college support services and resources helps students to get an idea of what types of services they might be able to receive instead of just wondering and never knowing what to ask for. The section on foreign language requirements and possible options was also very helpful.

Some students come to college with no diagnosis, and this book supplies the undiagnosed student with a brief but informative description of what to do to possibly get help. This population is often forgotten, and it was wonderful to find this information in this book. By providing individual chapters on specific diagnoses, a student can easily navigate this book to try to find out what he/she might have to do to receive services as well as what types of accommodations might be available. In addition, the student is given helpful suggestions regarding their responsibilities if they want to experience success.

The specific information in Ms. Ingersoll's brief book can be helpful for many students with disabilities seeking a higher education, and I especially appreciate the advocacy section toward the end. Many students with disabilities who think they might want to pursue a college degree should be given this book so they can begin to prepare for success as an adult.—**Donna J Kearns**

C, P

84.   **Learning Disabilities Sourcebook.** 5th ed. Keith Jones, ed. Detroit, Omnigraphics, 2016. 544p. index. (Health Reference Series). $85.00. ISBN 13: 978-0-7808-1520-9; 978-0-7808-1521-6 (e-book).

The fifth edition of the *Learning Disabilities Sourcebook* represents the latest consumer health information on neurological disorders and how learning is affected. It is part of Omnigraphics' Health Reference Series, which provides titles in specific areas of the medical field that are useful to the general public. An advisory board was created for development of the series.

All titles in the series are similar in format and the *Learning Disabilities Sourcebook* maintains that structure. The 544-page book has 50 chapters spread over five main parts. The primary sections are: Understanding and Identifying Learning Disabilities; Types of Learning Disabilities; Other Disorders That Make Learning Difficult; Learning Disabilities and the Educational Process; and Living with Learning Disabilities. Part six, Additional Notes and Information, contains a glossary, directory of resources, and "Sources for College Funding for Students with Disabilities."

This reference book defines learning disabilities and states the causes, facts about diagnosing, and what the learning process looks like for individuals. Initial chapters explain brain function, learning milestones, and what to watch for in diagnosing disabilities. Chapters also include common disabilities like dyslexia with subtopics for greater clarity of information. Chapters may also cover lesser-well-known disabilities like XYY Syndrome. Entries describe how disability happens (inherited, chromosomal disorders, brain injuries, etc.) and possible learning delays. For those seeking information on specific neurological problems, this will serve only as introduction. Certain chapters are sure to be used, particularly those that offer guidance to caregivers and families on such topics as early intervention strategies and the transition to adulthood.

Recommended.—**Janis Minshull**

6 Ethnic Studies and Anthropology

Ethnic Studies

General Works

Dictionaries and Encyclopedias

C, P, S

85. **Ethnic American Food Today: A Cultural Encyclopedia.** Lucy M. Long, ed. Lanham, Md., Rowman & Littlefield, 2015. 2v. maps. index. $170.00/set; $169.99 (e-book). ISBN 13: 978-1-4422-2730-9; 978-1-4422-2731-6 (e-book).

This 700-page set, written by over 120 contributors, explores the food from scores of countries—its origin, its arrival in America, its place and importance in today's culture and society—from simple dining at home to ceremonial meals (holidays, weddings, etc.). An interesting element of these accounts is the adaptation of immigrants' cooking to a new set of conditions, particularly the availability of ingredients. Articles range from two to nine pages, based on the importance of the particular cuisine within the entire foodways of the United States. Articles range from France and India to Cornwall and the Comoros Islands. Some entries may include recipes of typical dishes. Most articles include sources for further reading.

A quite minor issue: the maps are not very easy to read, and the one for India employs city names that were changed to others in the 1990s. Otherwise this is a rich resource for anyone interested in a broad look at the culinary world in the United States. Public libraries, high school libraries, and college libraries should consider it for their collections.—**Mark Schumacher**

C, S

86. Michaud, Jean, Margaret Byrne Swain, and Meenaxi Barkataki-Ruscheweyh. **Historical Dictionary of the Peoples of the Southeast Asian Massif.** 2d ed. Lanham, Md., Rowman & Littlefield, 2016. 556p. (Historical Dictionaries of Peoples and Cultures). $140.00; $139.99 (e-book). ISBN 13: 978-1-4422-7278-1; 978-1-4422-7279-8 (e-book).

Written and edited by Jean Michaud, Meenaxi Barkataki-Ruscheweyh, and Margaret Byrne Swain, this second edition, part of the Historical Dictionaries of Peoples and Cultures, is a significant addition to the series as much has changed in the 10 years since the first edition.

The A-Z entries define events, institutions, places, politics, and social issues. The opening pages offer useful supplemental information for students including a chronology and maps. In addition to maps, visual information includes photos and tables with data. Appendixes are also found. The introduction, by the primary author, Jean Michaud, is written not only as a beginning point but provides solid contextual information not found elsewhere; Michaud states on page seven that "the Massif covers approximately 2.5 million square kilometers, around the size of Western Europe." Such discourse makes the introduction very pragmatic for background research. An extensive bibliography and author biographies round out the work.

Geographical areas covered are: Bangladesh, Burma (Myanmar), Cambodia, China, India, Laos, Malaysia, Taiwan, Thailand, and Vietnam. Topics in the dictionary are often very specific to a group such as the Na People or a place like the Kachin State. The entries also explain the many diverse languages in the region. General subjects such as gender are worthy overtures and provide a springboard to further inquiry. Tradition and historical entries use contemporary information. Within submissions, related topics are in bold type which lets students know of the option to follow this lead to another topic in the book.

Historical Dictionary of the Peoples of the Southeast Asian Massif, as a reference text, provides inclusive introductory information about this diverse geographical region. Designed for easy access and with over 250 new entries in the second edition, this is a useful tool for high school and college students. Areas of studies may include anthropology, archaeology, historical or current southeast Asian studies, and sociology.—**Janis Minshull**

C, S

87.   Williams, Victoria. **Celebrating Life Customs around the World: From Baby Showers to Funerals.** Santa Barbara, Calif., ABC-CLIO, 2016. 3v. index. $294.00/set. ISBN 13: 978-1-4408-3658-9; 978-1-4408-3659-6 (e-book).

This large, three-volume encyclopedia focuses on documenting traditions, rituals, rites of passage, and life customs from various countries around the world. The scope of the book is on rituals related to women, men, children, and animals whether as individuals or in groups. Volume one examines customs related to birth and early childhood, volume two discusses customs related to early adulthood and adolescents, and volume three explicates customs related to aging and death. Each volume is a self-contained alphabetical encyclopedia, and each has a centrally located group of color plates. The author indicates that some may find the descriptions and even photos of some of these rituals and customs disturbing and even distasteful, but the publication is an objective documentation of these practices. Both researchers and general readers will find this encyclopedia useful, as each entry is self-contained with cross-references and short bibliographies. A select bibliography for each volume and a comprehensive index for the three volumes are included in each volume. This is an excellent encyclopedia for both high school and college/university libraries as a starting point for initial research in global world cultures and customs.—**Bradford Lee Eden**

Handbooks and Yearbooks

C, P, S

88.   **D-Place: Database of Places, Language, Culture and Environment. https://d-place.org/home.** [Website] Free. Date reviewed: 2017.

This database, developed with support from the National Evolutionary Synthesis Center and the Max Planck Institute for the Science of Human History, aims to provide users with a means to compare and contrast a large variety of cultural characteristics of many societies across the globe. The site holds a vast amount of data (cultural, linguistic, environmental, and geographic) for over 1,400 localized "societies." Examining the data sources page on this site is very helpful in attaining a good comprehension of the data gathering. The site makes strong use of visuals to share its data, using tables, maps, and unique icons to help users navigate. The Search tab allows users to select a Places, Language, Culture, or Environment tab or to make their own entry if their search has already narrowed. Each of these tabs then offers further categories from which to refine the search. For example, selecting the Language tab leads users to then select a Language Family, which narrows the search to the societies connected by tongue. For users unfamiliar with the site, the How To tab walks them through different types of searches (e.g., Simple Search or Targeted Search). This site would be useful to advanced students, researchers, and educators in anthropology, linguistics, and more.—**ARBA Staff Reviewer**

C, S

89.   **People of Color in the United States: Contemporary Issues in Education, Work, Health, and Immigration.** Kofi Lomotey and others. Santa Barbara, Calif., Greenwood Press/ABC-CLIO, 2016. 4v. $399.00/set. ISBN 13: 978-1-61069-854-2; 978-1-61069-855-9 (e-book).

U.S. census experts claim that the white majority will be gone by 2043. In July of 2011, the Census Bureau reported: "Most Children Younger than Age 1 are Minorities." Given these developments, Greenwood (ABC-CLIO) appears to be capitalizing on the growing interest in diversity by introducing *People of Color in the United States: Contemporary Issues in Education, Work, Communities, Health, and Immigration.* Each of the four volumes is dedicated to a different aspect of the minority experience in America: Education, Social Life (employment, housing, family, and community), Health/Wellness, and Immigration/Migration.

Though published as a set, each volume can stand on its own, with its own editor(s) and contributors. The format for every volume, however, is exactly the same. The bulk of each is a collection of 50-60 signed "Essays" that run four to eight pages. They are written by professors, professionals, and "emerging scholars" (graduate students), and end with "Further Readings" and *see also* references when necessary. Students who are looking for term paper topics may browse the "Perspective & Debates" section following the essays. Here the editors have commissioned authors to write from a given perspective or on a current debate topic, such as "Is home schooling good for students of color?" The editors have selected a dozen of these for their respective volume. To make the set easier to use, the publisher has included a "Guide to Related Topics" at the beginning of each volume that lists entry titles under similar topics together. Volumes end with "Recommended Readings" (books, articles, websites, and films/videos), a list of contributors with credentials, and a comprehensive index.

People of Color in the United States is aimed at students, especially high school and undergraduates, and the general public. The overarching goal of the set is to educate. Topics have been selected to highlight issues of particular importance to minorities in America, such as racism, tracking, school-to-prison-pipeline, ethnic identity, hazing in African American fraternities, domestic violence, addiction and substance abuse, and affirmative action, to name only a few. Given the hundreds of contributors to this massive effort, the quality is bound to be uneven. The ratio of professional to "emerging scholar" entries varies per volume. For example, in volume three, health and wellness, most of the entries are written by professionals, while in the other volumes the ratio is closer to 50/50. Even so, a cursory reading of entries revealed clear and concise writing on topics that are unique to people of color in the United States. *People of Color in the United States* is an excellent place to begin doing research on a topic in this area.—**John P. Stierman**

African Americans

C, P, S

90.   **Documenting Ferguson. http://digital.wustl.edu/ferguson/index.html.** [Website] Free. Date reviewed: 2017.

This is a freely accessible online digital repository initiated by librarians at Washington University in collaboration with other St. Louis-area organizations and universities. The goal of *Documenting Ferguson* is to make available digital media captured and created by members of the Ferguson-area community after unarmed African American Michael Brown was shot to death by white police officer Darren Wilson on August 9, 2014. For those interested in knowing more, a link to a report explaining the project is available under the Our Purpose tab. The project team members are Rudolph Clay, Head of Library Diversity Initiatives and Outreach Services and African & African American Studies Librarian; Shannon Davis, Digital Library Services Manager; Chris Freeland, Associate University Librarian; Nadia Ghasedi, Associate University Librarian; Sonya Rooney, University Archivist; Andrew Rouner, Director of Scholarly Publishing; Rebecca Wanzo (faculty advisor), Associate Director for The Center of the Humanities; and Micah Zeller, Copyright Librarian.

Clicking View the Collection on the main page takes users to links for Browse All, Browse by Date Added (ascending), Browse by Tag, and Browse Map. There are audio files, letters, video files, photographs, and more. Items include a title, a description, the name of the creator, a date, format information, and a citation. The Contributor tab allows community members to upload images, audio, video, and stories. This page links to terms and approval criteria and to image use conditions. There is also a tab that takes users to additional resources, including articles, a resource guide on policing, community protest, and unrest, and more.—**ARBA Staff Reviewer**

C, P, S

91.   **Georgetown Slavery Archive. http://slaveryarchive.georgetown.edu/.** [Website] Free. Date reviewed: 2017.

The *Georgetown Slavery Archive* is a digital archive devoted to the stories of the slaves owned by Maryland Jesuits and Georgetown University. The archive is an ongoing project which hopes to add to its collection over time. The home page displays Recently Added Items, a Featured Item, and a Featured Exhibit. Users can also choose from several tabs on the header bar. The Gallery displays a sample of nine archived items. Viewers can select a thumbnail of the artifact to learn descriptive information: its subject, source, date, tags, geolocation, and more. Users will find maps, bills of sale, manifests, letters, photographs, and other materials. Archived manuscripts have been transcribed. Alternatively, users can select from a longer Inventory to peruse other items, similarly annotated. Selecting Browse Collections leads to five curated collections, such as "Descendants Stories" and "Slavery at Georgetown College." The Descendants tab explains the project's ongoing mission to find and work with descendants of these particular Maryland slaves in order to enhance the archive for the public good. A Map tab allows users to find artifacts by location. The site reflects an important part of the American slave era.—**ARBA Staff Reviewer**

C, P

92. Knoblock, Glenn A. **African American Historic Burial Grounds and Gravesites of New England.** Jefferson, N.C., McFarland, 2016. 322p. illus. index. $45.00pa. ISBN 13: 978-0-7864-7011-2; 978-1-4766-2042-8 (e-book).

Although Knoblock is best known for his work on African Americans in the military—he was the top military contributor to the multivolume *African American National Biography* (see ARBA 2009, entry 14)—he also writes on regional history, as evidenced in this current volume. The author visited graveyards, mostly little known, in six New England states (Connecticut, Rhode Island, Massachusetts, New Hampshire, Vermont, Maine) to discuss the individuals buried there and their significance to local history, making this volume extremely important for beginning and experienced researchers in cultural history and genealogy and the sociology of death. But perhaps just as important if not more so are Knoblock's introductory essays on African American funerary rites and customs in the select states. Readers will certainly be fascinated by the history of African American gravestones, and the author includes a generous selection of photographs of these monuments to accompany the texts. Although the scope and range of the research are obviously limited, users will find much useful information here that can serve as models for other regional studies. An excellent contribution to the small but growing library on African American localized funerary customs and cemeteries, including Lynn Rainville's *Hidden History* (University of Virginia Press, 2014).—**Anthony J. Adam**

C, P

93. Prahlad, Anand. **African American Folklore: An Encyclopedia for Students.** Santa Barbara, Calif., Greenwood Press/ABC-CLIO, 2016. 413p. illus. index. $100.00. ISBN 13: 978-1-61069-929-7; 978-1-61069-930-3 (e-book).

Designed as an introductory guide to the field of African American folklore for undergraduate students, University of Missouri professor Prahlad's single-volume encyclopedia covers a wide range of topics in a variety of fields. The 134 essays are relatively short at about one or two pages each, but all of these well-written essays by a series of academic scholars provide sufficient information to launch further investigation. Each signed essay includes a brief secondary bibliography, and many feature additional cross-references and black-and-white photographs. Topics range from the general, such as "Legends" and "Prayer," to the more specific, such as "Grave Decorations" and "Field Hollers." Although the volume is designed for students, the writing follows a fine balance between the popular and the scholarly, making it accessible to anyone searching for these topics. The volume concludes with a summative secondary bibliography and index for ease-of-use. Libraries which already own Prahlad's three-volume *Greenwood Encyclopedia of African-American Folklore* (see ARBA 2007, entry 1019) should seriously consider acquiring this single volume as an update to that set, considering the wealth of information here. A welcome addition to all folklore collections, recommended for all undergraduate and public libraries.—**Anthony J. Adam**

C, P

94.   Tipton-Martin, Toni. **The Jemima Code: Two Centuries of African American Cookbooks.** Austin, Tex., University of Texas at Austin, 2015. 246p. illus. index. $45.00. ISBN 13: 978-0-292-74548-3.

This volume presents scores of cookbooks created by African American women and men between 1827 and the twenty-first century. Along with the striking images of these publications and many of their authors, another strength of this work is the provision of the sociocultural and economic contexts which surround the publication of these works. Arranged chronologically, with most chapters covering the twentieth century, the book shows the key role African American cooks played in the evolution of Southern cuisine, and the growth of publications offering a look at this style of cooking. Images of numerous recipes from the cookbooks are included, as well occasional menu ideas.

Both public libraries, and academic libraries with interest in the culinary arts, will benefit from this volume, as will any institution supporting history and African American studies. The author, whose personal collection forms the content of this book, has presented a lively and accessible look at this subject.—**Mark Schumacher**

C, P

95.   **Understanding 19th-Century Slave Narratives.** Sterling Lecater Bland, Jr., ed. Santa Barbara, Calif., Greenwood Press/ABC-CLIO, 2016. 311p. index. $89.00. ISBN 13: 978-1-4408-4463-8; 978-1-4408-4464-5 (e-book).

According to *The Oxford Companion to African American Literature,* under the entry for "Slave Narrative," it is said of these autobiographical affidavits that they "...have provided some of the most graphic and damning documentary evidence of the horrors of slavery, America's 'peculiar institution'" (Andrews, Foster and Smith, eds., Oxford: Oxford University Press, 1997). Some titles have become classics of the genre, such as *Narrative of the Life of Frederick Douglass, an American Slave, Written by Himself* and *Up from Slavery* by Booker T. Washington. Indeed, many, if not most, among the college educated have read these volumes, or are at least cognizant of them. Magnificent and influential as they are, however, Douglass and Washington are not the only voices that yet echo down the hall of centuries; many others likewise bear witness and deserve to be heard. With this in mind, editor Bland has collected six lesser-known antebellum memoirs of bondage and deliverance, those of Nat Turner, Lundsford Lane, William Wells Brown, Henry "Box" Brown, James W. C. Pennington, and William and Ellen Craft. Evidently intended for use as a classroom text, Bland states in his preface that "Instructors and the students they teach will find a volume that presents a collection of unabridged, annotated, primary documents in conversation with scholarship that contextualizes its literary and historical significance. In doing so, these documents become part of a larger discussion that makes this collection of nineteenth century narratives relevant to the contemporary ways African American literature is taught and understood" (pp. xi-xii).

In addition to the narratives themselves, which obviously take up the bulk of the volume, there is a very nicely written introductory essay entitled, "Bearing Witness: The Fugitive Slave Narrative and Its Traditions," a biographical sketch of each author preceding the narrative proper, an ample bibliography, and an index.

Bland is well suited to helm this type of project. Holding a doctoral degree from New York University, he is currently an associate professor of English, African American Studies, and American Studies at Rutgers University in Newark, New Jersey. In addition, Bland has been widely published in his field of study, an example being *Voices of the Fugitives: Runaway Slave Stories and Their Fictions of Self-Creation* (Praeger, 2000).

As a set, these little-known narratives shed valuable light on a dark chapter in American history. The unique perspectives from which each author views the new world holocaust will help both students of American history and armchair historians better understand the causes and consequences of human bondage. Therefore, this volume is strongly recommended for purchase by all public and academic libraries.—**Michael Francis Bemis**

Africans

C, P, S

96. **Encyclopedia of the Yoruba.** Toyin Falola and Akintunde Akinyemi, eds. Bloomington, Ind., Indiana University Press, 2016. 371p. maps. index. $50.00pa. ISBN 13: 978-0-253-02144-1; 978-0-253-02156-4 (e-book)

The two editors of this volume have brought together the work of 118 contributors, predominantly Nigerian academics from Nigeria and the United States, providing readers with 285 articles on the history, culture, social life, and politics of the Yoruba people, in Nigeria and abroad. From gourds to gender, from linguistics (several entries) to livestock, and from work songs to women (several entries), the breadth of coverage is clearly very broad. Each entry has at least one reference for further reading. The "Introduction" by the editors provides a useful overview of many themes explored in the volume.

A couple of minor shortcomings: the lack of images within the text, and entry titles that do not stand out on the page. This volume is quite readable despite the large number of Yoruba words and names that necessarily appear. High school, public, and academic libraries with an interest in world affairs or life in African countries should certainly consider this volume.—**Mark Schumacher**

Asian Americans

C, P, S

97. **Asian American Culture: From Anime to Tiger Moms.** Lan Dong, ed. Santa Barbara, Calif., Greenwood Press/ABC-CLIO, 2016. 2v. illus. index. (Cultures of the American Mosaic). $189.00/set. ISBN 13: 978-1-4408-2920-8; 978-1-4408-2921-5 (e-book).

This two-volume set provides the reader with 170 articles written by scholars from at least nine different countries. As the editor states, this work "provide[s] comprehensive coverage of a variety of Asian American cultural forms." From art and literature, to folk traditions and popular culture, one can learn about the lives of Cambodian, Japanese, Filipino, Asian Indian Americans, and many other groups. Each of the entries contains cross-references and "further reading" suggestions, the latter leading to both print and Internet resources. From "Judo" and "Kimchi" to broader subjects such as "Japanese American Literature" and "Chinese American Women," these articles offer much insightful information.

There is an extensive index (almost 60 pages) to topics and individuals mentioned, although occasionally there are omissions (e.g., Jeremy Lin, an NBA player, pictured on the cover of the volumes). This is a minor drawback, however. Reasonably priced, this work will serve readers in many settings: public libraries, secondary schools, and institutions of higher education. It is recommended to all.—**Mark Schumacher**

C, P, S

98.   **Densho. http://www.densho.org/.** [Website] Free. Date reviewed: 2016.

Densho, a free and publicly accessible resource documenting the Japanese American experience during World War II, launched in 2012 with 300 articles. As of this review in 2016, the site housed 650 articles. Funding for this curated site comes from the Japanese American Confinement Sites Grant Program. The National Parks Service and the California State Library, through the California Civil Liberties Public Education Fund, administer the site.

Under the Core Story tab on the home page users can find articles that address a variety of topics, including Japanese migration to Hawaii and the western United States, prevalent racism, the internment camps and other wartime experiences, the postwar period, redress, and the enduring importance of learning about this chapter in American history.

The site has a well-developed encyclopedia searchable by author, subject, or topic. Material is easily discoverable and the entries are quite thorough. For example, the entry for Monica Sone, author of *Nisei Daughter,* contains biographical details, discusses the importance of her work, and links to other materials.

An incredibly valuable feature of the site is discoverable under the Archives search button, which takes users to the Densho Digital Archive and the Densho Digital Repository. The digital archive is an astounding trove of more than 1,700 hours of interviews, which are segmented and transcribed. All the material is indexed by topic, location, and chronology. Key word searching is available. In the digital repository users will find thousands of letters, newspapers, documents, photographs, and other primary sources. Much of this material is available for reuse by teachers, students, and researchers for educational purposes. Terms of use are clearly stated under the Terms of Use/Privacy Policy link at the bottom of the home page.

The site also includes a Learning Center tab with another amazing collection of resources for teachers and students. Here one can register for an hours-long course on how to teach about the internment. The learning center additionally provides video clips on how to teach with primary sources, a Sites of Shame link that allows users to use an interactive map, a timeline, and a site locator to investigate the detention facilities, a newspaper collection link, a civil liberties curriculum link, and a link to an exhibit by artist Roger Shimomura that pairs his grandmother's journal with his paintings of the internment.

This site is highly recommended for teachers, high school and college students, and anyone interested in this subject.—**ARBA Staff Reviewer**

Asian Canadians

C, P, S

99.   **Chinese Canadian Artifacts Project. https://ccap.uvic.ca/.** [Website] Free. Date reviewed: 2017.

Sixteen museums throughout western Canada have contributed to the Chinese Canadian Artifacts Project, a collection of over 6,000 objects and documents which help to tell the story of the Chinese in Canada. The project has digitized nearly 4,000 individual artifacts, resulting in a rich virtual gallery of items such as business documents, letters, textbooks, houseware, personal photographs, and clothing. The content is free to all users. The site offers a number of ways to examine its contents, and users can conduct a general search from the top of the page. The Archival Descriptions tab presents a listing of all items, even those that are not yet digitized. Users can scroll through artifact descriptions arranged alphabetically, by date or by reference number. They can also choose from a generous list of filters to enhance the search, such as museum of origin, creator, place, and subject. Selecting an item enlarges the thumbnail photograph alongside a variety of item details including title, physical description, and more. Authority Records allows access to the artifact via a listing of the owner (authority) of the artifact. Archival Institutions provides information on the museums involved in the project, including contact information, museum type, and description. It further provides an inventory of the artifacts the museum has contributed to the project. The digital archives are also searchable by Functions, Subjects, Places, and Digital Objects. This website shines a spotlight on a unique archival collection that would have broad appeal.—**ARBA Staff Reviewer**

Indians of North America

C, S

100.   **50 Events That Shaped American Indian History: An Encyclopedia of the American Mosaic.** Donna Martinez and Jennifer L. Williams Bordeaux, eds. Santa Barbara, Calif., Greenwood Press/ABC-CLIO, 2017. 2v. illus. index. $189.00. ISBN 13: 978-1-4408-3576-6; 978-1-4408-3577-3 (e-book).

One way to trace history over time is to highlight important events that have shaped people and places. This two-volume encyclopedia chronicles the history of American Indians through 50 important events, from the mound builders of early Native America to the canonization of Junípero Serra in 2015.

According to the editors, the entries were selected to chronicle the various legal and educational strategies used by Native Americans to retain their land, resources, cultures, and religions. The 50 events are arranged chronologically and divided into eight sections. The scope of the encyclopedia is indigenous people in America. The American mosaic promised in the subtitle is achieved by including many different tribes from various geographical regions of America and by including events related to a variety of general topics, including war, education, protest movements, discrimination, relocation, self-determination, and religion. Each article is approximately 15 pages long and includes a timeline to provide historical context. The essays are enhanced with sidebar highlights related to the event. In addition, the entries include biographies of important people connected to the event, excerpts from primary documents, and a list of additional readings.

The encyclopedia is easy to navigate, with a table of contents in each volume and a comprehensive index. There is also a list of recommended resources at the end of the second volume. The editors also provide brief biographies of the contributors, who have a broad range of backgrounds, expertise, and impressive credentials. This two-volume set is a recommended addition to any Native American history collection, especially for its concise, valuable coverage of people and events that have shaped the American Indian experience.—**Theresa Muraski**

C, P, S

101.   **Indigenous Law Portal. http://www.loc.gov/law/help/indigenous-law-guide/ americas/north-america/united-states/.** [Website] Free. Date reviewed: 2017.

This page of the greater Library of Congress Law Library site offers researchers free access to information on American Indian legal constructs, constitutions, and other documents. It is generally organized as a portal leading to a number of "gateways" or paths to relevant sites, directories (e.g., tribal leaders), organizations (e.g., National Indian Justice Center), research guides, and much more. The site also links to materials concerning other topics as they relate to Native Americans such as health, education, and citizenship. Most importantly, the site allows online examination of the legal foundations of over 500 unique tribes spanning the contiguous states and Alaska. Users can access materials in a number of ways. They may scroll and click on a particular state, or scroll and click on individual tribes by region, state, or alphabetical listing. Doing so will lead to a listing of downloadable materials (charters, constitutions, bylaws, land cessions, etc.), important website links, and the tribe's geographic location. Users also have PDF access to the Classification Schedule referring to indigenous law material location and/or structure within the greater Library of Congress Law Library. This site would be highly useful to students, educators, and others interested in Native American historical, legal or cultural issues.—**ARBA Staff Reviewer**

C, S

102.   Kania, John, and Alan Blaugrund. **Antique Native American Basketry of Western North America: A Comprehensive Guide to Identification.** Albuquerque, N.Mex., Coiled & Twined LLC, 2014. 312p. illus. maps. index. $95.00. ISBN 13: 978-0-615-98457-5.

This compendium of information about Native American basketry focuses on basketry "made for sale" between 1890 and 1930 in Western North America. Its purpose is to gather as much information as possible in one place and to explain how to systematically identify basketry based on basket types, materials used, and weaving techniques employed. Basketry can be identified as belonging to a tribe or group of tribes based on these criteria. The book explains the principles on which the value of a basket is based—condition, documented attribution, age, tribal affiliations, weave, and symmetry.

The book begins with a preface that explains its purpose and introduces the authors. Acknowledgements follow. A brief history of basketry and basket collecting provides useful information about collecting and the marketplace where basketry can be obtained. This is followed by an in-depth explanation of basketry materials and weaving techniques. Beautiful photographs illustrate the materials and techniques discussed.

The authors divide the American West into regions where materials available and cultures in proximity created similar types of basketry. The regions are: Southwest and Great Basin; California; Greater Northwest Coast. Within these regions are "complexes" of groups in smaller areas. Individual tribes are listed within these complexes. Photographic examples of basketry from each tribe and complex are included. Each photo caption includes the dimensions, tribe, material used, technique, and function of the item. There are map insets to show the locations of the regions, complexes, and tribes.

An appendix contains diagnostic tables that show the attributes of typical basketry for specific tribes. This tabular format helps the reader to compare and contrast the basketry produced from tribe to tribe and region to region. An eight-page bibliography follows the appendix. The book is completed with a comprehensive index.

This book will be useful to collectors of baskets, high school and college students studying Native American artifacts of the western United States, artists, and anthropologists.

Recommended.—**Joanna M. Burkhardt**

C, S

103.   Keenan, Jerry. **The Terrible Indian Wars of the West: A History from the Whitman Massacre to Wounded Knee, 1846-1890.** Jefferson, N.C., McFarland, 2016. 492p. illus. maps. index. $49.95pa. ISBN 13: 978-0-7864-9940-3; 978-1-4766-2310-8 (e-book).

The Indian wars of the trans-Mississippi West are a fascinating and sad chapter in American history. The destruction of the many indigenous peoples and cultures, and the plight of the remnants of both of these that remain today is a national tragedy. Although much has been written about the hundreds of battles, skirmishes, and incidents that occurred during the last half of the nineteenth century throughout the West, the author proposes to bring it all together in a single volume accessible for the interested layman.

The volume is divided by region—Central Plains, Southern Plains, Pacific Northwest, etc. Each section begins with a prologue overview before addressing individuals, incidents, and actions in that region. The chronological timeline is very valuable and the book has a good index and a solid list of recommended readings.

Full of interesting stories about individuals and events and the author's candid commentary, the book is engaging and a useful reference source.—**Joe P. Dunn**

P

104.   Leahy, Todd, and Nathan Wilson. **Historical Dictionary of Native American Movements.** 2d ed. Lanham, Md., Rowman & Littlefield, 2016. 302p. illus. maps. (Historical Dictionaries of Religions, Philosophies, and Movements series). $90.00; $89.99 (e-book). ISBN 13: 978-1-4422-6808-1; 978-1-4422-6809-8 (e-book).

Todd Leahy, conservation director for the New Mexico Wildlife Federation, and Nathan Wilson have authored a second edition of a work first published in 2008, (see ARBA 2009, entry 308). The title is somewhat misleading as the dictionary focuses specifically on American Indians. There are no entries for other Native American groups in the United States such as Native Hawaiians or Inuit peoples.

The work begins with four introductory sections. The first is a map of the United States' 48 contiguous states entitled "Map of Native American Movements." There are 16 spots on the map but there is no explanation as to why those locales are significant. It is followed by "Acronyms and Abbreviations." The "Chronology" begins with the occupation of Monte Verde in present-day Chile at c. 12,500 B.C.E. and concludes with a mention that in 2015 the health of American Indians continues to be an issue. It is important to note that many of the peoples or events mentioned in the chronology are not addressed within the dictionary. The final section is the "Introduction," which is a 34-page essay that provides an overview of American Indian history. While the authors do not take the opportunity to define what constitutes a "movement" for the purposes of this work, they do contextualize the entries included in the main body of the work. The dictionary includes approximately 250 entries. The coverage of American Indian history and culture is spotty at best. For example, in the Southeast, there are few, if any, entries on the Chickasaw, Choctaw, Creeks, or Seminoles. The Cherokees are discussed at length in "Boudinot, Elias (1804-1839)," "Cherokee Advocate," "Cherokee Constitution (1827)," "Cherokee Male Seminary," "Cherokee Nation v. Georgia," "Cherokee Phoenix," "Keetoowah Society," "Old Settlers," "Ross, John (1790-1866)," "Treaty of Holston (1791)," "Treaty of Hopewell (1785)," "Treaty of New Echota (1835)," and "Worcester v. Georgia." Six documents are included in "Indian Voices from Native American Movements": "Pontiac: You Must Lift the Hatchet Against Them, 27 April 1763"; "Tecumseh: Speech to Colonel Henry Proctor, 18 September 1813"; "Crazy Horse: We Preferred Our Own Way of Living, 5 September 1877"; "Clyde Warrior: We Are Not Free, From Testimony Before the President's National Advisory Commission on Rural Poverty, 2 February 1967"; "Proclamation: To the Great White Father and All His People, 20 November 1969"; and "A Summary of the Twenty Points, 31 October 1972." The work concludes with an 18-page bibliography. Fewer than 15 books and articles included in that section were published within the last 10 years. Of those, many are obituaries. Despite its shortcomings, this work would serve as a good ready-reference tool for public libraries due to its coverage of the American Indian Rights movement of the twentieth and twenty-first centuries.—**John R. Burch Jr.**

C, P, S

105.   **National Indian Law Library. http://www.narf.org/nill/.** [Website] Free. Date reviewed: 2017.

The National Indian Law Library (NILL) is located in Boulder, Colorado, and is run by Library Director David Selden. Its purpose is to serve the public and the Native American Rights Fund (NARF), an organization that since the 1970s has provided legal assistance to Indian tribes, individuals, and organizations. There are several tabs on the home page of this freely available website: Indian Law Bulletins, Tribal Law Gateway, Research Guides, Research Help, About NILL, and Catalog. The Bulletin tab provides archived and current information on new developments in Indian Law. Archival materials extend back to the 1990s, and the page is updated regularly. For instance, one of the most recent links as of this January 2017 review is to an article on the likelihood that the Supreme Court will rule in favor of the Washington Redskins keeping their name. Tribal Law Gateway allows users to search tribal law materials by tribal name via A-Z clickables. Once a tribe is accessed, there are further links as is the case of the Seminole Nation of Oklahoma where there are connections to the tribe's website and the materials available at NILL. There are more resources on the right side of the page, including a link to the *Tribal Leaders Directory* at the Bureau of Indian Affairs. The Research Guides section offers guides to resources by topic: Tribal Recognition, Tribal Enrollment, Citizenship & Borders, Indian Trust Responsibilities, Indigenous Peacemaking, Jurisdiction in Indian Country Prisoner Issues, Tribal Education, Indian Child Welfare, Religion & Sacred Places, International Indigenous Rights, Environment & Climate Change, and Water

Rights & Indian Land. There are also links to Tracing Native American Family Roots and Finding Legal Help. Additionally, pages offer a place to ask library staff a question. The About NILL tab provides a rather extensive history of both NILL and NARF, while the Catalog allows users to search all titles held in NILL online. For the novice, there are video tutorials on how to search the catalog and how to request documents.

Highly recommended to all libraries.—**ARBA Staff Reviewer**

C

106.   **The Routledge Companion to Native American Literature.** Deborah L. Madsen, ed. New York, Routledge/Taylor & Francis Group, 2016. 524p. illus. index. $230.00. ISBN 13: 978-1-13-802060-3; 978-1-315-77734-4 (e-book).

Deborah L. Madsen, Professor of American Literature and Culture at the University of Geneva, Switzerland, and editor of *Native Authenticity: Transatlantic Approaches to Native American Literary Studies,* is joined by 42 other scholars in producing this volume in the Routledge World Literature Series. It is comprised of an introduction and 41 essays, each concluding with notes and bibliographic references.

The editor's introduction dwells upon the definition of the terms "native," "American," and "literature." Written from a neo-colonial perspective, Madsen even targets the use of the phrase "Native American literature," which is part of the book's title. Her reason is that the generic phrase does not convey the writings of the more than 550 identified native groups in North America that are lumped together under that heading. Central to her perspective is that native writers convey their cultures to the masses, yet that ideal is not reflected in her choice of contributors, as less than a fourth are of native descent.

The essays are organized into five parts: Identities; Key Moments; Sovereignties; Traditions; and Literary Forms. The first part includes essays, such as "American Imperialism and Pacific Literatures" and "Recovering a Sovereign Erotic: Two-Spirit Writers 'Reclaim a Name for Ourselves,'" that focus on how native peoples view themselves, including feminist and LGBTQ perspectives. Key Moments focuses on events that shaped relations between native peoples and the United States, such as the passage of the Native American Graves Protection and Repatriation Act of 1990 (NAGPRA). In the third section, sovereignty is widely defined, as evidenced by the articles "'That We May Stand Up and Walk Ourselves': Indian Sovereignty and Diplomacy after the Revolutionary War" and "A Seat at the Table: Political Representation for Animals." Traditions examines the canon of Native American literature, as evidenced by "The Historical and Literary Role of Folklore, Storytelling, and the Oral Tradition in Native American Literatures." The final section turns its attention to specific forms of communication, including poetry, film, graphic novels, and digital media. Following the essays is a 14-page bibliography that provides a comprehensive view on the relevant published literature. The work concludes with a comprehensive index.

This collection of essays has limited use as a reference tool for undergraduate libraries but should be acquired by any institution serving graduate students in the fields of American Literature and/or Native American Studies.—**John R. Burch Jr.**

Italian Americans

C, S

107.   **Italian Americans: The History and Culture of a People.** Martone, Eric, ed. Santa Barbara, Calif., ABC-CLIO, 2017. 554p. illus. index. $100.00. ISBN 13: 978-1-61069-994-5; 978-1-61069-995-2 (e-book)..

With articles written by 55 contributors, this book is divided into five broad sections: emigration, civic and economic life, cultural and religious life, contributions to science and the humanities, and sports and popular culture. The last section contains the most entries—67 of 180. Entries on individuals, such as Tony Bennett, Joe DiMaggio, and Anne Bancroft, total 50. Entries usually have cross-references and further reading suggestions, while an eight-page bibliography supplements those references. The volume also includes 19 primary documents, ranging from 1493 (a letter by Christopher Columbus) to 2011, and information on 20 Italian American museums and historical sites.

Any library with readers interested in the role of Italians in the development of the United States should consider this volume. It is clearly written, while providing useful presentations of diverse topics concerning the contributions of Italian Americans. The one curiosity of the volume is an entry on the mathematician Fibonacci, who died in 1250, and was most closely connected to Mediterranean and Middle Eastern mathematicians of his day.—**Mark Schumacher**

Latin Americans

C, S

108.   Acuña, Rodolfo F. **U.S. Latino Issues.** 2d ed. Santa Barbara, Calif., Greenwood Press/ABC-CLIO, 2017. 317p. index. $61.00. ISBN 13: 978-1-4408-5322-7; 978-1-4408-5323-4 (e-book).

This second-edition book (see ARBA 2004, entry 323) explores contemporary issues of Latino peoples living in the United States in 12 chapters. Chapters open with background information, followed by debatable topics such as contested identity, cultural and linguistic diversity, assimilation, and immigration. Beyond essays supporting both sides of the presented issue, chapters are structured in a question-and-answer style to promote scholarly debate and encourage further inquiry. Black-and-white tables provide data such as a 2010 table from the U.S. Census where the broad spectrum of "Latino" nationalities is broken out by population and percent. Chapters conclude with notes, a bibliography, and an index. In addition, the book addresses the image of the United States and what makes it an attractive destination for immigrants. Moreover, *U.S. Latino Issues* pulls in information from migrations of different people (Central Americans, Cubans, Ecuadorians, Mexicans, and others) into the United States and identifies controversies surrounding culture, assimilation, acceptance, policy, and fear. For example, since the 1970s, "anti-immigrant organizations and politicians have fanned nativist fears in reaction to the heavy migration of people from Mexico, Central America, and Asia. The rise of immigration swelled the ranks of nativist organizations devoted to immigration control" (p. 93). Identifying that with contemporary political thought will lead to solid opportunity for debate and inquiry. Throughout the book, historical representation of the trajectory of government initiatives is included.

A very topical title, *U.S. Latino Issues* is well suited for high school and undergraduate students. Educators seeking ideas for student research and debate on immigration will also benefit from this recommended title.—**Janis Minshull**

C, P, S

109. **Bracero History Archive. http://www.neh.gov/explore/bracero-history-archive.** [Website] Free. Date reviewed: 2017.

A hugely important slice of twentieth century history, the Bracero program brought millions of Mexican workers over the American border to fill the vast demand for agricultural labor for more than 20 years starting in 1942. This award-winning website helps tell the stories of the Bracero program, archiving over 3,000 items and collecting more every day. A project of the National Endowment for the Humanities, the site offers easy access to these materials. Users can simply browse the archive by Images, Documents, Oral Histories, or Contributed Items. Here they will find contracts, paystubs, photographs, audio recordings, and many individual stories of life in American fields. Other tabs on the page allow users to contribute to the growing archive with their own stories or mementos, or to create their own personalized archival timeline. Users can also access Resources which offers links to video tutorials on how to add to the archive, how to interview for oral history, and more. A History tab leads to a bibliography, and a Teaching tab offers information for educators such as grade-level activities. The material gathered here on the Bracero program—the largest foreign worker program in history—is an excellent source for the broader study of immigration and American agricultural history. The complete site is also available in Spanish translation.—**ARBA Staff Reviewer**

C, S

110. **Latinos and Criminal Justice: An Encyclopedia.** José Luis Morín, ed. Santa Barbara, Calif., Greenwood Press/ABC-CLIO, 2016. 506p. $100.00. ISBN 13: 978-0-313-35660-5; 978-0-313-35661-2 (e-book).

Latinos and Criminal Justice: An Encyclopedia brings together an assemblage of information from experts, scholars, practitioners, and others knowledgeable about Latina/o incarceration history.

Divided into two parts, general information examines social, economic, historical, and other dimensions in relation to Latinas/os and criminal justice. Part one, Essays on Latinas/os and Criminal Justice, is comprised of lengthy essays organized in topical format. Chapters end with further readings and cases cited, which effectively point researchers to more sources. The chapter also includes highlighted tables and data groupings. Part two lists entries in a typical A to Z format. Examples of entries include drugs, the death penalty, gangs, policing, and racial profiling. Cross-referencing offers practical paths for further study. Visuals such as data tables continue in part two though are no longer highlighted. General research topics may include: racism, alien criminals, criminal justice, stereotyping, Latin Americans, and the need for change in perceptions and the criminal system. A table of contents, overview of the book's two parts, a guide to related topics, and an index facilitate searches and topic identification.

Latinos and Criminal Justice collects insights into the Latina/o experience within the U.S. criminal justice system. The well-documented information is both historical and contemporary and comes at a time when high rates of incarceration and recidivism lead to questions about the criminal justice system itself. Undergraduate and graduate students, social activists, political leaders, and those interested in Latin American issues will find this book particularly valuable because of the lack of resources on this topic. This book will provide very useful information for those studying history, sociology, law, anthropology, or political science.

Highly Recommended.—**Janis Minshull**

7 Genealogy and Heraldry

Genealogy

C, P, S

111. **Kindred Britain. http://kindred.stanford.edu/#.** [Website] Free. Date reviewed: 2017.

Created by Nicholas Jenkins, Elijah Meeks, and Scott Murray of the Stanford University Libraries, this database is a virtual network of nearly 30,000 individuals, many of whom are iconic figures in British culture. The site demonstrates connections between people by blood, marriage, and affiliation. The database spans more than 1,500 years, but the densest concentration is in the nineteenth century. The site's design encourages users to move around and discover connections. Overall, it gives users a sense that British history can be considered a family affair.

The site can be searched via a basic text box or by curated searches locatable under People, Connections, or Stories. People is further divided into Families, Professions, Most Viewed, Sisters, and Firsts and Lasts. Connections can be searched by Opponents, Judges and Accused, Author and Subject, Sitter and Artist, Doctor and Patient, and Graves: Buried Side-by-Side or in the Same Ground. Stories is grouped into Historical and Cultural stories and Conceptual stories. The information found in the curated searches is quite extensive and fascinating. For example, one story "Rival Relations: Washington and Cornwallis" provides an in-depth account of the two men, opponents in the Revolutionary War and distant cousins.

It takes some time to get comfortable searching but there is quite a bit of valuable guidance under the help icon. It is also highly recommended that first-time users practice navigating by clicking on one of the curated searches before embarking on a search using the basic search option.—**ARBA Staff Reviewer**

Personal Names

P

112. **Baby Name Wizard. http://www.babynamewizard.com/.** [Website] Free. Date reviewed: 2017.

For students looking to research the history of their names for a homework project or for parents-to-be struggling to find a name, look no further than *Baby Name Wizard,* a free-to-use database of national and international names that is searchable in a variety of ways. New users should register as members free of charge in order to take advantage of all search tools. There is some advertising, but it is not terribly distracting. There are four main tabs (Name Finder Tools, Name Lists, Baby Names Blog, and Forum) along with a basic search screen. Under Name Finder Tools, users will find Name Finder (both basic and advanced) and NameVoyager, which looks at name trends historically. Members can also take advantage of Expert NameVoyager, the Name Matchmaker (find names that work well together), or Namipedia, which allows searchers to click on a letter of the alphabet to see a list of names for boys or girls. Whatever way a name like Kathryn is accessed, users will see a set of data that includes information about related names, as well as the name's meaning, origin, and popularity (the popularity of the name Kathryn peaked in the 1950s). The unique part of this site is that it allows one to search for name criteria. If, for example, a user wants a girl name that is somewhat popular and indicative of strength, these traits can be typed into the Name Finder to produce a list of options. The site also offers an entertaining Blog, with entries from 2004-2017. This is a great place to find information about spelling trends, the potential top 2017 names (Elia, Prescott, Brontë, Winston, Aviania, Caoimbe, pronounced Keeva, and Wolf), and much more.— **ARBA Staff Reviewer**

8 Geography and Travel Guides

General Works

Handbooks and Yearbooks

C, S

113.   Kerski, Joseph J. **Interpreting Our World: 100 Discoveries that Revolutionized Geography.** Santa Barbara, Calif., ABC-CLIO, 2016. 386p. maps. index. $89.00. ISBN 13: 978-1-61069-919-8; 978-1-61069-920-4 (e-book).

Contributions to the field of geography have been many over the past several thousand years. To distill these discoveries down to 100 is a significant undertaking. That is the task the author set for himself in *Interpreting Our World,* which includes individuals, systems, ideas, events, artifacts, and more. In the book's introduction the author discusses the difficulty of editing down the final entries, but he still seems a bit vague about why and how the inclusion decisions were made. The author acknowledges this by saying that others may find a different set of contributions appropriate. Organized alphabetically, each entry is approximately one to two pages in length. Entries include an outline of the contribution, related entries to consult for expanded understanding, and a brief bibliography for further research. Several of the entries include black-and-white illustrations and photographs, which enhance the text visually. Embedded within several of the entries are mini-entries on a related person, idea, or event; for example, within the Magellan entry is a one-paragraph entry on Pedro Alvares Cabral, a contemporary. Another example is information on the laser rangefinder within the entry entitled surveying. The mini-entries are not listed in the table of contents or, more unfortunately, in the keyword index, so locating is best accomplished by skimming the volume. A selected chronology of events, dating from 2300 B.C.E. to the present, continent location maps, and an introduction open the volume. A bibliography and an extensive keyword index complete the volume. The binding and presentation of the material are up to the usual standards of ABC-CLIO. The volume is recommended for collections supporting geography, GIS, and cartographic research. Librarians will need to decide whether to place this in the reference area or the circulating collection due to the readability of the material. Some patrons may want to read the volume as a good, general introduction to many lines of inquiry within geography rather than use the volume in a quick consultancy manner in ready reference.—**Gregory Curtis**

C, S

114.   World Geography: Understanding a Changing World. http://www.abc-clio.com/ABC-CLIOCorporate/Forms/Preview/ZipLookup.aspx?pc=solutionsdatabases. [Website] Santa Barbara, Calif., ABC-CLIO, 2016. Price negotiated by site. Date reviewed: 2016.

ABC-CLIO's *World Geography* database is a useful resource for users to explore the world around them. The *World Geography* database does not limit itself strictly to geography in the traditional sense—the entries on each nation include reflections on history, politics, and culture.

The database is broken down, sensibly, by continent. In each continent is contained an entry on each country in that continent. For example, take the expansive entry on Germany. The entry contains a landing page with an overview of the country, and many links off to the side of the page that allow the user to explore other relevant topics pertinent to the country at hand. In the country landing page, the user can explore the geography of the nation, the history and issues of the nation, the society and culture of the nation, and the government and economy of the nation. The tab also contains a facts and figures sheet that the user can quickly access. The facts and figures sheet contains some predictable information including population numbers and the country's largest exports. In addition to these facts, the fact sheet contains an entry on communications, which includes access to telephones, the Internet, and Facebook. In Germany, 83% of the German population (or right around 65 million people) have access to the Internet. Further, 26 million people maintain Facebook accounts. This information is useful to determine how connected a society is and how quickly its members can access important information.

The database also contains important perspectives on pressing issues in each country. For the entry on Germany, the pressing issues are: the geopolitics of World War II alliances, which includes a discussion of Germany's relationship with the Allies after World War II; the Fall of the Berlin Wall and the efforts to remake Germany into a united nation with shared prosperity despite years of Communist rule in the East; the Eurozone Crisis, namely Germany's efforts to rebuild a Europe that has been decimated by currency crises; and mitigating distrust between Muslims and the west, which is especially pertinent considering Germany's stance on Syrian refugees in the midst of the Syrian civil war.

The *World Geography* database also contains entries from advisory board members. These advisory board members, all experts in their chosen field, provide guidance on current issues that may affect geography. For example, material examines the transmission of the Zika virus—how it is transmitted, what happens when it is transmitted, and where it is likely to be transmitted based on geography and patterns. Recommended for high school and academic libraries.—**Sara Mofford**

Travel Guides

General Works

Handbooks and Yearbooks

P

115.   **World Heritage Sites: A Complete Guide to 1031 UNESCO World Heritage Sites.** 7th ed. New York, Firefly Books, 2015. 928p. illus. maps. index. $29.95pa. ISBN 13: 978-1-77085-817-6.

This 2015 guidebook to more than 1,031 UNESCO world heritage sites opens with a usage guide, a foreword, and several color maps that indicate the location and type of site covered (cultural, natural, or mixed) as well as a page number reference for the sites in Europe, North American and the Caribbean, South America, Africa, Oceania, and Asia, the Middle East, and the Arabian Peninsula. The sites are organized by the year they were first listed by UNESCO, starting with the Galápagos Islands, a World Heritage Site since 1978, and ending with the Blue and John Crow Mountains in Jamaica, designated a World Heritage Site in 2015.

All sites include an inset color map and most have a captioned color photograph. A color band, green, red, or blue, indicates type of site-natural, cultural, or mixed, respectively. Selection criteria are listed under the name of each site. Sites can easily be accessed by either index, one which lists sites by country and the other which lists sites by name in alphabetic order. Many users, however, will wish to thumb through this attractive volume. Some sites, like Carthage in Tunisia, cover two full pages, while some like the archaeological site of Olympia get one page and the Lushan National Park in China gets half a page. The book also includes a copy of the World Heritage Mission statement prior to the indexes and lists the different selection criteria used by UNESCO.

The inclusion of a further readings section would enhance this volume; nevertheless, it is highly recommended for public libraries.—**ARBA Staff Reviewer**

Canada

P

116. Early, Chris, and Tracy C. Read. **100 Nature Hot Spots in Ontario: The Best Parks, Conservation Areas and Wild Places.** New York, Firefly Books, 2016. 224p. illus. maps. index. $29.95pa. ISBN 13: 978-1-77085-705-6.

The authors selected 100 nature spots that highlight the natural beauty and diversity of· Ontario. The book is organized by region and sites within regions are listed alphabetically. Each section starts with a colored map that identifies by number the location of each nature hot spot. Each entry has a two-page spread that includes captioned color photographs and a text box "What Makes This Hot Spot Hot?" along with basic information about the place (physical address, telephone number, and website address). The authors take readers on a journey from the Devil's Punchbowl Conservation Area, part of the Niagara Escarpment in Southwestern Ontario, to one of the last remaining intact hardwood forests (Happy Valley Forest) in Central Ontario South, to the Niagara Region's Woodend Conservation Area, which saw a good deal of action during the War of 1812, to a stand of old growth white pines in Gilles Grove (Eastern Ontario), to the Thirty Thousand Islands archipelago in Central Ontario North, to Ouimet Canyon, often referred to as Canada's Grand Canyon, in Northern Ontario. Short entries (a few paragraphs) accompany each hot spot. In addition to relaying what makes the place special, readers may also get an idea of the best time of year to visit, the place's geography, its place in history, or how to find a location. Though admittedly there are more than 100 beautifully unique nature hot spots in Ontario, this book showcases the province and all it has to offer. Recommended to public libraries.——
ARBA Staff Reviewer

Italy

P

117.   Arena, Romina. **Where Did They Film That? Italy: Famous Film Scenes and Their Italian Movie Locations.** Fresno, Calif., Quill Driver, 2016. 143p. illus. maps. index. $18.95pa. ISBN 13: 978-1-61035-182-9.

Like any good guide book, this reference covers the basics such as sights to see, hours of operation, modes of transportation, restaurants, and hotels. What differentiates this travel guide from the many others available is the author's inside knowledge from having lived many years in Italy and her interesting twist of tying in movies made on location in popular Italian locales. The author uses a breezy, first-person narrative to engage us and make us feel as though we are experiencing the country first hand with her as our guide. She provides practical advice on navigating the country as well as insider tips such as how to get advance tickets to see da Vinci's *Last Supper* when you visit Milan; how to get an audience with the Pope and bypass the lines at the Coliseum in Rome; and where to learn how to be a gondolier in Venice. For each region, the author showcases well-known films shot at that location and gives advice as to how to visit those scenes. For example, we are told where to find the Mouth of Truth from *Roman Holiday*; the Naples restaurant where Julia Roberts eats pizza in *Eat, Pray, Love*; the bar in Sicily where *The Godfather's* Michael Corleone first meets his beautiful but doomed wife; the charming restaurants we glimpse in Woody Allen's *To Rome with Love,* and many more. The author also sprinkles in recipes and interviews with Italian directors and actors. For those of us who fell in love with Italy by watching movies, this guide tells us how we can see for ourselves the locations that originally enchanted us while introducing us to new "must-sees."—**Adrienne Antink**

United States

P

118.   Poggioli, Kristine, and Carolyn Eidson. **Walking San Francisco's 49 Mile Scenic Drive: Explore the Famous Sites, Neighborhoods, and Vistas in 17 Enchanting Walks.** Fresno, Calif., Craven Street Books, 2016. 272p. illus. maps. index. $16.95pa. ISBN 13: 978-1-61035-279-6.

The Downtown Association of San Francisco originally designed this 49-mile route for visitors to the 1939-1940 Golden Gate International Exposition. Though designed as a drive, as the authors of this book illustrate, the 49 miles along the route (which has changed slightly over the years) are ideal for walkers, whether individuals, couples, friends, or family groups.

The compact and easy-to-carry book details 17 walks, two to four miles each. The authors provide street-by-street directions, color photographs and maps, starting and ending points, a list of important places, San Francisco history facts, and more for each walk. The introduction includes important information about traffic, hills, weather, and getting to and from each walk, as well as a one-page color map showing the whole route and a smaller color map that outlines one walk with explanations of the map legend.

Seven of the 17 walks are indicated as "must-see" for visitors. These include walk two from Chinatown through Nob Hill to North Beach; walk three, Fisherman's Wharf, the Marina, and the Palace of Fine Arts; walk four, the Presidio to the Golden Gate Bridge; walk six, Legion of Honor, Sutro Baths, Cliff House, and Playlands; walk 11, Golden Gate Park 2—East End Museums and Carousel; walk 13, Twin Peaks Meander to Market Street; and walk 16, the Ferry Building, Financial District, and South of Market. Walk four nicely captures the fun and usefulness of this engaging guide. For the 2.5-mile, 50-minute walk that starts at the Presidio's Lombard Gate and ends at the Golden Gate Bridge Welcome Center, there are 13 color photographs; a one-page, easy-to-follow color map; and a list of 10 sites to note. There is also a paragraph on the history of the Presidio and one on the earthquake shacks built by the army to house residents displaced after the 1906 trembler. Like most chapters, this one concludes with a bonus section called *The Daily Crab,* where interesting history tidbits are presented in a tabloid format.

This charming and extremely useable book will be welcomed by visitors and residents of the City by the Bay. Highly recommended for public libraries.—**ARBA Staff Reviewer**

9 History

American History

Dictionaries and Encyclopedias

C, P

119.   Blume, Kenneth J. **Historical Dictionary of U.S. Diplomacy from the Civil War to World War I.** 2d ed. Lanham, Md., Rowman & Littlefield, 2017. 558p. illus. (Historical Dictionaries of U.S. Politics and Political Eras). $130.00; $129.99 (e-book). ISBN 13: 978-1-4422-7332-0; 978-1-4422-7333-7 (e-book).

Kenneth J. Blume, Professor of History and Humanities at Albany College of Pharmacy and Health Sciences, saw the first edition of this work published in 2005 (see ARBA 2006, entry 742). The new edition is expanded to include more than 1,000 entries. Like all volumes in Rowman & Littlefield's Historical Dictionaries of U.S. Politics and Political Eras, the entries are supplemented by a chronology, introduction, and an extensive bibliography. Particularly notable in this work are the seven appendixes, which include the "U.S. Diplomatic Corps, 1861-1914," "U.S. Wars, Conflicts, Interventions, and Military Engagements, 1860-1920," and "U.S. Treaties, Conventions, and Agreements, 1860-1914." This excellent ready-reference tool is recommended for public and academic libraries.—**John R. Burch Jr.**

C, P

120.   Buel, Richard, Jr., and Jeffers Lennox. **Historical Dictionary of the Early American Republic.** 2d ed. Lanham, Md., Rowman & Littlefield, 2017. 507p. maps. (Historical Dictionaries of U.S. Politics and Political Eras). $125.00; $124.99 (e-book). ISBN 13: 978-1-4422-6298-0; 978-1-4422-6299-7 (e-book).

This second edition (see ARBA 2007, entry 346), published 11 years after the first edition, has added a new coeditor and greatly expanded the number of inclusions to more than 500 cross-referenced entries. The single most important expansion has been the bibliography on the War of 1812. Only a small number books on this confusing and misunderstood conflict existed at the time of the first edition, but the bicentennial of the war resulted in many new volumes and articles on the subject.

The volume follows the common format for this series of forward, preface, maps (two only), chronology, lengthy introduction, dictionary items, an appendix (which includes the cabinets of each of the first five presidential administrations), and an extensive bibliography. Typical of all the volumes in this series with which I am familiar, it is an excellent work. The popularity of the Broadway musical *Hamilton* has brought attention to early American history to a whole new audience and generation. This volume can expand upon that introduction.—**Joe P. Dunn**

C, P

121.   Cheathem, Mark R., and Terry Corps. **Historical Dictionary of the Jacksonian Era and Manifest Destiny.** 2d ed. Lanham, Md., Rowman & Littlefield, 2017. 534p. illus. (Historical Dictionaries of U.S. Politics and Political Eras). $120.00; $119.99 (e-book). ISBN 13: 978-1-4422-7319-1; 978-1-4422-7320-7 (e-book).

     This book, part of the Historical Dictionaries of U.S. Politics and Political Eras series, is now in its second edition. It deals with the years 1829-49 in United States history, and era of five presidents: Andrew Jackson, Martin Van Buren, William Henry Harrison, John Tyler, and James K. Polk. During this time period, the concept of manifest destiny was initiated, the federal government became more active and stronger, and various industries such as banking and manufacturing grew and flourished. It was also a time when issues around the treatment of slaves and Native Americans began to influence policy and public opinion, which would culminate in the Civil War. An extensive chronology is provided at the beginning of the book, along with a fairly comprehensive introduction on the people, issues, and topics of these two decades. The dictionary proper follows, with cross-references in bold; there are numerous black-and-white pictures and artwork throughout. An appendix lists the five presidents and their administrations, along with election results. Finally, a thorough bibliography divided into various sections is provided at the end. This series in total provides an in-depth examination of the entire history of the United States.—**Bradford Lee Eden**

C, P, S

122.   **The World of the American West: A Daily Life Encyclopedia.** Bakken, Gordon Morris, ed. Santa Barbara, Calif., Greenwood Press/ABC-CLIO, 2017. 2v. illus. index. (Daily Life Encyclopedias). $198.00/set. ISBN 13: 978-1-4408-2859-1; 978-1-4408-2860-7 (e-book).

     Edited by the late Gordon Morris Bakken, this two-volume work focuses on the daily lives of ordinary people who resided west of the Mississippi River during the nineteenth century. Like other Daily Lives Encyclopedias, such as *The World of the American Revolution* and *The World of the Civil War*, these volumes are organized by topical sections including Arts, Fashion and Appearance, Politics and Warfare, and Science and Technology. Divided between the respective sections are approximately 230 signed articles that include cross-references and bibliographic citations for further reading. Interspersed through the articles are illustrations, photographs, and a number of sidebars. Also notable is the inclusion after the entries of 12 primary sources, including "John O. Sullivan's First Use of the Term 'Manifest Destiny' (1845)"; "Morrill Act (1862)"; and "Newspaper Accounts of the Devastating Cattle Kill during the Winter of 1886-1887." The encyclopedia concludes with a six-page bibliography and an index. Written at a level accessible to high school students, this reference tool would be a beneficial resource for high school, public, and undergraduate libraries.—**John R. Burch Jr.**

Handbooks and Yearbooks

C, S

123.   **American History. http://www.abc-clio.com/ABC-CLIOCorporate/SearchResults. aspx?type=a.** [Website] Santa Barbara, Calif., ABC-CLIO, 2016. Price negotiated by site. Date reviewed: 2016.

The history of the discovery, exploration, and development of what is now the United States covers several centuries and a multiplicity of events large and small. ABC-CLIO Solutions, under the supervision of an advisory board, has created the newly updated and curated *American History* database which affords readers easy access to searchable data within this broad expanse of information. The three primary components of this database are: a comprehensive reference library, a textbook course companion, and multiple perspectives on key issues. Intuitive in design, this interface is an excellent resource with extensive primary and secondary information relating to the history of the United States. Periods of time are not lacking for details of challenges, choices, and first-hand offerings of the American experience.

A logical place for students to start with the *American History* database is with Student Tools which define how to use the many options. At the bottom of the topic page, educators and students will find Check Your Understanding, a useful quiz to assist with retention of information. When a wrong answer is given, students are directed to the correct answer. Weird Words and Primary Sources will heighten learning. Additionally, there are standard research features for exporting, listening, saving, sharing, translating, printing, and citing works (including APA, Chicago, and MLA styles with definition).

Information about the vast and storied past of the United States might leave students crippled, not knowing where to begin their research. Not so with the *American History* database! Thoughtfully structured for ease of use with well-defined data, information is easily found. A carousel of 11 tiles presents overlapping time periods from Exploration and Colonization (1350-1760) through the Age of Globalization (2001-Present). Under each of these epochs are specific wars, events, or issues of concern. An upper-right search bar within data will further define information. A left sidebar offers multiple filters such as under the header Research: General Resources, Media, and Documents. Today, in our very visual and auditory world, students will find the photos and illustrations, political cartoons, posters, documents, audio, video, maps, and visuals in the Media section effective in their research experience. Also on the sidebar are opportunities to explore, find various perspectives, and a vast library of additional resources; for example, in researching FDR and the New Deal, there are links to an additional 695 resources in the library!

Students and teachers of American history will find this database rich with content and extremely user friendly. This is highly recommended for advanced students in middle school, high school, and college. Educators in the fields of social studies, American history, and government will find this resource platform advantageous to curriculum development.—**Janis Minshull**

C, P

124.   **American History through Its Greatest Speeches: A Documentary History of the United States.** Jolyon P. Girard, Darryl Mace, and Courtney Smith, eds. Santa Barbara, Calif., ABC-CLIO, 2017. 3v. index. $294.00/set. ISBN 13: 978-1-61069-969-3; 978-1-61069-970-9 (e-book).

This three-volume set is an impressive source for over 250 important speeches in American history. Organized chronologically, each volume contains relevant information about every speech, highlighting its source and circumstances. Biographical sketches appear at the end, along with a useful and extensive index to the complete set. Compared to the much smaller *American Speeches* collection in the Library of America series (2006), this volume's entries are edited for easier reading by modern audiences. In Patrick Henry's "Give Me Liberty or Give Me Death" speech of 1775, *American Speeches* reprints its first transcription, published some 40 years later; this set reprints an 1880 publication that changed the speech to a first person voice, making it more effective. Eugene Debs' "Statement to the Court" (1918) introduces a question about which source to use: an authorized version of his life and letters (*American Speeches*) or US District Court records (the review set). *American Speeches* contains 128 speeches, including six by Martin Luther King, Jr.; the review set has twice as many speeches, but unfortunately none by King, due, according to the introduction, to prohibitive rights costs. Copyright issues have likely prevented the republication of other modern speeches, as well.

Some speeches have been changed. Editors significantly modified the dialectic writing and word choice of Sojourner Truth's "Ain't I a Woman?" oration, for example, and they replaced terms now considered inappropriate.

This set will be a useful addition to all academic libraries, and most publics.—**Peter H. McCracken**

C, S

125.   Buckley, Jay H., and Jeffery D. Nokes. **Explorers of the American West: Mapping the World through Primary Documents.** Santa Barbara, Calif., ABC-CLIO, 2016. 321p. illus. maps. index. $100.00. ISBN 13: 978-1-61069-731-6; 978-1-61069-732-3 (e-book).

Part of the series, Mapping the World through Primary Documents, *Explorers of the American West* is written by Jay H. Buckley and Jeffrey D. Nokes, both U.S. history professors at Brigham Young University.

The book begins with preface, acknowledgements, introduction, and a selected chronology. Chapters conclude with a selected bibliography; an index rounds out the work. Chapters include 10 episodes and biographical case studies of North American explorers and travelers. Common explorers (Lewis and Clark, chapter one) are interspersed with chapters devoted to lesser-known people (e.g., Susan Shelby Magoffin, chapter seven). Each person is introduced with a biography, followed by an introduction to the document, the primary source itself, and historical analysis. Documentary evidence is well organized; field diaries, journals, memoirs, letters, scientific surveys, cartographic depictions, or maps lead to strong evidence-based representation of the American westward movement. Researchers need to be aware that sources may occasionally be from a contemporary of an explorer.

Western exploration and travel cannot be analyzed without incorporating American Indians into the discussion. The vital knowledge and aid of indigenous peoples was critical to the federal government's push to acquire lands through purchase and "just and lawful wars." Primary sources provide access to studies of American Indians who were rich in oral histories but often lacked written documentation. Detailed documentation records the dispossession of native peoples. For example, in describing the Amuchaba Indians' homes, Jedediah Smith writes "their summer lodges about 3 feet high are made of forks and poles covered with grass weeds and dirt flat on the top." Smith's description of their village, clothing, physical appearance, tools, and food brings to life the culture of the Amuchaba.

Altogether, *Explorers of the American West* is a user-friendly collection of documentation that shares the experience of the explorer or traveler in the westward expansion in the nineteenth-century United States. The primary sources are engaging and bring the reader in to the experience. Sourcing information is well organized and clear. This collection of written documentation and analysis will be extremely useful for scholars, researchers, and historians seeking primary source information on United States westward exploration.

Highly recommended.—**Janis Minshull**

C

126.   Cheathem, Mark R. **Andrew Jackson and the Rise of the Democrats: A Reference Guide.** Santa Barbara, Calif., ABC-CLIO, 2015. 309p. index. (Guides to Historic Events in America). $58.00. ISBN 13: 978-1-61069-406-3; 978-1-61069-407-0 (e-book).

This book documents in great detail the state of politics, political groups, and important politicians in the United States in the early nineteenth century, centered around the career of the seventh president, Andrew Jackson. The formation of Jackson's Democratic Party (not to be confused with today's modern understanding of that political party) is described, including the 1824 presidential election which Jackson lost to John Quincy Adams due to what has been labeled the "corrupt bargain." Jackson's status as the "Hero of New Orleans" as well as his well-known military victories helped him to secure the support of prominent politicians so that he could win the 1828 presidential election. The book then documents many of Jackson's struggles and challenges as president, including his character and penchant for explosive anger. Partisanship and the national economy dominated his presidency, along with the treatment of Native Americans and the constitutional authority of the chief executive. Jackson has been labeled the most significant president of the pre-Civil War era, and this book brings out that history and those issues that have left subsequent generations with their impressions of Andrew Jackson and the mark that he left on the development of the United States.

Recommended for academic libraries.—**Bradford Lee Eden**

C, P, S

127.   **Defining Documents in American History: The Cold War (1945-1991).** Michael Shally-Jensen, ed. Hackensack, N.J., Salem Press, 2016. 2v. index. $295.00/set. ISBN 13: 978-1-61925-858-7; 978-1-61925-859-4 (e-book).

The Salem Press Defining Documents in American History volumes constitute a fascinating series. All follow a common pattern of important documents that are put in context with critical essays (generally written by classroom teachers at the college or secondary level) that include a summary overview, the defining moment, biography of the author of the document, analysis of the document, and themes that emanate from the document. Appendixes include a chronology, bibliography, web resources, and an index.

This two-volume contribution identifies 86 primary source documents to trace the Cold War from 1945 until the end of the Soviet Union in 1991. The sources include official government documents, letters, memos, speeches, and other genres. The supporting features that put each source in context are very valuable. At the end of each entry is a brief listing of usually four sources for further study.

With the overwhelming number of reference volumes pouring out, one wonders how a library can decide what to acquire when free online sources are readily available. To that question, I can only state that unlike many other reference books that are dated by the time of acquisition, the documents in this reference source will remain historical fixtures; therefore, this hard copy reference work will have a long shelf life.—**Joe P. Dunn**

C, P, S

128. **Defining Documents in American History: Environment & Conservation.** Michael Shally-Jensen, ed. Hackensack, N.J., Salem Press, 2016. 222p. index. $175.00. ISBN 13: 978-1-61925-854-9; 978-1-61925-855-6 (e-book).

This book is a presentation of 45 primary source documents related to the environment and conservation movement in the United States from its origins to the present. Each document has a critical essay attached that includes a summary overview, defining moment, author biography, document analysis, and essential themes. These diverse texts include letters, court opinions, laws, government reports, speeches, journal entries, treaties, and international resolutions. The documents are organized under three broad categories: Beginnings, The Middle Years, and The Modern Era. A bibliography and additional readings section follow each essay. A number of appendixes are included, such as a chronological list of the source documents, an annotated list of web resources, and an overall bibliography. Some of the most important documents on this topic are presented and discussed, including the Homestead Act of 1862, the establishment of Yellowstone National Park, one of John Muir's many letters regarding Hetch Hetchy and Yosemite, and Jimmy Carter on the Three Mile Island Incident. This book represents an excellent addition to the reference collection of any library, and provides K-12 and higher education students with access to some of the most important documents in the American conservation movement.—**Bradford Lee Eden**

C, P, S

129. **Defining Documents in American History: The 1950s** (1950-1959). Michael Shally-Jensen, ed. Hackensack, N.J., Salem Press, 2016. 257p. index. $175.00. ISBN 13: 978-1-61925-886-0; 978-1-61925-887-7 (e-book).

Examining a decade known for conformity, confidence, communism, and civil rights, *The 1950s* is the latest in a series of titles that examines discrete periods of American history through a close reading of the primary documents produced therein. Previous volumes by Salem Press include the Reconstruction Era (1865-1877), the decade of the 1920s, and others.

A standard format allows the user of any one work to be familiar with the entire set. An "Editor's Introduction" sets the scene by giving an objective overview of the period in question. Each chapter takes an in-depth look at a single speech (President Dwight David Eisenhower, "The Chance for Peace"), government report ("A 'New Look' at National Defense Policy"), congressional legislation (Civil Rights Act of 1957), or other document, and uses this as a springboard to discuss not only the primary source itself, but also the social, cultural, and political ramifications that later came to be.

A "Summary Overview" gives the researcher a snapshot of the contents of the document, while "Defining Moment" fleshes out the background that led up to its creation. This is followed by "Author Biography" (if appropriate, as some documents are created by committees or other groups, as opposed to an individual writer), "Document Analysis," which is self-explanatory, and "Essential Themes," which discusses the significance and historical import of the document. Lastly, a "Bibliography and Additional Reading" section lists resources helpful for further research. The core of each chapter, however, is a shaded box that contains the verbatim text of the primary source under examination. Shorter pieces appear in their entirety, while the more lengthy are excerpted, which can still run to several pages.

Editor Michael Shally-Jensen holds a doctorate in cultural anthropology from Princeton University. He has assembled a competent crew of academics whom likewise hold advanced degrees and that have contributed to the contents of this work.

As with previously published volumes in this series, *The 1950s* is well written, exhibits solid scholarship, and presents an engaging read. As an understanding of our nation's past is central to becoming a well-rounded citizen, this volume is strongly recommended for purchase by all public and academic libraries.—**Michael Francis Bemis**

C, P, S

130. **Defining Documents in American History: The 1900s (1900-1909).** Michael Shally-Jensen, ed. Hackensack, N.J., Salem Press, 2016. 298p. index. $175.00. ISBN 13: 978-1-68217-185-1.

This single-volume edition edited by Michael Shally-Jensen is one of 22 titles that currently make up the Defining Documents in American History Series. The book is crafted like other volumes in the larger series. As the title states, the focus is on the opening decade of the 1900s. The work offers up an in-depth analysis of a wide range of 30 historical documents and the historical events that shaped American history at the dawn of the twentieth century. The documents cover a diverse range of topics such as Politics and Reform, Foreign Challenges, African American Debates, Native American Life, and Religion and Philosophy. Each of these topics serves as a chapter in the book and is presented in such a manner that allows students and educators to neatly isolate and focus on one particular area. As broad as the topics are, so too are the genres of documents, including journals, letters, speeches, government legislature, and court opinions. The wide array of documents exposes the issues which would come to define the social, political, and cultural themes important not only in the early part of the 1900s but throughout the century.

The format of the work is straightforward and easy to understand. Shally-Jensen provides the user with prologue before each topic area to set the stage. Individual entries provide the following information: subject title, date of the document, and genre of the document. Then the entry offers up a Summary Overview of the time of the document's creation as well as the Defining Moment, which explains to the reader the exact reason or cause for which the document being viewed came to be created. The entry also offers up an author biography. Then comes the document; the text of the document is re-created in full and formatted in a gray text box. This allows the reader to distinguish the document from the analysis that goes along with it. At the end of the text box, a glossary can be found to aid the researcher in understanding particular terms that may be unique to the time period. Next the reader will find a substantial Document Analysis, which helps the reader fully grasp the importance of the selected text as it relates to American history. This is followed by the Essential Themes section of the entry. It is within this area that the themes (often complex in nature) are presented so the reader can understand the underlying meaning of both the document, this moment in time, and how it relates to the large picture of American history. Last but definitely not any less important to the researcher is the Bibliography followed by the Further Readings section, which provides a starting point from which to begin more in-depth research. The book also offers appendixes and a chronological list of events, useful to anyone who wants to see how any particular document fits into the overall 1900-1910 timeline. There is also a section that offers the researcher a list of electronic resources. This if especially useful for researchers born in the time of Google and the digital age. The websites offered have been evaluated for their credibility and value. Like any research tool, a substantial bibliography and well-crafted index round out the volume. The overall craftsmanship is clearly a mark of Salem Press and the work they publish.

This work is a valuable asset to any collection not only for the documents but also for the presentation. It instructs readers in how to analyze a primary document—a valuable tool applicable to any level of research.—**Lawrence Joseph Mello**

C, P, S

131.   **Defining Documents in American History: The 1970s.** Michael Shally-Jensen, ed. Hackensack, N.J., Salem Press, 2016. 373p. $175.00. ISBN 13: 978-1-61925-890-7; 978-1-61925-891-4 (e-book).

As explained in the editor's introduction, the 1970s are often thought of as a transitional period between the 1960s and the 1980s. However, *Defining Documents in American History: The 1970s* is a collection of primary source documents and analyses that show this transitional outlook on the decade may be selling the time period short.

Through analysis of 49 primary documents and events of the 1970s, this book encourages high-school students and college-level students to analyze the decade through the lens of its most important events. The 49 primary documents and events are categorized into six broad categories. These include The Vietnam War, Nixon and Watergate, The Cold War and The Middle East, Domestic Affairs, Environmental Developments, and Science and Technology.

Each document or event is introduced by a summary overview and followed by a description of the defining moment, a brief biography of the document's author, the primary source document itself, a document analysis, and essential themes of the document. The defining moment entry is especially impactful because it provides readers with the context of the document. The analysis to follow then takes the context and the document together to provide information on significance.

The goal of helping high school and college students analyze primary documents and events is certainly achieved. The features of each entry, combined with the documents and topics chosen, facilitates the learning of not only the historical content of the decade, but also of how to analyze primary sources. High school teachers and college professors will be pleased when their students use *Defining Documents in American History: The 1970s* in their research of the decade.—**James D'annibale**

C, P, S

132.   **Defining Documents in American History: The 1960s (1960-1969).** Michael Shally-Jensen, ed. Hackensack, N.J., Salem Press, 2016. 331p. index. $175.00. ISBN 13: 978-1-61925-888-4; 978-1-61925-889-1 (e-book).

Examining a turbulent and eventful decade for our nation, *The 1960s* is the latest in a series of titles that examines discrete periods of American history through a close reading of the primary documents produced therein. Previous volumes by Salem Press include the

Reconstruction Era (1865-1877) and the decade of the 1920s.

A standard format allows the user of any one work to be familiar with the entire set. An "Editor's Introduction" sets the scene by giving an objective overview of the period in question. Each chapter takes an in-depth look at a single speech (John F. Kennedy, "The New Frontier"), government report ("The Tet Offensive: A CIA Assessment"), Congressional legislation (Civil Rights Act of 1964), or other document, and uses this as a springboard to discuss not only the primary source itself, but also the social, cultural, and political ramifications that later came to be.

A "Summary Overview" gives the researcher a snapshot of the contents of the document, while "Defining Moment" fleshes out the background that led up to its creation. This is followed by "Author Biography" (if appropriate, as some documents are created by committees or other groups, as opposed to an individual writer), "Document Analysis," which is self-explanatory, and "Essential Themes," which discusses the significance and historical import of the document. Lastly, a "Bibliography and Additional Reading" section lists resources helpful for further research. The core of each chapter, however, is a shaded box that contains the verbatim text of the primary source under examination. Shorter pieces appear in their entirety, while the more lengthy are excerpted, which can still run to several pages.

Editor Michael Shally-Jensen holds a doctorate in cultural anthropology from Princeton University. He has assembled a competent crew of academics who likewise hold advanced degrees and that have contributed to the contents of this work.

As with previously published volumes in this series, *The 1960s* is well written, exhibits solid scholarship, and presents an engaging read. As an understanding of our nation's past is central to becoming a well-rounded citizen, this volume is strongly recommended for purchase by all public and academic libraries.—**Michael Francis Bemis**

S

133.   **FactCite: Defining Moments in U.S. History.** [Website] Cleveland, Ohio, Lincoln Library Press, 2016. $249.00 (annual subscription).

Databases are clearly a preferred resource format for students today. FactCite: The Lincoln Library Online has partnered with Omnigraphics to create *Defining Moments in U.S. History* based on the Defining Moments print series by Omnigraphics. This database includes 2,800 entries and more than 1,000 photos evaluated by an elite advisory board. *Defining Moments* is exceedingly easy to search. Topics are discoverable via a keyword search, from an alphabetical list (Civil War: Gettysburg to Zoot Suit Riots), or a timeline (1804-2011). Once a topic like Gilded Age is selected, researchers can click on a variety of sublinks: Topics in Depth, Timeline, Topic Spotlights, Primary Sources, Biography, Glossary of People, Places, and Terms, Research Topics, and Resources. Each of these sublinks connects to further sources of information. Topics in Depth, for instance, links users to eight essays on such issues as the rise of labor, robber barons, and the legacy of the Gilded Age. The ten primary sources include Andrew Carnegie's "Gospel of Wealth," the text of the Sherman Antitrust Act, and much more. As of this review in October 2016, the database covers 34 major events in American history; more topics will be added annually and updates will be made as needed. None of these changes affects the moderate annual subscription price of $249.00.

Information is thorough and will make history come alive for students. Features that will be most captivating for educators and students are the primary source documents.

Important documents, journal entries, memoirs, and speeches bring the account to life. An abstract before the primary source content will provide an engaging overview for students. Secondly, the Glossary of Peoples, Places and Terms shows students the relationships during that era and clarifies wording. The Research Topics and Resources sections will provide teachers and students with extended subject ideas and further avenues for classroom investigation. Lastly, citing may be linked to Noodle Tool, a certain advantage to this historical database.

Defining Moments in U.S. History is both easily navigated and richly engaging for middle school and high school students. Lesson plans and teaching information make this invaluable for history teachers.

Additional databases available from FactCite, will further enhance the usefulness of *Defining Moments in U.S. History* when used in combination.

Recommended.—**Janis Minshull**

C, P, S

134.   **Family Ties on the Underground Railroad. http://still.hsp.org/still.** [Website] Free. Date reviewed: 2016.

William Still, a free black man, moved to Pennsylvania in 1844 and in 1847 started work as a clerk in the Philadelphia Anti-Slavery Society. He also served as secretary and chairman of the Vigilance Committee, which aided slaves escaping on the Underground Railroad. His 1872 book *The Underground Rail Road* and "Journal C" kept while working for the Vigilance Committee form the basis of this Historical Society of Pennsylvania digital history prototype project that tells the story of three family groups—the Shephard family, the Taylor family, and the Wanzer-Grigsby family—selected from the pages of Still's journal and book.

From the home page, users can access a series of essays that help contextualize the information: "Family, Slavery, and Flight," "5 Myths about the Underground Railroad," "On the Border of Slavery and Freedom: What Conductors and Passengers on the Underground Railroad in Pennsylvania Were Up Against," "Slavery, Abolition, and William Still: A Timeline," "To Render the Private Public: William Still and the Selling of the Underground Rail Road," and "A Brief History of the Underground Railroad." The top of the page provides several search buttons: Documents, Reference, Places, Relationships, and Education Tools alongside a simple search screen. These buttons take users to primary sources, maps, definitions, an A-Z list of biographies, and a clickable relationships graphic that uses color-coding to indicate the ties between the people in the selected excerpts from "Journal C" and *The Underground Rail Road*. Educator tools include three unit plans: *Using Primary Sources in the Classroom, From Fugitive Slaves to Free Americans,* and *The Pennsylvania Abolition Society and the Free Black Community.*

This site will serve many users from students to teachers to researchers. Highly recommended.—**ARBA Staff Reviewer**

S

135.   Hillstrom, Laurie Collier. **Defining Moments: Reconstruction.** Detroit, Omnigraphics, 2016. 228p. illus. index. $60.00. ISBN 13: 978-0-7808-1510-0.

Hillstrom presents a detailed overview of the tumultuous 12-year period from 1865 to 1877 that followed the American Civil War. The Narrative Overview tells the story of postwar Reconstruction, detailing seven aspects: slavery, the presidents, southern resistance, Reconstruction, segregation, the civil rights movement, and the legacy of Reconstruction. She relates these to the Jim Crow south and twentieth-century civil rights movement. Biographies of key figures include presidents (Andrew Johnson and Ulysses S. Grant), former slaves (Joseph Rainey, Robert Smalls), other politicians (Wade Hampton, Thaddeus Stevens), and a reformer (Frances Harper).

The volume is completed with 15 primary sources, a glossary, and chronology. Teachers of secondary (high school) students will find this a quality narrative for the basics of Reconstruction. Further details may be ascertained from *Reconstruction: A Historical Encyclopedia of the American Mosaic,* edited by Richard Zuczek (see ARBA 2016, entry 119) and the section on Reconstruction in *Revolts, Protests, Demonstrations, and Rebellions in American History: An Encyclopedia,* edited by Steven L. Danver. (see ARBA 2012, entry 461).—**Ralph Hartsock**

C, P, S

136.   **Histories of the National Mall. http://chnm.gmu.edu/histories-of-the-national-mall/.** [Website] Free. Date reviewed: 2017.

A genuine showpiece of the Center for History and New Media, this site acts as a virtual tour guide to the National Mall, a premier fixture of America's National Park Service. Users have the option to explore the National Mall and its many offerings in a variety of ways. They can simply click on one of four options to begin their virtual tour. One option, Maps, fills a page with a large interactive map of the National Mall and its environs. Holding 345 points of interest, users can click on an area to zoom, then click again on a point to access information about it. Users can also customize the map with a selection of filters to suit their particular interests. Explorations presents five pages of questions about the National Mall, such as "Who takes care of the Mall?" or "Why was the Mall important during the Civil War?" Users simply click on a question to access the summary answer. Alternatively, users currently visiting the Mall can choose one of four Scavenger Hunts to find and learn about items within specific exhibits such as the Korean War Memorial. People features brief biographies of nearly 90 figures whose stories intersect with the National Mall; from landscape designer Frederick Law Olmsted to singer Marian Andersen. And Past Events offers a chronology of nearly 100 events connected with the National Mall, from The Women's Suffragist Parade of 1913 to the display of the AIDS quilt in 1987. Each event is tagged for easy reference. The ease of viewing and navigation makes this site ideal for users to access via their mobile devices as they visit the Mall. But the good variety and clarity of the content may also appeal to armchair travelers, educators, students of American history, and others.—**ARBA Staff Reviewer**

C, P, S

137.   **History Matters: The U.S. Survey Course on the Web. http://historymatters. gmu.edu/.** [Website] Free. Date reviewed: 2017.

History Matters melds a large variety of resources with a selection of organizational and analytical tools. Its collection of over 1,000 primary source items, in conjunction with many other features, works to create a website ideal for students and educators of American history. A joint endeavor from the American Social History Project/Center for

Media and Learning of the City University of New York and the Center for History and New Media at George Mason University, *History Matters* also receives funding from the National Endowment for the Humanities, the W. K. Kellogg Foundation, the Rockefeller Foundation, and the Visible Knowledge Foundation.

Users can simply click on the particular feature that suits their needs, or conduct a search. Many Pasts is the main crux of the site, offering a good variety of primary source items such as newspaper articles, tracts, diary entries, memoirs, photographs, and prints. The items tell the stories of common people who had a part in the building of the American nation, from Native Americans and colonists to religious leaders, slaves, business women, and many others. Organized from oldest to most recent, each item is accompanied by a succinct paragraph of contextual information. Making Sense of Evidence offers an interactive, multimedia examination of how students can best use the many types of primary sources, while www.History offers a generous catalog of over 850 vetted and reviewed websites valuable towards the teaching of U.S. History. Other content includes archived discussion forums, strategies, and techniques regarding teaching and researching history, web-based assignments, history quizzes, and much more.—**ARBA Staff Reviewer**

C, P, S

138.   **Open Parks Network. https://openparksnetwork.org/.** [Website] Free. Date reviewed: 2017.

This site allows free access to over 200,000 items of cultural interest in addition to well over a million pages of technical reports, evaluations, and other documents pertaining to 18 national parks, historic sites, national monuments, and more. The Institute of Museum and Library Services, together with Clemson University and the National Park Service, has contrived this project to open a window on the pioneering days of the greater U.S. National Park system and the figures that would contribute to their greater ideal. The site holds materials derived from the archives and libraries of such places as the Abraham Lincoln Birthplace National Historic Park, Cape Hatteras National Seashore, Mammoth Cave National Park, and Yellowstone National Park. Users can conduct a general keyword search, or may choose to examine the material by specific location or collection. Some of the noteworthy collections include Congaree Photographic Prints, Jimmy Carter Memorabilia, Civil War Era Maps, and Carl Sandburg's Collection of Stereographs. Within each collection, users will find photographs, maps, government signage, park iconography, records, and other resources. Clicking on a specific item will show a high resolution image in addition to available metadata, such as subject, location, associated collections, format, etc. While focusing on only 18 major sites, the materials are numerous and fascinating, and offer a good source for research on "America's best idea." The website is connected with several social media platforms.—**ARBA Staff Reviewer**

S

139.   **Smithsonian Primary Sources in US History. https://www.gale.com/c/ smithsonian-primary-sources-in-us-history.** Farmington Hills, Mich., Gale/Cengage Learning, 2016. Price negotiated by site. Date reviewed: 2016.

This database brings the Smithsonian's most interesting and important photographs, documents, maps, and artwork into your school library. From a 1612 map of Virginia drawn by John Smith himself to a piece of the levee broken in New Orleans from the aftermath of Hurricane Katrina, these primary sources are divided into important eras in US history from 1450 to the present. Each item has a description outlining its importance as well as critical thinking questions. Curriculum connections are made to national and individual state standards. Special features include having the entries read aloud, downloading the text and citations, making highlights and notes, and being able to translate into many other languages. Educators can also connect to Google Classroom and Apps for Education to create assignments. The database itself is easy to navigate and search for relevant resources with key words. Educators can request a free trial before purchasing; price is dependent on enrolment and starts at $500 a year. This is a useful, high quality database to share with students to show them the value of using primary sources in their learning. Recommended.—**Kasey Garrison**

P, S

140.   **This is Who We Were: In the 1980s.** Amenia, N.Y., Grey House Publishing, 2016. 570p. illus. index. $155.00. ISBN 13: 978-1-61925-934-8; 978-1-61925-935-5 (e-book).

This Is Who We Were: In the 1980s is part of Grey House Publishing's This Is Who We Were series. If one wants to take a gentle stroll down memory lane and visit the 1980s or begin their research on what historians call the transformative in American History, *This is Who We Were: In the 1980s* is the place to begin their stroll. The 1980s were known as a decade of patriotism, prosperity, and peace; it was vibrant, it was big, and the Cold War was coming to an end. This work will begin to shed light on areas of the economy, music, television and movies, and social change. Within this volume one will be able to discover and view economic classes, dozens of occupations, and all regions of the nation. The volume will provide a comprehensive look at the decade known at the 1980s. This work is broken down into five sections: Profiles, Historical Snapshots, Economy of the Times, All Around Us, and Census Data. Each of the 28 biographical profiles is arranged in three categories: Life at Home, Life at Work, and Life in the Community. The researcher will learn about the 1980s through the photographs and original advertisements used to support each chapter, many of which include industry or social timelines and contemporary articles. This is a very useful way to open up the decade up to the reader regardless of their level and ability in the research process. The quality of the work is well crafted and the 28 profiles help shed light on the 1980s especially to those in younger generations who did not live through it firsthand. Besides the individuals, the real gold mine lays in the photographs of 1980s pop culture. These photos truly help open up the generation to the reader. Another aspect of the work, the Census Data, makes up three quarters of the volume. While census data can be found in the official governmental record, the ability to have it in the same volume as the 28 profiles helps the researcher to delve deeper into the 80s well beyond the cultural surface. This blend of materials makes this book a perfect resource. Overall this work is a very useful tool to any reference collection and to any level of researcher. Whether one is unable to remember the 1980s or was born long after the Berlin Wall came down, *This Is Who We Were: In the 1980s* is a volume you will want to add to your collection.—**Lawrence Joseph Mello**

P, S

141.   **This is Who We Were: In the 1970s.** Amenia, N.Y., Grey House Publishing, 2016. 488p. illus. index. 155.00. ISBN 13: 978-1-61925-749-8; 978-1-61925-750-4 (e-book).

Like the other titles in the This Is Who We Were series, this one focused on the 1970s captures the essence of the decade through its creative blend of biographies, historical snapshots, economic and census data, and inclusion of newspaper and magazine articles, speeches, and other documents. Black-and-white photographs and reproductions of advertisements further engage the reader. The eclectic mix of personal profiles from the creator of Sesame Street to a Vietnam prisoner of war, elementary school principal, and family business owner give a broad look at the decade as does data on annual incomes and prices for essentials like food, clothing, and housing. All of this is followed by a bibliography and index. This mix of primary and secondary data makes for a fun read as well as a reliable place to find out about the 1970s. Recommended for public and school libraries.—**ARBA Staff Reviewer**

C

142.   Vile, John R. **The Early Republic.** Santa Barbara, Calif., ABC-CLIO, 2016. 309p. index. (Documents Decoded). $81.00. ISBN 13: 978-1-4408-4346-4; 978-1-4408-4345-7 (e-book).

The Early Republic is part of the ABC-CLIO series Documents Decoded. This work, like others in the series, pairs key documents with in-depth examination. *The Early Republic* is authored by the distinguished John R. Vile, professor of political science and the dean of the University Honors College at Middle Tennessee State University. He has also authored such works as *The Men Who Made the Constitution* and *The Writing and Ratification of the U.S. Constitution,* as well as other titles for the Documents Decoded series. This series will "give readers a front-row seat to their own investigation and interpretation of each essential document line-by-line," allowing readers to use critical thinking skills.

Vile uses the documents to show how different the Founders were, while showing their similarities when it came to preserving their fragile new nation. The author lays out in the introduction his schematic for his book, as it is highlights key events in the early American republic. He also notes that while he could have easily stopped with the first five presidents, he decided to include John Quincy Adams because most historians see the election of Andrew Jackson in 1828 as ushering in a new era in American politics. He also points out that John Quincy Adams, as secretary of state under Monroe, played a huge role in the foreign policy that bears Monroe's name. The introduction's inclusion of synopses of the six presidents gives necessary background information to novice readers and provides a refresher for more advanced researchers. Another unique aspect to the introduction is the section where Vile points out the lessons he has drawn. This shows the reader a little about what the author was hoping to show through his work and just what he learned by the end of its creation. He tells the reader the presidents are used as markers, to chronologically explain the time periods. It is noted in this section that not every document is from the sitting president; for example, in some cases readers will find a passage from either Congress or the Supreme Court. This is done to emphasize the importance of other branches of government and their interactions with a particular president. Vile also exposes the contradiction between proclamations of human liberty and equality and the enslavement of African Americans, the marginalization and treatment of Native Americans, and the fact that women did not have the right to vote.

Each chapter begins with an introduction of the president under discussion. This introductory text is clearly identified as secondary material. The text of a particular letter, speech, or diary entry is presented in a separate bluish box. This allows the reader to designate it as primary and of importance. Then the author provides in blue text a little insight and analysis right next to the primary text. This format runs through the entire book. Then, between primary document passages, Vile provides linking text to help narrate or guide the reader to the next passage. This keeps the reader on track and provides continuity to the overall chapter. The chapters are not only well crafted by the author but are well-cited with sources provided throughout the individual chapters. John Vile provides the reader of this resource with a substantial and diverse "Further Reading" section. This will greatly aid both the novice researcher as well as the hardened faculty member who is doing research on the era of the early republic and its presidents. The source is well indexed and will allow the reader to clearly make the jump to a distinct topic of his or her choice if the need should arise. *The Early Republic* is a clear must have for any academic library's reference collection, let alone a historian who specializes in this era of American history.—**Lawrence Joseph Mello**

C, S

143.   Vile, John R. **The Jacksonian and Antebellum Eras.** Santa Barbara, Calif., ABC-CLIO, 2017. 280p. index. $81.00. ISBN 13: 978-1-4408-4981-7; 978-1-4408-4982-4 (e-book).

John R. Vile, Professor of Political Science and Dean of the University Honors College at Middle Tennessee State University, has compiled and edited two other volumes of the Documents Decoded series: *Founding Documents of America* and *The Early Republic.* His latest contribution focuses on one of the most turbulent periods of United States history, 1828 to 1861. That epoch begins with the ascension of Andrew Jackson to the presidency and concludes with Abraham Lincoln's first year in office.

The volume is comprised of 52 chronologically arranged documents, some in excerpted form, divided into three sections. The Jackson Years section contains 17 documents, including Andrew Jackson's Speech to Congress on Indian Removal and the Texas Declaration of Independence. Section two, Years of Expansion, Nascent Reform, and Manifest Destiny, includes 14 documents, ranging from the song lyrics to "Go Down Moses" to an excerpt from Henry David Thoreau's *Civil Disobedience.* The final section, Prelude to Irrepressible Conflict, focuses primarily on the sectional conflicts that ultimately erupted in the Civil War. Among its notable documents are the Compromise of 1850, an excerpt from Harriet Beecher Stowe's *Uncle Tom's Cabin,* and the Know-Nothing Party Platform of 1855. Each of the documents is accompanied by both analysis and commentary. The work concludes with a chronology, bibliography, and index.

As with any compilation of primary resources, one might quibble with what was selected for inclusion and what was not. For example, none of the Fugitive Slave Acts were included. It would have helped if there had been an explanation of the criteria utilized to select the respective documents. Still, this is a useful reference that will prove an excellent acquisition for libraries serving high school students and undergraduates.—**John R. Burch Jr.**

African History

Dictionaries and Encyclopedias

C, S

144. **Encyclopedia of African Colonial Conflicts.** Timothy J. Stapleton, ed. Santa Barbara, Calif., ABC-CLIO, 2017. 2v. illus. maps. index. $189.00/set. ISBN 13: 978-1-59884-836-6; 978-1-59884-837-3 (e-book).

    This encyclopedia of African colonial conflicts starts in time with some entries about Portuguese activity in Africa during the 1500s and 1600s but focuses mainly on the activity in the nineteenth century especially on the Scramble for Africa. Some colonial invasions and anticolonial armed rebellions in the early twentieth century are covered but not the African campaigns of World War I and World War II. There is a list of entries, a guide to related topics (battles/sieges; campaigns/wars; themes; treaties and conferences; organizations/institutions/groups; individuals). There are 367 entries, some on familiar people and events such as Charles George Gordon and the Zulu rebellions; others are on lesser-known people and events, such as Luka Jantjie and the Battle of Kuono. Each entry is signed. Each has a list of a few related entries (though not all are cross-referenced) and some suggestions for further readings at the end of the entry. The first volume has a short introduction. The second volume ends with a chronology, a bibliography, a list of contributors, and an index. The publication provides a convenient source for basic information about African colonial conflicts with helpful references for further information.—**J. E. Weaver**

Central African Republic

C

145.   Bradshaw, Richard, and Juan Fandos-Rius. **Historical Dictionary of the Central African Republic.** 4th ed. Lanham, Md., Rowman & Littlefield, 2016. 735p. (Historical Dictionaries of Africa). $175.00; $174.99 (e-book). ISBN 13: 978-0-8108-7991-1; 978-0-8108-7992-8 (e-book).

    Though called "new," this edition is the fourth in the series and updates the previous (3rd) edition (2005). Sections on acronyms and abbreviations, terminology, two maps, a chronology, and a detailed introduction to the country and its people precede the dictionary entries. Appendixes of rulers, constitutions, foreign peace-keeping support, and an extensive bibliography complete the book. Author Bradshaw was a professor of world history at Centre College in Kentucky who spent several years in the Central African Republic (CAR) while in the Peace Corps; many of his publications also centered on the CAR and Cameroon. For libraries with African and/or Africana studies programs.—**Michael W. Handis**

Morocco

C, P, S

146.   Boum, Aomar, and Thomas K. Park. **Historical Dictionary of Morocco.** 3d ed. Lanham, Md., Rowman & Littlefield, 2016. 927p. (Historical Dictionaries of Africa). $225.00; $224.99 (e-book). ISBN 13: 978-1-4422-6296-6; 978-1-4422-6297-3 (e-book).

The *Historical Dictionary of Morocco,* now in its third edition continues to be an easy-to-use, reliable reference. The dictionary incorporates new material to reflect changes since the second edition (see ARBA 2007, entry 88). In just under a thousand pages, users can find people, places, industries, and other things related to this North African country. The front matter includes a list of acronyms and abbreviations, notes on transliteration, maps, a solid introduction, and a chronology. The text is enhanced by the use of figures, such as a graph of cereals production from 1965 to 2016. Helpfully, cross-referenced terms appear in bold-face type; the text also employs *see* and see also references. The book concludes with a glossary and a bibliography that will facilitate deeper research, followed by information about the authors. Recommended for school, academic, and public libraries.—**ARBA Staff Reviewer**

Ancient History

Dictionaries and Encyclopedias

C, S

147.   **Conflict in Ancient Greece and Rome: The Definitive Political, Social, and Military Encyclopedia.** Iain Spence, Douglas Kelly, Peter Londey, and Sara E. Phang, eds. Santa Barbara, Calif., ABC-CLIO, 2016. 3v. illus. index. $310.00/set. ISBN 13: 978-1-61069-019-5; 978-1-61069-020-1 (e-book).

This large, three-volume series is meant to provide a standard reference work on Greek and Roman military history that is accessible to nonspecialists, namely advanced secondary students and undergraduates. There are two parts spread out over the three volumes: part one is on conflict in ancient Greece and presents an alphabetical encyclopedia of the major authors, battles, sieges, individuals, groups, cities, kingdoms, leagues, alliances, peoples, politics, treaties, wars, and campaigns; part two deals with conflict in ancient Rome and also provides an alphabetical encyclopedia of the above topics. One of the nice inclusions is a chronology of conflict in both ancient Greece and ancient Rome. At the end of each part, a number of appendixes contain quotable quotes, primary documents, maps, glossary, and bibliography. Each entry contains cross-references and a short further reading section. The volumes contain numerous black-and-white pictures and photographs of surviving sculptures, coins, cities, and artwork from the time period. The depth and breadth of the content is geared towards high school and undergraduate students who are interested in a quick reference source on these subject areas.

Recommended for high school and college libraries.—**Bradford Lee Eden**

C

148.   The World of Ancient Egypt: A Daily Life Encyclopedia. Lacovara, Peter, ed. Santa Barbara, Calif., Greenwood Press/ABC-CLIO, 2016. 2v. illus. maps. index. (Daily Life Encyclopedias). $198.00/set. ISBN 13: 978-1-61069-229-8; 978-1-61069-230-4 (e-book).

The civilization of ancient Egypt has for centuries mystified both academics and lay people with its towering monuments, larger than life rulers, and its intricate mythology and religion. Amongst the stories of great wars and pharaohs, however, it is the daily life of the common Egyptian that is often left out of the narrative. How did aspects of their technology, arts, religion, or economics affect their lives? It is the goal of this two-volume work to provide answers to these questions and to give the student a clearer picture of the Egyptian's everyday life.

The World of Ancient Egypt is divided into two volumes each with a comprehensive table of contents. Each volume is further divided into themed sections, beginning with their own introduction, that then contain the individual, alphabetically listed entries. Entries are highly detailed with many containing captioned illustrations to provide further description. Spread throughout the entries are also sidebars with more in-depth information related to nearby topics. Each topic also ends with a list of books for further reading into the subject. In addition to the entries the work also possesses a timeline from ancient to modern-day Egypt as well as several appendixes for such topics as a list of kings and the location of important museum exhibits. Also included at the end is a glossary, select bibliography, and a comprehensive index.

This is an excellent addition to any academic collection on ancient history. The organization is top notch allowing the reader to easily locate or discover important topics through contents, by section, or through a very efficient index. Entries are extremely well written to allow a combination of ease of use for the nonprofessional and depth for the academic while the suggested readings provide a clear path for those interested in further research.—**W. Cole Williamson**

Handbooks and Yearbooks

P, S

149.   Ancient World News. http://news.nationalgeographic.com/ancient-world/. [Website] Free. Date reviewed: 2017.

The National Geographic Society, long respected for promoting science, geography, history, and world culture across the globe, has focused this page on news, features, and other content related to ancient world cultures. Users simply scroll down through the page to access content across several categories. Recently Published brings news regarding recent discoveries of the ancient world such as the latest uncovering of Egyptian statuary, as well as general features. From the Magazine showcases longer features from the National Geographic print magazine. From History Magazine selects features from a sister publication focused on the historical narrative behind other National Geographic interests. Users can also browse the archive of National Geographic History for complete online editions. Archaeology features articles emphasizing the work of this field-based discipline, and History of Religion focuses on rituals and beliefs of world religions both well-known and obscure. There is also a video feature near the top of the page relating to noteworthy news of historical flavor. It is worth noting that the same article may appear across several categories within the page. Also, as this is a commercial site, the page contains wraparound advertisements, many of which promote National Geographic product sales (subscriptions, expeditions, etc.), which may visually interfere with the content. While this may seem disruptive to users, the value of National Geographic reporting and photography cannot be discounted, and the site remains a good choice for those pursuing a variety of scientific, historical, or other interests.—**ARBA Staff Reviewer**

C, S

150.   Kia, Mehrdad. **The Persian Empire: A Historical Encyclopedia.** Santa Barbara, Calif., ABC-CLIO, 2016. 2v. illus. index. (Empires of the World). $198.00/set. ISBN 13: 978-1-61069-390-5; 978-1-61069-391-2 (e-book).

The Empires of the World Series explores the defining characteristics of the greatest empires in world history, so it is only logical that *The Persian Empire: A Historical Encyclopedia,* is included alongside that of Rome, Spain, Ottoman, and British. Each work contains a timeline, overview essays, reference entries arranged by topic, and a series of primary source documents. By Persian, this work refers to the great dynasties of pre-Islamic Iran, but the author does make mention of Islamic and Royal Iran, but not to what is the modern country of Iran. The rich tapestry of ethnic, linguistic, and religious is given to the reader alongside that of history, culture, customs, politics, economics, science, literature, and traditions. Such entries as Nisa; Dura Europos; Samarquand; Chorasmia; Iranian Cuisine; Persian Gardens; Sports; Xerxes II; Vologeses V; Peroz; Seleucus I Nicator; Alexander of Macedon; Sacred Birds; and the Kushan Empire paint a far more complex picture of the empire.

A wonderful addition to this subject, especially for the novice.—**Scott R. DiMarco**

Asian History

Dictionaries and Encyclopedias

C

151.   **The Mongol Empire: A Historical Encyclopedia.** Timothy May, ed. Santa Barbara, Calif., ABC-CLIO, 2017. 2v. illus. maps. index. (Empires of the World). $198.00/set. ISBN 13: 978-1-61069-339-4; 978-1-61069-340-0 (e-book).

This set, containing 192 articles, is divided into eight sections: Government and Politics, Organization and Administration, Individuals, Groups and Organizations, Key Events, Military, Objects and Artifacts, and Key Places. Also included are 48 primary documents, dating from 1205 to 1406 C.E., and a chronology (1125-1480 C.E.) The presumed readership of these volumes is not totally clear. For example, Genghis Khan is referred to as Chinggis Khan, perhaps confusing newcomers to the subject. Many of the entries, such as Karachi Begs, Ulus, Alginchi, Chagatai Khanate, and Kumiss, may require consulting the glossary before undertaking the articles themselves. Brief overview essays for each of the sections do help to some extent to outline the articles that follow, while the "Further Reading" lists at the end of all the articles, as well as a comprehensive bibliography in volume two, will help readers considerably if they wish to explore the Mongol world further.

This volume will be most useful in academic libraries, particularly at institutions studying Asian history. Other libraries will find it too focused on details, without an overarching setting to guide readers.—**Mark Schumacher**

Korea

C, S
152.   Matray, James I. **Crisis in a Divided Korea: A Chronology and Reference Guide.** Santa Barbara, Calif., ABC-CLIO, 2016. 389p. index. $89.00. ISBN 13: 978-1-61069-992-1; 978-1-61069-993-8 (e-book).

This book starts with the earliest history of the Korean Peninsula and moves forward to the governments of Pak Geun-hye and Kim Jong Un, the current leaders of the two Koreas. In the course of the narrative, Matray identifies recurring themes that have shaped the peninsula's history. These include the country's geostrategic position in Northeast Asia making it the target of invasion and foreign domination since its beginnings; patriarchal and hierarchical traditions that can be traced back to its Confucian past; historical reliance on isolation from the outside world; four decades of Japanese colonialism, the destruction of the Korean War and the ongoing presence of the United States in South Korea that have created strong feelings of nationalism and anti-imperialism in both Koreas; and both Koreas' top priority for reunification made secondary to Cold War and post-Cold War global politics. The story of this peninsula can be summed up by the Korean proverb, "A shrimp is crushed in the battle of the whales." Features include a chronology of Korean history from 1866 and its first experience with the West to the present; biographies of key individuals, Korean and foreign, who have played pivotal roles in the peninsula's history; and a selection of primary documents from the 1882 Korean-American Treaty to President George W. Bush's Axis of Evil speech. This book helps the reader better understand current U.S. relations with South Korea as well as gives insights into the North Korean Kim dynasty, its ability to last through three generations, and its current nuclear posturing.—**Adrienne Antink**

European History

Former Yugoslav Republics

C, S
153.   **Bosnian Genocide: The Essential Reference Guide.** Paul R. Bartrop, ed. Santa Barbara, Calif., ABC-CLIO, 2016. 355p. illus. maps. index. $89.00. ISBN 13: 978-1-4408-3868-2; 978-1-4408-3869-9 (e-book).

This encyclopedia of persons, ideas, events, and places revolves around the wide range of war crimes associated with the civil wars that followed the collapse of socialist Yugoslavia in the 1990s. The title understates the extent of coverage, which ranges beyond genocide to include other war crimes, pays proportional attention to other regions such as Croatia and Kosovo, and offers a record of events after the 1995 Bosnian ceasefire through the 1998-1999 Kosovo War and the outcome of war crimes trials up to 2015.

There are 127 articles in alphabetical order, signed by the contributors, who are chiefly American and British academics. The editor is an accomplished scholar of genocide studies. Half of the entries are concise biographies of political and military leaders, war criminals, world statesmen, and lawyers. Other articles discuss the historical background, competing ideologies, key figures on all sides, and crucial events. The emphasis is on the emergence of post-communist regimes, ethnic tensions, the fighting in Bosnia-Hercegovina from 1991 to 1995 and in Kosovo during 1998-1999, torture and rape as instruments of ethnic cleansing, the eventual NATO interventions against Serbia, and subsequent war crime prosecutions at the Hague. Substantial detail is provided about the massacre at Srebrenica, the sieges of Sarajevo and Vukovar, and the careers of Milosevic, Mladic, and other leaders. Some material discusses Tito and the context of Yugoslav history, but for a thorough understanding of political and social causes, readers will need to turn to other works. One such source is *Conflict in the Former Yugoslavia: An Encyclopedia* (see ARBA 2000, entry 472): the present volume under review extends and updates this 1998 publication, while reprinting selected articles (such as "Chetniks"). *Bosnian Genocide* provides more biographies and offers coverage subsequent to 1998, notably the crisis in Kosovo and the prosecution of war criminals.

The articles are supported by six outline maps, 25 black-and-white photographs (many of them portraits), a chronology from 1944 to 2015, a bibliography, an index, 10 primary source documents (such as the Dayton Peace Accords), and summary essays on causes, consequences, and the roles played by perpetrators, victims, and the world community. Available in hard cover or as an e-book. Comparable entries in free sources like Wikipedia generally are shorter, lack references to scholarly monographs for wider reading, and assume that readers already recognize key personal and place names.— **Steven W. Sowards**

Germany

C

154. Lewis, Derek, and Ulrike Zitzlsperger. **Historical Dictionary of Contemporary Germany.** 2d ed. Lanham, Md., Rowman & Littlefield, 2016. 770p. (Historical Dictionaries of Europe). $180.00; $179.99 (e-book). ISBN 13: 978-1-4422-6956-9; 978-1-4422-6957-6 (e-book).

This second edition (see ARBA 2008, entry 128), part of the Historical Dictionaries of Europe series, contains everything one needs to know or wants to know about modern-day Germany from 1961 (building of the Berlin Wall) to the present. It focuses mainly on the Federal Republic of Germany (FRG), but also includes information on the former German Democratic Republic (GDR). A fairly large chronology of events from 1961 to March 2016 is included, as is a comprehensive acronyms and abbreviations list.

The Introduction is 30 pages, a very nice summary of Germany's history in the last 65 years. The dictionary entries themselves contain numerous cross-references in bold, and detail events, people, leadership, resources, treaties, states, and natural resources. Two appendixes list the German presidents, chancellors, and their dates in the FRG. Finally, a comprehensive bibliography divided into detailed sections on history, topical studies, and references closes the book. An excellent reference work for college and university libraries.—**Bradford Lee Eden**

Great Britain

C, P, S

155.   **Collage: The London Picture Archive.** [Website] Free. Date reviewed: 2017.

The London Metropolitan Archives (LMA), operated on behalf of the City of London, manages this online archive of London images. The archive includes maps, prints, drawings, photographs, and images of paintings, watercolors, and sculptures of greater London and adjoining counties. Materials extend back to the sixteenth century and are drawn from both the Guildhall Art Gallery and the LMA. Like the physical archive, the site is free to use and open to the public.

Navigation is quite simple. Users will find seven links at the top of the home page: Advanced Search, Search Tips, Galleries, Collections, London Picture Map, About Collage, and Help and Support. Along the left side of the page, there is another refined search option along with links to popular searches and galleries. There are also thumbnails of the Galleries, which can be clicked to access the curated materials. Examples of galleries include: Iconic London landmarks, London Gothic, London Fire Brigade, 1866-2016, First World War, and Shakespeare and London. If a researcher prefers to find materials via collection, they will find clickable thumbnails that link to the materials in the Granger Portrait Collection, the Baddeley Collection, the London Metropolitan Railway collection, and many others, all in the LMA or the Guildhall Art Gallery. Once an image is accessed, a user will find a title, description, date of work (if known), the location of the piece, acquisition information, and more. There are hyperlinked subject terms for each image as well, so it is easy to jump, for example, from an 1893 photograph of Tower Bridge construction to images of other road bridges. A selected and limited number of images are viewable by clicking on the London picture map. Curators have linked images to particular areas; in some cases, the images might be of buildings no longer in existence, so users can get a sense of what is referred to as "Lost London."

Materials in the archive are intended for personal use. Any other use must be approved by the LMA; this can be done by filling out a form under the Request a License link. Users can print images, download PDF copies of images, or buy a digital copy (the price varies based on the quality desired).—**ARBA Staff Reviewer**

C, P, S

156.   **Six Degrees of Francis Bacon. http://www.sixdegreesoffrancisbacon.com/.** [Website] Free. Date reviewed: 2017.

This website offers an inventive way to track societal relationships of the early modern era in England (generally the late 1400s to the late 1700s). It is designed to provide a fluid and collaborative examination of scholarship on these nearly 200,000 relationships revolving around roughly 13,000 individuals (so far). Users who create an account (free) may contribute to or download the data, but all users may view the data. It is important to note that this site is in the beta stage of development and content and/or design is subject to change at any time. The site employs visualizations via colored nodes to link individuals or groups. Selecting View Records from the header bar will provide a list view of the extensive data. Variables on a sidebar allow users to discover basic information of a selected individual (such as birth date and historical significance) as well as links to further information. Users can also conduct a search from the sidebar via network or group. Specialized mechanisms (e.g., the Relationship Confidence Slider) help enhance the search process. It is essential for beginning users to select the "?" tab at the top of the page. Here they can access an Introductory Video and tutorials explaining the nature of the site and how to utilize and expand the data. This website would be of great interest to historians, social scientists, Anglophiles, and many others.—**ARBA Staff Reviewer**

C, P, S
157.   **Voices of Medieval England, Scotland, Ireland, and Wales: Contemporary Accounts of Daily Life.** Linda E. Mitchell, ed. Santa Barbara, Calif., Greenwood Press/ABC-CLIO, 2016. 263p. index. $79.00. ISBN 13: 978-1-61069-787-3; 978-1-61069-788-0 (e-book).

Like the other volumes in Greenwood's Voices of an Era series, such as *Voices of Civil War America* (see ARBA 2012, entry 474) and *Voices of Revolutionary America* (see ARBA 2012, entry 475), this reference work seeks to illuminate the lives of ordinary people rather than dwelling on cultural, political, or social elites. Its focus is the British Isles during the Middle Ages, which was a period that saw the region impacted by numerous distinct cultures, including the Celts, Anglo-Saxons, and Scandinavians.

Edited by Linda E. Mitchell, the Martha Jane Phillips Starr Missouri Distinguished Professor of Women's and Gender Studies and Professor of History at the University of Missouri—Kansas City, this reference tool begins with a detailed introduction and a chronology of the British Isles from 500 to 1500 C.E. that contextualize the 63 primary sources excerpted in this work. The documents comprise the heart of the volume and are arranged in eight topical sections: "Domestic Life and the Medieval Household"; "Education and Professional Training"; "Economic Life"; "Religious Life and Religious Conflict"; "Politics, Law, and Administration"; "Warfare, Conquest, and Diplomacy"; "Crime, Disorder, and Deviance"; and "Popular Culture and Literature." The text of the respective documents is supplemented by an introduction that provides background information, an aftermath that examines its impacts on society, and bibliographic citations for further research. Following the documents are two appendixes that greatly add to the usefulness of this work: "Appendix 1: Biographical Sketches of Important Individuals Mentioned in the Text" and "Appendix 2: Glossary of Terms Mentioned in the Text." Concluding the reference is a disappointing bibliography, which includes citations for 17 monographs and 10 websites, and an index.

This reference work would be extremely useful for school and public libraries serving a high school clientele. Academic libraries supporting undergraduate courses in British history or literature should consider obtaining a copy to circulate.—**John R. Burch Jr.**

Spain

C, P, S

158.   **The Spanish Empire: A Historical Encyclopedia.** H. Micheal Tarver and Emily Slape, eds. Santa Barbara, Calif., ABC-CLIO, 2016. 2v. illus. maps. index. (Empires of the World). $198.00/set. ISBN 13: 978-1-61069-421-6; 978-1-61069-422-3 (e-book).

As part of the Empires of the World series, this two-volume set covers the Spanish Empire from the fifteenth century forward. It is organized around the following themes: government and politics; organization and administration; individuals, groups, and organizations; key events; military; objects; and key places. The set also includes 34 primary documents and a list of monarchs and rulers of Spain from 1479 to the present that help contextualize many of the entries. The work also includes a glossary, selected bibliography, list of editors and contributors, and an index.

The introduction to the set covers the general history. This 18-page summary highlights the creation of the united kingdom of Spain, the voyages of Columbus, settlements in the new world, multiculturalism and ethnic mixing, religion, education, decline of local populations in the new world and the import of African slaves, colonial administration, nineteenth-century revolts and independence, World Wars I and II, and the Spanish Civil War. It also underlines two major world-changing results of the expansion of the Spanish Empire: the Columbian Exchange (trade between previously separated countries) and the social consequences of the mixing of races. This essay concludes with a list of recommended readings and is followed by a chronology of events relevant to the Spanish Empire.

Each thematic area that follows begins with a general essay on the topic, with suggestions for further reading. The signed entries in each section are in alphabetical order. Most include photographs, drawings, and/or pictures relevant to the entry. There is often an inset in the entry that details something significant to the entry. *See also* recommendations and further readings complete each entry.

Entries are written by school and college/university faculty and independent scholars from several countries. The editor is a professor of history at Arkansas Technical University and the assistant editor is an independent historian and documentary editor. This encyclopedia is aimed at high school and college undergraduate students and general readers. It offers a good starting point for basic research on aspects of the Spanish Empire. Recommended for public, school, and academic library collections.—**Joanna M. Burkhardt**

Latin America and the Caribbean

Dictionaries and Encyclopedias

C, S

159.   Kohut, David, and Olga Vilella. **Historical Dictionary of the Dirty Wars.** 3d ed. Lanham, Md., Rowman & Littlefield, 2017. 448p. illus. (Historical Dictionaries of War, Revolution, and Civil Unrest). $110.00; $109.99 (e-book). ISBN 13: 978-1-4422-7641-3; 978-1-4422-7642-0 (e-book).

The third edition of this book still focuses on the content of the previous two, but with more up-to-date information. The scope is the time period of 1954-1990, the continent is South America, and the countries are Argentina, Paraguay, Brazil, Bolivia, Uruguay, and Chile. The editors bring detailed knowledge and expertise on the dictatorships that governed these countries during the indicated time period, examining the little-known federation formed between them (along with Peru and Ecuador) nicknamed "Operation Condor," which assisted these dictators in the kidnapping, torture, disappearance, and death of one another's political rivals. An extensive list of acronyms and abbreviations, a chronology, and an introduction where the term "dirty war" is defined and discussed prefaces the dictionary proper. Each entry in the dictionary is concise, with bolded items indicating cross-references. The bibliography provides both general works and country-specific resources. This book is an excellent reference work on this specific topic and time period in South America.—**Bradford Lee Eden**

Handbooks and Yearbooks

C, P, S
160.   **Ecclesiastical & Secular Sources for Slave Societies. http://www.vanderbilt. edu/esss/index.php.** [Website] Free. Date reviewed: 2017.

This ongoing project via Vanderbilt University is working to digitize thousands of centuries-old documents connected to the non-European (primarily African) slave populace in the Spanish-Portuguese colonized lands of South America and the Caribbean. This site offers users a look at the many documents from maps to death certificates that the project has been able to digitally preserve. Much of the archive is borne of church records: the Catholic insistence on baptism for all African slaves in the region instituted the need for marriage, death, and other sacramental documentation. Many secular records, such as land transfers, slave sales, business disputes, and wills are also included in this collection.

Visitors to this site can select their country of interest from the tabs at the top of the page: Brazil, Colombia, Cuba, or Spanish Florida. For each country, users can access contextual information about the project (such as people involved, history, etc.), additional resources, transcriptions (if available), and document images. Documents within each country may be further organized by region or parish. The Additional Resources tab offers Useful Links, Teaching Tools, and recent site-based scholarship, among other things.

The grand scope of this project, coupled with the ease of navigation, makes this site a worthwhile stop for those with genealogical, historical, or other interest in South American/Caribbean slave societies.—**ARBA Staff Reviewer**

World History

Handbooks and Yearbooks

P, S
161.   Eaton, Gale. **A History of Ambition in 50 Hoaxes.** Thomaston, Maine, Tilbury House Publishers, 2016. 271p. illus. index. $24.95. ISBN 13: 978-0-88448-465-3; 978-0-

88448-492-9 (e-book).

The story of humanity shows that the route to success varies greatly. History is certainly rife with stories of noble leaders, brilliant thinkers, and others whose intelligence, hard work, and integrity led to achievement. But there are also stories of those who opted to take an easier route, no ethics required. This volume in the engaging History in 50 series offers 50 examples of some of the more dubious human attempts at pulling a hoax throughout history. The series is adept at concisely connecting centuries of civilization via a particular theme.

Opening with the legend of the Trojan Horse and culminating 49 chapters later with the perhaps all-too-familiar scourge of cyber-scams, the book takes readers chronologically through some of history's most noteworthy hoaxes. Chapters are brief, but contain a host of interesting details and facts. The chapter "Fairies Are Caught on Camera," for example, shares details of contemporary photographic technology, sensational journalism, and a heightened interest in the supernatural in post-World War I society. Other chapters include "Michelangelo Fakes an Antiquity," "The Original Ponzi Scheme," "Martians Attack," and many more. While the volume shows that many hoaxes are debunked in due time with no lasting damage, it also reveals, as in the case of Benjamin Franklin's "hoax diplomacy" (which furthered years of enmity toward Native Americans), how many can indeed come at a cost.

Each chapter includes color illustrations and shaded text boxes sharing further insight. Supplementary material at the book's close includes a glossary, a chapter-by-chapter list of sources and additional resources, extensive endnotes, and an index. While not delving too deeply into its topics, the book manages to both inform and entertain readers and can certainly pique their interest in further research.—**ARBA Staff Reviewer**

C, S

162. Lang, William L., and James V. Walker. **Explorers of the Maritime Pacific Northwest.** Santa Barbara, Calif., ABC-CLIO, 2016. 303p. illus. maps. index. (Mapping the World through Primary Documents). $108.00. ISBN 13: 978-1-61069-925-9; 978-1-61069-926-6 (e-book).

This is the second title in the ABC-CLIO series Mapping the World through Primary Documents which supports Common Core Standards relating to primary source analysis as well as National Geography Standards. Students in geography, American history, and social studies classes will find the series extremely useful. In this series the reader will explore the vastness of untamed lands and uncharted waters, and all their exploration is crafted through the use of primary documents. This will allow the researcher to work on his or her critical thinking skills while learning about the early days of exploration. This book is co-authored by William L. Lang and James V. Walker. Lang is professor emeritus of history at Portland State University. The author or editor of seven books on Pacific Northwest history, Lang was director of the Center for Columbia River History (1990–2003) and founding editor of *The Oregon Encyclopedia.* Walker is a retired physician and map collector living in Eugene, Oregon, with research interests focusing on the Pacific Northwest and early-nineteenth-century Trans-Mississippi West material. He is a member of the steering committee of the Philip Lee Phillips Map Society of the Library of Congress.

Before the reader crosses over the ship's gangplank, he or she is provided with a substantial introduction, which gives a brief yet substantial history of exploration leading up to sea exploration of the seventeenth-eighteenth centuries. Not only will the key sea commanders be mentioned in the introduction, so will key themes like "How National Interest Shaped Exploration," or "Why Maps Have Power." Those two themes and others provide the reader with the necessary basic understanding of the time period and the expeditions. Right before the sails are raised and the exploration begins the reader is also supplied with a selected chronology of key dates and events of sea exploration, covering 1494 to 1803.

The uniqueness that is the *Explorers of the Maritime Pacific Northwest* is the selection of 10 major exploratory experiences, which greatly expanded mankind's understanding of the world. This work also expands significantly the cartographic knowledge about the North Pacific, an area which often is overlooked during the studies of world explorations. In most chapters which cover a single voyage, simplistic maps are offered to the researcher to relive the journey of the crew. These maps also include geopolitical and cultural information, such as place-names, that reflected competition among imperial maritime nations exploring the Pacific Northwest. The reader is able to earn his or her "sea-legs" through the incorporation of various primary documents including but not limited to diary entries, ship's logs, and royal decrees. It is these documents which will take the reader right on the deck of the ship on the high seas, from on-the-scene descriptions of the mariners' experiences at sea to their often tenuous encounters with native inhabitants to their return home with information of a distant land and new world. Each chapter stands on its own merits and is a story unto itself. Chapters open with a brief biography of the ship's captain or commander. The chapter then dives right into the heart of the journey and offers the primary documents to re-create and bring to life the journey. The researcher will take from the documents the main results of the exploration, and, importantly, how the expedition expanded the world's cartographic understanding of the North Pacific. The truly amazing feature of the chapters is how the documents reveal personal reflections of the principal actors. This will help bring an often distant part of history alive. Then after the reader is drawn into the exploration the authors offer up analysis that aids understanding. The authors clearly cite the primary documents used and offer the citation at the end of each themed section of the chapter. This information allows the reader to dig deeper into the event and learn more about the larger primary document. A "Further Reading" section also offers readers the opportunity to dive deeper into the exploration or gain a more in-depth understanding of the particular event. One interesting point is the authors' use of small "Did you know?" boxes within the chapters. For example, "Did you know, one Manila galleon ship carried 50,000 pairs of silk stockings, from China to Spain." While not directly important to the chapter, this information is nonetheless interesting.

This is a well-crafted book, written in a manner suitable for both a young novice student and a more seasoned researcher. The material offered is well vetted and while the chapters are but small windows to larger explorations or expeditions, the reader is provided with a substantial biography, which will allow him or her to take on another exploration during the Great Age of Sail and Exploration. This work is one that can prove valuable to any reference collection.—**Lawrence Joseph Mello**

C, S

163. **World History: The Modern Era.** http://www.abc-clio.com/ABC-CLIOCorporate/product.aspx?pc=WOHSW. [Website] Santa Barbara, Calif., ABC-CLIO, 2016. Price negotiated by site. Date reviewed: 2016.

World history scholarship is a colossal undertaking; textbooks can labor over topics and discourage students who are seeking a topic within a topic. The ABC-CLIO database *World History: The Modern Era* gives students a digital collection which can easily be searched with many options for access. An advisory board has assisted with the assemblage of the modern history collection from 1500 to the present.

The strong presence of help tools for students will make this a successful research experience and the support options will give students confidence in their world history studies. All resources can be accessed, filtered, and evaluated via the Explore the Library bar, and more assistance is found in Tools for Students and News You Can Use. Correlating with topics, the glossary has rudimentary terms such as printing press or democracy, and also more challenging terms such as *encomienda*.

Resources are found via General Resources, Media, or Documents which includes cultural information, narratives and letters, reference articles, biographies, speeches, quotes, and more. For example, in the section on The Spread of Transportation, Henry Ford is quoted as saying "a business that makes nothing but money is a poor kind of business" which could be used as a springboard to study of business, transportation, and the industrial age, among other topics. In carousel and tile form, the periods range from The Emergence of Modern Europe (1500-1700) to A New Millennium (1991-present). Beyond chronological categories, information encompasses different geographical areas around the globe, times of war, and times of prosperity. Subtitles are found under each epoch; The Industrial Revolution includes a subtopic of Breakthroughs in Science where, for example, you will find Edison's advertisement for a phonograph or his invention of the vitascope, a precursor to a motion picture projector. Tools are ones that most students will be familiar with; the standard search bar is found in the upper right with the advanced search option for more detailed filtering. Options for sharing, emailing, and printing are found on information pages. Citation styles include APA, Chicago, and MLA.

This recommended database complements *World History: Ancient and Medieval Eras* and the combination of the two will provide a variety of resources, both primary and secondary. *World History: The Modern Era* will be useful to junior and senior high school students studying world history in what we consider the modern era. Teachers and professors will find this database easy for students to use and a worthy resource for extending classroom learning.—**Janis Minshull**

C, S

164. **World War I: The Essential Reference Guide.** Spencer C. Tucker, ed. Santa Barbara, Calif., ABC-CLIO, 2016. 397p. illus. maps. index. $89.00. ISBN 13: 978-1-4408-4121-7; 978-1-4408-4122-4 (e-book).

The indefatigable Spencer Tucker, the senior fellow in military history at ABC-CLIO, is a machine that produces military history reference works. This is his 56th volume. I have reviewed a large number of them and I have run out of new things to say. All the ABC-CLIO reference works follow a common proven model that includes entry list, an introduction that is a thorough introduction to the topic, maps, documents, chronology, bibliography, contributors, index, and the (always valuable) alphabetically arranged entries. Unlike others, this volume does not have a glossary, but it has a new feature—a series of brief essays on major questions about World War I. Examples include "What was the primary cause of World War I?" and "Was the Treaty of Versailles a success or failure?"

The author begins by stating emphatically that "World War I was the most important single event of the 20th century." He later reemphasizes this by claiming that "In a very real sense, World War II was simply a continuation of World War I." The subject is clearly important. For libraries, the question is, as always, how many of these bound reference volumes does one purchase vs. online sources?—**Joe P. Dunn**

10 Law

General Works

Handbooks and Yearbooks

P

165.   **California State Law Library. http://www.library.ca.gov/collections/law_coll. html.** [Website] Free. Date reviewed: 2017.

The Law Collection page of the greater California State website offers indirect access to California legislative and judicial history in addition to some limited information on U.S. legislative history. The page is very basic, as it merely provides a listing of links to other pages both within and without the main California website. Still, it is convenient for assessing one's research options relative to California law. Off-site links will help users Find A Lawyer and/or discover basic information regarding California Courts and Court Forms. Clicking on California Legislative Information will redirect users to another site with floor and committee hearing schedules, bill search capabilities, and more. California City/County Ordinances will direct users to sites providing listings of California-applicable laws, codes, statutes, courts opinions and large city (San Francisco, Los Angeles, Sacramento and San Diego) ordinances. And California Code of Regulations (CCR) directs users to the complete code of 28 titles covering such issues as administration, education, industrial relations, motor vehicles, and public works. From this page, users can also access www.congress.gov for federal legislative information. Finally, clicking on California Library Laws directs to the portion of the CCR covering library administration and usage.—**ARBA Staff Reviewer**

P

166.   **CourtHelp. New York State Courts. www.nycourts.gov/courthelp/ .** [Website] Free. Date reviewed: 2017.

CourtHelp offers free online access to information regarding a host of legal issues, procedures, and concepts relative to New York State Courts. Its user-friendly design allows searchers to conduct a basic search, or simply click on any topic from the homepage listing. Many topics and subtopics are covered, such as Name Change, Abuse & Harassment, Guardianship, Small Claims, and Criminal. Users can learn straightforward information about court procedures, forms, fees, finding the appropriate assistance, and much more.

Specialized topics, like Families & Children, explain the legal basics of topics like adoption, custody, visitation, support, and divorce. Each topic is cross-referenced. A Court Locator, where users can input county and court type, is found on the right sidebar, as are a selection of Quick Links to a Legal Glossary, DIY Forms, A to Z Topics, Help Centers, and further resources. This website stresses that it offers general legal information, not advice. This is a good source of reliable and regularly updated information for a variety of users.—**ARBA Staff Reviewer**

C, P, S

167.   **Famous Trials. www.famous-trials.com.** [Website] Free. Date reviewed: 2017.

This recently updated site is an excellent source of information on 76 of the most famous court trials in history, cataloging proceedings ranging from the trial of Socrates in 399 B.C.E. to the 2013 Florida murder trial of George Zimmerman. This well-curated selection covers a diverse array of prosecutions focused on criminal indecency, police brutality, espionage, domestic terrorism, tax evasion, murder and much more. Most of the 76 trials focus on cases in the United States.

Users can simply scroll through the page and click on the trial of interest, marked by its name (e.g., the Scopes-Monkey trial), date, and an illustration. Once users access a trial, they will see a concise but thorough summary. Links on the right side of the page direct users to further resources, which can include trial excerpts, interviews, chronologies, bibliographic materials, museum exhibits or videos, and more. Each trial's page presents a concise but thorough summary of the alleged crime and subsequent trial. Content is also searchable by trial classification: Free Speech, Murder, Race, Religion and War/Corruption/Politics. The site's attractive design and clean interface—users can scroll through fine art depictions of several trials on the home page—well-defined structure and generous content will appeal to educators, students, librarians, and researchers.—**ARBA Staff Reviewer**

C, P

168.   **Florida Law Collections. http://ufdc.ufl.edu/flaw1.** [Website] Free. Date reviewed: 2016

Florida Law: Laws and Legal Heritage of the State of Florida is comprised of *The Florida Historical Legal Documents* collection, a Florida Water Law collection, and the *Journal* of the Florida House of Representatives. *Florida Law* aims to document the laws and legal heritage of Florida using digitized texts from university, government, and private collections. Users can search the entire collection via basic or advanced search screens on the home page or search within the three subcollections. The home screens of the collection and subcollections also offer researchers an option to view items via hyperlinks, which is a good choice for someone who wants to browse or is unfamiliar with the material. When "View Items" is selected users can choose from a variety of filters on the left side of the page to narrow results. The House *Journal* found in the Florida House of Representatives subcollection comes from the printed holdings of the University of Florida Library, the State Library and Archives, and the Florida House of Representatives. An outside link takes users to the Florida House of Representatives where current *Journal* issues are located. The Florida Water Law subcollection is a digital archives project with several contributing collections, including that of the Northwest Florida Water

Management District (NWFWMD). This archive is a joint project between the five Florida water management districts. The Florida Historical Legal Documents provides access to over a dozen documents like the *Bibliography of Florida Government* from 1960 or the *Ordnance of Secession.* In the latter case, viewers can look at an image of the original document or read a transcript.

    Florida Law provides a wide range of legal materials to novice or advanced researchers in history, political science, or law.—**ARBA Staff Reviewer**

P

169.   Grimaldi, Judith D., Joanne Seminara, and Pierre A. Lehu. **5@55: The 5 Essential Legal Documents You Need by Age 55.** Fresno, Calif., Quill Driver, 2016. 142p. index. $12.95pa. ISBN 13: 978-1-61035-258-1.

    In a clear, straightforward manner, this book guides readers through the potentially overwhelming but absolutely necessary process of estate planning. Six brief chapters thoroughly explain the legal and financial details behind such end-of-life matters as health care, inheritance, and more. Specifically, the book details the five indispensable legal documents crucial to this preparation: the health care proxy, the living will, the power of attorney, the will, and the digital diary.

    The short chapters clearly define the nature of these documents and their various forms while illustrating their value via real life examples. In the case of Jared, for example, his lack of a will resulted in a vindictive widow evicting his elderly mother from her long-time home. Chapters also detail the methodology behind obtaining these documents and discuss contemporary complexities such as domestic partnerships and blended families. The information also does a good job of laying out the responsibilities of the professionals used to create the documents.

    Appendixes are extremely helpful, and include sample, standardized copies of the aforementioned documents, in addition to a sample layout for one's Digital Diary (which organizes passwords and ids for various online accounts). Appendixes also include information regarding the roles of the estate executor and trustee as well as a listing of charter and founding members of the 5@55 Campaign, which serves to build greater public awareness of the need for these legal documents by the age of 55.

    Recommended for public libraries.—**ARBA Staff Reviewer**

C, P, S

170.   **Justia. www.justia.com/.** [Website] Free. Date reviewed: 2017.

    Justia acts as a warehouse of legal matters, research, and personnel. It offers a generous amount of free but basic information regarding U.S.-based lawyers, laws, law schools, regulations, and more (some resources are available for Latin America). Users can select from a large variety of Legal Practice Areas, such as injury, business, immigration law, criminal law, and estate planning. Upon doing so, they will be able to search relevant resources, read a summary definition, and view a listing of current cases on the docket, related legislation, regulations, articles, and blogs. Legal Research & Law Practice provides definitions and examples of Laws: Cases & Codes, U.S. Courts, Law Schools, Law Blogs, Legal Forms, etc. Lawyers, Legal Aid & Pro Bono Services links to information by category (Personal Injury, Business Law, etc.) or state. Cases in the News highlights some of the better-known legal matters impacting society (e.g., Facebook lawsuits), and Public Interest and Pro Bono Projects supplies information on such matters as copyright information and recall warnings. Users are also able to quickly Find a Lawyer, searchable by legal issue, lawyer name, and state, or Ask a Lawyer, where site-registered lawyers may provide general answers to user-submitted questions. Verdict, an auxiliary blog, has articles related to law in current events, politics, and more. The site would greatly appeal to users with either a general or specific interest in the law and would be an excellent starting point for many types of legal research.—**ARBA Staff Reviewer**

C, P

171. **National Center for State Courts. http://www.ncsc.org/.** [Website] Free. Date reviewed: 2017.

The National Center for State Courts' (NCSC) website houses a large variety of research options, information services, and education aimed at state court administrators as they seek to enhance court operations. Information here addresses a wide variety of courts (municipal, probate, etc.), management issues (budgets, workflow, etc.), and specific topics (adoption, human trafficking, marriage & divorce, etc.). The vast amount of information on this site may appear daunting, but it is generally well organized. Users can select from a number of tabs on the header bar. Information and Resources has a drop-down menu of several browsing options (A-Z Topics, Category, State) and applications such as State Court Comparisons and a court management diagnostic tool. Services & Experts aim planning guides, best case practices, projects, reports, surveys, and more toward many court-related concerns, such as statistics, civil justice, case flow management, and language access. Users can also explore Education & Careers and Conferences & Events. Other features from the site include NCSC Highlights, which offers a selection of broader court-based news and a link to the 2016 NCSC Annual Report. This Week at NCSC allows users to side scroll through court-related news stories. Users can also access an NCSC podcast, find courses offered by the NCSC's instructional affiliate, locate associations, and do much more. This website would be a vital resource for legal and administrative professionals, law students, and educators alike.—**ARBA Staff Reviewer**

C, P, S

172. **Oyez. www.oyez.org/.** [Website] Free. Date reviewed: 2017.

This ideal research tool, www.oyez.org, is home to audio archives of U.S. Supreme Court sessions dating back to 1955, when proceedings were first recorded. Users can hear for themselves the arguments and decisions that uphold and interpret the U.S. Constitution as it pertains to a host of issues, from civil rights to business law and more. Selecting the Cases tab allows access to cases beginning with the most recent, or users can browse by date, case name, term, or issue. Users can also conduct a general search. Each case is annotated with information about petitioner, respondent, docket number, lower court, and advocates, among other things. There is also a "plain English" summary of the case providing background information including the essential question put toward the court. If a decision has been rendered there is a conclusion summary including the justices' vote. The site currently features a curated exhibit called *The Body Politic,* highlighting four cases focused on abortion law. The main highlight within Cases, however, is the audio recording of the proceedings (where available). Recordings come with complete and searchable transcripts and offer a truly essential window into the history of the court.

The Justices tab presents a biographical sketch of each justice and lists their argued cases. The Tour tab takes users on a virtual inside and out tour of the Supreme Court building. News links to an excellent blog covering Supreme Court news of the day and a well-organized topical archive covering such things as Confirmation Hearings, Drama in the Court, and the Affordable Care Act. With information that is accessible, engaging, and vitally important to understanding the American judiciary and its role in history, the site would be highly valuable to a variety of students and educators.—**ARBA Staff Reviewer**

C, P

173. The State and Federal Courts: A Complete Guide to History, Powers, and Controversy. Christopher P. Banks, ed. Santa Barbara, Calif., ABC-CLIO, 2017. 513p. index. $105.00. ISBN 13: 978-1-4408-4145-3; 978-1-4408-4146-0 (e-book).

As the subtitle indicates, this is a wide-ranging overview of the American judicial system, extending beyond the courts per se to discussions of legal procedures and doctrines. The chapters or subchapters are attributed to any of a large number of contributors (Banks himself has written quite a few of them), although many of the 26 listed contributors do not appear as authors. The first three chapters cover the history, roles, functions, powers, structure, and process of the judiciary. The fourth and longest chapter ("Political Issues and Controversies of the Judicial Branch") is subdivided into four parts: Constitutional Politics and Democratic Principles; Judicial Access, Independence, and Accountability; The Politics of Judicial Selection and Removal; and Political Controversies (this last briefly covering the judicial history of 17 prominent issues such as same-sex marriage, the Affordable Care Act, and affirmative action). This book cannot really be considered a reference source; it more resembles a traditional textbook. Except for a glossary of legal terms it contains no tabular material, although the torrent of percentages in the 15-page section on the makeup of the judiciary (e.g., socioeconomic status and demographic characteristics of judges) would have been better displayed in such a form. There is not a single illustration or sidebar to enhance the text. The book is well written; the authors are good about providing examples to illustrate their points. There is some repetition, particularly between chapters two and three, and there are a few other glitches (three of the cited references in chapter three do not appear in the list of references at the end of the chapter; an occasional malaprop, such as "principle" instead of "principal"; and a failure to note that after a defendant enters a plea the judge has other options besides setting bail or keeping in jail (e.g., release upon personal recognizance or home monitoring). Also, since this is not an alphabetically arranged source, the *see also* references at the end of sections can only be accessed by referring to the index at the end of the book. All this notwithstanding, this source is packed with accessible information and is recommended for public and academic libraries.—**Jack Ray**

P

174. State of Oregon Law Library Digital Collection. http://digitallawlibrary. oregon.gov/. [Website] Free. Date reviewed: 2017.

This website allows users to search the vast collection of legal briefs and opinions rendered by the Oregon Court of Appeals and Oregon Supreme Court. All documents are downloadable as PDFs. Users can conduct a broad search via a Google Custom Search or Index (court) search, or they can narrow their search by Case File number, Case Citation, or Keyword. There are no browsing options. A list of Oregon Appellate Court Management System (OACMS) abbreviations helpful in further identifying the type of legal brief is included on this page, as well as a short list of helpful links such as the State of Oregon Law Library. This narrowly focused site would appeal to users with specific interest in Oregon law.—**ARBA Staff Reviewer**

C, P, S

175.   **Virginia Decoded. https://vacode.org/ .** [Website] Free. Date reviewed: 2017.

This website represents a clever and contemporary way to disseminate the laws of the Commonwealth of Virginia. Simply constructed, users can conduct a search by keyword, phrase or title, and can browse an alphabetized listing of the 79 chapters of the entire code. Chapters address Aviation, Commercial Code, Education, Eminent Domain, Juvenile Justice, Mines and Mining, and much more. Multiple sections within each chapter are well distinguished on the site, and users can easily navigate to any and all of them. Special features include pop-up, plain English definitions of code legalese and a selection of downloading capabilities. It is important to note that the website is currently in beta development, and some errors may be present. Nonetheless, this site would appeal to law students, policy-makers, Virginia historians, educators, and those with a broad interest in state law (or a particular interest in the laws of Virginia).—**ARBA Staff Reviewer**

C, P, S

176.   **WashLaw. http://www.washlaw.edu/.** [Website] Free. Date reviewed: 2017.

This free site brings a comprehensive listing of resources related to law and government together in one place. Users can select a location from one of two map graphics to conduct a geographic search, or they can scroll through a well-organized series of sidebar options. Under U.S. Government, users can select from a series of topics covering the three branches of government and including a listing of links to federal agencies (e.g., Census Bureau, Environmental Protection Agency, etc.) and legislation (e.g., U.S. Tax Code, U.S. Constitution, etc.) as well as general government resources such as Veterans Resources and Consumer Issues. The State tab offers a full listing of sources pertaining to a chosen's state's executive, legislative, and judicial branches in addition to links to general state information (e.g., demographics, directories, etc.) and state agencies (such as boards and commissions), law schools, and more. The Foreign tab presents a map of designated region alongside a similar listing of resource links. International focuses on the United Nations and other resources. Users can also find a wide variety of options under the Resources for Lawyers and Law Links tabs, including legal forms, Bar resources, and legal directories. *WashLaw* is easy to use, and would be an ideal starting point for researchers across a number of legal or governmental disciplines.—**ARBA Staff Reviewer**

Criminology and Criminal Justice

Chronology

C, S

177.   Mickolus, Edward. **Terrorism, 2013-2015: A Worldwide Chronology.** Jefferson, N.C., McFarland, 2016. 571p. index. $150.00. ISBN 13: 978-1-4766-6437-8; 978-1-4766-

2589-8 (e-book).

Terrorism remains an ugly reality in our world and its influence affects the political process and governmental policy-making in most countries. Many Americans have associated this phenomenon with events in overseas countries and continents. However, recent events including the bombing in New York City's Chelsea neighborhood, the attack at Orlando's Pulse nightclub, and murders in San Bernardino, California, irrefutably demonstrate that this scourge now afflicts the U.S. homeland.

This work continues an ongoing compilation documenting international terrorist incidents between 2013 and 2015 and updating developments occurring between 1971 and 2012. Entries are arranged chronologically in the 2013-2015 session, such as a succinct description of a May 20, 2013, detonation of two bombs in Makhachkala, Dagestan, Russia, killing four police officers and a lengthier description of a May 22, 2013, attack in London when a Nigerian Islamist killed British soldier Lee Rigby (pp. 55-56). Besides describing terrorist attacks, these entries also list events such as government policy announcements declaring certain organizations to be terrorist groups, and major news reports on terrorism-related developments.

The section updating terrorist attacks between 1971 and 2012 mentions how Italian police arrested a Pakistani Al-Qaeda suspect at Rome's Leonardo da Vinci Airport on June 25, 2015, for his role in a 2009 attack on a Peshawar market which killed more than 100 people (p. 526), and the November 25, 2013, conviction and sentencing in a Baku, Azerbaijan, court of 29 individuals for plotting to assassinate that country's president and bomb the Eurovision music contest in 2012 (p. 536).

The conclusion features a detailed bibliography of scholarly and governmental works on terrorism ranging from general analyses to terrorism in specific geographic regions. The work concludes with an extremely helpful index of terrorist incidents by countries including the dates of terrorist events in these countries between 2013 and 2015 along with a supplemental index of terrorist groups and organizations and the dates they attempted or executed attacks between 2013 and 2015.

This is an exhaustively researched and documented compilation which will be very beneficial to students and scholars wishing to study terrorists and terrorism on a chronologically oriented basis during these years.—**Bert Chapman**

Handbooks and Yearbooks

C, P, S

178. **Global Terrorism Database. www.start.umd.edu/gtd.** [Website] Free. Date reviewed: 2017.

The *Global Terrorism Database* (GTD) site considers itself "the most comprehensive unclassified database on terrorist events" and offers users access to over 150,000 cases of domestic, transnational, and international acts of terror. Created by START (the National Consortium for the Study of Terror and Responses to Terror), the site houses information from terror acts documented from 1970 through 2015. From the homepage, users can access video tutorials on how best to use the site, data visualizations depicting how terror acts are concentrated across the globe, and chronological information. Users can conduct a basic or advanced search which will lead them to relevant reports. Each terror report notes date of event, country, and other location details and includes an incident number and a GTD identification number. Further report information is available by tab, such as type of attack, property damage, weapon information, and perpetrator and casualty statistics. Another tab leads to media sources of the terror incident. General searches can also direct users to a variety of line, bar, or pie charts marking data for a number of variables. This is a valuable starting point for researchers interested in the numbers behind global terrorism.— **ARBA Staff Reviewer**

C, S

179.   **Police Psychology and Its Growing Impact on Modern Law Enforcement.** Cary Mitchell and Edrick Dorian, eds. Hershey, Pa., Information Science Reference/IGI Global, 2017. 345p. index. (Advances in Applied Psychology, Mental Health, and Behavioral Studies (APMHBS) Book Series). $190.00 (individual chapters available for purchase in electronic format). ISBN 13: 978-1-52250-813-7; 978-1-52250-814-4 (e-book).

Police Psychology and Its Growing Impact on Modern Law Enforcement represents a distinguished volume in the Advances in Psychology, Mental Health, and Behavioral Studies Book Series. It is edited by two experienced scholars, Cary Mitchell and Edrick Dorian. Mitchell, PhD, is a Professor of Psychology at Pepperdine University. A licensed psychologist, he has been conducting pre-employment psychological screenings of law enforcement applicants for departments throughout California for over 25 years. Formerly a Veterans Administration psychologist, he has worked in two federal prisons and has been a consultant for the U.S. Department of Justice's COPS program. Dorian, PsyD, ABPP, is a police psychologist with the Los Angeles Police Department (LAPD) and a clinical psychologist in private practice. He is board certified in both Clinical Psychology and Police & Public Safety Psychology by the American Board of Professional Psychology, and a diplomate of the Academy of Cognitive Therapy.

In 1972, Robert Reiser, widely considered the father of police psychology, wrote in his pioneering book *The Police Department Psychologist*, that the book's main purpose was to "explicate some of the dimensions of this fascinating position for psychologist … with the expectation that in the future the psychologist will be less of a rare bird in the police profession." Over four decades later, the editors produce a volume that supports Reiser's position. The police psychologist is no longer a rare bird, but rather an integral contributing figure in present-day police agencies. Police psychologists provide support in the areas of personal assessment, individual and organizational intervention, consultation, and operational assistance.

The unique content in this volume emphasizes key elements of police psychology as it relates to current issues and challenges in law enforcement and police agencies and is an essential reference source for practicing police psychologists, researchers, graduate-level students, and law enforcement executives. The book covers a vast array of topics, including emerging ethical issues, police suicide, police interactions with the mentally ill, mass casualty events and first responders, and so much more. The book is divided into 6 sections and 16 chapters. Readability is enhanced by the font size, a clear writing style, subject and topic bold font type, abstracts at the beginning of chapters, and the use of bullet formats, charts, and graphics. Moreover, the resources used are current.

Police Psychology and Its Growing Impact on Modern Law Enforcement is ideally suited for upper-level undergraduates and graduate students. Recommended for university library collections as well as for people serving in the mental health profession, school librarians, and law enforcement executives. *Police Psychology* could easily be incorporated into graduate-level courses. Multiple copies of this book should be on the top shelf of every police resource center in the nation.—**Thomas E. Baker**

C, S

180.   Shoemaker, Donald J., and Timothy W. Wolfe. **Juvenile Justice: A Reference Handbook.** 2d ed. Santa Barbara, Calif., ABC-CLIO, 2016. 314p. index. (Contemporary World Issues). $60.00. ISBN 13: 978-1-4408-4074-6; 978-1-4408-4075-3 (e-book).

Part of the Contemporary World Issues series, this book offers general as well as informed readers essential current research on a topic that affects the lives of everyday citizens. The major objective of the book is to explore youthful misbehaviors and planned responses to cope with criminal violations. The second edition provides the most recent statistical data and a new chapter entitled "Perspectives." The authors are Donald J. Shoemaker, professor of sociology at Virginia Tech, and Timothy W. Wolfe, currently an associate professor of sociology and director of the Human Services Program at Mount St. Mary's University

Seven informative chapters address problems, controversies, and possible solutions for juvenile justice. In addition, the authors present diverse perspectives from leading experts, and profile important figures in the juvenile justice system. Furthermore, the text offers primary documents that identify offenders who move through the juvenile justice system and track their offenses. The title also provides a chronology of key moments in the history of juvenile justice in the United States along with a glossary, extensive footnotes and references, and an index. The clear and concise writing style, use of illustrative pictorial images, and appropriate font sizes enhance usability.

Juvenile Justice: A Reference Handbook is ideally suited for undergraduates, high school students, and general nonspecialists. High school, community college, and university library collections would benefit and inquiring minds will consider this book to be essential reading. This book provides a good starting point for research by high school and college students, scholars, and general readers as well as practitioners, activists, and others. The writing style is easy to understand and the content offers thought-provoking issues.—**Thomas E. Baker**

Human Rights

Handbooks and Yearbooks

C, P, S

181.   **The Syrian Archive: Preserving Documentation of Human Rights Violations** **https://syrianarchive.org/.** [Website] Free. Date reviewed: 2017.

Nonpartisan and opportune in its mission, this website offers free access to materials related to any crimes and human rights violations occurring throughout the ongoing Syrian conflict. Its main focus is a database, continually updated and holding basic information, such as date of record, location, violation type, and more, for roughly 4,000 incidents.

The database also includes a brief description of each incident. Users can click on an accompanying reference code which will direct them to further incident details in addition to multimedia (videos, maps, etc.) documentation. The database covers a variety of violations from the use of illegal weapons to attacks on civilians. Users can also access the database information through the interactive map of Syria, allowing for a clearer perspective on the conflict's geography. The Investigations tab consolidates certain data into thematic investigations, shows how data can be used to fact check media or state reports, and shares a Syrian Archive press release covering a chemical weapon attack in Damascus. The site is available in English or Arabic and will likely continue to grow into a valuable resource for journalists, historians, activists, and others.—**ARBA Staff Reviewer**

International Law

Handbooks and Yearbooks

C, P, S

182.   **Nuremberg Trials Project. http://nuremberg.law.harvard.edu/.** [Website] Free. Date reviewed: 2017.

From the Harvard Law School Library comes the *Nuremberg Trials Project*—a vast undertaking that consolidates and presents the many photographs, legal briefs, evidence files, transcripts, and more which tells the story of the Nuremberg Trials The project is a work in progress but at the time of this review 650,000 pages have been digitized and five trials out of 13 total are searchable. The site offers a number of ways to approach information. Besides the basic search bar, users can click on the type of material they are interested in: Trial Documents, Evidence File Documents, Trial Transcripts, and Photographs. Users may also choose to explore via Trial Issues, which looks at particular themes (e.g., epidemic jaundice experiments) or specific people like Reich Minister Hermann Goering. The site also allows users to filter search results in many ways, such as trial date, defendant name, document author, and related issues. With its sophisticated but simple design, the site is an excellent resource for researchers, students, and educators interested in the legal and historical relevance of the Nuremberg Trials.—**ARBA Staff Reviewer**

C, P, S

183.   **Piracy Trials. https://www.loc.gov/law/help/piracy/piracy_trials.php.** [Website] Free. Date reviewed: 2017.

This page from the Library of Congress presents a collection of digitized records relating to piracy matters concerning several nations. The collection focuses on documents dated before 1923 that are generally representative of eighteenth and nineteenth century incidents, with a few exceptions. The collection consists of a variety of documents—some quite dramatic—including newspaper accounts, letters, arguments before the court, confessions, indictments, exhibited articles, and much more. Most records are in the English language, with some in Dutch, French, and German as they may relate to multinational proceedings. Users can easily scroll through a list of 57 items which display a thumbnail photo of the document cover, the Library of Congress identification number, a brief title, and date of publication. Users can then view the record or examine it as a PDF. Documents are not transcribed. One highlight of the collection is an account of the trial of the infamous Captain William Kidd. The primary source contents of this site provide an engaging look at the history of international maritime law, and would be of great interest to historians, students, educators, and others.—**ARBA Staff Reviewer**

11 Library and Information Science and Publishing and Bookselling

Library and Information Science

General Works

C, P, S

184. Cooke, Nicole A. **Information Services to Diverse Populations.** Santa Barbara, Calif., Libraries Unlimited/ABC-CLIO, 2017. 166p. index. (Library and Information Science Text Series). $65.00pa. ISBN 13: 978-1-4408-3460-8; 978-1-4408-3461-5 (e-book).

Author Nicole A. Cooke, assistant professor at the School of Information Sciences at the University of Illinois, Urbana-Champaign, and a faculty affiliate at the school's Center for Digital Inclusion, focuses her research and teaching on three topics: "human information behavior (particularly in the online context), critical cultural information studies, and diversity and social justice in librarianship (with an emphasis on infusing them into LIS education and pedagogy" (p. 167). This volume in the Library and Information Science Text Series includes typical front matter which gives way to the body of Cooke's research and advocacy in diversity in the LIS profession in six chapters. Well-researched and well-presented chapters have solid introductions and conclude with references. Three appendixes support curricula for library professionals and networking options. The index is significant as a navigational entryway. This excellent resource advocates for diversity in libraries, both in the inclusion of all people and the recruitment of minority library staff. Promotion of cultural competency and social justice in library settings is given multifaceted exposure so whether discussing marginalized people, community needs, or professional development curriculum, this book addresses the essential need for modification in libraries to best represent our communities.

The twenty-first century is a time of global expansion and libraries must reflect societal diversity. *Informative Services to Diverse Populations* is required reading for LIS students, as well as academic, public, and school library administrators and librarians.

Highly recommended.—**Janis Minshull**

Reference Works

Bibliography

P, S

185. **Graphic Novels Core Collection, First Edition.** Kendal Spires, Gabriela Toth, and Maria Hugger, eds. Bronx, N.Y., H. W. Wilson, 2016. 1391p. index. $295.00. ISBN 13:

978-1-68217-070-0.

H.W. Wilson has expanded its Core Collection series to include a new volume on graphic novels, aimed primarily at school and public libraries. *Graphic Novels Core Collection* provides entries for more than 3,500 titles, divided into four age groups: children. middle school, high school, and adult. The titles were selected by collection development librarians from titles in English, published in the United States, Canada, or the United Kingdom and distributed in the United States. There are also bilingual titles and translated works, including Japanese manga. The collection covers a wide variety of genres including nonfiction, fantasy, adventure, superhero, mystery, romance, science fiction, and coming of age. The list also includes a selection of works about the history and culture of comics and graphic novels.

Each entry includes bibliographic information, grade level recommendations, Dewey classifications, Sears subject headings, ISBN, publisher, availability, and price. In addition to this basic information, there is a short annotation describing each graphic novel, often using information from the publisher. The entries also include quotes and evaluations from reviewing sources when they are available. Series information, which is especially critical for graphic novels, is also provided.

This handbook would be an invaluable tool for beginning or assessing a graphic novel collection, one of the most popular, fastest growing formats for many libraries. An important feature that enhances the value of this list as a collection development tool is that the most highly recommended titles are noted, providing a short list of essential purchases.

Like other titles in the Core Collection series, this volume is made even more useful as a reader's advisory tool by the inclusion of author, title, and subject indexes. The print volume is an abridgement of the corresponding EbscoHost database.—**Theresa Muraski**

P, S

186.   **Senior High Core Collection.** 20th ed. Bronx, N.Y., H. W. Wilson, 2016. 2005p. index. $295.00. ISBN 13: 978-1-68217-239-1.

Wilson's Core Collection series are standard collection management tools for school and public libraries. They are now also available online in Ebscohost as a database which is updated weekly and includes expanded content such as additional metadata, reviews, and "Supplementary" and "Archival Materials." The printed version, continuing to be updated every two years, covers "Most Highly Recommended" and "Core Collection" titles. This edition covers over 8,600 titles, including an expanded professional aids section (bibliographies and selection & evaluation resources, library management and programming, library building design, and use of the Internet in instruction); significant revisions in the computers and STEM sections; and graphic novels. The volume excludes most non-English titles, adult fiction not widely read or used in curricula for senior high students, computer program manuals, topics that date quickly, and "classic literature," leaving greater emphasis on current and less easily identified materials. Part one is the classified section, arranged by the abridged Dewey classification and followed by fiction and short story collections. Part two is the author, title, and subject index. The use of Dewey and Sears headings makes this an easily navigable resource. The editors and 11 Advisory Board members have put together an edition worthy of the history of this resource; it continues to be an essential resource for collection management in high school and public libraries. Librarians will want to consider the database for access to greater numbers of titles and resources. Essential.—**Rosanne M. Cordell**

Libraries

College and Research Libraries

C
187.   **Bridging Worlds: Emerging Models and Practices of U.S. Academic Libraries around the Globe.** Raymond Pun, Scott Collard, and Justin Parrott, eds. Chicago, American Library Association, Association of College and Research Libraries, 2016. 204p. $50.00pa. ISBN 13: 978-0-8389-8842-8.

This volume explores different initiatives in a variety of areas of librarianship as applied to international campuses of American universities. The focus is on efforts by New York University; most of the authors of these 16 chapters are affiliated with the university. From interlibrary loan service and building library collections (including special collections) to library instruction, tech support, and licensing online resources, these essays explore the challenges (and their solutions) facing libraries located far from their American home campus. Even time difference and varying work weeks can cause problems!

In this increasingly international era, academic libraries, particularly those with programs in library and information science, will certainly benefit from this volume, despite its somewhat steep price.—**Mark Schumacher**

C
188.   Eshleman, Joe, Richard Moniz, Karen Mann, and Kristen Eshleman. **Librarians and Instructional Designers: Collaboration and Innovation.** Chicago, American Library Association, 2016. 240p. index. $65.00pa.; $58.50pa. (ALA members). ISBN 13: 978-0-8389-1455-7.

This book establishes the compelling parallels between the professions of librarians and instructional designers in college and university settings. Authors Joe Eshleman, Richard Moniz, Karen Mann, and Kristen Eshleman disclose a key collaboration for providing value to career and digital learning growth on and off campus.

Providing a purposeful introduction and index, the authors also give evidence in nine solid chapters on how to cultivate relations with curriculum development in mind. Chapters have a clean design with satisfactory balance between white space and text using subtopic divisions, visual figures, and highlighted information boxes. Chapters include inspiration and inclusiveness with intentional areas of overlap between librarians and instructional designers.

Collaboration has been around for eons. A new pathway for partnerships is highlighted in this professional development title as the authors anticipate the need for liaisons to enhance the design of instructional systems. This book embarks on a mission to demonstrate why college and university librarians should be included in higher education design and how to become an active leader in the networked world of digital education. Relationship opportunity and development are key to innovative learning and starting with the glossary of roles defined in the highlighted information box on page xiii, the argument for librarian and instructional designer as partners is inherent (but not necessarily obvious). Titles aside, curriculum design is crucial to effective learning and higher education value; developing partnerships with instructional design players will bring emerging trends and technologies for best teaching practices to the forefront. Librarians and those creating curriculum are no longer lone practitioners; breaking from static, traditional roles, faculty and staff roles are evolving almost as quickly as the digital learning environment. Innovation is vital to robust higher education offerings and also to the value of professions in education.

Librarians and Instructional Designers: Collaboration and Innovation is an excellent resource for administrators, librarians, and instructional designers at the collegiate and postcollegiate level. Highly recommended.—**Janis Minshull**

C, S

189.   Reale, Michelle. **Becoming an Embedded Librarian: Making Connections in the Classroom.** Chicago, American Library Association, 2015. 128p. index. $54.00pa. ISBN 13: 978-0-8389-1367-3.

This is a professional level book geared to the librarian embedded in a research classroom. It includes 12 chapters that range from explaining what an embedded librarian should be, to how important they are, to how to facilitate and set goals. Embedded librarianship facilitates a collaborative learning community that is extremely beneficial to the students. Each of the chapters has practical steps to follow and includes a bibliography for additional reading. Told from the viewpoint of the author in a college seminar class made up of students doing their senior theses, it delves into both the successes and problems inherent in sharing a classroom. It was not smooth sailing on the part of either the librarian or the professor, but after a long semester fraught with obstacles, both considered the embedding a success worth repeating. I see aspects of this as an activity being very successful in a high school setting as well as at the college level. Highly recommended.—**Cynthia Foster**

C

190.   **Technology-Centered Academic Library Partnerships and Collaborations.** Brian Doherty, ed. Hershey, Pa., Information Science Reference/IGI Global, 2016. 309p. index. (Advances in Library and Information Science (ALIS) Book Series). $165.00 (individual chapters available for purchase in electronic format). ISBN 13: 978-1-52250-323-1; 978-1-52250-324-8 (e-book).

Technology-Centered Academic Library Partnerships and Collaborations is an insightful look at academic libraries, technological innovation, and collaborative measures. Under the editorship of Brian Doherty, a Dean of the Jane Bancroft Cook Library at New College of Florida and the University of South Florida, Sarasota-Manatee, contributors to this compilation have undergone a stringent process of inclusion to find research and case studies that offer contemporary, unmitigated empirical and conceptual options in technological partnerships for academic libraries.

The book commences with the usual front matter; the addition of a detailed table of contents aids the researcher in evaluating content. The back matter includes references, notes on contributors, and an index. Chapters include multiple writers and in addition to the research topic, extended study is possible through "Future Research Directions" and strong reference sections.

Academic libraries must seek the latest methodologies and tools to be progressive with twenty-first-century education. This resource provides professional support, organization needs, and information resource development in the context of collaboration. Librarians are notorious in their efforts for resource sharing, and models like the Boston Library Consortium are creating innovative modules of what partnerships in today's libraries look like.

Challenges and benefits of collaboration, and the necessity of reaching beyond physical space, bring library services to the forefront of technology-centered relationships. *Technology-Centered Academic Library Partnerships and Collaborations* examines place (Boston, Caribbean, Estonia, New York, etc.), school type (liberal arts, online, etc.), and specific scenarios including library service in times of disaster. The samplings of collaboration demonstrate a new paradigm of librarian, faculty, and outside partnerships in the community.

Librarians are leaders in interdisciplinary studies, technology, and innovation, and they foster curriculum with technology. With less fiscal tenacity, libraries are finding partners in academic libraries, communities, government, and business. Colleges and universities, more than ever, need to educate for the work force and "it is imperative that both faculty members and librarian work to ensure that graduates not only have the distinct disciplinary skills that they need to succeed in their field of choice, but that they also have the applied learning skills that employers seek" (p. 96). *Technology-Centered Academic Library Partnerships and Collaborations* will support collaborative efforts between academic libraries and the global community; offering a multiplicity of avenues for learning and research through resource sharing means improved technological education and greater influence on employment of highly skilled workers beyond graduate studies. This volume will be well used by faculty members, IT, librarians, researchers in education development, technologists, and university administrators.

Highly recommended.—**Janis Minshull**

Public Libraries

C, P

191.   Alvarez, Barbara A. **Embedded Business Librarianship for the Public Librarian.** Chicago, American Library Association, 2016. 120p. index. $40.00pa. ISBN 13: 978-0-8389-1474-8.

The stated purpose of *Embedded Business Librarianship for the Public Librarian* by Barbara A. Alvarez, is "to introduce those who are completely new to this type of librarianship to the mission, purpose, and practice of embedded business librarianship in public libraries." Embedded business librarianship "means that a librarian leaves the physical library space and becomes integrated within the business community and its dialogue." Barbara A. Alvarez has served at the Barrington Area Public Library and taught job seekers, assisted local business owners and professionals in research, presented professional networking events on business librarianship, and contributed to *Public Libraries Online, Library Journal,* and *Illinois Libraries Matter.* Alvarez's guide to embedded business librarianship includes advice on how to research major industries in the library's business community, how to prepare and conduct informational interviews of businesspeople in the area, and how to create a networking list. There are also tips about preparing outreach programs and events, becoming a liaison ("serving as a point of reference between various people and organizations"), and networking with library professionals who also work with business communities. There are Q and A' sections throughout the book; for example, "How can librarians adjust the public library to be more adaptable for coworking spaces" and "When I am networking in the community, how should I introduce myself and explain what I do?" In addition, the author has compiled a list of continuing education sources including books, articles, websites, videos and podcasts, online courses, business news sources, blogs, discussion lists, and associations. This resource is highly recommended for business librarians in public libraries, but those from academic and special libraries should benefit from this as well. Students of library and information should also find this book very informative.—**Lucy Heckman**

P

192.   Marquis, Kathy, and Leslie Waggener. **Local History Reference Collections for Public Libraries.** Chicago, American Library Association, 2015. 146p. index. $55.00pa.; ($49.50pa. ALA members). ISBN 13: 978-0-8389-1331-4.

Public libraries have a long history supporting and building local history collections which create a special place in their collections. Such local collections offer an important service to their communities with unique and specific collections of local historical material not available anywhere else. Originating from an article in *Public Libraries* magazine in 2011, Marquis and Waggener "offer a one-stop shop of advice and resources that can get you started with your local history collection building" and do so in a concise, methodical, and slim volume of 146 pages.

The authors present what they call the Local History Reference Collection (LHRC) model, which emphasizes open and accessible history resources mainly in print (books, periodicals, pamphlets, etc.), with techniques, guides, and policies aimed at making a more effective collection that libraries can grow and that users will be attracted to and use.

In nine chapters and six appendixes, the elements that make up this LHRC model are explained. Chapter one begins with a survey of current trends in local history collections; chapter two differentiates archival collections from local history collections; chapter three focuses on creating a mission statement and collection development policy; and chapter four addresses audience and users. Chapter five examines ideas on collaboration with other local history collections. Facility needs and preservation are addressed in chapter six. Chapters seven, eight, and nine examine reference and access, marketing and outreach, and creating a virtual (online) collection presence, respectively.

The six appendixes provide excellent resources for those who want a guide to building collections. Resources include policy templates, sample surveys, and ALA guidelines for local history collections.

Highly recommended for public libraries and local history collections.—**William Shakalis**

School Libraries

S

193.   Deskins, Liz, and Christina H. Dorr. **Linking Picture Book Biographies to National Content Standards.** Santa Barbara, Calif., Libraries Unlimited/ABC-CLIO, 2016. 153p. index. $45.00pa. ISBN 13: 978-1-4408-3523-0; 978-1-4408-3524-7 (e-book).

Over the past 10 years or so, quality nonfiction written for children and young adults has flourished, and there are now many picture book biographies that can help engage students and meet national content standards. The authors begin the book by describing the great resurgence of quality nonfiction in education and the many options available to teachers. Additionally, they detail the researched benefits of reading aloud to students of all ages. The picture book biographies listed in the book meet national content standards in science, social studies, English, fine arts, and physical education. The book is broken down into chapters by subject and each chapter shows the standards a particular picture book biography meets as well as bibliographic information, a short description of the book, essential questions that could be paired with a unit, and additional biographies. This could be a great resource for the teacher resource section of a school library or for anyone looking to incorporate read-alouds and picture books into existing curriculum. Recommended.—**Jianna Taylor**

C, S

194.   Farmer, Lesley S. J. **Information and Digital Literacies: A Curricular Guide for Middle and High School Librarians.** Lanham, Md., Rowman & Littlefield, 2016. 143p. index. $35.00pa.; $34.99 (e-book). ISBN 13: 978-1-4422-3981-4; 978-1-4422-3982-1 (e-book).

Literacy in the information age takes on a wide spectrum and school librarians must be prepared to develop curriculum encompassing the information and digital literacies. An expert on the topic, professor and author Lesley S. J. Farmer has research interests in information literacy, assessment, and educational technology. Her overview in *Information and Digital Literacies* and inclusion of lessons and unit plans makes curriculum plans readily available for librarians in middle and secondary school environments.

Available in hardcover, paperback, and digital format, this 2016 handbook is published by Rowman & Littlefield with practical content for professional and curriculum development. Consisting of 143 pages, this reference opens with a brief introduction to the continuous evolution of literacy, school librarians, and information retrieval. Contents' pages offer patent chapter and subset headings that will be easily accessed; chapters two and three address information literacy and digital literacy, respectively, with subsequent chapters building toward standards based curriculum chapters. Chapters start with a clear introduction and chapters close with an extremely useful paragraph on "Implications for School Librarians," and "References" where applicable. Back-end reference information includes a typical bibliography, index, and author information. Black-and-white figures and charts are well balanced and break up the text agreeably.

This text is a great manual on the how-to of integrating new literacy instruction as many schools change to standards such as the Common Core State Standards (CCSS), American Association of School Librarians (AASL) standards, and others. The introductory chapters are useful and provide clarity and definition, but the chapters on middle school and high school curriculum are the heart of this book. Curriculum development for digital and information literacies is offered in the form of stand-alone courses, instructional units, and learning activities. The grade level for lessons is clear, and week-by-week structure for lengthier units increases the likelihood of use for librarians who wish to easily replicate or modify curriculum. Tables and figures are well placed and correlate with informational text. For example, topics such as student assessment for a lesson are augmented with a rubric in Table 7.1 to assist with evaluation of lesson proficiency. Variations in lessons and planning for diverse learners make these curriculum plans open to adaptation.

Information and Digital Literacies is unequivocally a guide that will be well used and loved by school librarians developing and teaching curriculum for the middle school and high school student. Teachers will also find this very pertinent for strategy and skill development in teaching research to prepare students for college, life, and work in the real world.

Highly recommended.—**Janis Minshull**

C, S

195.   Maniotes, Leslie K., LaDawna Harrington, and Patrice Lambusta. **Guided Inquiry Design in Action: Middle School.** Santa Barbara, Calif., Libraries Unlimited/ABC-CLIO, 2016. 158p. illus. index. (Guided Inquiry). $40.00pa. ISBN 13: 978-1-4408-3764-7; 978-1-4408-3765-4 (e-book).

Guided Inquiry Design in Action: Middle School is a hands-on professional development tool containing useful classroom inquiry plans. Published by Libraries Unlimited in 2016, this is the newest of the Guided Inquiry series. Written by Leslie K. Maniotes, LaDawna Harrington, and Patrice Lambusta, the authors meld teacher and librarian collaboration together to create a strong guide of support and action for classroom learning in the middle school setting.

A comprehensive professional development resource on Guided Inquiry Design (GID), this 176-page book is organized in a very practical manner for the beginner or the expert who seeks new ideas on inquiry lessons. After the usual introductory information, the table of contents shows the book is divided into nine chapters with useful chapter headings and subheadings for further delineation. The book closes with a reference and index of typical stature.

Useful for the beginner into inquiry learning or those wanting reinforcement, the first chapters deal with setup, the building of a professional team, and how GID looks in the middle school. The GID process is clearly defined with icons representing different steps in the learning: Open, Immerse, Explore, Identify, Gather, Create, Share, and Evaluate. These same graphics are found in the actual lesson plans of chapters five, six, seven, and eight which have detailed inquiry lesson plans. These chapters provide engaging research-based guides for educators of students in grades six through eight in the areas of science, math, language arts, and social studies. Students will be involved with using inquiry journals, logs, and charts for documenting their research process. Chapters are rich with step-by-step planning and provide valuable work forms for different stages of the process. The book is full of figures and charts both for the use of educators or their students such as the "6th Grade Presentation Checklist" on page 51. A few black-and-white photos are sprinkled throughout the text but add no significant value. The final chapter bestows encouragement for engaging with middle school students and support for implementing the GID with your team. It also offers limited suggestions for extending this professional development study.

With the strong emphasis on Common Core State Standards and the growing momentum toward more inquiry based learning, *Guided Inquiry Design in Action* collects classroom-tested lessons and unit plans and will be very useful to educators wishing to take action with middle school GID. The companion, *Guided Inquiry Design: A Framework for Inquiry in Your School* is a useful addition to the implementation of inquiry in schools.

Highly recommended.—**Janis Minshull**

Special Libraries

C, P

196.   Hartnett, Cassandra J., Andrea L. Sevetson, and Eric J. Forte. **Fundamentals of Government Information: Mining, Finding, Evaluating, and Using Government Resources.** 2d ed. Chicago, American Library Association, 2016. 424p. index. $85.00pa.; $76.50pa. (ALA members). ISBN 13: 978-0-8389-1395-6.

This book's primary purpose is to provide sources and strategies for finding and using government information; the operative word here is information, since it transcends documents per se. In addressing the issue of approaching the field of government documents by branch or by topic, Hartnett (University of Washington), Sevetson (ProQuest), and Forte (OCLC) opt for both. The first half, "Overview of Key Government Information Resources," focuses on publications of the congressional, judicial, and executive branches of government, including laws and regulations (a structural revision from the first edition). The second part, "Government Information in Focus," though technically concerning agencies falling under the auspices of the executive branch, includes separate chapters on the most frequently consulted subject areas of government information: statistics; health; education; environment and energy; scientific and technical information; business, economic and consumer information; census; and patents, trademarks, and intellectual property (which surprisingly doesn't include copyright). Its coverage of 13 primary statistical agencies has two more than Hernon et al *United States Government Information.* An effective system of cross-references refers users to topics from one chapter to further mentions in others. Its usefulness is enhanced by almost 50 figures that illustrate key points, useful sidebars, and end-of-chapter exercises designed to clarify the concepts covered in the chapter and to give readers a chance to apply information resources.

This resource is notable for three factors. First, although it focuses on federal information, it also provides sources for state and local information. Next, the personal, informal style diffuses the normally dry tone of the material. Finally, it casts a broad net, covering not only specific government-issued resources but also many alternative print and online ones, many of which are free.

Changes from the first edition are relatively minor: some bibliographies have been updated, the order of presentation of topics has been changed, and the topics of intellectual property and case law now have their own chapters.

A quick spot-check of the index, however, reveals some shortcomings. The Statutes at Large produced by the Government Publishing Office is listed under both US Statutes at Large and United States Statutes at Large with unique page references. The topic of "online census" appears as its own entry in the index without being included under the broader topic of "census." Users must look under both "depository libraries" and "Federal Depository Library Program (FDLP)" to get all the relevant references as there is little overlap between the two. The index includes WorldCat.org in the index but not two other relevant references to OCLC/WorldCat on page 33 and 284. Likewise the index does not mention one of the few references to copyright on page 375. A more rigorous system of authority control coupled with better cross-references would have substantially enhanced the usefulness of the index.

This is now the only up-to-date book on this topic, since the latest editions of the classic texts in this field are now woefully out of date. Judith Schiek Robinson's *Tapping the Government Grapevine* (3d ed., Oryx, 1998), Jean Sears and Marilyn Moody's *Using Government Information Sources* (see ARBA 2002, entry 53), Joe Morehead's *Introduction to United States Government Information Sources* (see ARBA 2001, entry 44), and Peter Hernon et al *United States Government Information: Policies and Sources* (see ARBA 2004, entry 47) still provide useful historical perspectives but lack the currency required to keep up with the rapidly changing developments in the provision and dissemination of government information (like even something so relatively minor as the 2014 name change from the Government Printing Office to the Government Publishing Office).

The book is probably most useful as a textbook in government documents library school courses but it will also serve public and academic librarians working with government information and general researchers looking for quality vetted information.—**Lawrence Olszewski**

Special Topics

Cataloging and Classification

C, P, S
197.   Brenndorfer, Thomas. **RDA Essentials.** Chicago, American Library Association, 2016. 376p. index. $105.00pa.; $94.50pa. (ALA members). ISBN 13: 978-0-8389-1328-4.

In *RDA Essentials,* the cataloger needing quick points of reference and the student first learning how to catalog using the FRBR entity-relationship model will find a handbook that distills down to the essentials the rules of Resource Description and Access cataloging. Author Thomas Brenndorfer, an experienced cataloger and advocate for FRBR and RDA, first provides a short history of RDA's development as well as definitions of concepts and terms. The 384-page softcover then offers an accessible instructor and guide. Readers have the impression that Brenndorfer is reading the instructions aloud: terms are provided in gloss at the start of each chapter, grey boxes provide information on how these instructions will support your library's user, and throughout the text tips, cross-references, exceptions, and examples are given. As he explains, you first consider the resource in terms of its acquisition, access, content, and the people associated with it. You then proceed to describe the relationships of that resource to work, expression, manifestation, and item, and among the connected people groups (person, family, and corporate body).

RDA Essentials does not claim to be a one-stop, RDA cataloging reference, and the introduction clearly defines what the book does and does not cover. This primer should be used with the RDA Toolkit, the full RDA text and appendix, the RDA Registry, and perhaps even the RDA Database Implementation Scenarios document. With these resources, it is hoped that cataloging under RDA will become as natural as following AACR2. I would recommend this text for libraries with an in-house cataloging group and for students of library science.—**Amy Koehler**

P, S
198.   Houston, Cynthia. **Organizing Information in School Libraries: Basic Principles and New Rules.** Santa Barbara, Calif., Libraries Unlimited/ABC-CLIO, 2016. 186p. index. $55.00pa. ISBN 13: 978-1-4408-3686-2; 978-1-4408-3687-9 (e-book).

Created for the solo librarian working in a school or small public library, this book will assist with cataloging a variety of materials efficiently. Current library systems allow users to search the library catalog from anywhere on any device, and includes social networking features that are embedded in the catalog allowing users to tag, blog, or review materials. With all these features, users will benefit from having a variety of resources in one place. This book takes the guesswork out of creating records for Internet resources, print materials, DVDs, audio books, picture books, graphic novels, and electronic streaming resources. Cataloging rules and procedures are discussed at length, followed by a how-to section for a variety of resource types such as print and Internet. Each section includes additional resources, discussion questions, and exercises, allowing the reader to practice with examples. This is a handy resource for anyone looking to streamline the current library system for users. An appendix, glossary, reference, and index round out the work. Recommended.—**Karen Alexander**

C, P
199.   Kaplan, Allison G. **Catalog It! A Guide to Cataloging School Library Materials.** 3d ed. Santa Barbara, Calif., Libraries Unlimited/ABC-CLIO, 2016. 231p. index. $60.00pa. ISBN 13: 978-1-4408-3580-3; 978-1-4408-3581-0 (e-book).

Catalog It! is the updated third edition for modern cataloging and the changes that have occurred in the cataloging world in the last 30 years. The nine chapters in this edition provide a history, trends in cataloging, resources in cataloging, vendors in cataloging, different access points, and the future of cataloging. The author Allison G. Kaplan is a MLIS professor and has over 20 years of experience teaching cataloging to students. Kaplan's main objective in this edition is to cover the broad spectrum that is cataloging and give the reader enough strong and affordable information to guide them in choosing the best type of cataloging for their specific library. Kaplan covers every popular form of cataloging, and the changes (most notably) from AACR to RDA. The supplementary items include references, exploratory sidebars, a glossary, and an index.

This book covers cataloging techniques that could apply to any type of library including public, academic, school, or special. There is constant reference to this text being a great resource for school libraries, but this book would be extremely useful for librarians in many types of settings. It could also be a welcome textbook for any class teaching contemporary cataloging techniques. The most interesting and possibly the most beneficial additions to this book are Kaplan's in-depth explanations of how to construct certain cataloging techniques for most materials found in a library. As an appendix, Kaplan includes a hint sheet that details the most commonly used MARC fields for book materials with descriptions and illustrations, then explicates the RDA rules that should be applied. There are two other appendixes that include MARC templates and answers to cataloging questions that are asked throughout the book.

This book is highly recommended for both academic libraries and public libraries.— **Sara Mofford**

C
200.   Weihs, Jean, and Sheila S. Intner. **Beginning Cataloging.** 2d ed. Santa Barbara, Calif., Libraries Unlimited/ABC-CLIO, 2017. 149p. index. $60.00pa. ISBN 13: 978-1-4408-3844-6; 978-1-4408-3845-3 (e-book).

This second edition, (see ARBA 2010, entry 558), introduces current standard cataloging practice. The first chapter is a cataloging introduction, and the following chapters in this title include: "Cataloging-In-Publication," "Computer Coding," "Descriptive Cataloging," "Access Points," "Subject Headings," "Classification," and "Copy Cataloging and Copyright Issues." Chapters have introductions where practical, and some chapters end with exercises for sensible hands-on training. The answers to exercises are found in the appendix. Answers are explained well and provide actual examples of cataloging for review. Additionally, chapters two through seven have figures introducing verso, title page, and different examples of catalog records. The glossary is useful to the beginner as it explains terms and acronyms. Two indexes provide either topical access or navigation for systematic study of figures and examples to learn the rules.

While the original concept standardized cataloging articulated by Charles Cutter in 1876 holds true for the twenty-first century, this title is essential due to the development of the Resource Description and Access (RDA) cataloging rules released in 2010 and revised in 2013. For beginners, the introduction of RDA, the online public access catalog (OPAC), Machine-Readable Cataloging (MARC) format, examples of classification, Dewey Decimal Classification, Library of Congress Classification, copy cataloging, and other relevant topics make this a superior handbook for introduction to materials cataloging.

Beginning Cataloging is a strong tool for students in library technical programs and LIS programs. This is an impeccable choice for beginning catalogers and for those who are cataloging but have no formal training. Highly recommended!—**Janis Minshull**

Children's and Young Adult Services

P

201.   Foote, Anna, and Bradley Debrick. **Six Skills by Age Six: Launching Early Literacy at the Library.** Santa Barbara, Calif., Libraries Unlimited/ABC-CLIO, 2016. 228p. index. $45.00pa. ISBN 13: 978-1-61069-899-3; 978-1-61069-900-6 (e-book).

This would be a wise purchase for libraries looking to increase their early literacy programming, education, and community outreach. A hybrid of the Every Child Ready to Read program, the Kansas State 6 by 6 Program focuses on librarians as early literacy experts, outreach to preschools and other organizations, and parental and caregiver education. The authors explain the program in detail, including age-group definitions (Early Talkers, Talkers, Pre-Readers), and the six skills, with a chapter dedicated to each. An informative chapter on storytimes is great for a beginning children's librarian and a good refresher for seasoned storytellers. Finally, the book gives 18 storytime plans. While some of the information is clearly for larger library systems, much of the information can be used to implement a 6 by 6 Program at any size library. At the very least, learning to be an advocate for libraries and teaching librarians that they are early literacy experts makes this book an excellent purchase for any size library.—**Karen M. Smith**

C, P, S

202.   **Libraries, Literacy, and African American Youth: Research and Practice.** Sandra Hughes-Hassell, Pauletta Brown Bracy, and Casey H. Rawson, eds. Santa Barbara, Calif., Libraries Unlimited/ABC-CLIO, 2017. 250p. index. $50.00pa. ISBN 13: 978-1-4408-3872-9; 978-1-4408-3873-6 (e-book).

This title highlights the current state of services to African American youth, examines current library practices, and suggests ways to improve them. The authors compile a series of case studies which examine the concept of educational debt present in libraries servicing nonwhite patrons, with specific attention paid to cultural deficits within the curriculum. The book is divided into two sections—the first focusing on research, the second on practice—and each chapter begins by laying out the intent of the material presented, and ends with concrete ideas for librarians to move forward in acting on the content. A strong thread of literacy ties together the various aspects of interest within this topic, including social justice, ethnic and racial development, and community outreach. There is a need within the educational and library system to allow for all patrons to share their voice, and the authors support this by including excerpts from current youth and adult literature which provide illustrations of the research discussed in each chapter. Although the title focuses on African American youth, the action items suggested are equally beneficial to all minorities, as well as the majority class solely by shining a spotlight on a frequently overlooked need, especially in areas of racial homogeny. This is a must-read for any current or future librarian. The book concludes with references and an index.

Highly Recommended—**Michaela Schied**

Collection Development

S
203.   Mardis, Marcia. A. **The Collection Program in Schools: Concepts and Practices.** 6th ed. Santa Barbara, Calif., Libraries Unlimited/ABC-CLIO, 2016. 330p. index. $65.00pa. ISBN 13: 978-1-61069-823-8; 978-1-61069-824-5 (e-book).

Thoroughly written and researched, this text is easy to understand and well organized, covering a variety of topics necessary to develop and maintain a school library collection. While the Common Core State Standards have driven collection development in the past, the text explores the latest shift to Next Generation Science Standards (NGSS) which have been adopted by 28 states. Mardis has worked hard to maintain information from previous editions but updated and expanded as library usage and needs continue to change over time. Updated chapters include information regarding diversity in a collection, the learning environment and its shifts with technology, and opening, reclassifying, moving, or closing a collection along with discussion regarding current technology and digital resources. Mardis has included a smattering of helpful "anecdotes, scenarios, lessons learned, and best practices" taken from the LM-NET email list archives. Users will find useful information throughout the book; however, the section on criteria by source format with advantages and disadvantages is particularly helpful. This latest edition will not disappoint and is perfect for those just entering the profession and veterans of the field. The book includes an appendix "Resources and Further Reading," as well as an index. Highly recommended.—**Karen Alexander**

S
204.   Ross, Sheri V. T., and Sarah W. Sutton. **Guide to Electronic Resource Management.** Santa Barbara, Calif., Libraries Unlimited/ABC-CLIO, 2016. 159p. index. $55.00. ISBN 13: 978-1-4408-3958-0; 978-1-4408-3959-7 (e-book).

This book is a comprehensive electronic resource guide. The book is written in 11 chapters beginning with the "Emergence and Entrenchment of Electronic Resources in Libraries" and concluding with the "Future Directions of Electronic Resource Management." This resource includes everything the beginning librarian needs to know when starting or maintaining an electronic resource collection. Chapters of particular interest include the "Information Standards," "Identifying and Selecting Electronic Resources," "Acquiring and Licensing Electronic Resources," "Providing Access to Electronic Resources," and "Managing Access and Discovery." Also included are assessment measures of the resources and ways to preserve the resources. This title is a good choice for beginning librarians or experienced librarians who need more information regarding electronic resources. Recommended.—**Shelly Lee**

Customer Service

C, P
205.   Radford, Marie L., and Gary P. Radford. **Library Conversations: Reclaiming Interpersonal Communication Theory for Understanding Professional Encounters.** Chicago, American Library Association, 2017. 168p. index. $75.00pa.; $67.50pa. (ALA members). ISBN 13: 978-0-8389-1484-7.

A 2017 ALA imprint (Neal-Schuman), *Library Conversations: Reclaiming Interpersonal Communication Theory for Understanding Professional Encounters* examines communication in library settings and demystifies challenges of understanding customer requests and how to give library patrons the best service possible.

Communication is Challenging! authors Marie L. Radford and Gary P. Radford investigate the function of communication in all types of library settings. This 168-page, soft cover book has standard front matter. Part one, Reclaiming Theory for Library Contexts defines and discusses several theoretical frameworks for interpersonal communication while part two, Applying Theory to Reference Encounters, focuses on communication in the all important reference scenario. Back matter includes an appendix, author information, and a solid index for unearthing subtopics. Chapters include tables, charts, and situational dialogues; chapters end with conclusions and references for further exploration.

Comprised of seven chapters, the first chapter explores age-old theories on communication with Aristotle leading the way with observation on "practical wisdom" and how vital it is to communication. Phronesis, a type of wisdom relevant to practical things, incorporates virtue and the ability to discern how or why to act, essential to the reference conversation. Radford & Radford relay that interpersonal communication in libraries must go beyond simply disseminating information.

Librarians are the custodians of communication and the prerequisite to service excellence is, in part, communication in both the reference encounter and routine customer meetings. In *Library Conversations,* readers will have the opportunity to consider different types of communication encounters; face to face, virtual, and blended opportunities (where more than one mode of communication is used) with many examples of interpersonal communication with results categorized as unsuccessful, mixed, and successful.

Return library customers come back because of the quality of their interaction with library staff. The twofold purpose of excellence in communication in libraries is to build a positive relationship and provide customers with the convenience, information, or instruction that they desire. This professional title observes the importance of greetings, politeness, eye contact, nonverbal cues, body language, and positive closings to communication. The human wild card can bring or take from any interaction which makes this a useful tool for the most positive outcome.

Library Conversations: Reclaiming Interpersonal Communication Theory for Understanding Professional Encounters will be best used by library staff, administrators, students, and researchers in both academic and public library settings. This will be beneficial to those who seek information on communication theories, and how to implement the best possible communication and reflective practices for each unique scenario.

Recommended.—**Janis Minshull**

Digitization and Digital Libraries

C

206.   **Exploring Discovery: The Front Door to Your Library's Licensed and Digitized Content.** Kenneth J. Varnum, ed. Chicago, American Library Association, 2016. 292p. index. $95.00pa.; $85.50pa. (ALA members). ISBN 13: 978-0-8389-1414-4.

Exploring Discovery: The Front Door to Your Library's Licensed and Digitized Content provides an introduction to licensed and digitized content in a library setting. The goal of the book is to provide a roadmap to implement and service new discovery methods in libraries. Made up of 19 chapters that each describe a library project, the book can be looked at in two ways: as a book to sit down and read in implementing a new discovery project, or as a book to refer to from time to time as new projects are implemented. In this way, the book can serve as both a guidebook from project beginning to project end, or as a quick reference resource to be referred to during a project. As such, the book is malleable for many different situations and is adaptable to any situation.

The book's 19 chapters are made up as case stories, authored by a group of individuals who have implemented new discovery methods in their libraries. The case studies include large public libraries, small community libraries, large university libraries, and small university libraries. The case studies range from tips for creating a "punch list" for discovery needs from working with salespeople of licensed and digitized content. The book dips into the theoretical, which has some value, but centers on the practical. As such, the book is geared toward working library professionals. One useful tool that several chapters include is a framework for evaluating and implementing the system that the chapter advocates. This tool includes costs, processes, integrations, resources, technology, and strategic planning. Not only is this a useful shorthand way for professionals to refer back to an article they have read in the past, it is also a useful tool for implementing programs and policies that are tedious and require deep attention to detail.

Exploring Discovery is a useful tool for evaluating existing discovery systems, implementing new discovery systems, and calibrating those existing discovery systems to maximum effectiveness. The book is geared toward library professionals who do not devote their entire days to thinking about data, and that is a good thing. Overall, *Exploring Discovery* is an essential tool for individuals who manage their library's discovery systems. This book is recommended for academic libraries.—**Sara Mofford**

P

207.   Hoffman, Alex. **Digitizing Your Community's History.** Santa Barbara, Calif., Libraries Unlimited/ABC-CLIO, 2016. 140p. index. (Innovative Librarian's Guide). $55.00pa. ISBN 13: 978-1-4408-4240-5; 978-1-4408-4241-2 (e-book).

This volume from the Innovative Librarian's Guide series outlines the process of digitizing for everyone from the novice to the archival curator. Author Alex Hoffman frames the introduction with emphasis on the importance of libraries today and their evolving relevance with trending technologies. He observes "libraries are now thriving community centers, still full of books, stories, and wisdom, but also cultural programs, access to new tools, and opportunities for education" (p. vii). Starting with basics of what digitization is and why it is important, Hoffman straightforwardly leads readers through the importance of digital projects, digital preservation, and the future of such projects. Extended research and navigation of this handbook is enhanced by the bibliography and the index.

A do-it-yourself manual, *Digitizing Your Community's History* is the impetus for librarians to address digital projects of local histories, genealogies, and personal information preservation. Information here will allow for the recording of text, images, audio, video, and ephemera with step-by-step details for saving historical materials for future generations. Recommendations for hardware and software alternatives are described and the simplicity of scanner and hand-held devices are encouraging. Digital preservation and discussion of options for reliable storage are addressed. Consideration for the future of digital projects with technological advancements such as 3D scanning will bring a whole new "dimension" to recording of actual objects to preserve shape, size, and likeness.

Digitization of information is sensible and easily available, affordable, and accessible today. As a guide, this resource not only describes and details options for such a project, but also serves as stimulus for librarians or small institutions considering the diversity of digital projects and best practices for garnering community support. Archival records connect people, history, time, and place; with libraries as community centers, this reference tool on digitization will create another valuable service for local connection.

Digitizing Your Community's History is an excellent tool for archival curators, librarians, and community members seeking to preserve personal and local histories.

Highly recommended.—**Janis Minshull**

P

208.   Meister, Sam, Tammy Ravas, and Wendy Walker. Caro, Suzanne, comp. **Digitizing Your Collection: Public Library Success Stories.** Chicago, American Library Association, 2016. 163p. index. $55.00pa.; $49.50pa. (ALA members). ISBN 13: 978-0-8389-1383-3.

Digitizing Your Collection is a credible resource for library staff considering development of online collections. Information is presented in seven chapters: "What to Consider before Digitizing," "Digitizing Copyrighted Materials," "Overcoming Staffing Limitations," "Getting Your Community Involved," "Funding Opportunities," "Marketing Your Collection," and "Digital Preservation." The chapters provide introductory information, plausible ways to tackle each chapter's topic, valuable case studies where appropriate, a well-delineated synopsis (which readers may want to read first to get an overview of the chapter), and notes. The resources section at the end of the book provides avenues for additional research. An index that provides customary access rounds out the book.

Libraries dealing with small staff, fiscal challenges, and lack of time will appreciate this book, which shows that digital projects in public libraries are both possible and pragmatic. In the twenty-first century, "digital access redefines a library community from geographically-based to interest-based" (p. x). Reasons for developing digital projects such as these are then supported by nuts-and-bolts information about technology, questions of copyright, and potential collection ideas with emphasis on organization. The book also discusses such topics as grants and funding, marketing, outsourcing, and volunteers.

Public library administrators, staff, nonprofit groups, and volunteers will unequivocally benefit from the information, ideas, and examples presented here. Highly recommended.—**Janis Minshull**

C, P

209.   Purcell, Aaron D. **Digital Library Programs for Libraries and Archives.** Chicago, American Library Association, 2016. 256p. index. $85.00pa.; $76.50pa. (ALA members). ISBN 13: 978-0-8389-1450-2.

Digital Library Programs for Libraries and Archives is a necessary resource for navigating the emerging landscape of digitalization of library collections. Published in 2016, it provides frameworks for two different situations: those where a library is starting a digital collection from scratch and those situations where a library is adding to an already digitized collection. Purcell is a well-respected digital librarian, currently serving as professor and director of special collections at Virginia Tech in Blacksburg, Virginia. Purcell approaches the digitization of collections as an ongoing effort, and provides a framework for librarians to properly do so.

Numbering 218 pages, the book is as practical as it is readable. Purcell, as a working librarian himself, understands the value of time for the librarians he writes for and it shows. The book is broken down into three parts: the theory and reality of digital libraries; building digital library programs: a step-by-step process; and digital library planning exercises. Within those three parts are eleven chapters and eight exercises. The chapters flow logically—from planning the work, to speaking with stakeholders about the work, to executing the work.

One of the useful features of the book is that it not only presents a tremendous amount of useful information, it also serves a dual function as a journal. Most chapters end with a set of "questions." These questions could be better termed "reflections" as there is no objectively right or wrong answer. Nevertheless, their function remains useful for two reasons: it engages the reader with the book in a way that is deeper than simply read and (hopefully) retain, and it allows the reader to go back and refer to thoughts at the time they were reading the material.

The exercises are where the workbook portion of the book genuinely shines. As a practicing librarian, Purcell understands that while portions of the digitization process are applicable to all libraries, each library will have its own set of circumstances, making the book relevant to the daily lives of the digitization professionals.

Digital Library Programs for Libraries and Archives is a tremendously helpful resource for those individuals who are digitizing their collection for the first time, or for those who are adding to their current digital collection. By applying a framework to the digitization process, Purcell sets out a formula for a successful and sustainable digital future.—**Sara Mofford**

Fundraising

C, P, S

210.   Gerding, Stephanie K., and Pamela H. MacKellar. **Winning Grants: A How-To-Do-It Manual for Librarians.** 2d ed. Chicago, American Library Association, 2017. 248p. index. $108.00pa.; $97.20pa. (ALA members). ISBN 13: 978-0-8389-1473-1.

Grant writing for library programs and projects has just gotten easier! Updated by authors Stephanie K. Gerding and Pamela H. MacKellar, this handbook demonstrates how library staff can write successful grants.

The book is divided into three parts. The first covers the phases of the grant process cycle, the second shares six real-life examples of successful grants, and the third supports grant writing by providing checklists, forms, and worksheets. Chapters are laid out well, adequately balancing white space, black-and-white graphics (figures, photos, tables, and charts), and text. Chapter sidebars display chapter topics, grant overviews, credits, and other pertinent information. Resource information at the close of the book is useful and the glossary supports those seeking definitions for terms like challenge grant. The glossary also defines different roles, letters, and buzz words that will be most useful for inexperienced grant writers.

Dynamic libraries devote time and energy to strategic planning and goal setting. Grant writing is an integral part of that process and "it is more important than ever for librarians to master the skill of grant work and build it into their everyday jobs" (p. xv). This template of practical grant information will lend itself to busy librarians. Grant sourcing ideas are found throughout but additional suggestions will help greatly. For example, "Tips for Grant Success" states that "when completing grant proposals or award applications, follow the guidelines explicitly and answer all questions" (p. 138). Well-researched and well-written proposals also advocate for community projects and successful collaborations which might just lead to more sustainability and funding options!

Grant writing is not for the faint of heart and *Winning Grants* is a comprehensive resource for novice or expert grants writers seeking inspiration, examples, and other useful tools. This book will be best suited for administrators, grant writers, and librarians in all library sectors. Library nonprofits will also gain advantage from this material.

Highly recommended.—**Janis Minshull**

Information Literacy

C, P

211.   **Being Evidence Based in Library and Information Practice.** Denise Koufogiannakis and Alison Brettle, eds. Chicago, American Library Association, 2016. 208p. index. $75.00pa.; $67.50pa. (ALA members). ISBN 13: 978-0-8389-1521-9.

Librarians of all types seek to provide best services and to grow and evolve their physical and virtual libraries. A timely and useful guide, *Being Evidence Based in Library and Information Practice* demonstrates both the model for Evidence Based Library and Information Practice (EBLIP) and different library settings for development of this ongoing research practice. It is an extremely useful guide for developing evidence-based library improvements and a lifetime of professional growth.

Editors Denise Koufogiannakis and Alison Brettle are also the authors of the first seven chapters in part one where the background for EBLIP and the model are clearly represented. This section effectively communicates the new framework for this practice. The authors/editors state "being evidence based involves: questioning our practice, gathering or creating the evidence (through research or evaluation) if we don't have it already, using information or evidence wisely, and using our professional skill wisely to help others (often to make their own evidence-based decisions" (p. 3-4). The chapters in part one are sequential and flexible for individual library scenarios, ending with chapter seven, "Adapt" where evaluation of your EBLIP helps determine impact, what didn't work, and improvement options for next time. It is clear that Koufogiannakis and Brettle believe that librarians must embrace the philosophy behind EBLIP as a lifelong career model. Part two, written by contributing scholars and practitioners, brings the evidence-based practice into action with LIS examples from academic, health, public, school, and special libraries. Individual cases are filled with concrete lessons and techniques provide adaptability to other library settings.

Being Evidence Based in Library and Information Practice is a sensible and long-term commitment to improving library services of all types through implementation of evidence-based research. The approach has evolved since its original conception for use in the medical field in 1997 and this contemporary book will be well received by administrators, practitioners, and students of LIS seeking to find tangible impacts for improved funding and services in libraries.

Highly recommended.—**Janis Minshull**

Information Science and Information Systems

C
212.   Zeng, Marcia Lei, and Jian Qin. **Metadata, Second Edition.** Chicago, American Library Association, 2016. 555p. index. $84.00pa.; $75.60pa. (ALA members). ISBN 13: 978-1-55570-965-5.

Zeng and Qin provide a substantial revision to their earlier book of the same title, originally published in 2008 (see ARBA 2009, entry 574). The new edition reflects changes in technologies and standards in the intervening eight years, as well as the increasing popularity of the Semantic Web (p. xxv). The book provides an exhaustive explanation of metadata, assuming no lower or upper limits on the reader's prior knowledge—metadata is defined (pp. 11-14), but the authors also explain how to achieve interoperability between metadata repositories supporting multiple formats without record conversions (p. 364).

The book is divided into five parts, comprising ten chapters. "Fundamentals of Metadata" provides a conceptual introduction to metadata, metadata vocabularies, and creating metadata descriptions. "Metadata Vocabulary Building Blocks" examines metadata structure, semantics, and schemas. "Metadata Services" explains how metadata is stored, searched, and retrieved, quality measurement and improvement, and systems interoperability. "Metadata Research" details innovative efforts to better understand metadata architecture, modeling, semantics, and data-driven approaches. "Metadata Standards" discusses current standards for nine different purposes (e.g., Preservation and Provenance Metadata).

Metadata, Second Edition should work well as a textbook for aspiring librarians or a reference work for early-career information professionals, because of its broad scope.

The writing is engaging and memorable, especially when considering the technical nature of the subject matter. Visual learners will also appreciate the numerous illustrations, examples, and tables. No practitioner could ever hope to master every concept herein, but careful readers will undoubtedly feel their horizons expanding.—**Richard Nathan Leigh**

Information Technology

C, P

213.   Burke, John J. **The Neal-Schuman Library Technology Companion: A Basic Guide for Library Staff.** 5th ed. Chicago, American Library Association, 2016. 218p. index. $80.00pa.; $72.00pa. (ALA members). ISBN 13: 978-0-8389-1382-6.

John J. Burke, Director and Principal Librarian for the Gardner-Harvey Library on the Middletown Campus of Miami University (Ohio) modifies *Neal-Schuman Library Technology Companion: A Basic Guide for Library Staff* for this well-updated fifth edition. Librarians tend to be organized and Burke has rearranged, updated, and improved this latest edition for ease of use.

This 2016 edition provides a contemporary look at library technology and also includes new chapters on free technology (chapter three) and makerspaces (chapter 10). This reference material is available in paperback, PDF, e-book, or Kindle format. The set-up for this book is traditional with the addition of a handy list of illustrations and figures in the beginning and a basic guide to technology terms in the glossary. Visuals include tables such as those found in chapter two where Burke surveyed librarians to gain a broader understanding of how library staff members use technology. Screenshots are common as well but beyond chapter seven visual images are scant. The index is standard fare and concise.

The 17 chapters are laid out in five parts. The introductory chapters provide a strong path to what library staff do and what they need to do to keep their libraries relevant. Common system functions such as website management or interlibrary loan are examined and latest options like 3-D modeling or adaptive/assist technologies are also covered. Equipment, design, planning, and implementation are extremely current and all chapters end with review questions and valuable sources for further research. Ending chapters convey the speed at which technology becomes obsolete; Chapter 15 ("The Death of Technologies: Preservation Issues and Saying Goodbye") is a refreshing reality check but will make some library staff cringe to think what is still in their library. Looking to the future, Burke reminds us in the last chapters of what is yet to come.

Technology advances at a startling rate, and this book provides a timely overview of what is taking place in libraries. Whether it's staff using ILL programs or learning about free information options, assisting a patron with setting up a digital projector, or teaching someone how to use social media, library staff are the technocentric community option for all people. This information is essential for keeping libraries vital and this should be required reading for all library staff. The book is an excellent basic guide for librarians and support staff, archivists, information managers, and those seeking information about technology in libraries.

Highly recommended.—**Janis Minshull**

C, P

214.   Wittman, Stacy Ann, and Julianne T. Stam. **Redesign Your Library Website.** Santa Barbara, Calif., Libraries Unlimited/ABC-CLIO, 2016. 120p. index. $50.00pa. ISBN 13: 978-1-4408-3856-9; 978-1-4408-3857-6 (e-book).

Redesign Your Library Website proposes to do what the title says: walk local librarians through redesigning their local library's website. The authors, Wittman and Stam, redesigned the Eisenhower (Illinois) Public Library System's website during the 2012-2013 year. Wittman and Stam claim that they have no special qualifications other than being public librarians. Despite this modesty, a quick spin around the book shows they are eminently qualified to help librarians redesign their website.

At 116 pages before the index, the book is on the short side. However, readers need not correlate the author's brevity with a lack of content. Indeed, the book is designed for busy librarians who are doing much more than simply redesigning their library's website. The book contains 15 chapters and starts at the beginning: "Why does my library need a website?" From there, the book explores marketing of the website, the budget for a new website, the content that should be contained on the website, measuring the website's effectiveness, and usability testing. Finally, the book ends with a chapter called "What We've Learned," where the authors share lessons they've learned from redesigning their library website and helping other professionals do the same.

Wittman and Stam make the point that any good library website is informational and the goals are threefold: to provide information regarding location(s), contact information, and programs; to provide information regarding the administration of the library; and to provide access to the online catalog. With these overarching goals in mind, the authors set out best practices on how to redesign a website.

One chapter that provides very interesting albeit overlooked information is chapter 14: "Postlaunch and Usability Testing." This is understandably important for any individual redesigning a library website. It is one thing to say that the website is up and running, but it is quite another to constantly try to improve that website. This is the goal: a constantly improving website that is responsive to the needs of the patrons it serves. In fact, the authors suggest that libraries engage in usability testing every year or so and submit that finding patrons to participate in this testing is easier than it may initially seem. In addition, the authors suggest that libraries include their website in their annual communications review to gain honest feedback.

Redesign Your Library Website should be on the bookshelf of every library professional tasked with redesigning any library's website. It is a necessary tool. This book is recommended for academic and public libraries.—**Sara Mofford**

International Librarianship

C

215.   **Academic Library Development and Administration in China.** Lian Ruan, Qiang Zhu, and Ying Ye, eds. Hershey, Pa., Information Science Reference/IGI Global, 2017. 391p. index. (Advances in Library and Information Sciences (ALIS) Book Series). $195.00 (individual chapters available for purchase in electronic format). ISBN 13: 978-1-52250-550-1; 978-1-52250-551-8 (e-book).

Chinese academic libraries have made an excellent progress since the 1970s with the introduction of technology and the construction of many new library buildings. The book under review discusses various aspects of academic libraries and library administration. It has 19 chapters and is divided into six sections. All chapters are well written and are scholarly with many references, black-and-white photographs, charts, figures, and tables. Section one has three chapters and they discuss three major projects of the Ministry of Education: The China Academic Library and Information System, The China Academic Digital Associative Library, and The China Academic Social and Humanities Library. Section two has four chapters and they deal with user services and buildings. Section three has five chapters and the focus is on digital libraries and resources. Section four entitled Education and Research has three chapters and they deal with the analysis of academic education and research. Two chapters of section five discuss leadership and assessment of professional development of academic libraries and librarians. They show that the new trend has helped the growth of Internet technology, digital libraries, and career planning of academic librarians. Even academic library leadership has also developed and improved which in turn has helped libraries to grow and develop faster. The last section, with two chapters, discusses the International Communication and New Model of Cooperation between academic and public libraries to give joint service to students and other users. It also deals with the growing partnership between Chinese and American academic librarians through conferences, exchange visits, and the contributions of library pioneers. This book is an excellent addition to the library literature and is recommended for all academic libraries.—**Ravindra Nath Sharma**

Library Education

C, P

216.   **The Library's Role in Supporting Financial Literacy for Patrons.** Carol Smallwood, ed. Lanham, Md., Rowman & Littlefield, 2016. 358p. index. $95.00; $49.99 (e-book). ISBN 13: 978-1-4422-6591-2; 978-1-4422-6593-6 (e-book).

The Library's Role in Supporting Financial Literacy for Patrons is "an anthology of articles by practicing public, academic, school, and special librarians as well as LIS faculty in the United States that fills a gap in the literature on patron financial literacy." Financial literacy is sought after by consumers of all ages and all socioeconomic levels in making decisions that include: savings and investment, retirement planning, obtaining loans, credit card management, tax planning, and avoiding financial scams. The book is designed to examine how libraries can organize and present programs on financial literacy. The articles are arranged within three parts: Overview of Financial Literacy; Library Resources; and Case Studies, with descriptions of actual financial literacy programs in libraries. Each article includes bibliographical references. Part one includes chapters on planning of financial literacy programs in academic libraries; financial literacy as a lifetime skill; presenting library employee education programs; myths and realities of consumer credit; and why financial literacy matters. Part two contains articles on financial literacy collection development; core resources in career information; financial literacy for homebuyers; teaching career information literacy in an academic library; and U.S. government resources on financial literacy. Part three provides chapters on specific cases of financial literacy programs at Patchogue-Medford Library, Quinby Street Resource Center Library, Lane Library at Ripon College, and San Diego Public Library. Included also is an index and a section on "About the Editor and Contributors." This resource is a very informative, practical guide on how to plan programs for financial literacy in libraries. It is an excellent starting point for anybody interested in instructing patrons on financial literacy, through lectures and workshops, acquiring materials, assisting patrons at the reference desk, and advising them. *The Library's Role in Supporting Financial Literacy for Patrons* is highly recommended.—**Lucy Heckman**

Library Facilities

C, P

217.   **Creating the High-Functioning Library Space.** Marta Mestrovic Deyrup, ed. Santa Barbara, Calif., Libraries Unlimited/ABC-CLIO, 2017. 158p. illus. index. $70.00pa. ISBN 13: 978-1-4408-4058-6; 978-1-4408-4059-3 (e-book).

Creating the High-Functioning Library Space is an indispensable resource for any individual who is designing or renovating a library. The book is not only written for library professionals—the architects that those professionals hire will find the book useful as well! Realizing that designing a library balances several needs: present needs, future needs, specialized local needs (just to name a few) editor Marta Mestrovic Deyrup has compiled a book that will make any library professional feel seasoned in this foreign and often scary venture. Deyrup, currently the head of Technical Services at Seton Hall University Libraries (South Orange, New Jersey), has extensive experience in designing libraries to meet local needs. The book walks professionals through every step in the library building process, from crafting their request for proposal and selecting an architect for the project to developing the proper financial plans. With essays written by some of the most accomplished library designers in the field, the book makes a very intimidating task a little less so.

The book numbers 148 pages. It is broken down into 13 chapters that flow in a logical pattern. The first chapter is a history of American library design that helps to "center" the reader in the principles, both historical and present, of library design. The book then explores the visioning process and the rarely considered but equally as important aspects of the library experience such as lighting, technology, and storage options.

It goes without saying to library professionals that all libraries, even those in the same system, are unique and tailored to the needs of the community served. In fact, in an essay in the book titled "Library Programming," Daria Pizzetta of the New York design firm H3 Hardy Collaboration Architecture claims that libraries do not "design" libraries, but rather they "program" these libraries. By programming libraries, the variables of cost, quality, and quantity in a building project are considered and measured. In this way, according to Pizzetta, costs can be managed and expectations controlled.

Overall, the book is a useful resource for any professional tasked with the daunting task of redesigning a library. By adapting the ideas put forth in the book to the needs of the individual library, the new library will properly serve patrons for years to come.—**Sara Mofford**

Library Instruction

C

218.   Schmidt, Randell K., Emilia N. Giordano, and Geoffrey M. Schmidt. **A Guided Inquiry Approach to Teaching the Humanities Research Project.** Santa Barbara, Calif.,

Libraries Unlimited/ABC-CLIO, 2015. 192p. index. (Libraries Unlimited Guided Inquiry Series). $45.00pa. ISBN 13: 978-1-4408-3438-7; 978-1-4408-3439-4 (e-book).

Guided Inquiry is an approach that continues to gain momentum in education. Part of the Guided Inquiry Series, *A Guided Inquiry Approach to Teaching the Humanities Research Project* is a pragmatic handbook that supplies solid information and high school lessons on research writing with Common Core State Standards (CCSS) intersections. The first part of the book offers educators the trajectory from traditional humanities research papers to measuring metacognition, while the second part is a compilation of 20 sequential workshops. Following these empirical inquiry lessons, three appendixes offer very solid tools for teachers and librarians on training, planning, teaching, accessing, and extended professional development. A works cited section and an index round out the work.

Teaching is not a passive process and this curriculum resource affords secondary educators a clear path for teaching contemporary research. While the focus is on humanities, the material can be applied to social science disciplines. Within the pedagogical process, teachers and educators initially are heavily vested in student support and engagement with a goal of more reliance on the student as research confidence and independence develops. The Guided Inquiry methodology is chronological and closely aligns with the Information Search Process (ISP). The stages of ISP include: initiation, selection, exploration, formulation, collection, presentation, and assessment. From introduction to research and through assessment, each lesson plan is well defined. This is a robust resource for teachers, librarians, and curriculum designers in the course area of humanities or social studies. Because of the step-by-step process and the plethora of handout options, this book is valuable to both the student teacher and expert educator.

Highly recommended.—**Janis Minshull**

Library Management

C, P, S

219. Almquist, Arne J., and Sharon G. Almquist. **Intrapreneurship Handbook for Librarians: How to be a Change Agent in Your Library.** Santa Barbara, Calif., Libraries Unlimited/ABC-CLIO, 2017. 156p. illus. index. $55.00pa. ISBN 13: 978-1-61069-528-2; 978-1-61069-529-9 (e-book).

Innovation is what librarians are all about! The intrapreneurial concept was introduced by Steve Jobs in the 1980s and "many organizations, non-profit and for-profit, embraced the concept, that is, the concept of creating effective change through passion, perseverance, promotion, planning, and professionalization within an organization" (p. 21). Authors Almquist and Almquist share historical context, and also write of library and community experiences from their own efforts as agents of change. Concepts for vision and action are found in examples from public libraries in Kentucky. Assessment, funding, feasibility, team building, and other steps are explicitly laid out for library staff seeking nuts and bolts of twenty-first century program and project paths. This book provides inspiration, confidence, examples, and coaching steps for successful, new library and community collaborations. The book has nine chapters which end with notes for extended reference study. The text makes effective use of subtopics, bulleted lists, and multiple figures, providing a clean, easy visual for readers while also providing practical information. For example, Figure 1.3 compares the characteristics of the entrepreneur, intrapreneur, and the conventional manager; the two-page spread clarifies the parallels between and the diversity among these roles. The book ends with two appendixes that present intrapreneurship "tests," and librarians will want to share these at staff meetings or professional development workshops. An adequate index rounds out the work.

As a professional development tool, *Intrapreneurship Handbook for Librarians* is very useful for library administrators and librarians from all types of libraries.

Highly recommended.—**Janis Minshull**

C

220.   Soehner, Catherine, and Ann Darling. **Effective Difficult Conversations: A Step-by-Step Guide.** Chicago, American Library Association, 2017. 112p. index. $28.00pa.; $34.20pa. (ALA members). ISBN 13: 978-0-8389-1495-3.

Effective Difficult Conversations provides a useful framework that allows library professionals to perform effectively in difficult conversations with other library staff. These difficult conversations, while often awkward, can lead to growth and leadership in an unanticipated and unforeseen way. The authors, Catherine B. Soehner and Ann Darling, are both accomplished library professionals and conflict managers. Soehner and Darling bring a wealth of "on the ground" experience to managing conflict in libraries. Using their experience in both conflict management and library management, Soehner and Darling set out a concrete plan to be used by professionals in managing these difficult conversations. While "soft" skills are often necessary and useful, they are not always preferable especially in deeply emotionally charged situations. In discussions of emotional intelligence and other necessaries, a mindset that prioritizes a formulaic approach to such an emotionally charged issue may seem counterintuitive. However, this formulaic approach can provide a "centering" mechanism to bring some levity.

Numbering 104 pages, the book is designed for library professionals who may not have time to dive into the theoretical implications of conflict management in a library setting, but who nevertheless recognize the importance of having difficult conversations. As mentioned earlier, the book provides a formulaic method of structuring a difficult conversation: from defining the difficult conversation, to determining what the party initiating the difficult conversation wants to say, to the ebbs and flows of said difficult conversation, to documenting the results of the conversation. By relying on a formula and preplanning the conversation, difficult conversations can be structured in a way that does not digress into an emotional shouting match.

The last chapter of the book contains a profoundly important chapter titled "Managing Up: How to Have Difficult Conversations with Your Boss." The vast majority of the book is centered around the best ways to have conversations with peers or inferiors, which is of great value. However, a legitimate chunk of conversations must be had with superiors. This chapter attempts to deal with that. While the authors do not paint an overly rosy picture (they concede at one point that if an individual does not get along with her boss one solution may be to "get a new job and leave your current institution"), there are useful tips contained in the short chapter.

Overall, *Effective Difficult Conversations* is a useful tool for all library professionals. The skills discussed in the book help librarians perfect the soft skills that are necessary to serve all patrons. This book is recommended for academic libraries and professional development collections.—**Sara Mofford**

Library Outreach

P

221.   Barbakoff, Audrey. **Adults Just Wanna Have Fun: Programs for Emerging Adults.** Chicago, American Library Association, 2016. 116p. index. $49.00pa.; $44.10pa (ALA members). ISBN 13: 978-0-8389-1391-8

Adults Just Wanna Have Fun is an activity book designed for public librarians to structure programs for one of the most underserved demographics in the library system: the patron in their twenties and thirties. The author of the activity book points out the discrepancy that exists in the library patron demographic: as a general rule, the library does a wonderful job of serving young children; students at the K-12, college, and graduate school level; and senior citizens. However, for myriad reasons such as time restrictions, lack of interest, or too few programs, adults in their twenties and thirties have chosen to disengage with the library. To counter this, *Adults Just Wanna Have Fun* delineates programs designed to bring adults back into the library fold.

The preface of the book makes the case for adult programming. It also explores how adults play, encourages librarians to look in specific established directions for inspiration, and suggests ways to convince funders that adult programs are worthwhile.

The book is broken down into three parts containing 18 chapters: get dirty (activities that build), get out (essentially adult field trips), and get together (social activities for adults). The activities include homemade spa products, DIY hot cocoa mix, book-to-action, and tabletop gaming. Each entry is thoroughly researched and vetted. Each entry follows a consistent pattern that considers community need, materials required for the project, the process the project goes through, and further reading. Some of the entries represent twists on traditional library functions, such as the "book club in a bar," suggesting ways to reach the target market and best practices to select a location for the book club. Other adult activity suggestions include speed dating.

The book is very useful to all library professionals looking to broaden their base and reach out to underserved populations. It will prove itself an indispensable resource in engaging adults in their twenties and thirties. This book is highly recommended for public librarians.—**Sara Mofford**

C, P, S

222.   **How to Launch an Author Awards Program at Your Library: Curating Self-Published Books, Reaching Out to the Community.** Stam, Julianne and Elizabeth Clemmons, eds. Santa Barbara, Calif., Libraries Unlimited/ABC-CLIO, 2016. 160p. index. $45.00. ISBN 13: 978-1-4408-4164-4; 978-1-4408-4165-1 (e-book).

Librarians are always on the lookout for adult service programs that are vibrant and relevant. As the publishing world evolves, self-publishing is gaining interest quickly. *How to Launch an Author Awards Program at Your Library* provides a step-by-step guide to understanding and embracing the self-publishing trend and opening it up to a library community.

Edited by Julianne T. Stam and Elizabeth Clemmons, this reference tool consists of eight chapters with contributions from experts on libraries and self-publishing. The focus of the text is the Soon To Be Famous (STBF) project based in Illinois. Available in both hard copy and in digital format, this 160-page book will be useful for librarians seeking ways to enhance writing and literacy efforts for adults but can be modified for other applications including a school community. The handbook focuses on the how-to of learning about self-publishing and bringing that information to the community through extensive planning and marketing; causation leads to the journey of this group of Illinois librarians to create an effective self-publishing program.

Chapter one, the "why chapter," examines the importance of keeping libraries relevant in the twenty-first century and how this self-publishing program can engage community. This chapter also introduces why librarians need to be knowledgeable about self-publishing. Sequential information will be easily accessed and the personal experiences of contributors make this manual convincing for library colleagues. The creation of a plan unfolds with sidebar charts and figures as well as black-and-white photos. The program is well documented with information such as a project timeline on page 21. Extensive promotion of collaboration and marketing may be useful in other avenues for programming. The final chapter brings the self-publishing program full circle with practical thoughts on outcomes and assessments. Appendixes A through F provide more in-depth access to resources, marketing plan creation, and the history of self-publishing.

The Soon To Be Famous (STBF) project provides a clear template for others who wish to start self-publishing programs. *How to Launch an Author Awards Program at Your Library* explores the promotion of reading and writing with a germane program to educate library teams and expand community outreach. This book will be of interest to public, school, and academic librarians who seek current program ideas and want to enhance their knowledge of this popular trend in publishing.

Highly recommended.—**Janis Minshull**

Museum Studies

C, P

223.   Yerkovich, Sally. **A Practical Guide to Museum Ethics.** Lanham, Md., Rowman & Littlefield, 2016. 329p. index. $35.00pa.; $34.99 (e-book). ISBN 13: 978-1-4422-3163-4; 978-1-4422-3164-1 (e-book).

This volume, divided into 10 chapters, explores a wide range of areas in the museum world, from acquisition of collections and deaccessioning items to fundraising, external pressures on museums, collection conservation, and diversity and access. Issues of cultural heritage, censorship, and management responsibility are also addressed. Also included are four codes of ethics developed by various American museum organizations. The book employs "hypothetical and real-life cases" (p. x) to wrestle with all of these issues. It also provides a multistep framework for analyzing and resolving potential ethical issues in the museum setting.

Although focused on museums, this volume could also interest others studying ethics, as the topics examined here are not ones generally discussed in broader analyses of ethics. Their real-life setting should expand the reader's reflection. Academic and some public libraries should consider this reasonably priced work.—**Mark Schumacher**

Public Relations

C, P

224.   Solomon, Laura. **The Librarian's Nitty-Gritty Guide to Content Marketing.** Chicago, American Library Association, 2016. 120p. index. $50.00pa.; $45.00pa. (ALA members). ISBN 13: 978-0-8389-1432-8.

The Librarian's Nitty-Gritty Guide to Content Marketing attempts to answer the age-old question that library patrons ask: "What's in it for me?" There is no doubt that the programs, content, and resources offered at libraries are of great worth. However, the significant challenge that library marketers have and continue to face is how to get the content in the hands of the consumer. The guide, published in 2016 by the American Library Association, attempts to walk library professionals through the steps involved in content marketing. Author Laura Solomon provides extensive "ground up" training in how to market library content and leads with the attention-grabbing chapter headline "Get over Yourself." (In this chapter, Solomon provides a framework for librarians to reject the tired paradigm that they do not need to market their libraries and services in the traditional "build it and they will come manner" that was the norm previously.)

The book contains seven chapters, including the aforementioned "Get over Yourself," "Should You Care about Content Marketing?", "Identifying Your Audiences," "Planning Not to Fail," "Writing So People Might Give a Damn," "Common Mistakes," and "Are You Actually Succeeding?" The chapters and book are succinct—the book only contains 120 pages in total. However, Solomon's 120 pages pack a powerful punch. The book is written for library professionals, and focuses heavily on the transactional rather than the theoretical. Busy professionals will appreciate its succinct and to-the-point style.

The last chapter, "Are You Actually Succeeding?" provides a useful way to measure content marketing. Traditional marketing metrics—namely, income—are not present in library marketing and there must be alternative ways to measure the success of marketing campaigns. Even though consumer spending may not be an available metric, there are other metrics that libraries can consider to determine if their marketing campaign is a success. Some examples that Solomon provides are engagement (comments, likes, shares, Tweets, forwards, clickthroughs), patron loyalty (percent of content consumed, repeat website visitors, email subscriptions), and brand awareness (website traffic, page views, and video views). Solomon makes the salient point that metrics cannot be a one-time evaluation; rather, metric evaluation must be continually monitored. These evaluations can also be useful in budget discussions with funding authorities to justify library spending.

The Librarian's Nitty-Gritty Guide to Content Marketing is a useful tool for librarians in a changing world. As the way that libraries operate evolves, so does the way that libraries market themselves. Advanced marketing techniques will help libraries maintain their relevance and continue to be a useful harbinger of information for all people. This book is recommended for academic and public libraries.—**Sara Mofford**

Reference Services

C, P, S

225.   Goldsmith, Francisca. **Crash Course in Contemporary Reference.** Santa Barbara, Calif., Libraries Unlimited/ABC-CLIO, 2017. 183p. index. (Crash Course Series).

$45.00pa. ISBN 13: 978-1-4408-4481-2; 978-1-4408-4482-9 (e-book).

Crash Course in Contemporary Reference examines the redefined roles, strategies, practices, and resource options for reference librarians in the twenty-first century.

One volume of the professional development series, Crash Course, this resource is comprised of a dozen chapters. The first chapter relates to service provision and outlines the critical reference value found in dynamic communication. The author presents a list of actionable practices in the reference interaction process that covers, among other things: body language, tone of voice, and language. In a world of ever-changing technology, information sources are a necessary discussion and chapter five extends beyond print resources to the exploding plethora of electronic references. This extension of library reference beyond physical space makes this professional development title timely. Reference strategies and reference models are included, and the value of staff training through a variety of networks and professional development technologies is the focus for chapter 12.

Professional reference success is determined by far more than a simple reference question. Librarians, essentially the purveyors of information, must be current and forward thinking so students, scholars, and the general public obtain the most relevant information. *Crash Course in Contemporary Reference* belongs in professional development collections for academic, public, and school librarians seeking best reference practices for the twenty-first century.

Recommended.—**Janis Minshull**

C

226.   **Reference and Information Services: An Introduction.** 5th ed. Linda C. Smith and Melissa A. Wong, eds. Santa Barbara, Calif., Libraries Unlimited/ABC-CLIO, 2016. 880p. index. $75.00pa. ISBN 13: 978-1-4408-3696-1; 978-1-4408-3697-8 (e-book).

This latest version of a book first published in 1991 examines the changes in the world of reference since the last edition (2011), with an additional 100 pages of information. The 29 chapters are written by 28 contributors, predominantly academic librarians and faculty in library science departments. While examining all the aspects of reference work, this volume focuses on "rapidly developing technologies and increasing volumes of digital content" (p. ix). The two major sections are those used in the 1990's: "Concepts and Processes," including the reference interview, services for different populations, marketing reference services, and "Information Sources and Their Use," examining resources in a variety of fields: business, health, biography, archives, law. etc. This book will be most useful in academic libraries, particularly those supporting programs in library and information science programs. Other large libraries may also find it useful for its rich information.—**Mark Schumacher**

C

227.   **Teaching Reference Today: New Directions, Novel Approaches.** Lisa A. Ellis, ed. Lanham, Md., Rowman & Littlefield, 2016. 360p. index. $60.00pa; $59.99 (e-book). ISBN 13: 978-1-4422-6392-5; 978-1-4422-6393-2 (e-book).

It's no secret that traditional reference and information service providers are having to adapt to rapid changes in technology and society. Gone are the days when a librarian or other reference professional held the keys to the warehouse of knowledge! Google and other search engines put a wealth of information at an individual's hand. Is there even a place for the reference professional anymore?

Teaching Reference Today believes there is. But only if today's reference professionals are trained properly. *Teaching Reference Today* aims to educate those who are teaching tomorrow's reference professionals about what their students will need to know to be successful in a rapidly changing environment.

It is broken up in to five parts, each focusing on a broad topic. A number of contributors (four to five on average) then provide a chapter on a discrete subtopic. The first part focuses on the Evolution of Reference Values and Roles and the last on Exploring Reference Education: Here and Beyond. The parts in between discuss the teaching, training, and design aspects of educating future (and current) reference professionals. Footnotes and a bibliography are included at the end of each chapter, and a comprehensive index is provided at the end of the volume.

Teaching Reference Today is an excellent tool both for those who are teaching others about providing reference services and those learning about the topic. It discusses the pedagogy of teaching reference and information services and provides answers to difficult questions that will continue to occur in a quickly changing information environment. It is recommended for any college which has a library school and for students interested in the library profession.—**Alicia Brillon**

Storytelling

P, S

228.   Hovious, Amanda S. **Transmedia Storytelling: The Librarian's Guide.** Santa Barbara, Calif., Libraries Unlimited/ABC-CLIO, 2016. 142p. index. $45.00pa. ISBN 13: 978-1-4408-3848-4; 978-1-4408-3849-1 (e-book).

This book introduces and explains the new twenty-first-century way to tell a story. Transmedia storytelling is defined as "a new form of storytelling where fictional story worlds are built and delivered across multiple media platforms to create an immersive and interactive narrative universe that blurs the lines between fantasy and reality." The author then goes into describing this new form of storytelling and its foundations and applications. The second half of the book provides ideas, detailed plans, and various ways in which to create and utilize this new exciting tool. Specific plans for various program examples, such as maker activities and transmedia storytime, are also provided. All ideas and plans can be used in both a school library and a public library setting. This would be a good resource for school librarians of all age levels and for public librarians. The book has two appendixes, "Transmedia Storytelling Resources" and "Technology Tools" along with a references section, including websites, and an appendix. Recommended.—**Chris Dexter**

Publishing and Bookselling

Handbooks and Yearbooks

C, P, S

229.   Grover, Robert J. and others. **Libraries Partnering with Self-Publishing: A Winning Combination.** Santa Barbara, Calif., Libraries Unlimited/ABC-CLIO, 2016. 154p. index. $65.00pa. ISBN 13: 978-1-4408-4158-3; 978-1-4408-4159-0 (e-book).

Libraries Partnering with Self-Publishing demonstrates how librarians can assist writers with the process of self-publishing, a growing contemporary trend. Librarians have always had a prudent interest in the traditional publishing industry. No longer passive, the active verb in the title, "partnering," exhibits the dynamic possibilities for another aspect of community building for librarians. The author team, in 10 chapters, covers the writing process from initial writing to completed manuscript, and explores actual avenues for nontraditional publication. The case studies, interviews, technology, and resources presented will support writers and library staffing seeking new ideas for programs. References to well-known writing promotions such as NaNoWriMo (National Novel Writing Month) are reintroduced in the context of creating robust and knowledgeable library programs as stimulus for writers. The book also discusses social media marketing, virtual exchanges using tools like Google Docs, and the impact of the Open Access Movement. In addition to the index, six appendixes supplement project information such as "Community Novel Project Details" where librarians may consider aspects of self-publishing examples from the Topeka and Shawnee County Public Library Model.

An excellent tool for expanding writing programs, this book is well suited for school, public, college and university librarians, as well as special libraries. The wealth of self-publishing information will also be worthwhile for authors.

Highly recommended.—**Janis Minshull**

C

230.   **Open Book: A Librarian's Guide to Academic Publishing.** James Wiser and Rolf Janke, eds. Santa Barbara, Calif., Mission Bell Media, 2017. 200p. index. (Peak Series). $49.95pa. ISBN 13: 978-0-9971757-1-4.

One of the premises of this volume is as follows: "librarians know little of what happens behind the doors of academic publishers and the vendors who play a vital role in distributing their content" (p. vii). The 14 chapters in this slim volume are mostly written by members of the academic publishing industry. Topics range from university presses and open access to e-books, copyright, and the role of journals in academic publishing. Usefully, most of the chapters present "top take-aways in this chapter" to guide readers through the text. A few case studies involve individual companies or academic institutions, but most of the time the approach is more general and even anonymous.

Any library with readers interested in librarianship and/or the world of publishing should consider this book. Academic libraries are the most likely ones to purchase this work, but others might also find it useful.—**Mark Schumacher**

12 Military Studies

General Works

Dictionaries and Encyclopedias

C, P, S

231. **World War II: The Definitive Encyclopedia and Document Collection.** Spencer C. Tucker, ed. Santa Barbara, Calif., ABC-CLIO, 2016. 5v. illus. maps. index. $520.00/set. ISBN 13: 978-1-85109-968-9; 978-1-85109-969-6 (e-book).

This five-volume tome is a revision of the five-volume 2004 title—*Encyclopedia of World War II: A Political, Social, and Military History*—by the same editor. This revised edition has added 212 new entries, and most of the 2004 entries have been revised and their bibliographies updated. Besides the excellent essays, there are a number of additional features detailed in the foreword and preface. Volume one includes some general maps, along with overview essays on the origins of World War II, a summary of World War II, and the legacy of World War II. Volume four includes information on medals and decorations, military organization, selected belligerents, chronology, glossary, overall bibliography, and a list of editors and contributors. Finally, volume five contains numerous important primary source documents related to World War II. There are numerous maps, black-and-white photos, charts, and tables interspersed throughout. This reference work is the definitive work on the subject of World War II; it should be included in any reference collection from high school up through university libraries.—**Bradford Lee Eden**

Handbooks and Yearbooks

C, P, S

232. **Library of Congress World War I Collection. www.loc.gov/topics/world-war-i.** [Website] Free. Date reviewed: 2017.

As part of the 100th anniversary of the United States' entry into World War I, the Library of Congress recently unveiled this new portal to their virtual resource collection. This collection includes many rare materials such as lectures, film programs, recordings, speeches, exhibitions, and veterans' stories. These are all easily searchable and displayed clearly on the main World War I homepage. Social studies teachers will find the variety of primary and secondary sources extremely easy to share with students and other teachers using the "save/share" option located near the top of every page. Teachers will also find the lesson plans located on this site valuable as they include overviews, preparation plans, procedure instructions, and evaluation information. Articles from the Library of Congress blog are also featured and are updated with new information regularly. The Library of Congress' new exhibition "Echoes of the Great War: American Experience of World War I" is also included in this collection. This is an impressive, completely free resource that should be utilized in every U.S. and world history classroom and posted on every school library website's list of online resources for students. Highly recommended.—**Angela Wojtecki**

C, P

233.	**The Soldier in Later Medieval England. http://www.medievalsoldier.org/.** [Website] Free. Date reviewed: 2016.

This newly refreshed website and database stem from a larger project funded by the Arts and Humanities Research Council. Professor Adrian Bell, Henley Business School, University of Reading, and Anne Curry, University of Southampton, led the project that studied the emergence of professional soldiery in England between 1369 and 1453.

The site is easy to use. There are three main tabs—About, Database, and Help. The About tab takes users to five different places: Project, Publications, Soldier Profiles, Agincourt 600, and Miscellanea. Here users can read about the project and see the publications of those involved with it. In addition, the Soldier Profiles link takes users to mini-biographies by "citizen" historians and academics. Each is approximately 2,000 words in length and is fully cited. Moreover, the Agincourt 600 connects to detailed datasets of the French and English soldiers at the battle; information provided includes titles, biographical details, ransom information, and much more. At the time of this review, Miscellanea was still under development. The database itself is searchable by name or by a variety of other criteria, such as status or rank. The results are downloadable. It might be best to consult the information in the Help tab first, as four different links describe the datasets, as well as how to search and cite the material.

Highly recommended.—**ARBA Staff Reviewer**

C, P, S

234.	Tucker, Spencer C. **The Roots and Consequences of 20th-Century Warfare.** Santa Barbara, Calif., ABC-CLIO, 2016. 545p. illus. index. $100.00. ISBN 13: 978-1-61069-801-6; 978-1-61069-802-3 (e-book).

Noted historian Dr. Spencer C. Tucker made an astute observation concerning the twentieth century when he stated it has "arguably the two greatest wars in history and … a spate of comparatively minor ones." He begins with the 1904-1905 Russo-Japanese War and concludes with the Yugoslav Wars of 1991-1999, with two world wars taking center stage, but each conflict getting its own entry too. Wars on each continent are illustrated ranging from the Mexican Revolution (1910-1920) and the Russian Revolution (1917-1922) to the Indo-Pakistani Wars (1947-1949, 1965-1971), the Rhodesian Bush War (1965-1979), and the Persian Gulf (War 1991). Each entry is signed and contains an overview for the cause and its consequences; a list of casualties; a timeline; and a section of suggested further readings. An excellent example of an entry is the 12 pages concerning the Greek

Civil War (1946-1949). Overall, this is an excellent exploration of several conflicts that shaped the twentieth century and beyond.—**Scott R. DiMarco**

C, P

235.   **The Vietnam War in Popular Culture: The Influence of America's Most Controversial War on Everyday Life.** Milam, Ron, ed. Santa Barbara, Calif., Praeger/ ABC-CLIO, 2017. 2v. index. $164.00/set. ISBN 13: 978-1-4408-4046-3; 978-1-4408-4047-0 (e-book).

Editor Ron Milam, a combat veteran of the Vietnam War, associate professor of history at Texas Tech University, and author of *Not a Gentleman's War: An Inside View of Junior Officers in the Vietnam War* (University of North Carolina Press, 2009) is joined by 18 other scholars in producing a fascinating look at how popular culture first reacted to the Vietnam War and was later affected by the conflict's legacy. Since the work was not intended to be a comprehensive resource, the contributors of the 37 essays (each ranging from approximately 8,000 to 9000 words) were apparently given the freedom to explore the respective topics as they saw fit. It is particularly notable that the contributors also include individuals from Vietnam, thus giving some perspectives usually missing from works produced in the United States.

Although the work is comprised of two volumes, each volume stands on its own. Volume one contains 19 essays that explore popular culture during the war years. The entries are subdivided into six sections: From the Soldiers; From the Press with Words and Photos; The Sounds; Some Fun; Some Dissension; and Some Propaganda. Specific essays include "Isolated Images: The Photos of My Lai in American Memory," "The Cult of Playboy: Exploring Playboy Magazine's Popularity," and "'Hanoi Jane' and the Myth of Betrayal: The Cultural War on the Home Front." Volume two's focus is the legacy of the conflict. Its 18 essays fall under four categories: The Spoken Word through Film; The Spoken Word through Film and Television; The Written Word; and Everyday Life. Among the essays can be found "At Alamo Bay-Love is Not Enough: Reflections of an ARVN Officer's Daughter about War and Peace," "The Slow Integration of Vietnam War Films," and "Vietnam Veterans, Agent Orange, and Public Awareness of the Dangers of Toxic Chemicals in the United States."

Although this title has some utility as a reference work, this highly recommended set is probably better suited for circulation in both academic and public libraries with collecting interests in popular culture or the history of the Vietnam War.—**John R. Burch Jr.**

C, P, S

236.   **The Virtual Vietnam Archive. http://www.vietnam.ttu.edu/virtualarchive/.** [Website] Free. Date reviewed: 2017.

Texas Tech University, home to the Vietnam Center and Archive, has created a virtual archive of over four million pages of materials relevant to the Vietnam War era of United States history. This site offers access to many of these materials, which include photographs, documents, video and audio recordings, and maps.

This page of the greater archive's site offers technical information on how to search for, browse, and utilize the materials. As the scope of this archive is quite impressive, the site has created several useful options for searching and browsing. Users can also watch a video tutorial for navigation assistance.

Users can conduct a general search from the left sidebar, or they can browse via collections, which are essentially alphabetized by donor (individual or organization) name. The archive has further created several specific collections itself, such as The Maps Collection or the Operations Database. In addition, users can narrow their browsing options by Association Donations, Digitized Audio, Digitized Moving Images, and Oral Histories.

When perusing the collections, users will note them marked with an item number, a brief description of the materials, and the date the collection was added to the archive, as well as other technical information. Users can click the Finding Aid icon to access the physical location of the material in the archive or the downloadable format (e.g., PDF, audio file, etc.) if available.

The wealth of information held in this site is truly impressive, and would hold great appeal to history or military researchers, veterans groups, students, and many others.—**ARBA Staff Reviewer**

Army

C, P, S

237. **Mapping Occupation. http://mappingoccupation.org/.** [Website] Free. Date reviewed: 2017.

This highly focused website amasses data on the location and nature of U.S. federal troops stationed throughout the southern states after the Civil War. The project aims to clarify the role of the U.S. Army in the south during Reconstruction. The site displays a series of interactive maps of the southern states that locate and measure U.S. troop presence throughout. Maps provide information on the composition of troops (cavalry, black, etc.), general population figures, location of rail lines, and more. Maps help clarify zones of occupation and troop access to the general population. The left sidebar offers a running narrative which provides ample context to the data on the maps. Other maps and illustrations are dispersed throughout this narrative. This site offers a fresh perspective on the aftermath of the Civil War and would definitely be useful to anyone studying the Reconstruction period.—**ARBA Staff Reviewer**

13 Political Science

International Organizations

Handbooks and Yearbooks

238.   **UNBISNET.http://unbisnet.us.org/.** [Website] Free. Date reviewed: 2017.

This site allows easy entry to a large selection of records regarding the United Nations (UN) and its various councils. Users will find Bibliographic Records of UN documents and publications and other relevant non-UN-sourced documents held at the Dag Hammarskjöld Library in New York. Users can also access the Voting Records for all UN General Assembly and UN Security Council resolutions, with links to full-text versions, declared since 1946. Finally, users can examine the Index to Speeches made to the General Assembly, Security Council, and other councils since 1983, also with links to full-text versions. Keyword Searching and List Browsing are available for each of the records categories. A sidebar offers a number of further resources, including a Thesaurus, Research Guides on a number of topics (e.g., Peace & Security), UN Resources (searchable in a number of ways), and over 800 tagged FAQs. Available in the six official languages of the United Nations (Arabic, Chinese, French, English, Russian, and Spanish), the site is an excellent source for students, educators, global policy-makers, historians, and many others.—**ARBA Staff Reviewer**

International Relations

Dictionaries and Encyclopedias

239.   Hahn, Peter L. **Historical Dictionary of United States-Middle East Relations.** Lanham, Md., Rowman & Littlefield, 2016. 345p. illus. (Historical Dictionaries of Diplomacy and Foreign Relations). $95.99; $94.99 (e-book). ISBN 13: 978-1-4422-6294-2; 978-1-4422-6295-9 (e-book).

Peter L. Hahn, professor of history and dean of arts and humanities at Ohio State

University, has authored a second edition of a work first published in 2007, (see ARBA 2008, entry 663). Its scope of coverage begins with the establishment of the Syrian Protestant College, later American University of Beirut, in 1866, and continues to July 2015, when the Islamic State in Iraq and Syria (ISIS) began destroying some of the monuments in Palmyra, Syria, that had such significance that the ruins had been designated a World Heritage site by United Nations Educational, Scientific and Cultural Organization (UNESCO).

Like other volumes in the Historical Dictionaries of Diplomacy and Foreign Relations series, it begins with four introductory sections: Map, Acronyms and Abbreviations, Chronology, and Introduction. The main part of the text is the dictionary with approximately 330 entries on such topics as conflicts, diplomatic efforts, key personalities, nongovernmental organizations, and migration. The text is supplemented by pictures. The work concludes with an extensive 44-page bibliography. This work is recommended for public and academic libraries as a quick-reference tool. The respective entries do not contain enough information for in-depth research.—**John R. Burch Jr.**

Handbooks and Yearbooks

C

240.   **The SAGE Handbook of Diplomacy.** Costas M. Constantinou, Pauline Kerr, and Paul Sharp, eds. Thousand Oaks, Calif., Sage, 2016. 684p. index. $175.00. ISBN 13: 978-1-4462-9856-5.

Editors Costas M. Constantinou, professor of international relations at the University of Cyprus, Pauline Kerr, emeritus fellow in the Asia-Pacific College of Diplomacy at the Australian National University, and Paul Sharp, professor and head of political science at the University of Minnesota Duluth and senior visiting fellow at the Netherlands Institute of International Relations, and 59 distinguished scholars from around the world have collaborated to produce a valuable reference designed for academics and practicing diplomats. It is comprised of 53 essays, which range from 9 to 16 pages, divided into four parts: Diplomatic Concepts and Theories; Diplomatic Institutions; Diplomatic Relations; and Types of Diplomatic Engagement. Each essay concludes with an extensive list of references. Also included are abstracts of the respective articles and an index. This authoritative and comprehensive reference work is an essential purchase for academic libraries supporting programs in political science and diplomacy.—**John R. Burch Jr.**

C, P, S

241.   Steed, Brian L. **Isis: An Introduction and Guide to the Islamic State.** Santa Barbara, Calif., Praeger/ABC-CLIO, 2016. 197p. index. $58.00. ISBN 13: 978-1-4408-4986-2; 978-1-4408-4987-9 (e-book).

This book offers general as well as well-informed readers contemporary information about the Islamic State. In addition, the book explores the rise of ISIS and its influence globally and throughout the Middle East. ISIS—also referred to as ISIL, the Islamic State, or Daesh—began to assert its power and gain recognition for its militant and terroristic activities in April of 2013. ISIS captured the full attention of Western observers after the coordinated attacks in Paris on November 13, 2015.

The book explores the following basic questions: what is ISIS, what are its goals, what do their members believe, and why are their ranks growing. Readers will gain an understanding of how ISIS as a dedicated terrorist group seeks to advance extremist views that reflect growing frustrations with life in the Middle East. After reading this book, one concludes that there is no quick fix to very complex ISIS political issues. The author, Brian L. Steed, is assistant professor of military history at the U.S. Army Command and General Staff College and a U.S. Army Middle East foreign area officer. He served eight-and-a-half consecutive years in the Middle East and in Iraq in 2005, 2010–2011, and 2014-2015. Steed was a Jordanian Army advisor as part of the Military Personnel Exchange Program for two-and-a-half years. He has written numerous books on military theory, military history, and cultural awareness.

The introduction documents the origins of ISIS within the larger Al Qaeda organization during the Iraq War. Other entries discuss individuals, events, and organizations that put ISIS in historical context in terms of contemporary events since the Iraq War and explain the group's position within the complex conflict currently boiling in the Middle East. Chapters analyze the origins, development, and territorial expansion of ISIS in Syria and Iraq and assess the ideological motivations behind the emergence of ISIS, giving readers an understanding of the importance of ISIS in contemporary history. The reference entries are especially helpful, as is an appendix, the "Obama Administration Strategy Report, March 24, 2016." The book additionally offers a chronology of events and an index.

This introduction and guide to ISIS is ideally suited for undergraduates, high school students, and general nonspecialists. High school, community college, and university library collections would benefit. School librarians would do well to incorporate this book in their acquisition budget for the academic year. Library acquisition decision-makers responsible for the selection and purchase of materials or resources will consider this book a welcome addition to their research collection. Moreover, the book should be required reading for every commissioned and noncommissioned officer of the United States Armed Forces. Law enforcement agencies will consider this book insightful when addressing domestic terrorism. Public safety and homeland security organizations assuredly would benefit from acquiring this timely reference book. University instructors could easily incorporate it as supplementary reading material. This excellent book presents a current, balanced, and reliable collection of material to help readers understand a complex subject in an easy-to-understand, thought-provoking manner. The topic is timely, essential, and meets the immediate needs of a global and interconnected population to a very real threat.—**Thomas E. Baker**

Politics and Government

Europe

C

242. **The Handbook of European Intelligence Cultures.** Bob De Graaff, James M. Nyce, and Chelsea Locke, eds. Lanham, Md., Rowman & Littlefield, 2016. 496p. index. $115.00; $114.99 (e-book). ISBN 13: 978-1-4422-4941-7; 978-1-4422-4942-4 (e-book).

This book, part of the Security and Professional Intelligence Education Series (SPIES), is meant to provide detailed information on a number of little-known European intelligence agencies, as well as allow readers to make comparisons regarding the different approaches of the various organizations. For those who think that libraries have too many acronyms, the 15-page list of abbreviations/acronyms in regards to the multitude of European intelligence agencies provided at the beginning of this book is astounding. The editors provide an excellent review of the literature on this topic, examining each tome in detail and why their book is better and more current (p. xxxi-xxxii). The 32 chapters are arranged alphabetically and provide a wealth of information on the following countries and their intelligence agencies: Albania, Austria, Belgium, Bosnia and Herzegovina, Bulgaria, Croatia, Czechoslovakia, Denmark, Estonia, Finland, France, Germany, Greece, Iceland, Ireland, Italy, Lithuania, Luxembourg, Montenegro, The Netherlands, Norway, Poland, Portugal, Romania, Serbia, Slovakia, Slovenia, Spain, Sweden, Switzerland, Ukraine, and the United Kingdom. This reference work is an essential addition to any college or university library.—**Bradford Lee Eden**

United States

Dictionaries and Encyclopedias

C, P
243.   Conley, Richard S. **Historical Dictionary of the U.S. Constitution.** Lanham, Md., Rowman & Littlefield, 2016. 474p. (Historical Dictionaries of U.S. Politics and Political Eras). $105.00; $104.99 (e-book). ISBN 13: 978-1-4422-7188-3; 978-1-4422-7187-6 (e-book).

Richard S. Conley, Associate Professor of Political Science at the University of Florida, has produced a number of volumes in Rowman & Littlefield's series Historical Dictionaries of U.S. Politics and Political Eras, including *Historical Dictionary of the Reagan-Bush Era, Historical Dictionary of the George W. Bush Era, Historical Dictionary of the Clinton Era* (see ARBA 2013, entry 609), and *Historical Dictionary of the U.S. Presidency* (see ARBA 2016, entry 469). His latest offering focuses on the United States Constitution, beginning with the obvious need for such a document in the wake of the Articles of Confederation. The volume begins with an introductory section that includes a listing of acronyms and abbreviations utilized, a chronology, and a general introduction to the topic. The bulk of the work is a dictionary with approximately 300 alphabetically arranged entries that explores not only the Constitution itself, but how it has been shaped and interpreted by politicians and Supreme Court Justices. The entries are supplemented by 29 appendixes, which include "Federalist No. 15: The Insufficiency of the Present Confederation to Preserve the Union" and "Anti-Federalist No. 85: Concluding Remarks: Evils Under Confederation Exaggerated; Constitution Must be Drastically Revised Before Adoption." A strength of this reference work is the bibliography which is 42 pages long. This excellent ready reference tool is recommended for academic libraries serving undergraduates and for public libraries.—**John R. Burch Jr.**

C, P, S

244.   **Religion and Politics in America: An Encyclopedia of Church and State in American Life.** Frank J. Smith, ed. Santa Barbara, Calif., ABC-CLIO, 2016. 2v. illus. index. $189.00/set. ISBN 13: 978-1-59884-435-1; 978-1-59884-436-8 (e-book).

Even the casual observer of the American experience today senses the dynamic tension between church and state or religion and politics. This is especially true during an election cycle or when the President has nominated a Supreme Court justice. For students, citizens, and scholars who would like to know more about the relationship between religion and politics and how the culture is shaped by it, they now have a worthy two-volume encyclopedia entitled *Religion and Politics in America: An Encyclopedia of Church and State in American Life,* edited by Frank J. Smith, a Presbyterian minister and author of *The History of the Presbyterian Church in America* (1985).

Religion and Politics in America contains 360 entries, signed by college professors, seasoned writers, and independent scholars, whose credentials precede the index. The 109 contributors have a wide range of academic training, with a breadth of perspective, both ideological and religious, according to the editor. The coverage is comprehensive, spanning from colonial times to the present. The reader is advised to peruse the Guide to Related Topics at the beginning, as some topics, such as "separation of church and state," are not listed as such in the index. Under the broad topic of "Church and State," the user finds "Disestablishment" and "Wall of Separation." Other "Related Topics" include education, events, government/legal and judicial, groups and organizations, ideas and movements, issues, literature and films, people, political organizations, religion and denominations, science and the environment, and theology and religious governance.

The average entry is a page or two in length and has approximately six references to related articles and books. A few have photographs or primary documents. Other entries, such as abortion and African Americans, are lengthy at four to five pages. At the end of volume two is an extensive index, including *see also* suggestions. Users would have been better served by the liberal use of *see* references. For example, there is no *see* reference to "Wall of Separation" under the phrase "Separation of Church and State." The final volume also has a page and a half of recommended resources.

One can always quibble with entries included and excluded. This reviewer was surprised by the lack of a biographical entry on Roger Williams, one of America's earliest proponents of the separation of church and state. In the index under "Williams, Roger," the reader is referred to the entry on "Disestablishment," which is appropriate, but most students of American religious history would expect the historically significant Williams to have his own entry. This, however, is a minor point. Given the current political climate, this encyclopedia is an important and useful addition to the humanities reference shelf.— **John P. Stierman**

Directories

C, P

245.   **Federal Regulatory Directory: The Essential Guide to the History, Organization, and Impact of U.S. Federal Regulation.** 17th ed. Thousand Oaks, Calif., CQ Press / Sage, 2016. 1044p. index. $215.00. ISBN 13: 978-1-4833-8477-1.

Now appearing in a 17th edition, this reference classic provides a comprehensive roadmap to our national government's rule making apparatus: the alphabet soup of regulatory agencies, boards, and commissions; their organization and areas of responsibility; and biographical sketches of major actors and complete contact information, including postal addresses, e-mail addresses, telephone numbers, and websites.

The volume format follows a well-established pattern familiar from earlier editions. "Federal Regulation: An Introduction" is a 43-page primer covering the rationale for governmental control, how this oversight has evolved through the years, regulatory tools, implementation techniques, and so forth. The bulk of the book consists of agency profiles; one appealing aspect of these is the unusually full historical background presented, which allows the reader to trace a particular organization's wax and wane over the decades. A lengthy series of appendixes covering such topics as ordering government publications, use of the Federal Register, and verbatim text of presidential executive orders that are relevant to regulatory matters round out this sizable tome.

A number of special features add to this title's usefulness. In addition to a standard table of contents, there is also a thematic table of contents that lists topics alphabetically by subject, such as agriculture, business, civil rights, and so on, with appropriate agencies appearing under said headings. Separate indexes are provided for names of individuals (commissioners, agency heads, etc.) and subject matter. Organization charts give an at-a-glance overview of agency hierarchy and an annotated list of relevant legislation concerning each agency provides evidence of their accomplishments. Agency publications and libraries, if any, are listed and described.

Careful editing, up-to-date hard data, and ease of use all combine to lend credence to this volume's subtitle: *The Essential Guide to the History, Organization, and Impact of U.S. Federal Regulation.*—**Michael Francis Bemis**

Handbooks and Yearbooks

C, S

246. **American Government. http://www.abc-clio.com/ABC-CLIOCorporate/ product.aspx?pc=AGOVW.** [Website] Santa Barbara, Calif., ABC-CLIO, 2016. Price negotiated by site. Date reviewed: 2016.

ABC-CLIO's *American Government* database provides a thorough overview that students and researchers alike will find useful. The database is broken down into subheadings, which include Foundations of American Government, Legislative Branch, Executive Branch, Judicial Branch, Rights and Liberties, Political Behavior, Domestic and Foreign Policy, Political and Economic Systems, and State and Local Government. Under these broad headings, there are subheadings that allow further exploration of each topic.

One of the many useful features of this database is that it carefully explores reality. Every American schoolchild was taught the basic maxim of American government: Congress makes the laws, the Judiciary interprets the laws, and the President enforces the laws. While the basic maxim remains useful as a roadmap to American government, the current state of our government presents complexities that deserve more than quick platitudes. This complexity is illustrated by the *American Government* database's entry on the Legislative Branch. There are two subtopics: "Congress" and "Congress in Action." The entry on Congress details the basics about Congress—its constitutional authority, the split between the House and the Senate, and the way that districts are apportioned.

The Congress in Action subtopic explores the way that Congress goes about its business on a daily basis. The subtopic includes entries about how a bill becomes a law, the powers of Congress, and congressional committees. Since so much of American government is wrapped up in debate and differing perspectives, there is also a lengthy discussion about whether the filibuster (a common way that the minority party in Congress stalls legislation if they do not have the votes to block legislation outright) is good or bad for democracy and the American system. The entries also contain quizzes so that students can test themselves on what they've learned in addition to a "name that quote" feature that allows visitors to match up a quote with the source of the quote.

The main page of the database also provides a useful blog source, updated frequently, that explores a current topic in American government. For example, in the weeks before the election of 2016, the blog explored the American Electoral College. The blog explored the rationale for the Electoral College as well as arguments for its continued existence and arguments for its abolition. The blog provided cases where the Electoral College served its purpose as envisioned by the founders and cases where the Electoral College provided a different result from the popular vote, including the elections of 1876, 1888, and 2000. Disagreements are presented in a rational, thoughtful manner. Such presentation allows students to consider both sides of a hot-button issue and form their own opinion based on reason.

Overall, the *American Government* database is a helpful resource for students. This database is recommended for academic and high school libraries.—**Sara Mofford**

C, P, S

247. **Ballot Measures Database.** http://www.ncsl.org/research/elections-and-campaigns/ballot-measures-database.aspx. [Website] Free. Date reviewed: 2017.

The *Ballot Measures Database* is hosted by the bipartisan National Conference of State Legislatures. The database is searchable by state, topic (abortion, criminal justice, insurance, military and veterans affairs, term limits), measure type, type of election, election year (the latest year as of this review was 2016), or by simple keyword. Users will find approximately 100 years' worth of data in this easy-to-use site. Selecting Environmental Protection from the Topics list yields, for example, 154 total results. Refining the search by California narrows the results to 38, listed in alphabetic order. The earliest measure, "Prohibiting Tideland Surface Oil Drilling," failed to pass in 1936. In addition to learning whether or not the measure passed or failed, users will find a summary of the measure, the number of the proposition, type of measure (initiative, legislative referendum, popular referendum), and voting percentages. A great place for basic information or for the beginning of a research project. Highly recommended for libraries of all types.—**ARBA Staff Reviewer**

C

248. Burgess, Susan, and Kate Leeman. **The CQ Press Guide to Radical Politics in the United States.** Thousand Oaks, Calif., CQ Press / Sage, 2016. 356p. illus. index. $185.00. ISBN 13: 978-1-4522-9227-4; 978-1-5063-5470-5 (e-book).

"Radical politics" is, by its definition, a nebulous term. One person's radical may be another person's mainstream. Further, calling an individual's politics "radical" may be considered offensive, so anyone writing about this topic must tread lightly—calling an individual "radical" is not often taken with a grain of salt. Nevertheless, Burgess and

Leeman write deftly about American radical politics in the *CQ Press Guide to Radical Politics in the United States.* Burgess and Leeman explore these radical politics through the lens of movements that were either wildly progressive or regressive at the time they were proposed.

These issues include: organized labor and farmer relations; socialism, communism, and other anticapitalist movements; anarchists, militias, and other anticapitalist movements; Native American and Mexican American resistance to U.S. sovereignty; resistance to slavery and black nationalism; the Ku Klux Klan, fascism, and white supremacy; nativism and immigration; gender and sexuality; peace and antiwar movements; environmentalism, environmental justice, and animal rights. The striking point of this list is that some of the movements that are listed, such as the antislavery movement, are seen as mainstream now. In fact, an individual who advocates for slavery nowadays would be seen as beyond radical. However, at the time the antislavery movement was at its peak, opposing slavery was radical. As such, Burgess and Leeman must set the stage to not only define the radical politics, but what makes (or made) the politics radical at the time. A politic can only be radical in comparison to the prevailing views of the day. This task is daunting at first blush, but Burgess and Leeman accomplish it deftly and concisely without sacrificing quality.

The book contains illustrative graphs and photos. These photos usually depict a historical event, though some represent other helpful and interesting historical tidbits. For example, in the early 2010s, the "Occupy" movement emerged to protest what it classified as capitalist greed. One graph contains a list of hand signals used during Occupy meetings to keep the meetings under control. By raising one's hand and forming a letter C, one can ask the speaker to clarify what they are discussing. This fact helps to immerse the reader in the issue at hand. It deepens engagement for the general good of the reader.

Overall, the book is a useful resource for anyone looking to learn more about radical politics in the United States and is a welcome addition to the bookshelf of any scholar of American politics. This book is recommended for academic libraries.—**Sara Mofford**

C

249.   **The CQ Press Guide to Urban Politics and Policy in the United States.** Palus, Christine Kelleher and Richardson Dilworth, eds. Thousand Oaks, Calif., CQ Press / Sage, 2016. 468p. index. $185.00. ISBN 13: 978-1-4833-5003-5.

This compilation examines "the social, political, institutional, economic, and administrative responses to the changing landscape of urban America" (p. 1). Beginning with historical legacies in different geographical areas, 44 chapters are categorized in the following seven parts: The Origins of Urban Politics and Policy, the Urban Political Landscape, City Governing Institutions, The Changing Shape and Place of Urban Governance, The Dynamics of Service Delivery, Balancing Economic Development and Social Justice, and The Interface between Cities and Natural Systems. Within chapters, black-and white-figures, photos, and tables comfortably divide up text; the occasional highlight box includes quotes or definitions. Chapters conclude with notes and suggestions for further reading, and a solid index rounds out the work.

Knowledge and understanding of the layers of government and how they relate to cities in the United States is a fairly new field of study. In an effort to better understand urban politics and policy, these studies explore government structure, specific leadership positions, boards and commissions, state and federal pressure, school districts, urban infrastructure, fiscal issues, resource allocation, and diminishing political engagement.

Humanitarian aspects of immigration, work, welfare, housing, culture, racial and economic segregation, neighborhoods and community development are included in this research collection. Going beyond historical study, this grouping includes chapters that look to the future of U.S. cities; for example, chapter 39 explores research on sustainability.

The CQ Press Guide to Urban Politics and Policy in the United States is best suited for scholars of urban studies, sociology, U.S. history, and political science. Practitioners of urban planning, governance, and public administration will also find this a current, useful resource.

Recommended.—**Janis Minshull**

C, P, S

250.   **C-Span Video Library. https://www.c-span.org/about/videoLibrary/.** [Website] Free. Date reviewed: 2017.

Cable network channel C-Span devotes round-the-clock coverage to the work of the American federal government. In addition to some moderated public affairs broadcasting, the channel offers extensive coverage of live political events. This database hosts over 200,000 videos of C-Span's political programming reaching back nearly 40 years. Users will find C-Span coverage of a host of events, such as press briefings, congressional debate, rallies, town hall meetings, new conferences, confirmation hearings, and much more. The site also includes videos for the network-moderated Washington Journal, a series including panel discussions and in-studio interviews with policy-makers, advocates, and other experts discussing the pressing issues of the day.

The site continually uploads videos and clips as they are made available. Users can scroll through a display beginning with the most recently uploaded videos, or can search for a particular video or clip using a variety of filters, such as tag, date, organization (e.g., the White House, U.S. Senate, etc.), location, and event type.

Access to the site is free, but creating an account allows users to create and save video clips for later use. This database is an ideal way to explore the mechanisms of the federal government up close and would be a vital source for students and educators in a number of fields, from media to public policy to history and beyond.—**ARBA Staff Reviewer**

C, P, S

251.   **Dark Money Watch. http://darkmoneywatch.org/.** [Website] Free. Date reviewed: 2016.

Limited Liability Corporations (LLCs) and political nonprofit organizations can receive unlimited amounts of money from individuals without ever disclosing donation information. *Dark Money Watch,* a project of the nonpartisan nonprofit, MapLight, is devoted to exposing the role of this dark money in politics and the influence hidden political donors have on the U.S. political system.

There is an impressive amount of easily accessible information on this freely available site. Importantly for those who might be dubious of claims about nonpartisanship, there is also a link to the MapLight main page where users can research sponsors, the advisory board, the tax returns, and major accomplishments of the organization that produces *Dark Money Watch.* Additionally, the site is easily navigable from tabs at the top of the main page: How Dark Money Works, Key Players, News Coverage, Data, and About Us. As users drill down from these main tabs, they will find bountiful information on the history of dark money; the people and companies behind super PACs; how much dark money is in political campaigns; dozens of news stories on dark money (updated regularly); tools for investigating dark money, including video of advertisements and the geographical areas in which they aired; and so much more.

Highly recommended to all public, high school, and college libraries.—**ARBA Staff Reviewer**

C, P, S

252. **Freedom of Information Act Electronic Reading Room. https://www.cia.gov/ library/readingroom/.** [Website] Free. Date reviewed: 2017.

The Freedom of Information Act (FOIA) Electronic Reading Room, accessible under the Library tab of the CIA's main page (https://www.cia.gov/index.html) is home to a wealth of materials, particularly CREST, the CIA records search system, made publicly accessible online in January 2017. Left-side navigation offers a list of such links as How to File a FOIA Request, Annual Reports of the Chief FOIA Officer, Frequently Requested Records, Historical Collections, FAQs, CREST, and a link to the Daily Presidential Briefings for Nixon, Ford, Johnson, and Kennedy. Frequently Requested Records include documents on Nazi war crimes, UFOs, human rights in Latin America, and accused spies Ethel and Julian Rosenberg, among others. Under the CREST link, researchers can access the subset of CIA records reviewed and released under Executive Order 13526, which requires the declassification of nonexempt, historically valuable records 25 years or older. CREST is currently home to more than 11 million pages of records, which are divided into collections. The collection names are listed once the CREST link is accessed. Advanced Search and Search Help links, which are quite useful with a database of this size, appear at the top of all pages.—**ARBA Staff Reviewer**

C, P, S

253. **The National Journal. www.nationaljournal.com.** [Website] Washington D.C., National Journal, 2017. Price negotiated by site. Date reviewed: 2017.

This site hosts paid access to expert research, tools, journalism, and data covering U.S. government affairs and policies. The site derives from the now obsolete *National Journal* magazine which was in circulation for nearly 50 years. Subscribers have access to a variety of daily journalism (*National Journal Daily, The Hotline,* etc.) covering current events and political issues. They can also make use of specialized tools (editable slides, studies, networks, etc.) helpful in advancing advocacy plan(s), among other things. One such tool is *The Almanac of American Politics*—a necessary who's who in American government. Other proprietary products available to subscribers include the Race Tracker, the Policy Brands Roundtable, The Network Science Initiative and more. Subscribers can customize their membership to include all or some of the online products. Nonsubscribers have limited access to article teasers (essentially, the headlines) and samples of *National Journal* resources and data. The content of this site would be extremely useful to many policy-makers, lobbyists, political science students, educators, and others, if the price is right.—**ARBA Staff Reviewer**

C, S

254.   **The Powers of the U.S. Congress: Where Congressional Authority Begins and Ends.** Brien Hallett, ed. Santa Barbara, Calif., ABC-CLIO, 2016. 298p. index. $89.00. ISBN 13: 978-1-4408-4323-5; 978-1-4408-4324-2 (e-book).

The Powers of the U.S. Congress is a manageable one-volume book which explains the 21 congressional powers enumerated in the Constitution of the United States. From the power to borrow money to the power to establish post offices and post roads, 19 authors (or teams of authors) take on a power and discuss not only its meaning but any controversies the power has encountered from the time of adoption to the present, as well as those that may be encountered in the future.

For instance, in chapter 11, author Brien Hallett discusses the power to declare war. This has historically been a confusing power. What constitutes a "legitimate" declaration? Who can make the declaration and are there specific steps that must be followed? How will property seized during wartime be treated–who will own it? The government? The captor of the property? These and many other issues are tackled in this one chapter.

The other 18 chapters go equally in depth about their specific topics and also include a list of further readings that may be of interest. Appendixes containing the Articles of Confederation and Perpetual Union and the Constitution of the United States are at the end of the volume, as well as a fairly detailed index.

The Powers of the U.S. Congress is an excellent resource both for those who are just beginning to study the powers of Congress as well as those whose scholarship touches on these issues. It would be a welcome addition to any high school or college library.—**Alicia Brillon**

C, P, S

255.   Wilson, Harry L. **Gun Politics in America: Historical and Modern Documents in Context.** Santa Barbara, Calif., ABC-CLIO, 2016. 2v. illus. index. $189.00/set. ISBN 13: 978-1-4408-3728-9; 978-1-4408-3729-6 (e-book).

The use of guns has remained a controversial issue in American politics and culture for over 225 years. Proponents of personal ownership of guns cite the U.S. Constitution's Second Amendment and the need for personal protection against criminal or terrorist acts to which law enforcement and the military cannot immediately respond. Opponents of personal firearms ownership maintain that too many mentally ill people owning guns are a threat to societal safety and cause the deaths of innocent individuals.

This work explores the historical and contemporary political controversies involving gun politics in the United States. It opens with a contextual introduction on this topic and features a historical chronology documenting important firearm, legal, legislative, and political developments between 1680 and 2014. Work contents are highlighted by chapters featuring documents on this perennially contentious political subject from the colonial era to the present. Each chapter begins with an introductory overview describing the political environment of the period in which the documents were produced. Chapter one "Guns in a Frontier Nation" features documents such as the Connecticut Firearm Impressment Law (1756); Divergent Views of the Citizen Militia: Webster (1787) and Madison (1788); and State Court Decisions Define the Right to Keep and Bear Arms (1822-1859).

Other subjects addressed in these volumes include firearms regulation in the post-Civil War South and the Western frontier; Prohibition Era violence; confrontational politics in the 1960s; intensified divisions over gun control in the 1980s-1990s; legal victories for gun rights in the 2000s; and first-term Obama Administration gun control and gun rights political debate. Additional work contents include public speeches, court decisions, congressional testimony, commission reports, the text of laws and political debate, statistical tables for sources such as the FBI's *Crime in the U.S.: Uniform Crime Reports.* photographs, and detailed bibliographic references representing multiple sources and perspectives.

Gun Politics in America is an even-handed, insightful, and valuable resource which will be useful to individuals discussing this contentious subject regardless of their political perspective. Highly recommended.—**Bert Chapman**

Public Policy and Administration

Handbooks and Yearbooks

C, P, S

256.   Levin-Waldman, Oren M. **The Minimum Wage: A Reference Handbook.** Santa Barbara, Calif., ABC-CLIO, 2016. 354p. illus. index. (Contemporary World Issues). $58.00. ISBN 13: 978-1-4408-3394-6; 978-1-4408-3395-3 (e-book).

The Minimum Wage: A Reference Handbook is a title within the ABC-CLIO Contemporary World Issues series, which is about important issues our society is currently facing. Other titles in the series include books on GMO food, fracking, illegal immigration, and prescription drug abuse. The author is from academia with experience in public policy and employment with an interest in wages. While it has a strong U.S. perspective it does include international content.

The book is well organized with a table of contents, preface, glossary, index, and author description. The chapter layout and titles are understandable, and the book provides a well-rounded description of the minimum wage including its history, controversies, arguments for and against it, interested parties on both sides, and a chronological history. It also includes statistics, related documents, and resources for further research. The glossary helps identify unfamiliar terms. This reference title provides a very good overview of what even novice readers may need to know surrounding the controversial issue of minimum wages plus help in identifying other resources for further research. This title is easy to read and would be appropriate for students researching the minimum wage issue.—**Breezy Silver**

P

257.   **USDA Disaster Reference Guide. http://www.usda.gov/wps/portal/usda/ usdahome?navid=reference-guide.** [Website] Free. Date reviewed: 2017.

This free site from the U.S. Department of Agriculture Disaster Reference Center offers a comprehensive guide to programs and information related to assisting farmers, ranchers, and their communities in case of a disaster. The page allows users to scroll through a listing of federal programs and the disaster-related issues they address. These issues are generally arranged under the broader themes of Technical Assistance,

Disaster Payments for Agricultural Losses, Loans/Credit, Risk Management/Insurance, Conservation and Land Management, and Household and Community Water Supplies. From the left sidebar, users can also search for resources affiliated with particular disaster events, such as Wildland Fire, Drought, Pests & Animal Disease, and more. They can also select from a listing of Local/State Help organizations like the American Red Cross. Users will also find links to a number of Resources & Factsheets such as blogs, reports, and apps. Browsing and search options seem to function within the greater USDA site. Users can also connect with this site via a good variety of social media.—**ARBA Staff Reviewer**

14 Psychology, Parapsychology, and Occultism

Psychology

Directories

P

258.   **The Complete Mental Health Directory 2016/2017.** 10th ed. Amenia, N.Y., Grey House Publishing, 2016. 587p. index. $165.00pa. ISBN 13: 978-1-61925-915-7.

Now in its 10th edition, this directory provides users with reliable and timely information in an easily navigable format. The book begins with an introduction and table of contents followed by a 40-page report, *The State of Mental Health in America 2016, State Mental Health Legislation 2015,* the *Bill of Rights for Children's Mental Health Disorders and Their Families,* and a list of mental disorders by category (cognitive disorders, psychotic disorders, etc.). There is also a user's guide followed by a user's key. The remainder of the nearly 600-page book is divided into eight sections: Disorders; Associations & Organizations; Government Agencies; Professional and Support Services; Publishers; Facilities; Clinical Management; and Pharmaceutical Companies. There are three indexes: "Disorder Index," "Entry Index," and "Geographic Index." This is followed by one appendix, "Drugs A-Z, by Brand Name." The indexes refer to entry numbers in the book, which are clearly marked. The 21 chapters in the first section, Disorders, begin with a description of the disorder (such as stress disorder, anxiety disorder, or suicide) followed by an alphabetic listing of such resources as associations & agencies, books, and websites. Details for each listing can include contact information, the name of the founder or director, a brief description, and more. This book gathers an enormous amount of information in one place, saving professionals and caregivers valuable time. The title is also available at http://gold.greyhouse.com. Recommended for academic, medical, and public libraries.—**ARBA Staff Reviewer**

Handbooks and Yearbooks

P

259.   Cullinane, Diane. **Behavioral Challenges in Children with Autism and Other Special Needs: The Developmental Approach.** New York, W. W. Norton, 2016. 350p. index. $37.95. ISBN 13: 978-0-393-70925-4.

Cullinane has developed a framework and details of methods to be used to shape a child's behaviors. The developmental approach has been described for many years with most recognizing Piaget as the father of this approach. Most public schools in the United States follow the ideals of the developmental approach, so this book can support those interventions and provide the necessary steps to provide consistency across settings. Though parents and professionals may have knowledge of typical developmental milestones, they often question that knowledge when one's own child shows signs of not meeting those milestones due to behavioral issues outweighing their progress.

Many parents of children with behavioral problems ask what they can do to help their child, and this book provides suggestions and step-by-step directions on how to use the techniques prescribed. Cullinane provides a healthy description of why some children exhibit more difficulty with self-regulation and a stronger inclination to our primitive fight-or-flight reactions. Helping parents to obtain historical information about the child's milestones may also help the parents to determine the skills their child demonstrates and those he/she may need help with. Providing parents with play-based observation guidelines could prove very useful in determining which skills to teach and what materials might help the child acquire those skills. Guidance regarding the need to understand intent or purpose of behavior is extremely important in order to enable parents to select the correct techniques that help the child adapt behaviors.

Though Cullinane provides great information about behaviors and why they happen at different developmental stages, one of the most helpful sections of the book is that on creating a plan from chapter nine. After identifying the underlying emotional functions of behaviors, it is important to develop a long-term plan including long- and short-term goals which are carefully described to each reader along with a table for modifiers for goals to help individualize the plan. Especially important is the description of the DIR (Developmental, Individual Difference, Relationship-Based) approach and the parents' role in helping their child with behavioral issues through play and natural environmental variables. This book offers parents and professionals another option to helping their child acquire acceptable behaviors through methods and techniques described.—**Donna J Kearns**

P, S

260. **Mental Health Disorders Sourcebook.** 6th ed. Keith Jones, ed. Detroit, Omnigraphics, 2016. 695p. index. (Health Reference Series). $85.00. ISBN 13: 978-0-7808-1484-4; 978-0-7808-1483-7 (e-book).

This sixth edition of the *Mental Health Disorders Sourcebook* presents the most recent advancements in mental health information. Managing Editor Keith Jones worked with an advisory board and a medical review team to enhance this latest edition. Entries note, in the subsection headings, the most recent review of information by senior medical professionals.

Following the template of other volumes in the Health Reference Series, this 695-page book begins with a table of contents where mental health subjects are divided into seven primary topics spread out over 55 chapters. "Part VIII: Additional Help and Information" includes chapters 56-58 where terms are explained, hotline information is listed, and contact information for further help is offered. Sections are further divided into chapter topics; for example, part one introduces positive brain health with seven chapters on how to create mental health wellness. Chapters are then divided into deeper detail with subsections such as Pets Are Good for Mental Health. The further delineation of topics is a practical tool for those searching for information. Categorization is effective in the *Mental Health Disorders Sourcebook* and the index will be the quickest access point with its very solid listings.

Mental illness encompasses a broad spectrum of illnesses and populations. This resource addresses common topics of suicide, addictions, and bipolar disorder. Less common psychiatric issues such as Pediatric Autoimmune Neuropsychiatric Disorders Associated with Streptococcal Infections make this book more valuable. Information on mental health is positive and practical with data on best practices, medications and alternative treatments, symptoms, therapies, and mainstream treatments. Useful for the layperson, explanation of professions of psychologist, psychiatrist, and therapist are found in both text and visual form.

The *Mental Health Disorders Sourcebook* will be best suited for the patient, caregiver, family, and general public. Whether newly diagnosed or a chronic condition, young or old, this is a worthwhile introduction to how the brain works and mental health concerns.

Recommended.—**Janis Minshull**

P

261.   Noonan, Susan J. **When Someone You Know Has Depression: Words to Say and Things to Do.** Baltimore, Md., Johns Hopkins University Press, 2016. 134p. index. $16.95pa. ISBN 13: 978-1-4214-2015-8; 978-1-4214-2015-5 (e-book).

As the title suggests, this quick read is designed to educate individuals who know someone suffering from depression. It is less a reference source and more a beginner's handbook written by an author who is a medical doctor and has a degree in public health. It is also meant to serve as a companion to the author's first book, *Managing Your Depression.* Intended for a general audience, the information is rich and serves as an excellent starting point for those unfamiliar with the manifold symptoms of mood disorders. This text is a much-needed addition to mental health literature, as depression is stigmatized and few understand how to support friends and loved ones who frequently do not obtain help on their own. This text also addresses care for the growing population of caregivers, making it even more valuable.

The language used is very basic, and the book is divided into nine chapters with a conclusion. The author skillfully provides psychoeducation about mood disorders and addresses signs and support for those afflicted, approaches for treatment, and recovery. Tables and charts, such as the Risk Factors for Suicide or the Sample Completed Mood Chart, can serve as useful tools that will help readers assess and assist loved ones who exhibit symptoms of depression. The brief glossary is comprised of terms that most readers have likely heard before, such as "Bipolar Disorder" and "Cognitive Behavior Therapy," but also includes jargon widely used in academia, such as "triggers" and "cognitive distortions." A resources page includes literature, organizations, and online information that could provide additional information. The index is understandably short given the length of this book, though the references page is thorough and organized by chapter.

This is an informative read that will better equip readers to notice symptoms of depression among peers and feel comfortable providing support. It is not intended to be a substitute for professional mental health treatment, but it will serve to spread awareness for growing mental health issues and is recommended for larger public libraries.—**ARBA Staff Reviewer**

P

262.   Rado, Jeffrey, and Philip G. Janicak. **Living with Schizophrenia: A Family Guide to Making a Difference.** Baltimore, Md., Johns Hopkins University Press, 2017. 144p. index. $17.95pa. ISBN 13: 978-1-4214-2143-8.

True to its title, this book is designed to assist caregivers and family members of those diagnosed with schizophrenia. It is a reference source that contains valuable, yet basic, information about a disorder that is still stigmatized today. While it is not intended to replace professional mental health or medical intervention, this guide addresses symptoms, causes, and medication treatments, as well as behavioral and psychosocial approaches families can implement. Without minimizing the lifelong difficulties individuals with schizophrenia face, Living with Schizophrenia equips readers with knowledge and optimism for the long-term.

The book has a brief preface, seven chapters that address causes and treatment options, and a short conclusion that summarizes the key points of the book. A small notes section contains additional resources that are more academic. The index is thorough and will be extremely helpful for readers who are particularly interested in exploring treatment options, as the majority of the terms reference medical/therapy interventions and describe the benefits and neurological side effects of each. This text would be an excellent addition for a Health/Wellness and Psychology section in a public library, and its brevity and affordability are huge selling points.—**ARBA Staff Reviewer**

C

263.   **SAGE Video Counseling & Psychotherapy Collection. http://sk.sagepub. com/video/counseling-psychotherapy.** [Website] Thousand Oaks, Calif., Sage. Price negotiated by site. Date reviewed: 2016.

SAGE has gathered this grouping of educational videos, the *SAGE Video Counseling & Psychotherapy Collection,* for use in counseling and exploration of differing methods and topics in counseling and psychotherapy. Publication dates are as early as 2001 with the vast majority of the videos from 2015.

Video selection involved finding and evaluating films from the Counseling & Psychotherapy Central Awarding Body and Psychotherapy Networker. Authors and editors of these films are from a vast network of sources around the globe. This collection includes more than 430 videos and 120 viewing hours. Many films are exclusive to this SAGE compilation though other collected works, such as *Dancing with Disappointment* (Urquhart Publishing), are part of this assemblage. Films range from a short discourse to films that are up to two hours in length.

The collection is easily accessed with five overall categories of Counseling Setting/Client Groups, Counseling Skills, Professional Issues, Research Methods for Counseling and Psychotherapy, and Theory & Approaches. Video titles are listed with a simple click to link to each video. Videos are of quality both visually and aurally. Each video has a brief abstract for further evaluation of the film. Films are well transcribed with a search option for finding specific information in the text. SAGE has clear page demarcation with large tabs for Add to List, Citation, Embed, Help, and Share options. A side tab, SAGE Recommends, suggests books, journals, and other materials related to the video topic.

The inclusion of multiple topics ensures that this collection will be useful to those in many areas of counseling, therapy, or study. Psychotherapy types (cognitive, dance, music, etc) give practical examples into use of therapies. The in-depth coverage of counseling gives substance to this collection; abuse, addiction, career, depression, grief, and trauma are covered as well as many more. Perhaps most useful will be films which cover active listening, assessment, reflective practice, therapeutic relationship process, and other hands-on counseling skills. Often in real-life context, videos show client and practitioner interaction.

This collection is a strong overview of contemporary practice in counseling methods and techniques. Insights into best practices and how to incorporate these therapies into a patient/practitioner session make these videos sensible for use. The Professional Issues header will be a supportive resource group for those in practice. These evidence-based films will be best put to use by both beginner and experienced therapists, students and scholars of psychotherapy, and others interested in current counseling style and methodology.

Highly recommended.—**Janis Minshull**

C, S

264.   **SAGE Video Psychology Collection. http://sk.sagepub.com/video/psychology.** [Website] Thousand Oaks, Calif., Sage. Price negotiated by site. Date reviewed: 2016.

SAGE Video has created a psychology collection that has over 400 videos containing 134 hours of material pertaining to all levels and types of psychology. The collection is divided into 11 subjects ranging from biological/physiological psychology to social psychology. Curated for the novice student each subject provides basic informational videos for the corresponding psychology subsubject and then digs deeper with case studies, tutorials, and interviews. An abstract, publisher information, publication year, content type, and subject accompany each video, along with keywords associated tagged to the video content. Viewers can also follow along with the interactive video transcript.

This collection encompasses an almost overwhelming amount of information concerning all different types of psychology. It is recommended for the novice learner, but the viewer needs to understand that they will be exposed to a copious amount of information. With the more challenging topics such as theories the collection has a nice range of presentations in the collection. For instance, Dr. Christian Kloeckner from the Norwegian University of Science and Technology explains the theory of planned behavior. Kloeckner regularly sites peer-reviewed research and even provides the viewer with research citation on the screen. Kloeckner explains the theory by providing the viewer with a graph and talks the viewer through each part of the graph. Along with explaining the graphs Kloeckner provides real life examples to help the learner relate the theory of social behavior to their life. This type of strategy in presentation creates a trustworthy and effective way of teaching the subject to novice pupils.

The collection also includes thought-provoking documentaries such as *A Great Mystery* which explores consciousness during sleep and sleep research/disorders. The video has interviews with experts, tutorials of research studies, past videos from actual cases/research studies, and illustrations. With all of the added supplemental items the viewer is able to not only listen to the speakers, but also to visualize the subject matter. In one portion of the video, viewers can relate to the point of view of someone who does not get enough sleep. The added supplemental material has a strong impact on new learners of psychology.

Instructors will find this collection useful to their curriculum as a supplemental component during classroom time. Instructors could also use it as part of a flipped instructional strategy in order that their students could view it outside of the classroom in order to prepare for in-class discussion and instruction.

Highly recommended for academic libraries and high school libraries.—**Sara Mofford**

P

265.   Trainor, Kathleen. **Calming Your Anxious Child: Words to Say and Things to Do.** Baltimore, Md., Johns Hopkins University Press, 2016. 249p. index. $18.95pa. ISBN 13: 978-1-4214-2010-3; 978-1-4214-2011-0 (e-book).

The idea that their children may not outgrow certain perplexing behaviors can overwhelm parents, as many of these behaviors can disrupt a child's social, academic, and emotional development. It is crucial that parents know how to distinguish between normal childhood fears and anxieties and those that can ultimately disrupt this development. This book offers clear, step-by-step guidance for navigating a child and their family through a variety of anxiety-related behaviors.

An early chapter explains the author's own methodology: the eponymous TRAINOR Method, which simplifies the standard Cognitive Behavioral Therapy and incorporates a whole family plan into a child's treatment. Chapters then segue into addressing many common forms of childhood anxiety, such as separation anxiety, obsessive compulsive disorder, and post-traumatic stress.

Chapters provide background on the particular disorder, introduce readers to a family dealing with it, then lay out the step-by-step plan that the family adopts to address it. Chapters also include brief follow-ups to the case and a listing of DSM-5 (Diagnostical and Statistical Manual of Mental Disorders, 5th edition) guidelines for identifying each chapter's disorder. A concluding chapter moves treatment beyond the family and therapist to discuss medications, school involvement, medical tests, alternative treatments and parental support.

Readability and usability is enhanced by the book's organization, accessible writing style, and index. Recommended.—**ARBA Staff Reviewer**

15 Recreation and Sports

General Works

Directories

P

266. **Parks Directory of the United States.** 7th ed. Pearline Jaikumar, ed. Detroit, Omnigraphics, 2016. 1157p. index. $195.00. ISBN 13: 978-0-7808-1424-0.

The seventh edition of *Parks Directory of the United States* is a treasured resource that is a necessary addition to the library of any individual who enjoys exploring nature in North America. When most hear "parks," they think of the great national parks so beloved and engrained in the popular culture, such as Yellowstone National Park. Yellowstone is a treasure to be enjoyed by all, but did you know about Eden Park in Cincinnati, Ohio, five miles east of downtown Cincinnati? Eden Park's 156 acres contain picnic areas, trails, lakes, gardens, a conservatory, an art museum, and a planetarium among other features. This is an example of the usefulness of the *Parks Directory of the United States.*

The book is large, which may make it inappropriate for frequent transport. It contains significant information on lots of natural sites for individuals to explore, including: national parks, state parks, national forests, national grasslands, national wildlife refuges, national scenic and historic trails, national marine sanctuaries, national heritage areas, Canadian national parks and national park reserves, parks and conservation related organizations and agencies, urban parks, and scenic byways.

Each entry contains details on location, size, facilities, activities, and special features as well as addresses, phone numbers, contact emails, and websites. While the entries on each park are admittedly short, the entries are intended to be a starting point for exploration of a park, not the extent of the reader's exploration of the park. The book serves as a more than sufficient jumping off point for further exploration.

One useful feature of the book is the number of maps it contains. This feature is especially useful for travelers who are looking to explore parks along their travel route. It is easy to imagine, for example, a traveler looking for a short respite during a journey and finding a convenient park for a short picnic, and a brief walk of the traveler's canine companion.

Overall, the book is useful for individuals who are frequent visitors to parks. The book provides a convenient directory for both casual and devoted park visitors. The updated seventh edition is valuable to all visitors as it contains useful internet links, email addresses, and updated phone numbers for the appropriate contact information at each park. This book is recommended to public and academic libraries.—**Sara Mofford**

Handbooks and Yearbooks

P

267. Harper, Richard. **Bizarre Competitions: 101 Ways to Become a World Champion.** New York, Firefly Books, 2016. 256p. illus. index. $19.95pa. ISBN 13: 978-1-77085-862-6.

"The Most Weird & Wonderful Championships From Around the Globe," screams out on the second page of this bizarre and eye-catching book like a warning of what is to come. Anyone who likes the unconventional, as most everyone does once in a while, will find this book hard to put down. Even the contents are unusual with a small picture of each contest in order from no.1) Bee Wearing to no. 101) Speed Knitting. So, by skimming the seven pages of the contents, you can go directly to the one contest that catches your fancy. How does Worm Charming in Cheshire, England, Outhouse Racing in Nevada, or Toe Wrestling in Derbyshire strike you? If you desire a less bizarre contest, there is Mountain Unicycling in Canada, Window Cleaning in Florida, Chainsaw Carving in Wisconsin, or Dog Racing in Alaska.

Each of the bizarre competitions is explained in one to four pages of colorful and often outrageous pictures, with explanations of the events printed usually on top of the pictures. A colorful banner on top of each page tells the basic facts: where, when, number of competitors, world record, equipment, dangers, etc. Several paragraphs of wit and whim about the competitions whet the appetite with tips for participants or viewers. An index and lists of websites for sources and further information is also helpful for readers who really want to compete or show further interest. However, anyone will get a chuckle out of this fun book even if they don't want to become a world champion.—**Georgia Briscoe**

C

268. **Sports Leadership: A Reference Guide.** Mark Dodds and James T. Reese, eds. Santa Barbara, Calif., Mission Bell Media, 2015. 560p. illus. index. $130.00. ISBN 13: 978-0-9907300-1-9; 978-1-78539-258-0 (e-book).

Sports is woven into the fabric of our everyday lives whether it be in the form of Cleveland's NBA championship or the recent 2016 Rio Olympics. Sports is big business at all levels and leadership is a major component of the process, among players, coaches, and fans. This one-volume reference guide includes over 100 entries by nearly 80 contributors on topics in sports ranging from high school to professional sports focusing on the issue of leadership among athletes, coaches, management, education, and business. The rather lengthy essays on leadership qualities include *see also* references and suggestions for further reading. Examples are a three-page entry on NASCAR and a set of four summaries of media portrayals on cable television, radio, women, and the print media. These represent some of the innovation presented in the volume. Other features include a brief chronology, a six-page resource guide, an index, and an extensive glossary with nearly 1000 listings. The glossary is unique in that there are virtually no sports references—the emphasis is on leadership concepts. Two examples reflect this emphasis—the My Lai Massacre and

Sigmund Freud. A different approach to reference literature, *Sports Leadership* is targeted at an academic audience and deserves a place in college and larger public libraries.—**Boyd Childress**

Baseball

C, P, S

269.   **Digitalballparks.com: Your Virtual Baseball Stadium Museum. http://www. digitalballparks.com/.** [Website] Free. Date reviewed: 2017.

Eric and Wendy Pastore, the authors of *500 Ballparks,* a 2016 Firefly publication, provide the contents of this virtual baseball stadium to the public free of charge. The database contains thousands of captioned black-and-white or color photographs of ballparks throughout the United States and Canada (with about a dozen more from Mexico, the Netherlands, and Germany). Many of the more recent photographs were taken by the Pastores. There are several ways to search the site from the home page, but there is no basic search screen. Searches can be conducted by state (ballparks are listed in alphabetic order), by major league team, by triple-A team, and by defunct leagues, among other options. A sample search of the San Francisco Giants, accessed under the link for major league teams, provides a sense of what can be found on the site. The photographs are grouped into four categories. The oldest are views of the ballpark where the Giants played in New York in the 1900s. There are also photographs of the spring training ballparks used by the Giants over the years and photographs of ballparks used by their triple-A, double-A, and other teams. Some of the captions that go along with the photographs are longer than others, but users will get a sense of the history of the ballparks and the franchise. The site is not entirely up to date. In the case of the Giants, for example, there are no photographs of the team's current ballpark.

The site is not terribly sophisticated, and it lacks the polish and definitive character of the authors' book. The lack of a basic search screen to allow for searches of something like Negro National Leagues seems particularly regrettable. Nevertheless, the sheer quantity of photographs makes this a site worth looking at, either for casual purposes or as part of a larger research project.—**ARBA Staff Reviewer**

P

270.   Pastore, Eric, and Wendy Pastore. **500 Ballparks: From Wooden Seats to Retro Classics.** 2d ed. New York, Firefly Books, 2016. 399p. illus. index. $39.95. ISBN 13: 978-1-77085-751-3.

This intriguing book provides information on 500 ballparks, listed in alphabetic order and ranging from early examples in the nineteenth century to modern stadiums. The ballparks covered include those played in by major league, minor league, and Negro league teams. Ballpark architecture lost much of its original character in the turn to steel and concrete in the mid-twentieth century, but the so-called retro movement in the late twentieth century brought back some of the original charm of the earlier parks. Ballpark design, according to the authors, is in the midst of another transformation.

Users can read the book cover to cover, use the alphabetic listing at the front of the book, or simply thumb through the pages. Colored tabs on the upper portion of each page indicate the ballpark under discussion. For each park, there is at least one captioned color and/or black-and-white photograph. A text box insert provides information about the ballpark that can include the location and address, the name it is also known as, the architect, the date opened, the capacity, the dimensions, and noteworthy games played. For some ballparks, this text box also indicates the demolition date. Entries range in length from approximately half a page to two pages. Descriptions are typically a few paragraphs.

Descriptions provide details about the structure but also about the teams and owners. For example, the Dyckman Oval (named for the family who owned the property for more than 400 years) was opened in 1920 in Manhattan and was the home field of the New York Cuban Stars who played in the Eastern Colored League. They were owned by Alejandro Pompez whose illegal activities forced them to withdraw from play in 1937 and 1938. New York City demolished the ballpark to create a parking lot in 1938.

The book concludes with just over seven pages that list information for ballparks that do not have more extensive coverage in the main part of the book. An index rounds out the work. While this would be a nice addition to a coffee table, there is a lot of information for someone interested in further research on the Negro leagues, ballpark architecture, baseball, or more. Recommended for public libraries.—**ARBA Staff Reviewer**

Hiking

P
271.   Brown, Michael H. Carrie L. Stambaugh. **Hiking Kentucky: A Guide to 80 of Kentucky's Greatest Hiking Adventures.** 3d ed. Guilford, Conn., Falcon Guides, 2016. 359p. illus. maps. index. $24.95pa. ISBN 13: 978-1-4930-1256-5; 978-1-4930-1451-4 (e-book).

This third edition treats readers to 80 hikes around the diverse and beautiful state of Kentucky, from the Appalachian Mountains to the bottomlands and rolling fields. The introduction briefly covers Kentucky geology, history, and weather, noting that the state is home to many rivers and lakes, two national parks, more than 12 U.S. Army Corps of Engineers reservoirs, and over 160 state parks, forests, wildlife areas, and nature preserves. There is also a section on how to use the guide that includes basic information about the best seasons to hike certain portions of the state, trail and safety ethics, and essential tips on how to leave no trace, keeping food away from animals, and more. For those who are interested in particular types of hikes, a table lists those that are best for backpacking, waterfalls, geology lovers, small children, great views, and for lovers of nature, history, and lakes. A map legend is also included. Individual hike descriptions include information on fees and permits, trailhead facilities, other trail users, difficulty level, where to find more detailed maps, hiking time and distance, parking, and directions. Each hike has a color photograph and a basic map that outlines the trail route.

This engagingly written book is recommended for public or personal libraries.—**ARBA Staff Reviewer**

P
272.   Gaug, Maryann. Sandy Heise. **Hiking Colorado: A Guide to the State's Greatest Hiking Adventures.** Guilford, Conn., Falcon Guides, 2016. 396p. illus. maps. $24.95pa.

ISBN 13: 978-1-4930-1419-4; 978-1-4930-1420-0 (e-book).

"Hiking is one of the best ways to explore Colorado," according to the authors and supported by this reviewer. Hikers of the 50 featured hikes in this guidebook will experience the wonderful scenery, geology, human history, flora, and fauna of Colorado. An additional 18 "honorable mention" hikes offer even more opportunities.

This book selects, organizes, describes, and illustrates with color photographs and maps some of the best hikes in the state. Hikes are organized by seven geographic regions, starting with the "Eastern Plains" and ending with the "Southwest." Nine to 12 hikes are described in each region. Each region begins with a sweeping overview of the area and a regional map. A "Trail Finder" chart by region allows one to find the best hikes for whatever your particular interest: waterfalls, fishing, geology, dinosaurs, bagging peaks, taking your dog, exploring canyons, etc.

Each description of the 68 numbered hikes starts with a quick overview and facts of the hike including: start location, distance, approximate hiking time, difficulty, elevation gain, trail surface, nearest town, canine compatibility, fees, and "Find the Trailhead" with GPS coordinates. This is followed with a longer narrative section of the author's impression of the trail which is well researched and written. There are excellent color maps and mile-by-mile directions telling the hiker what to expect at each turn. Finally, a "Hiker Information" section offers nearby restaurants, accommodations, and local events. The book is peppered with interesting fact boxes such as "Ute Indian History," "If you Meet a Rattlesnake," and "Bristlecone Pines."

There are many guides published for hiking in Colorado. This is one of the best that covers the entire state.—**Georgia Briscoe**

P

273.   Hansen, Eric, and Kevin Revolinski. **Hiking Wisconsin: A Guide to the State's Greatest Hikes.** Guilford, Conn., Falcon Guides, 2016. 261p. illus. maps. $22.95pa. ISBN 13: 978-1-4930-1873-4; 978-1-4930-1874-1 (e-book).

This second edition of *Hiking Wisconsin* from Falcon Guides is a full-color, fully updated description of 71 trails in the Badger State, retaining nearly all trails from the first edition. The full-color greatly enhances the quality the trail maps and the appeal of the trails themselves—the colors that you will actually see along the trail. Sixty trails are covered in detail (the text has been updated where needed) while 11 trails are "honorable mentions," having no accompanying map and little descriptive detail. In addition to the color, this second edition places all information about the particular trail within its section: GPS coordinates of trailheads; any local contact information (trail jurisdiction or responsibility, local tourist office); trail surface; nearest town; fees or permits; other trail users (is it a ski or snowmobile trail in the winter, equestrians, bicycles); land status; schedule (time the trail is open if there is such a limiter). The "hike finder" from the first edition has been replaced by a much easier to use "trail finder" which lets you find best hikes for kids, dogs, water lovers, birders, views, geology buffs, and nature lovers. The occasional stand-alone paragraph has been added, describing details (historical, geological) of the region near some hikes. A book of this nature must be selective, and the author's stated goals are "to find and catalog the best natural ambience in the state," find trails that offer a strong connection to the natural world, samples of what is unique, and what is pleasurable to the eye. This collection of hikes certainly shows off natural Wisconsin and will encourage the reader to search for more hikes in any particular area. While the chapters, and therefore the trails, have been divided into regions, the state overview map shows no defined regions. This guide (and other updated ones like it) will become dog-eared from much use.—**Bruce Sarjeant**

P

274.   Hurst, Robert. **Hiking through History Colorado: 40 Hikes from the Great Sand Dunes to Bobcat Ridge.** Guilford, Conn., Falcon Guides, 2016. 260p. illus. maps. $22.95pa. ISBN 13: 978-1-4930-2292-2; 978-1-4930-2293-9 (e-book).

The subtitle of this Falcon Guide is "40 Hikes from the Great Sand Dunes to Bobcat Ridge." These hikes include many enjoyable classic Colorado hikes. What makes this guide special is the historical explanation of each of the hikes and hiking areas. As someone who has hiked most of the 40 hikes, I learned a lot of fun history from reading the folksy historical information about each hike.

The hikes are divided into five geographic regions of Colorado. After selecting the region you want on the statewide map, you can browse the hikes by region or use the "Trail Finder" to find the best hikes for families, dogs, views, lakes and streams, etc. Each hike has the very useful Falcon Guide "Where to Hike Series" formulaic colored box. First is a general short description of the hike; second is a list of facts like the starting location, distance, hiking time, difficulty, canine compatibility, fees, etc. Last in the box is a detailed "Finding the Trailhead" with GPS coordinates.

After the handy box of information on the hike, comes the much longer description of the hike with all the historical and archaeological information. Mingled with the several pages of delightful history are color pictures and maps. Finally, each numbered hike has a "Miles and Directions" list giving mile-by-mile quick instructions.

A few historical pictures and sidebars add great interest for the reader. They cover topics like Doc Holiday, the Marksbury Incident, grizzlies, and local Indian legends. The author has published many popular Falcon Guidebooks and this one will surely be a winner.—**Georgia Briscoe**

P

275.   Julyan, Robert. **Hiking to History: A Guide to Off-Road New Mexico Historic Sites.** Albuquerque, N.Mex., University of New Mexico Press, 2016. 209p. illus. maps. index. $24.95pa. ISBN 13: 978-0-8263-5685-7.

Hiking to History takes readers to 22 off-road historic sites in the land of enchantment. In the vein of other books like Jeffrey Ryan's *Appalachian Odyssey* (Globe Pequot, 2016), this book nicely blends historical and personal narratives with hiking descriptions, producing a result as unique as it is difficult to classify.

There is much for both avid hikers and for lovers of New Mexico history. For those fascinated with the Taos Art Colony, for example, there is a chapter describing the author's quest to find the "Sacred Site," the place in the Sangre de Cristo mountain range where the wagon of the colony's founders broke down. For Civil War enthusiasts, there is a chapter tracing trails used in the Battle of Glorieta Pass while those interested in the Depression Era can trek to Civilian Conservation Corps camps in the Sandias. Some of the violence in New Mexico's past is evoked in the description of the expedition to find the marker for the murder site of John Tunstall, killed during the Lincoln County War. Indian and white clashes are recounted as the author tries to discover routes in Dog Canyon. Maps and black-and-white photographs enhance the tale telling. GPS coordinates and references to visitor centers and other guidebooks give readers a place to find more information on the hikes and the history.

Though not a hiking guide in the traditional sense, this work would be a great hiking companion. More likely to be found in the circulating collection than on the reference shelf, *Hiking to History* is highly recommended to public libraries in New Mexico and to anyone with a love of New Mexico history and hiking.—**ARBA Staff Reviewer**

P

276.   Molloy, Johnny. **Hiking through History New England: Exploring the Region's Past by Trail.** Guilford, Conn., Falcon Guides, 2015. 245p. illus. maps. index. $22.95pa. ISBN 13: 978-1-4930-0146-0; 978-1-4930-1441-5 (e-book).

The beauty of New England's natural environment and its history are a natural fit. From hikes around locks on canals in Connecticut to climbing Mount Katahdin in Maine individuals have unique opportunities to craft adventures of their own. Part of the Falcon Guide's Where to Hike series, *Hiking through History* covers 40 hikes spread throughout the six New England states, providing ample opportunities for a variety of historical and outdoor experiences. Each hike is a gateway into the region and its history and a pathway to enjoying the natural environment.

Well organized with color photographs, informative background material, trail maps, and route directions, the volume is a useful framework for the intersection of history and the natural world. The inclusion of a selection table in the introduction categorizing the hikes by subjects (stories of people, industrial history, dog friendly, etc.) is welcomed. Another handy feature of the volume is the appendix with standard information on what to bring for equipment, safety precautions and first aid, hiking with dogs, and trail etiquette. The connection with the American Hiking Society will bring additional readership to the volume. An interesting notice in the introductory material requests readers to contact the author or publisher of possible changes or updates to any of the hikes presented, an interesting way to connect a paper volume with its readership in this age of instant updates. *Hiking through History* is recommended for any library collection, but especially for those with collecting interests in history, New England, the environment, and outdoor recreation. Certain libraries may want to consider two copies, a reference and a general, circulating collection copy, due to the nature of the work and the potential interest in patrons taking it along on their hike through history.—**Gregory Curtis**

P

277.   Scheidt, Laurel. **Hiking Sequoia and Kings Canyon National Parks.** 3d ed. Guilford, Conn., Falcon Guides, 2016. 344p. illus. maps. index. $22.95pa. ISBN 13: 978-1-4930-2302-8; 978-1-4930-2303-5 (e-book).

This third edition starts with an introduction to the parks, a user guide, instructions on how to make a hiking or backpacking trip safe, a trail finder, lists of the author's favorite hikes, and a map legend. Here readers will find information on campfire rules, obtaining backcountry permits, interactions with wildlife, the best hikes for wildflowers, the best hikes for high altitude scenery, hikes to skip if you want to avoid other people, and much more.

The author provides information about 86 hikes, grouping them according to area:

the foothills, the giant forest, the central high Sierra Nevada, the Lodgepole and Dorst areas, Grant Grove, the Redwood Canyon area, Cedar Grove and Monarch Divide, the Mineral King and South Fork area, and the Jennie Lakes Wilderness. Reproduced color photographs and maps enhance the trail descriptions. An insert also provides necessary details, including hiking time and distances, fees and permits, and trail surface.

The book concludes with three appendixes that supply readers with additional contact information, further reading suggestions, and a checklist for hikers and backpackers.

This guide masterfully covers a large and incredibly diverse area and is recommended for public libraries.—**ARBA Staff Reviewer**

P
278.   Swedo, Suzanne. **Hiking Yosemite National Park: A Guide to 61 of the Park's Greatest Hiking Adventures.** 4th ed. Guilford, Conn., Falcon Guides, 2016. 308p. illus. maps. index. $22.95pa. ISBN 13: 978-1-4930-1772-0; 978-1-4930-1773-7 (e-book).

Updated and revised with color maps and images, this Falcon Guide to hiking Yosemite National Park is a must have for both day hikers and backpackers on extended trips. The author, Suzanne Swedo, is an experienced hiker, director of an adventure travel company, and has taught natural history seminars in Yosemite for 30 years. Hikes are grouped under geographical locations within the park, e.g. the Valley floor, South Rim of Yosemite Valley, High Sierra Camps, etc. The entry for each hike begins with a highlighted summary, including start location, total distance, difficulty, time to complete, elevation change, seasonal access, nearest facilities, permits required, relevant USGS map, and special considerations. Also included in the summary is a two-to-three sentence description of where to find the trailhead. All of this information is particularly handy when determining where to hike and whether a trail fits your abilities. Following the summary is a one-page description of the hike itself. Swedo provides incredible details about where to turn and what you will see at those points, along with trail conditions and scenic highlights. Each hike concludes with a colored trail map and a table of mile markers and navigation points. Added features include a brief overview of Yosemite, including life in the park, geology, history, and human impact considerations. A trail finder chart allows you to identify hikes by specific features: back country lakes, waterfalls, alpine areas, no hills, day hikes, solitude, early season accessibility, and areas known for wildflowers or wildlife. This chart makes it easy to identify hikes that meet your particular needs at the time. An appendix provides a further reading list on the flora, fauna, geology, and backcountry camping considerations for Yosemite. Another appendix provides a hiker's checklist of gear and supplies. Overall, it is hard to find anything negative about this book. It offers all the details necessary for identifying and navigating hikes, along with providing scenic descriptions and colored images. Highly recommended for all public libraries.—**Kevin McDonough**

Mountaineering

P
279.   Fitch, Nate, and Ron Funderburke. **Climbing: From Sport to Traditional Climbing.** Guilford, Conn., Falcon Guides, 2016. 152p. illus. $14.95pa. ISBN 13: 978-1-4930-1640-2; 978-1-4930-2527-5 (e-book).

This guide offers a handy resource for practitioners of one of the more technical pursuits of outdoor recreation: climbing. Specifically, the guide defines "sport climbing" and "traditional climbing" and lays out how enthusiasts can transition from the former to the latter as they develop in the sport.

An opening chapter reviews essential information readers presumably know to this point, emphasizing the need for interdisciplinary experience (bouldering, indoor climbing, etc.) and a progressive approach to skill mastery. Subsequent chapters explore more advanced topics along the lines of equipment, top belays, anchors, rappelling, emergency preparedness, and more.

The guide makes good use of such things as color photographs, charts, bullet points, and shaded text boxes to clearly organize and illustrate the information. Technical terms (e.g., load sharing, elongation, etc.) are defined, common errors (e.g., incorrect rope diameter) are explained, and equipment and methods are compared.

One in a series, this compact guide offers specialized information highly suited to readers seeking a concise and easily portable resource on the sport of climbing. Recommended.—**ARBA Staff Reviewer**

P

280.	Meehan, Chris. **Climbing Colorado's Fourteeners.** Guilford, Conn., Falcon Guides, 2016. 276p. illus. maps. $22.95pa. ISBN 13: 978-1-4930-1970-0; 978-1-4930-1971-7 (e-book).

Climbing one or more of the 14,000' high peaks in Colorado is a goal of many. Several excellent guidebooks are available. This new one is especially written for the novice. It is organized by difficulty (easy, hard, harder, hardest) rather than traditionally by mountain range. First timers therefore shouldn't find themselves on a difficult and dangerous peak by unknowingly selecting a peak that looks pretty or is close by.

The book has an initial 20-plus pages of introductory information to help beginners plan their trip. Included are the usual warnings of lightening and weather, discussion of the 10 essentials, briefings on flora and fauna, but also "How not to Hike a Deadly Fourteener." The author admonishes to "learn from my stupidity" and wear proper clothing, have proper gear and training, etc.

Following the Falcon Guide, "Where to Climb Series" formula, each fourteener has a chapter with a colored box containing a short description of the peak followed by data points (start, distance, time, elevation gain, difficulty, trail surface, maps, etc.) and a "Find the Trailhead" with GPS points. After the box is a more detailed and longer description of the hike or climb with a route map, color photo, and mile-by-mile points. The descriptions include interesting history and anecdotes. Many Colorado visitors and locals want to climb the highest peak in the state, Mt. Elbert, which is fortunately number eight in the "Easy" section and therefore doable by anyone with good fitness, endurance, and ability to handle the altitude. Lastly in the chapter for each peak are listed nearby outfitters and the most popular restaurants and breweries of the vicinity.

As someone who has climbed all the fourteeners, I will recommend this book to my grandsons and anyone heading out to bag a fourteener for the first time.—**Georgia Briscoe**

Outdoor Life

P

281.   Bartley, Natalie L. **Best Rail Trails: Pacific Northwest.** 2d ed. Guilford, Conn., Falcon Guides, 2015. 344p. illus. maps. $24.95pa. ISBN 13: 978-0-7627-9706-6; 978-1-4930-1478-1 (e-book).

Fortunately for outdoor enthusiasts, many abandoned railroad lines now serve as trails for hikers, bikers, runners, horseback riders, cross-country skiers, and others. This book highlights many of the best rails to trails routes in the Pacific Northwest—the states of Washington, Oregon, and Idaho.

The book's introduction summarizes the rails to trails movement, discusses trail etiquette, contains pointers for how to get involved in the rails to trails movement, and includes a how-to-use-the-book guide and a legend. The book is then organized by state, with Washington followed by Oregon and Idaho.

The entry for the Deschutes River Trail in eastern Oregon provides a nice example of the thorough information available in this guide. The trail description begins with a legend that indicates the activities allowed on the trail; here users will also find data about the GPS coordinates, the trail location and length, the terrain, whether or not the trail is wheelchair accessible, the location and availability of bathrooms and food, seasonal closures, and rental and bus route information. Users will also find directions and information about parking access. In addition, the author provides a well-written description of the trail. A full-page, easy-to-follow map and a reproduced photograph (in color) complete the description.

Highly recommended for public libraries in the Pacific Northwest.—**ARBA Staff Reviewer**

16 Sociology

Aging

P
282.   **AARP. http://www.aarp.org/.** [Website] Free. Date reviewed: 2017.

This freely available site acts as a clearing house for ideas and issues related to the interests of people of retirement age. A small menu tab leads to a wide range of lifestyle topics, such as Money, Politics & Society, Work & Jobs, Health, and Entertainment. Each of these menu topics leads to a wealth of more information in the form of tips, blog posts, product reviews, and more. AARP-specific topics, like member benefits, access to the magazine, Spanish translation, etc. can also be found under the menu tab. Users can also scroll through the page to peruse the same menu options.

The large amount of information is well managed into sections, opening with Today's Highlights, Your Membership, Daily Picks (related to previously mentioned menu topics), Working For You, Making a Difference, and more. The bottom of the page is a display of AARP member discounts and benefits, a popular component of the program. The site makes it easy to join AARP or renew a membership with Renew/Join tabs at the top of the page and throughout the site. Membership ($16 per year) is priced for affordability.—**ARBA Staff Reviewer**

C, P
283.   **Aging Stats. https://agingstats.gov/.** [Website] Free. Date reviewed: 2017.

Aging Stats is a freely accessible federal government site that links users to statistical information compiled on Americans 65 and older by the Federal Interagency Forum on Aging Related Statistics. The site is easy to navigate from the home page which features seven main search tabs. Under the Home tab, users will find links to downloads of the most recent report: *Older Americans 2016: Key Indicators of Well-Being.* Users can download the entire report (approximately 200 pages) or individual sections of the report (Population, Economics, Environment, Health Status, Health Risks and Behaviors, Health Care, Special Feature: Informal Caregiving, and Figures). Based on availability, users can request a hard copy of the report from the Government Publishing Office (contact information for copy requests is available under the Frequently Asked Questions tab). Those curious about the member agencies that comprise the interagency forum, such as the Department of Veterans Affairs, the Social Security Administration, and the Census Bureau, can find this information under the About tab. Previous reports for 2000, 2004, 2006, 2008, 2010, and 2012 are accessible by section or as a whole book under Data.

The Resources tab takes users to a glossary, links to the websites of federally sponsored surveys relevant to aging, and past reports like one from 2009 *Data Sources on Older Americans*. The Contacts tab not only provides information on agency contacts but also provides contacts by subject area like demographics, health, or economics. For those who want to look for a specific topic, there is a basic Search tab. This basic search is more useful if one is familiar with the report topics (prescription drugs, sources of income, marital status, long-term care providers), so it is advisable to open the current or older reports to view the table of contents.—**ARBA Staff Reviewer**

C, S

284.   **Gerontology: Changes, Challenges, and Solutions.** Madonna Harrington Meyer and Elizabeth A. Daniele, eds. Santa Barbara, Calif., Praeger/ABC-CLIO, 2016. 2v. index. $131.00/set. ISBN 13: 978-1-4408-3426-4; 978-1-4408-3427-1 (e-book).

Gerontology is the study of the social, psychological, and biological changes that take place as people age. The discipline represents an interdisciplinary field that draws from the expertise of multiple professions to encompass everything from research to care and advocacy for aging adults. The number of older adults in the world's population is higher than it has ever been, and that statistic will increase as medical advancements extend lifespans. The older population in 2030 will be twice as large as it was 2000. According to a report from agingstats.gov, it will grow from 35 million to 71.5 million and represent nearly 20% of the total U.S. population.

Gerontology was produced under the editorship of Madonna Harrington Meyer, professor and chair of sociology at Syracuse University and faculty associate of the Aging Studies Institute and senior research affiliate at the Center for Policy Research at Syracuse University, and Elizabeth A. Daniele, doctoral student and fellow in sociology at Syracuse University. The set provides an up-to-date, multidisciplinary, and forward-thinking look at the key areas and issues in gerontology; highlights links between topics and relevant demographic, social, economic, and health trends with implications for immediate and long-range work in aging; includes contributions from experts in the fields of sociology, psychology, medicine, education, politics, and government; identifies the key changes, challenges, and solutions in each subfield; includes an appendix containing lists of descriptions and contact information for aging organizations as well as an annotated list of documentaries about aging; and offers figures and tables, current references, and an expanded index.

This title makes a meaningful contribution to the humanitarian future and compassionate care of senior citizens. The publisher is primarily dedicated to creating unique, useful, and thoughtfully crafted resources that librarians and their patrons trust. The editors facilitate the discussion of a sensitive topic in an easy-to-understand and thought-provoking manner. This contribution is essential for twenty-first-century trends in psychology, social work, nursing, physical therapy, business, and sociology, etc. High schools, community colleges, and universities will value this set as an essential addition to their library reference shelves. Health care professionals, organizations, and public libraries will also benefit from purchasing this timely publication as a reference book.—**Thomas E. Baker**

P

285.   **Older Americans Information Directory.** Amenia, N.Y., Grey House Publishing, 2016. 1157p. index. $165.00pa. ISBN 13: 978-1-61925-907-2.

The *Older Americans Information Directory* is "designed for one of America's largest growing populations, with resources to help aging Americans lead happy and productive lives." This resource contains A Profile of Older Americans, analyzing statistical trends from sources including the U.S. Census Bureau, the National Center for Health Statistics, and the Bureau of Labor Statistics. Additionally, it includes directories of national organizations, government agencies, continuing education agencies, and more. There is also a Health Chapters section which includes listings of associations and organizations, books, directories, newspapers and magazines, websites, and resource centers related to health issues, including aging, AIDS, cancer, heart disease, hearing and visual impairment, and strokes; a directory of both independent and assisted living facilities, by state; legal aid resources; libraries and information centers; and travel and recreation agencies. Glossaries of health and medical terms as well as legal terms also serve as helpful research tools. Resources are indexed by entry name, geographic location, and subject. Each entry for agencies includes name, address, phone, fax, website, officers, purpose, and year founded. Each entry for publications includes: title, address of publisher, telephone number, fax, email address, editors, and annotation. The *Older Americans Information Directory* is an excellent resource and is of use to seniors looking for continuing education courses, travel opportunities, and ways to improve their quality of life. It also should be of great value to children caring for elderly parents. This resource brings together in one volume a wealth of information to assist elderly Americans. Highly recommended to public libraries, especially.—**Lucy Heckman**

Death

C, S

286.   Ball, Howard. **The Right to Die: A Reference Handbook.** Santa Barbara, Calif., ABC-CLIO, 2017. 369p. illus. index. (Contemporary World Issues). $60.00. ISBN 13: 978-1-4408-4311-2; 978-1-4408-4312-9 (e-book).

This volume in the Contemporary World Issues series is written by Howard Ball who is a political scientist with a specialization in constitutional law, the federal judiciary, civil rights, and the international community's responses to war crimes, crimes against humanity, and genocide. The book is divided into seven chapters. Chapter five provides data and documents, chapter six provides resources, and chapter seven is a chronology of right to die movements, legislation, court decisions, and more beginning in 1906. Customary back matter includes a glossary, index, and author biography.

Who decides when life is no longer of value? How does the U.S. Constitution fit in with the end of life debate? Is assisted suicide unlawful? Unethical? The battle in the right to die or live controversy is entrenched in ethical, medical, social, legal, and political debate. This handbook presents both sides of this life or death matter and examines the roles of individuals, groups, the country, and states. Aiding the process of death may have constitutional support but opponents provide a horde of ethical, religious, legal, and medical principles to counter this issue. This book guides researchers to both sides of the debate and options for extended study are available.

As a reference tool, *The Right to Die* will be useful to high school and undergraduate students studying medicine, sociology, and political science. This will also be beneficial to health care professionals, patients, and families concerned with options for those who are terminally ill.

Recommended.—**Janis Minshull**

Disabled

C, P

287.   **The Complete Directory for People with Disabilities,.** 25th ed. Amenia, N.Y., Grey House Publishing, 2016. 1044p. index. $165.00pa. ISBN 13: 978-1-61925-927-0.

This massive directory (more than 1,000 pages) begins with an introduction, glossary, user guide, and user key. The table of contents lists the 31 chapters and more than 100 subchapters, facilitating use. The directory will save busy caregivers and professionals time by providing reliable information in a straightforward manner. Here users will find information on such things as camps (listed by state), education (both general listings and listings by state), independent living centers (listed by state), services for veterans (including both federal and state), and federal and state agencies. The table of contents allows users to skip directly to an entry, but guide words at the top of the page help those who want to thumb through the volume. In addition there are three indexes that refer to directory listings by entry number: "Entry & Publisher Index," "Geographic Index," and "Subject Index." Once an entry is located, users will find basic contact information, the name or names of key executives, a brief description, and more (book listings, for example, will provide an ISBN number, price, and number of pages). The title is also available at http://gold.greyhouse.com. Recommended for academic, medical, and public libraries.—**ARBA Staff Reviewer**

Gay and Lesbian Studies

C, P, S

288.   Hillstrom, Laurie Collier. **Defining Moments: The Stonewall Riots.** Detroit, Omnigraphics, 2016. 234p. illus. index. $60.00. ISBN 13: 978-0-7808-1442-4.

This volume clearly provides a solid introduction to the modern struggle for LGBTQ rights that grew out of the events in New York City in June and July, 1969, tracing the impetus for many of the changes now in place to the Stonewall Riots. The text is straightforward and geared toward high school and undergraduate students. It also provides study topics to consider while reading the book, making it a possible textbook, too. Like other volumes in this series from Omnigraphics (Prohibition, *Roe* v. *Wade,* the Lewis and Clark Expedition, the Cuban Missile Crisis, etc.), this work is arranged in three sections: narrative overview, biographies, and primary sources. Included as well are a brief bibliography and a chronology running from 1869 to 2015. Numerous photographs enhance the narrative.

Libraries serving high school students and undergraduates, as well as public libraries, should consider adding this volume to their collections.—**Mark Schumacher**

C, P, S

289. **Wearing Gay History. http://www.wearinggayhistory.com/.** [Website] Free. Date reviewed: 2017.

This website, hosting a digital gallery of LGBT themed t-shirts, offers a novel approach to documenting the underserved history of the LGBT population. Users can choose from one of four menu categories to access the gallery. Exhibits presents seven curated virtual exhibits offering noteworthy perspectives on LGBT expression. "The Ones That Laughed: Humor in the LGBT Community" explores the use of comedy to advance its message and "A Lesbian Capital: 'Odd Girls' in Washington D.C." chooses shirts capturing lesbian advocacy in a city dominated by men's concerns. T-shirts displays the catalog of nearly 4,000 shirts of both domestic and international origins. Users can browse by tag or map and search by keyword, collection, tag, and more. T-shirt/artifact description includes thumbnail photographs (which can be enlarged), front and back text, general description, applicable tags, and collection of origin. Users are also able to send comments about each t-shirt. Collections provides a general description of 18 distinct collections from which this digital gallery drew. Clicking on a specific collection (e.g., Canadian Lesbian and Gay Archives—Toronto, Ontario) allows users to view its contents. T-shirt Map allows users to view collection locations and access them as well. A thought-provoking site, www.wearinggayhistory.com cleverly shows how a casual garment can signify the currents of social history. Helping to both celebrate the diversity within the LGBT culture and emphasize its union, the site would appeal to civil rights advocates, social scientists, and educators across a number of fields.—**ARBA Staff Reviewer**

Substance Abuse

C, S

290. Newton, David. **Prescription Drug Abuse.** Santa Barbara, Calif., ABC-CLIO, 2016. 370p. illus. index. (Contemporary World Issues). $60.00. ISBN 13: 978-1-4408-3978-8; 978-1-4408-3979-5 (e-book).

Drug problems impact all people and all nations and *Prescription Drug Abuse: A Reference Handbook* is a vital addition to the Contemporary World Issues series which is a diverse series including environmental, criminal, and cultural topics of the twenty-first century. Authored by David E. Newton, this entry into the series is a compendium of resources on the issue of prescription drug abuse.

Published by ABC-CLIO in 2016, this 392-page title is available in both hard copy and e-book format. The publisher's digital version allows for access to chapters and subsections with an easily navigated table of contents and a page scroll capability on the lower page. Tables provide statistical data as current as possible to enhance the dialogue. Black-and-white photos begin each chapter but add no value to the text.

Chapters begin with a brief one- or two-paragraph introduction. Each chapter concludes with extensive reference listings of books, studies, and websites. Prescription drug abuse appears as a modern problem, but chapter one introduces the researcher to the history of this problem in societies on a global level over the course of time. Chapters three and four provide essays and descriptions of individuals and representatives of organizations that deal with some aspect of nonmedical use of prescription drugs. People such as Felix Hoffman who first developed both aspirin and heroin in 1897 (p. 193) or groups such as the National Institute on Drug Abuse (p. 209) are gathered in these sections.

A true reference handbook, *Prescription Drug Abuse* looks at this issue as not a new problem but one that has taken on a different variation. With over 44,000 drug-related deaths in 2013 (as quoted from the CDC on p. 141), this is the leading cause of accidental death in the United States. Author Newton has incorporated information, essays, studies, resources, and references that address the abuse of drugs and the adverse effects that this has in society today. This resource is a strong collection of data which will provide a platform for furthering research.

Prescription Drug Abuse is a solid entry in the Contemporary World Issues series and will be of interest to students at the graduate and postgraduate level as well as for researchers in the areas of sociology, medicine, psychology, and cultural history. The vast resources may also be useful to those working in drug-abuse-related professions.

Recommended.—**Janis Minshull**

S

291. Newton, David. **Youth Substance Abuse: A Reference Handbook.** Santa Barbara, Calif., ABC-CLIO, 2016. 350p. index. $61.00. ISBN 13: 978-1-4408-3982-5; 978-1-4408-3983-2 (e-book).

This title, part of a multivolume set on contemporary world issues, provides a comprehensive look at youth substance abuse. This reference work includes sections on background and history (primarily in the United States), problems, issues, and solutions, individual perspectives, profiles, data, and documents pertaining to youth substance abuse. It contains an extensive annotated bibliography and chronology dating from 10,000 B.C.E. through the present. Also included are primary source documents resulting from laws and court cases dealing with youth substance abuse. This reference covers information on a wide range of drugs and their effects, causes, treatment, and prevention. This is a well-developed reference resource for high school libraries. Highly recommended.—**Cynthia Foster**

S

292. **Tobacco Information for Teens: Health Tips about the Hazards of Using Cigarettes, Smokeless Tobacco, and Other Nicotine Products.** 3d ed. Keith Jones, ed. Detroit, Omnigraphics, 2017. 362p. index. (Teen Health Series). $69.00. ISBN 13: 978-0-7808-1387-8; 978-0-7808-1413-4 (e-book).

Comprised of information on tobacco use and products, health consequences, cultural influences, and cessation, this title is directed at junior and senior high school students. Overseen by a medical review team, this third edition is revised for accuracy with the most current information available. The first 58 chapters are divided into the following sections: Facts about Tobacco and Nicotine, Nicotine Delivery Systems, Cancers Associated with Tobacco Use, Other Health Concerns Related to Tobacco Use, and Tobacco Use Cessation. Each chapter investigates one specific tobacco topic. Because of the health risks associated with the use of tobacco, all current products are discussed, and then chapters describe significant information on cancer and other diseases attributed to tobacco use. The final section, If You Need More Help or Information, includes chapters 59-61 where readers will find options for getting help, a directory for health effects, and smoking cessation resources.

Black-and-white tables and figures throughout help document data, and highlighted text boxes introduce significant facts. This title concludes with a comprehensive index.

This reference tool will be a useful addition to middle and high school libraries for use with all students, and especially for studies in health, sociology, and human development.

Recommended.—**Janis Minshull**

Youth and Child Development

P, S

293.   **Abuse and Violence Information for Teens: Health Tips about the Causes and Consequences of Abuse and Violent Behavior.** 2d ed. Keith Jones, ed. Detroit, Omnigraphics, 2017. 326p. index. (Teen Health Series). $69.00. ISBN 13: 978-0-7808-1456-1; 978-0-7808-1455-4 (e-book).

This second edition is a relevant tool for tweens and teens needing guidance, looking for information, or researching for a class assignment. The various sections categorize types of abuse, violence specific to teens, consequences of violence, prevention, safety, and legal rights for victims. Part five may be particularly useful for teens traversing the murky waters of abuse and violence as it lists state-by-state options for help. The index is a solid navigation tool for students seeking specific subject matter.

Students in middle and high school cope with a myriad of tough social issues today. Whether for personal use or for attainment of knowledge, this compilation will bring students to a better understanding of the tragedy of abuse and violence. Statistics are both sobering and critical. The use of U.S. government documents is reliable for research, and while the prevalence of abuse and violence is unsettling, the book brings the information into balance with pragmatic chapter topics on conflict resolution, helping others, knowing what healthy relationships look like, and other positive informational supports.

Abuse and Violence Information for Teens provides pragmatic information for middle school and high school students seeking preventive guidance, warning signs, medical statistics, and risk factors on abuse and violence. Librarians, guidance counselors, and health professionals working with this age group will want to have this resource available.

Recommended.—**Janis Minshull**

C

294.   **The SAGE Handbook of Early Childhood Research.** Ann Farrell, Sharon L. Kagan, and E. Kay M. Tisdall, eds. Thousand Oaks, Calif., Sage, 2015. 576p. index. $150.00. ISBN 13: 978-1-4462-7219-0; 978-1-4739-2085-9 (e-book).

Young children are catching the attention of researchers around the world. SAGE Publications, under the direction of editors Ann Farrell, Sharon Lynn Kagan, and E. Kay M. Tisdall, has amassed information on research and its implications on the early childhood community. In 31 chapters divided into five sections, international experts share conceptual and methodological challenges, discoveries, and direction of study in what is termed inclusively as "early childhood services"; with a broad variance of definition for this youngest population, the handbook targets research options for children from birth through age eight.

Articles, research theory, videos, and actual studies on topics of early intervention, cognitive and social development, and relational costs are specific to research with young children. Adherence to ethical means of research and a keen eye to human rights are considered in study approach. Program-based studies as well as longitudinal research are addressed here. Editors remark on the disproportionate amount of studies in the Global North, due to better education and economic strength, as opposed to the Global South. This gap is just one of the many reasons for the sharing of research information.

There is a sense of urgency in finding answers for challenges and taking theoretical information and transforming that into strong methodologies for research, analysis, and dissemination of information on a global scale. Section five looks to the future and considers what is next in this field of research. The UNICEF Report, "State of the World's Children" (2014), reports that 18,000 children under the age of five die every day. Sobering information, yet through confident tools, including *The SAGE Handbook of Early Childhood Research,* early childhood research will create a world of possibilities and opportunities.

This handbook will be very useful to scholars, researchers, and practitioners exploring the latest on research process and approach for this population. Highly recommended.—**Janis Minshull**

C
295.   **Youth Cultures in America.** Simon J. Bronner and Cindy Dell Clark, eds. Santa Barbara, Calif., Greenwood Press/ABC-CLIO, 2016. 2v. illus. index. $189.00/set. ISBN 13: 978-1-4408-3391-5; 978-1-4408-3392-2 (e-book).

Youth Cultures in America, a two-volume set, offers an extensive overview of the cultural traditions of modern and historical youth (defined as ages 2-30) groups. A valuable resource for students and researchers, this authoritative set aims to "guide users to the broad spectrum of groups, expressions, and issues in youth culture and fill in those gaps of knowledge as well as inspire future study along cultural lines for emergent communities and evolving traditions" (xxi). While its primary focus is on America (defined as the United States, Mexico, and Canada) this work recognizes the influence of other global cultures as is seen in the entries for Anime and Manga, Celtic Groups, and Francophone and French Heritage Groups, to name a few. The 165 alphabetically arranged entries examine youth identities in the cultural settings of home, school, work, and play. Entries fall into the following categories: challenges youth face (e.g., Bullying); shared interests (e.g., Occult and Supernatural); musical creativity and fandom (e.g., Emo Music); generational classifications (e.g., Gen X); sports and games (e.g., Martial Arts); and body and health (e.g., Disabled Groups). This set is unique in its focus on the cultural aspects of youth rather than psychological ones. This encyclopedia acknowledges the diversity of American youth cultures and explores issues such as race, class, gender, and cultural expectations. Each entry provides social and historical background information on the designated youth culture and includes examples of its traditions. See also and further reading references directing readers to related material are found at the end of each entry. The table of contents, list of entries, and topic finder are repeated in each volume. Volume two contains a detailed general index and a selected bibliography of books and websites related to youth culture in America. This resource provides a wealth of information on a topic that is not covered in great depth in other sources, thus making it a valuable addition to reference collections. This encyclopedia is recommended for academic and large public libraries.—**Lisa Morgan**

17 Statistics, Demography, and Urban Studies

Statistics

United States

C, P, S

296.   **Vital Statistics of the United States 2016.** 7th ed. Hattis, Shana Hertz, ed. Lanham, Md., Bernan Press, 2016. 408p. index. (U.S. DataBook Series). $121.00; $119.99 (e-book). ISBN 13: 978-1-59888-854-6; 978-1-59888-855-3 (e-book).

Published by the federal government as a multivolume work until 1993, now published as a single volume by Bernan Press, this 7th edition, like its Bernan predecessors, yields essential demographic and health information, compiled by various government agencies, about the population of the United States. Part one, Birth, includes 60 tables ranging from birth rates for teenagers to Cesarean births together with two pages noting sources of the data, notes on the data, and concepts and definitions. Part two, Mortality, offers 44 tables together with the sources, notes, concepts, and definitions on topics such as Life Expectancy and Death Rates from selected causes. Part three, Health, offers 78 tables on such subjects as Cancer Incidence Rates and Cigarette Smoking among Adults together with sources, concepts, and definitions. The relatively brief part four, Marriage, a new chapter in this edition, provides only three tables as well as sources, concepts, and definitions and could certainly be expanded in future editions. All tables are clearly identified first by part number and then in numerical sequence within each of the four parts of the book.

The most recent statistics date from 2014 but many tables reflect government figures compiled in earlier years. For some users this volume's utility may be hampered by the puzzling idiosyncrasies of its index. In the index, capitalized boldface headings lead to subtopics or cross-references and numbers indicate pages, not tables. Under index letter A, ALASKA NATIVES, AMERICAN INDIANS OR ALASKA NATIVES, and ASIAN OR PACIFIC ISLANDERS boldface headings appear, but African Americans do not appear at all. Under B, the reader finds BLACK RACE in boldface, no subtopics, and a single cross-reference to RACE. Under RACE are a host of subtopics leading to tables where results are reported by race, including Black or African American statistics. In contrast, under H, boldface entry HISPANIC ORIGIN yields many subtopics complete with page references. Index limitations aside, this dense, compact volume is a rich source of research data for readers ranging from high school students to scholars in many disciplines and has value for all but the smallest libraries.—**Julienne L. Wood**

International

C, P, S

297.   **OECD Factbook 2015-2016: Economic, Environmental and Social Statistics.** **http://www.oecd.org/publications/oecd-factbook-18147364.htm.** [Website] Free. Date reviewed: 2017.

The Organization for Economic Cooperation and Development has produced this online version of its *Factbook* covering the years 2015-2016. The report displays a wide array of economic, environmental, and social data for the 35 OECD-affiliated countries (in addition to Russia, Brazil, China, India, Indonesia, and South Africa if information is available). This edition has been updated with new indicators reflecting a more regional focus. Nearly 100 data points are encapsulated within 11 topical chapters: "Population and Migration," "Production," "Household Income and Wealth," "Globalization," "Prices," "Energy and Transportation," "Labor," "Environment and Science," "Education," "Government," and "Health." Chapters are similarly structured throughout, beginning with a textual summary of the indicators including an overview, definitions, and resources for further research, followed by a series of applicable tables and graphs. Individual data is downloadable and easily connected with various social media. The online information is free to all users but interested parties can purchase a print/PDF version as well. The up-to-date and easily accessible data in this website would be useful to a number of educators, policy-makers, social scientists, and others.—**ARBA Staff Reviewer**

Urban Studies

C, P, S

298.   **Atlas of ReUrbanism.http://forum.savingplaces.org/act/pgl/atlas.** [Website] Free. Date reviewed: 2017.

In concert with the National Trust for Historic Preservation (NHP), *The Atlas for ReUrbanism* functions as a dynamic data tool for use by city planners, urban leaders, redevelopment advocates, students, and others as they work to incorporate the NHP ReUrbanism Initiative into their work. The initiative directs the preservation and incorporation of older buildings into urban planning and development.

The free-to-use atlas is well designed and easy to navigate. Users can select from a basic menu to access data alongside a number of other features. Maps links to an interactive tool whereby users can "explore the built environment" of roughly 50 U.S. cities. Pins on the map identify those cities and allow users to mesh a building's "character score" (building size/age, diversity, etc.) with external demographic, economic, and environmental data. San Francisco, Los Angeles, Cleveland, Philadelphia, Austin, and Chicago are just some of the cities profiled, with others soon to be added. Downloadable Fact Sheets offer a graphic sketch of each city in terms of population density and diversity, economy, and more. This information is then matched up against a series of building/preservation data. The Summary Report gathers site data into one downloadable report. Stories contain a wide range of posts featuring such things as neighborhood profiles, webinars, project assessments, and book excerpts. And the Preservation Green Lab (PGL) is a hub of accessible research, policies, and tools promoting sustainable urban development from the individual building on up. Some of the PGL reports include "Saving Windows, Saving Money: Evaluating the Energy Performance of Window Retrofit and Replacement" and "The Greenest Building: Quantifying the Environmental Value of Building Reuse."—**ARBA Staff Reviewer**

C, P, S

299.   **City-Data.com. http://www.city-data.com/.** [Website] Free. Date reviewed: 2017.

This is a free-to-use database owned and operated by Advameg, Inc., an Illinois-based company founded in 2000. As of July 2016, more than 14 million users visited *City-Data.com* on a monthly basis. Its popularity has not gone unnoticed—the database has been featured in more than 120 books and by CNN and other news outlets.

Data is accessible from several entry points, including a number of tabs across the top of the home page: Cities, Schools, Neighborhoods, Assessments, Restaurants, Sex Offenders, Blog, Canada, and More. Much of the same information is found via other search tools, including a Quick Navigation map, an interactive data map, and a text box that allows searching by cities, schools, neighborhoods, assessments, and restaurants by state. By scrolling down the home page, users will also find the Blog on all sorts of city-related issues, a Forum, which is open to members (membership is free), and City Guides, which feature attractions, dining choices, and other information. Following this are two valuable features, the Advanced Search and the Compare Two Cities functions. *City-Data.com* also includes a number of Top 100 or Top 101 lists. Among other things, users can find the top 100 cities with the highest median income, the oldest residents, the longest commute time, the highest percentage of college students, and the biggest houses.—**ARBA Staff Reviewer**

18 Women's Studies

Biography

S
300. Atwood, Kathryn J. **Women Heroes of World War II.** Chicago, Chicago Review Press, 2017. 256p. index. $19.99. ISBN 13: 978-1-55652-961-0.

This title in the Women of Action biography series focuses on the often-overlooked war efforts of women on the Pacific front of WWII. The book is divided into sections based on geography, and each chapter focuses on a different woman's story. Stories of both Asian and Western women are balanced, although no Japanese women are included (this is explained in the back matter). Atwood's language is clear and precise, allowing the women's actions to speak for themselves while describing pivotal moments of the war. She does not shy away from the brutality of war or the Japanese army's horrific treatment of civilians and women, making this title a best option for older students. Each chapter includes a short bibliography for readers interested in learning more, while a map, chapter notes, and discussion questions are also included. Whether resistors, spies, nurses, or journalists, the uniting factor in these stories is the humanitarian spirit and audacity for hope these women possessed even on the front lines of some of the deadliest battlegrounds of WWII.

Highly Recommended—**Jessica Zubik**

C, P, S
301. **Great Lives from History: American Women.** Mary K. Trigg, ed. Hackensack, N.J., Salem Press, 2016. 3v. illus. index. $395.00/set. ISBN 13: 978-1-61925-944-7; 978-1-61925-954-4 (e-book).

This three-volume encyclopedia is part of the Salem Press Great Lives from History series, and combines biographical essays from those earlier volumes, many of them updated, with new ones written especially for this set. They highlight women's contributions over the past 350 years in a vast range of fields, including politics, religion, sports, suffrage, scholarship, science, business, and the arts. Although the set naturally features many of the great and famous women we expect, like Susan B. Anthony, Harriet Tubman, Hillary Clinton, and Meryl Streep, it also includes lesser-known but equally fascinating women like social reformer Rose Schneiderman and writer/scholar Lourdes Casal. Also, a third of the subjects are women of color. These factors give the set its uniqueness and make browsing it an adventure.

The editor is associate professor of women's and gender studies at Rutgers University and the author or editor of three other volumes on women's issues. The contributors are academics or independent scholars. The 524 biographies are signed and range from about one to four pages. They each begin with a short abstract and series of brief facts, followed by four sections. "Early Life" comprises facts about upbringing or, if these are unknown, historical context; "Life's Work," the essay's focus, describes how the subject became recognized in her field and her most important achievements; and "Significance" details the long-range value of her work and why she should be remembered. Essays conclude with an annotated bibliography called "Further Reading." The essays are well written and interesting. The only negative aspect about them is that not all contain information on the woman's personal life which makes for an incomplete picture.

The set includes a seven-page editor's introduction that provides valuable context and breadth, about 150 photographs, and many interesting sidebars. Each volume also contains an alphabetical list of all women profiled in the set. The appendixes in volume three are exceptional and include a chronological list of entries arranged by year of birth, a filmography of 71 notable and varied films about women, a list of organizations and societies related to women's professional and personal development, and a bibliography of resources both general and specific to the women profiled here. Finally, a useful category index lists the subjects under 59 areas of achievement; a broad-based subject index completes the set. Recommended for school, public, and college libraries.—**Madeleine Nash**

P, S
302.   Miller, Brandon Marie. **Women of Colonial America.** Chicago, Chicago Review Press, 2016. 256p. index. $19.95pa. ISBN 13: 978-1-55652-487-5.

Settling the new frontier was a rough job for the women of colonial America. Through 13 individual presentations of life during this time, plus anecdotal stories, readers are given factual information about daily life, jobs, hardships, family, and women's role in this newly formed society. With stories of Mary Rowlandson's capture by Native Americans, poet Anne Bradstreet, and New York merchant Margaret Hardenbroeck Philipse, each story provides a different, captivating treatment of colonial life. Part of the Women of Action Series, this book acquaints readers with primary source documents alongside research materials and reference documents, giving readers a complete picture of women who dared and made a difference. Appropriate for collections with research projects, as a supplemental text for classroom teachers, or for students with a special interest in either history or women's issues. Recommended for grades 6-12.—**Emily Cassady**

Dictionaries and Encyclopedias

C, S
303.   **Women in American History: A Social, Political, and Cultural Encyclopedia and Document Collection.** Peg A. Lamphier and Rosanne Welch, eds. Santa Barbara, Calif., ABC-CLIO, 2017. 4v. illus. index. $415.00/set. ISBN 13: 978-1-61069-602-9; 978-1-61069-603-6 (e-book).

While this massive, four-volume encyclopedia does not claim to be comprehensive, it certainly comes close. Chronologically arranged from precolonial North America to the present, with more than 750 entries and access to more than 195 primary documents, the four volumes are divided into 12 sections as follows: *Volume 1. Precolonial North America to the Early Republic* (Precolonial North America pre-1607, Colonial North America 1607-1754, Revolutionary America, the New Republic 1754-1819); *Volume 2. Antebellum America through the Gilded Age* (The Antebellum Era 1820-1860, The Civil War, Reconstruction 1861-1877, the Gilded Age 1878-1899); *Volume 3. Progressive Era through World War II* (The Progressive Era 1900-1929, The Great Depression and the New Deal 1930-1941, World War II 1939-1945); *Volume 4. Cold War America to Today* (Cold War America 1946-1962, Second-Wave Feminism 1963-1989, Third-Wave Feminism 1990-Present). Each entry includes *see also* references and further reading recommendations. Each of the 12 sections has a thematic issues area that covers 10 categories across the entire time period: childbirth and child rearing; clothing and fashion; courtship, marriage, and divorce; education; fertility and fertility control; gender roles; immigration and migration; legal and political power; violence, domestic and sexual; and work, waged and unwaged. The incorporation of primary documents throughout separates this encyclopedia from other similar reference works. Highly recommended for all high school and academic libraries.—**Bradford Lee Eden**

Handbooks and Yearbooks

C, P

304. **Overcoming Gender Inequalities through Technology Integration.** Joseph Wilson and Nuhu Diraso Gapsiso, eds. Hershey, Pa., Information Science Reference/ IGI Global, 2016. 324p. index. (Advances in Human and Social Aspects of Technology (AHSAT) Book Series). $185.00 (individual chapters available for purchase in electronic format). ISBN 13: 978-1-4666-9773-7; 978-1-4666-9774-4 (e-book).

Overcoming Gender Inequalities through Technology Integration explores novel ways to even the gender gap using the latest advancements. The book casts a special eye on gender inequities in developing countries, but is applicable to all nations working toward rectifying gender inequality. The book covers many different topics including cultural change, digital divide, feminism, gender equality, human rights, information communication technologies, self-empowerment, and social justice. The book contains 15 chapters, most of which take the form of case studies of female empowerment in the developing world. Not only do these case studies make the information infinitely more readable, they also make the information compelling in a useful way. The use of real stories of women on the ground in developing countries is infinitely useful in understanding the challenges and opportunities presented by our changing world.

Another positive is that many of the 15 chapters are authored by women in developing nations that include Zambia, Kenya, Ghana, and Nigeria. Further, the Editorial Advisory Board, with nearly 30 academics, is made up in significant portion of female academics from developing nations. This is important and adds credibility to the work. It is a common practice for western researchers to conduct "flyover research," or research on societies and countries that they may not have intimate familiarity with. This is not the case in many of the works contained in this book, and the work is better for it.

One interesting piece is "The Internet and the Rise in Self-Empowerment of Chinese

Women." Of course, China's "One Child" policy, in effect from 1979 and currently being phased out, is infamous. This policy's negative effect on women and girls has been well documented. The article explores women in China who have used technology to create community through their online blogs. The content explored in Chinese women's blogs is very similar to the content explored in western women's blogs: style; personal experiences, emotions, and reflections; love, marriage and sexual relationships; current events and news; parenting; and arts. The blogs have also cultivated female-to-female connections that result in empowerment and self-respect. The blogs are not all positive—some even encourage women to stop being manipulative in their relationships. While Chinese women's blogs still have a way to go, they are a good first start to foster connections between women in a society where it is still difficult to be female.

Overall, this book is a useful resource that allows researchers and students alike to understand the impacts of an emerging technology. This book is highly recommended for academic and public libraries.—**Sara Mofford**

Part III
HUMANITIES

19 Humanities in General

General Works

Dictionaries and Encyclopedias

C

305.   **The SAGE Encyclopedia of Intercultural Competence.** Janet M. Bennett, ed. Thousand Oaks, Calif., Sage, 2015. 2v. index. $395.00/set. ISBN 13: 978-1-4522-4428-0.

The SAGE Encyclopedia of Intercultural Competence is a useful reference for anyone seeking to communicate with a person of another culture or understand another culture. In this interconnected world where communication can be as simple as the click of a mouse or a few keystrokes, it is a tempting fallacy to assume that intercultural competence is no longer a salient topic. However, despite the ease of communication precipitated by technology, intercultural competence is more important, not less important. The encyclopedia provides a useful resource to promote intercultural competence, understanding, and communication.

The encyclopedia is an updated version of a piece that was published in 2001 and includes 300 to 350 features organized in A to Z fashion in two volumes, entries that include cross-references and suggestions for further reading, a chronology of the history of culture competence as a field of study, and an appendix and detailed index. A useful feature of the encyclopedia is the reader's guide, which provides a categorization of the entries. The encyclopedia contains 20 categories, including but not limited to culture change, identity development, and intercultural conflict and negotiation. The reader's guide categorization on intercultural conflict and negotiation, for example, contains 11 entries. The irony is that while workplace conflict is universal, the way that workplace conflict is handled is not similarly universal. The encyclopedia entry on workplace conflict attempts to find cross-cultural similarities in order to frame workplace conflict similarly so that it can be viewed through the lens of many cultures. Further, the entry makes clear the difference between occupational cultures and other cultures. This is a useful delineation, as not all workplace conflict can be chalked up to international cultural differences. Another useful entry in the encyclopedia is the entry on anxiety and uncertainty management. Considering the fact that in today's economy workers are estimated to work in multiple positions and with multiple companies over the course of their career, it is inevitable that this lack of job security and certainty will lead to anxiety-ridden, uncertain workers. This entry provides a framework for evaluating that uncertainty from the psychological perspective, and links to further reading to promote greater understanding of this emerging phenomenon.

Overall, the encyclopedia is a useful tool for the researcher and academic alike. Recommended for academic libraries.—**Sara Mofford**

20 Communication and Mass Media

General Works

Handbooks and Yearbooks

C, P, S

306. **American Rhetoric. http://www.americanrhetoric.com.** [Website] Free. Date reviewed: 2017.

Users need to scroll downward past the advertisements in order to find a virtual warehouse of important speeches and information related to public speaking. Users can click on categorized search boxes which lead to President Barack Obama Speeches, Movie Speeches, Top 100 Speeches, and a Speech of the Week. There is also a broader collection housed in the Online Speech Bank—a database/index of over 5,000 versions of a wide variety of public oratory. Users may also be interested in the Rhetorical Figures in Sound search box which shares over 200 audio/video clips of speech elements and styles. Clicking on one of the boxes will provide background about the collection of speeches, notes on the transcription process, and various groupings of the broader category (e.g., Top 100 Speeches shares them by rank, top women orators, and by decade). There are also links to audio files and transcripts in various downloadable forms. Users can access these categories from a sidebar menu as well. This menu further includes For Scholars, which offers definitions of rhetoric, a listing of communications journals and publishers, and more. Cool Exercises include fun items like a Rhetoric Quiz. Visually, there is a lot going on with this site. The use of many thumbnail photos, different colors and fonts, pulsating arrows, etc. may distract somewhat from the compelling content. Nonetheless, this site is a good place to start when conducting historical or rhetorical research, or just browsing some of society's best oratory.—**ARBA Staff Reviewer**

C, P, S

307. **Best Commencement Speeches, Ever. apps.npr.org/commencement.** [Website] Free. Date reviewed: 2017.

National Public Radio (NPR) has collected a compelling selection of commencement speeches for history buffs or others who may be at a loss for words. The diverse repertoire includes speeches from U.S. presidents, athletes, writers, entrepreneurs, a prisoner of the Gulag, a 1990's sitcom star, and many more. Similarly diverse are the particular institutions hosting the speakers: Harvard, Yale, Caltech, Ohio State, Liberty University,

Smith College, the Maine College of Art, and the Maharishi University of Management, among others. It is easy to search the site via name, school, year, or thematic elements (e.g., "change the world" or "YOLO"). Alternatively, users can scroll through a list of speakers alphabetized by first name. The search will bring users to a photograph of the speaker marked with the date of the speech and school, alongside a notable quote from the speech. A link directs users to read the speech or if possible, they can watch a video of it (there will be a video icon positioned within the entry if available). This site holds a broad appeal, particularly to anyone who could use a little encouragement.—**ARBA Staff Reviewer**

C

308.   **Impact of Communication and the Media on Ethnic Conflict.** Steven Gibson and Agnes Lando, eds. Hershey, Pa., Information Science Reference/IGI Global, 2016. 344p. index. (Advances in Media, Entertainment, and the Arts (AMEA) Book Series). $185.00 (individual chapters available for purchase in electronic format). ISBN 13: 978-1-46669-728-7; 978-1-46669-729-4 (e-book).

While there are other works that deal with media, conflict, and stereotypes this is the first that also incorporates new types of media. The book is made up of 17 chapters in three sections. The sections include, Communication Frameworks, New Media Impacts, and Ethnic Conflict Interventions. Most of the chapters deal with conflict in the Middle East and Africa, though some address events in the United States. A list of contributors with biographical information is located at the end of the monograph. Each chapter contains an abstract, an often lengthy reference section, and an additional readings section that is usually identified as suggested readings. The chapters conclude with a key terms and definitions section providing readers with additional information. Each chapter also has its own DOI for citing purposes. The book concludes with a compilation of references and a brief index. The monograph is hardback, and the print is large and easy to read. Overall the volume should hold up over time. The language and subject matter makes this a good addition to academic libraries and will probably be the first of many more monographs on this topic. Media libraries can skip this one.—**Melissa M. Johnson**

C, P, S

309.   **National Press Club Luncheon Recordings. https://www.loc.gov/rr/record/.** [Website] Free. Date reviewed: 2017.

Among the vast holdings of the Recorded Sound Research Center (RSRC) of the United States Library of Congress are recordings from the National Press Club Luncheons (NPCL), a series hosting government leaders and other prominent figures and consisting of speeches and moderated question-and-answer sessions. This page represents the RSRC collection titled "Food for Thought: Presidents, Prime Ministers, and Other National Press Club Luncheon Speakers 1954-1989." It allows free access to 25 of the nearly 2,000 recordings made of the NPCL since 1952. The online collection hosts speeches by Audrey Hepburn, Fidel Castro, Jimmy Carter, Nikita Khrushchev, Bob Hope, James Baldwin, Herbert Hoover, and others.

From the main page, users can select a subject (person) from a list which will direct them to an audio recording of the speech as well as a brief essay offering contextual analysis and ideas for further research. This essay is available to download in a PDF format. The total recording time of the speech includes cursory remarks and introductions in addition to the speech and questions and answers. Users are able to easily navigate to those three general sections of the speech, or to a particular listed topic. For example, within the Audrey Hepburn speech, topics range from her association with UNICEF, UNICEF's role in fighting AIDS, the World Economic Impact on Children, and much more. The subject page also includes a photograph.

While a relatively small segment of the center's total collection, the speeches on this site nonetheless offer a historical significance that many researchers, scholars, and educators would find compelling.—**ARBA Staff Reviewer**

Authorship

Style Manuals

C

310.   Gastel, Barbara, and Robert A. Day. **How to Write and Publish a Scientific Paper.** 8th ed. Santa Barbara, Calif., Greenwood Press/ABC-CLIO, 2016. 327p. index. $61.00. ISBN 13: 978-1-4408-4262-7; 978-1-4408-4263-4 (e-book).

This charmingly written and superbly organized volume leads the reader through the many steps of writing for the scientific community. Word choice (no jargon!), grammar, and overall structure of the work are well covered. It also addresses the needs of authors whose first language is not English. Beyond journal articles, the authors advise on theses, CVs, grant proposals, and letters of recommendation. Both the clear writing of this volume and the occasional inclusion of cartoons make it a wonderful text to read. Lists of accepted forms of abbreviation, vocabulary to avoid, and useful websites enhance the work.

Any library with readers who are seeking guidance in writing for publication in the sciences, and particularly academic libraries, will certainly benefit from adding this to their collections, even if it simply means updating an earlier edition.—**Mark Schumacher**

C, P, S

311.   **Purdue Online Writing Lab. https://owl.english.purdue.edu/owl/.** [Website] Free. Date reviewed: 2017.

The Writing Lab at Purdue provides writing resources and instructional materials free of charge via the Purdue Online Writing Lab (OWL) database. Users can easily navigate using links on the left-hand side of the main page—General Writing, Research and Citation, Teacher and Tutor Resources, Subject-Specific Writing, Job Search Writing, English as a Second Language, Purdue OWL Vidcasts—each of which has its own series of sublinks. Under General Writing, for example, users can access information about how to write research papers, book reports, annotated bibliographies, and more. This section also provides access to spelling, numbering, sentence structure, and sentence style exercises as well as grammar-related exercises. There are also sections on the writing process in general, academic writing, punctuation, and undergraduate and graduate applications, among other things. The Research and Citation link not only outlines the basics of the research process but offers links to the major style guides used across various disciplines, CMS, APA, AMA, and MLA. There is a wealth of information on the Teacher and Tutor Resources tab as well. For instance, one sublink takes teachers to exercises on how to contextualize and avoid plagiarism. A sublink under subject-specific writing connects users to many things including literary theory and schools of criticism (new historicism, Marxist criticism, post-colonial criticism, etc.). The OWL, moreover, is not just for coursework but has much to offer the job seeker, first time or otherwise, under Job Search Writing, which outlines best practices for resumes, cover letters, and applications. For those who learn by watching, it is worthwhile to investigate the OWL Vidcasts, which cover such things as how to analyze ethos and the semicolon. The Site Map for the OWL is particularly helpful since it functions as an index. Using the site map, users can go straight to subject-verb agreement, how to cite electronic resources in AMA style, how to close a cover letter, or a spelling exercise on "ible" and "able" word endings.

As many students, teachers, and parents/guardians already realize, the Purdue OWL is a treasure trove of writing resources and instructional materials. This resource is highly recommended to school, public, and academic libraries.—**ARBA Staff Reviewer**

Journalism

Dictionaries and Encyclopedias

C, S

312.   Banville, Lee. **Covering American Politics in the 21st Century.** Santa Barbara, Calif., ABC-CLIO, 2017. 2v. index. $189.00/set. ISBN 13: 978-1-4408-3552-0; 978-1-4408-3552-0 (e-book).

The country's current political climate and the rise of fake news make an encyclopedic reference guide about the state of politics and media more relevant than ever. *Covering American Politics in the 21st Century: An Encyclopedia of News, Media Titans, Trends, and Controversies* by Lee Banville provides users with current background knowledge, trends, and terminology to navigate journalistic coverage in this contentious political climate. This timely two-volume collection includes a variety of topics ranging from nonprofit journalism and NPR to TheBlaze and the Tea Party Movement and is organized in a narrative, A-to-Z format. This collection includes a guide to related topics for further research and investigation, and the second volume includes a selected bibliography and in-depth index. Each entry includes a *see also* reference for additional topics and a reference list for further reading. The volumes are easy to navigate, digestible for the average reader, and accessible to many audiences through effective critical analysis with consideration of objectivity and bias. Well-written and well-organized, *Covering American Politics in the 21st Century* offers patrons an easy-to-understand introspective into media and politics without delving too far into specific academic theories or study. Its roughly 200 entries cover a broad range of topics and provide a reader with a breadth of political and journalistic knowledge. It would be an appropriate addition to any library collection and particularly useful for journalism and media undergraduate students.—**Jessica Crossfield McIntosh**

Newspapers and Magazines

Handbooks and Yearbooks

C, P

313. **Digital Library of Danish American Newspapers and Journals. http://box2. nmtvault.com/DanishIM/.** [Website] Free. Date reviewed: 2017.

This archive is home to digital editions of several Danish American newspapers in addition to the scrapbook of noted Danish American tenor Lauritz Melchior. Included are editions of *Bien* and *Den Danske Pioneer,* both of which are publishing today, as well as editions of *Dannvirke,* published between 1880 and 1951, and *Danskeren,* published between 1892 and 1920. The Melchior scrapbook contains personal clippings such as performance reviews from a variety of newspaper sources. All in all, the archive is home to over 15,000 digitized items. Users can browse the collections via thumbnail views or browse titles filtered by year or month published. They can also conduct a simple search. Metadata for the material is accessible via the thumbnails. Most of the newspaper content is in the Danish language, although there is some English language content as well. As this particular site is strictly home to the digital archive, there is little context for the material. Users unfamiliar with the publications archived here or the legacy of Lauritz Melchior may wish to explore www.danishamericanarchive.com for further information. The archive could certainly appeal to those interested in Danish American history, genealogy, or expatriate journalism.—**ARBA Staff Reviewer**

Radio, Television, Audio, and Video

Handbooks and Yearbooks

C, P, S

314. **American Archive of Public Broadcasting. http://americanarchive.org/.** [Website] Free. Date reviewed: 2017.

This site allows free access to thousands of hours of public radio and television programming that shines a light on American heritage, culture, and public affairs. The media available in the site's Online Reading Room mainly represents local and regional programming covering topics from biography, business, and crafts to environmental issues, fine arts, geography, and much more. The online archive includes full episodes, promos, clips, and unedited footage, among other things. Users can find, for example, the full episodes of Chef Joyce Chen adapting Chinese recipes for the American kitchen in her eponymous WGBH television show or a 1975 Minnesota Public Radio feature with presidential candidate Jimmy Carter. The archive asks users to agree to the Online Reading Room Rules of Use before allowing access. Some of the programming has been consolidated into specific exhibits. The Voices from the Southern Civil Rights Movement exhibit collects programming from a variety of public radio sources to convey interesting perspectives on this pivotal era. Users can search via category selections on a sidebar of the page. The archive has made over 17,000 (and counting) audio and visual artifacts available online that would hold genuine appeal to researchers, historians, educators, and longtime fans of public broadcasting.—**ARBA Staff Reviewer**

21 Decorative Arts

Collecting

P

315. By Ron Keurajian. **Collecting Historical Autographs: What to Buy, What to Pay, and How to Spot Fakes.** Jefferson, N.C., McFarland, 2016. 405p. index. $45.00pa. ISBN 13: 978-1-4766-6415-6; 978-1-4766-2428-0 (e-book).

Based on the author's own personal experience, these guidelines present advice on identifying and collecting a specific kind of artifact. The book begins with a list of abbreviations used throughout the text; a preface and an introduction present an overview of the history and process of collecting. The main text begins with a discussion of techniques for building a collection and for discerning forgeries. The majority of the text examines more closely and thoroughly handwriting examples from individuals in such areas as various military conflicts, government officials (e.g., presidents), figures in American history, science, sports, literature, and music. There are a multitude of examples and black-and-white illustrations of signatures—along with detailed, knowledgeable discussions—that reflect a vast knowledge of the subject. A bibliography and index are available at the end.—**Martha Lawler**

Crafts

P

316. Adams, Katherine Jean. **Comfort & Glory: Two Centuries of American Quilts from the Briscoe Center.** Austin, Tex., Briscoe Center for American History/University of Texas Press at Austin, 2016. 320p. illus. index. $75.00. ISBN 13: 978-1-4773-0918-6; 978-1-4773-0919-3 (e-book).

This stunning volume presents 115 quilts from the Winedale Quilt Collection at the Briscoe Center for American History. Each entry provides information on the date and the quilter of the piece, when known, as well as a discussion of the techniques used and the place of the item in the history of quilting, often within the Texas setting. Beautiful photographs often include details of the stitchwork, beside the overall image of the piece. The author, the curator of the quilt collection, brings a vast knowledge to the text, providing clear yet insightful descriptions of these treasures.

Any library with an interest in the history of American textile art should consider this volume. Libraries in or near Texas may be particularly drawn to this work. Winedale Collection works can also be seen at http://www.quiltindex.org/search_results. php?collection=University%20of%20Texas%20at%20Austin   or   at   http://www.cah. utexas.edu/db/dmr/dmr_result.php?collection=e_wqh—**Mark Schumacher**

Fashion and Costume

C

317.   **A Cultural History of Dress and Fashion.** Susan J. Vincent, ed. New York, Bloomsbury Publishing, 2017. 6v. illus. maps. index. $550.00/set. ISBN 13: 978-1-4725-5749-0.

This six-volume series is a must-have reference work for any library. It encompasses the history of fashion and dress from antiquity to the present; it is richly illustrated with black-and-white photos, figures, and maps; and it offers extensive notes, comprehensive bibliographies, and indexes. The six volumes are titled: *Antiquity, Medieval Age, Renaissance, Age of Enlightenment, Age of Empire,* and *Modern Age.* Each volume is comprised of an introduction and 10 chapters by various experts and authorities; and the chapter titles in the volumes are the same throughout the series for clarity and overall structure: textiles, production and distribution, the body, belief, gender and sexuality, status, ethnicity, visual representations, and literary representations. This allows the reader to be able to compare and contrast the content and time periods of this topic in a relatively easy manner. While the price is rather high, I don't know of any other work of this kind with the content and comprehensiveness that this series offers; well worth the investment.—**Bradford Lee Eden**

C, P

318.   **Knitting Reference Library, https://archive.org/details/knittingreferencelibrary.** [Website] Free. Date reviewed: 2017.

Part of the Internet Archive, the Knitting Reference Library contains published works on knitting dating from 1840 to 2012—particularly books and patterns—from the Library Digitisation Unit at the University of Southampton (UK), which holds some 12,000 knitting patterns collected by Richard Rutt, Montse Stanley, and Jane Waller. While the Knitting Reference Library does not include the full university collection, it does contain some 300 items (and growing), including works on fashion, dress, needlework, and other topics related to the eponymous knitting.

As with other Internet Archive materials, items in the collection are available in a variety of formats such as PDF and kindle in addition to access via the Internet Archive's web-based reader. Items can be discovered by browsing or searching from the collection's home page and the pages of its two subcollections—Victorian knitting manuals and knitting patterns—or via the general Internet Archive search function by title, author, or other metadata. Once an item of interest has been identified, its text can be searched individually for a specific word or term, and full bibliographic records are available via links to the university's catalog.

Examples of items to be found in the collection include: *The Book of "Hows" or What May Be Done with Wools in Every Home: Learning to Knit by Miss Loch* (1900);

Fancy Dresses Described: What to Wear at Fancy Balls by Ardern Holt (ca. 1882); *Ladies Work for Sailors from the Missions to Seamen, London; The Lady's Assistant for Executing Useful and Fancy Designs in Knitting, Netting, and Crochet Work* (1863); and *The Woman's Book: Contains Everything a Woman Ought to Know* by Florence B. Jack (1911) as well as some 200 men's knitwear patterns published by Sirdar, a British yarn manufacturer, during the latter part of the twentieth century. Earlier works in the library, including the books in the collection, have been digitized and are provided in full. For works published after 1943 (in many cases staff had to estimate this date based on fashion styles), copyright concerns have limited digital publication, with the university contacting yarn companies individually for permission to reproduce portions of their published patterns. This work continues. Librarians should note that because the collection is intended for research, for most modern knitting patterns only the cover photo has been reproduced in the archive, leaving knitters and crafters seeking pattern instructions potentially disappointed. However, in addition to those studying knitting and needlework in general, this is a rich resource for those researching women's work and fashion in the mid-nineteenth or early twentieth centuries or for those studying men's fashion from the second half of the twentieth century.—**ARBA Staff Reviewer**

C, P, S

319. McKeefry, Aisling. **200 Skills Every Fashion Designer Must Have.** Hauppauge, N.Y., Barron's Educational Series, 2016. 272p. illus. index. $24.99pa. ISBN 13: 978-1-4380-0896-7.

This step-by-step guide covers all aspects of fashion design (both clothing and accessories) from initial concept and design to marketing and promoting the finished product. The main text includes ideas for inspiration and development of concepts, explicit explanations of design and construction techniques, and suggestions on how to market a collection and develop one's career as a designer. Excellent, helpful, easily understood illustrations are mostly in color and focus on particular aspects in minute detail. Sidebars (sometimes illustrated) give quick, efficient guidelines. The beginning section on getting started discusses what it takes to be a fashion designer, including the ability to think critically, to accept criticism, and to focus on the business side of designing as well as the creative side. The section on the actual mechanics of design and construction explains all kinds of details such as how to take and work with measurements, how to design and cut a pattern, how to create embellishments, how to choose the proper fabrics, etc. The final section deals with how to promote a collection, how to deal with rejection and with success, and how to continue to develop and expand skills. A glossary and index are included at the end. This handy, informative guide is highly recommended for anyone considering fashion as a career.—**Martha Lawler**

22 Fine Arts

General Works

Handbooks and Yearbooks

C, P, S

320. **Digital Fabergé Archive. http://faberge.vmfa.museum/.** [Website] Free. Date reviewed: 2017.

This Virginia Museum of Fine Art web page offers access to the Lillian Thomas Pratt Archives and her donated collection of late-nineteenth and early-twentieth-century Russian decorative art. The site does a fine job of displaying some of the gorgeous collection as well as illuminating the life of the museum's generous benefactor.

From the main Fabergé page, users may redirect to the collection itself, whereby they will see a visual gallery of over 180 Russian decorative objects, such as picture frames, cane handles, pendants, cigarette cases, and more. Users can hover over each photograph for object information. They will also see several of the famous Fabergé Easter eggs, designed by the house of Fabergé for the Romanov tsars of Russia. Lillian Pratt has five of the eggs in her collection, the largest in the western world. Users may also choose to search Pratt's archive of correspondence, receipts, item descriptions, price tags, and other items via a Finding Aid tab. The site also invites users to access videos for intimate display of each Fabergé egg in the collection. A standout, however, is the thoughtfully produced documentary—with a nearly 30-minute running time—telling the story of Fabergé and the American woman with a passion for Russian decorative art.—**ARBA Staff Reviewer**

C, P, S

321. **smarthistory. http://smarthistory.org/.** [Website] Free. Date reviewed: 2016.

With over 200 academic contributors, such as historians, archeologists, and curators, this site is a comprehensive resource for the study of art and cultural heritage. There are three main headings on the site: cultures, style/themes, and art history basics. A simple example search for "Introduction to Greek Architecture" results in an easy-to-read, visually appealing article with vivid pictures as well as an outline which breaks the general topic into subtopics. Another major benefit is that the images provided are all under Creative Commons Attributions. Students can also scroll to the bottom of the homepage and see the newly published articles, as well as popular articles trending on the site. The search tool is unique in that results are visible in the form of a small drop-down menu directly on the same page. All information is free of charge and there is no advertising on its site thanks to donations and grants. This resource would serve as a free, online alternative to expensive art history textbooks for high school teachers. Recommended.—**Angela Wojtecki**

Painting

C, P, S

322.   **Art UK .https://artuk.org/.** [Website] Free. Date reviewed: 2017.

This well-designed, free website offers a virtual tour of over 200,000 paintings from the United Kingdom's national collection. Visitors to the site also have access to complementary material, including information about the nearly 40,000 artists who created the works and about art issues in general. From the home page and other areas throughout the site visitors can conduct a basic search for a specific painting or artist. Clicking on the Menu tab, however, allows more focused searching and browsing. Selecting from the Discover category guides users to choose between Artworks, Artists, Stories, or Topics. Artworks offers the most direct access to individual paintings or curated thematic groups of paintings. It also allows users to refine their search by region, type, topic, or style. Artists offers a similar approach to the painter—allowing a general search, a search by nationality, or thematic browsing. Stories offers an engaging series of blog posts on varied art subjects, and Topics allows users to browse artwork by themes and subthemes such as People (Children, Groups, Men, etc.), Science and Knowledge (education, exploration, medicine, etc.), and much more. From the main menu, visitors are also able to shop an online store, engage with several interactive features, and note the locations of the galleries, museums, and other places that showcase the art. Several tutorials are available to teach users how to conduct specific searches. With its ease of use and abundant offerings, this site is an excellent choice for the remote study of paintings in the national collection of the United Kingdom.—**ARBA Staff Reviewer**

Photography

C, P, S

323.   **George Eastman Museum Collections Online.** https://www.eastman.org/collections-online. [Website] Free. Date reviewed: 2017.

Home to hundreds of thousands of photographs and photography-related objects, the George Eastman Museum in Rochester, New York, is a true celebration of the revolutionary art form. Thankfully, many pieces from the vast collection can be viewed online.

Currently, the website allows viewers access to over 250,000 images and objects. Photographs range from simple still lives to landscapes and portraits. Iconic subjects such as Marilyn Monroe, the John F. Kennedy funeral, or World War I are represented here, as well as those more ordinary. The work of notable photographers such as Ansel Adams, Matthew Brady, Margaret Bourke-White, or Edward Steichen is displayed, as is the work of many lesser-known, or even anonymous, photographers.

In addition to the many photographs, users can view artifacts from the technology portion of the museum's collection, such as Eadweard Muybridge's racetrack camera from 1884, and from the George Eastman Legacy Collection, such as his home furnishings, manuscripts, advertisements, films, and, of course, photographs. Users can conduct an advanced search if so desired.

The online collection is expected to expand and its review and maintenance are continuous.—**ARBA Staff Reviewer**

C, P, S

324. **Photogrammar Project. http://www.neh.gov/explore/photogrammar-project.** [Website] Free. Date reviewed: 2017.

Photogrammar is home to approximately 170,000 photographs commissioned by the U.S. Farm Security Administration and Office of War Information (FSA-OWI). Capturing the years between 1935 and 1946, and created to garner support for federal aid programs, the photos tell stories of American life during the merging epochs of the Great Depression and World War II. An Interactive Map of the United States allows access to the collection by county or photographer journey. Users simply click on a map location to bring up photograph thumbnails alongside information such as photographer, date, identification number, subject, and related photos. Alternatively, users can search the map by photographer name or narrow their search by date. From the homepage, users can also conduct a full-text or advanced search by photographer, location, date, and original classification identifications. Labs or Visualizations introduce users to the variety of state-of-the-art methods of examining the collection, such as a Treemap and the Metadata Dashboard. The collection includes the work of Dorothea Lange, Arthur Rothstein, Marion Post Walcott, Jack Delano, and others, and notably features Lange's iconic "Migrant Mother" (1936). Simple in structure, the site offers an innovative way to explore this essential collection of American history, and would have broad appeal to humanities educators and students alike.—**ARBA Staff Reviewer**

23 Language and Linguistics

General Works

Handbooks and Yearbooks

C, S

325. Wittmann, Anna M. **Talking Conflict: The Loaded Language of Genocide, Political Violence, Terrorism, and Warfare.** Santa Barbara, Calif., ABC-CLIO, 2017. 387p. index. $89.00. ISBN 13: 978-1-4408-3424-0; 978-1-4408-3425-7 (e-book).

This volume presents 265 articles on words and phrases found in discourse concerning war in the twentieth and twenty-first centuries and the related topics indicated in the title. Each entry contains "Further Reading" suggestions, which are supplemented by a 24-page bibliography. Many of the entries are euphemisms or propaganda terms created by individuals and governments: for instance, "Coalition of the Willing," "Signature Strike," "Interdictional Nonsuccumbers" and "Euthanasia" (in a Nazi context). The entries discuss many countries—China, Vietnam, Germany, Japan, as well as the United States—and many conflicts, from World War I to the present.

This volume serves as a fine introduction to the language (or jargon) of the topics it examines. School, public, and academic libraries will find it a useful tool for their readers exploring these topics. Given book prices today, this is reasonably priced.—**Mark Schumacher**

English-Language Dictionaries

Idioms, Colloquialisms, Special Usage

C, P, S

326. **Green's Dictionary of Slang. https://greensdictofslang.com/.** [Website] Price negotiated by site. Date reviewed: 2017,

This site is home to a vast and vastly engaging listing of over 100,000 slang terms of the English language. The 2010 three-volume dictionary by Jonathan Green forms the basis of the site. The site includes slang from American, British, Australian, West Indian,

Irish, and other versions of spoken English.

Basic users can browse for words via an alphabetized list of entries or conduct a basic search. These users can find the word, its derivation, a general timeline, and a definition. Paid subscribers, however, have access to much more, including more search capabilities (history, quotations, etc.), citation display, and a bibliography of over 9,000 sources. The site really encourages subscription as tabs throughout the site lead to the exclusive content. Individual subscriptions are currently priced at around $60 (American) dollars per year with student and institutional rates also available. The home page features a word of the week with definitions as well as links to news and other *Dictionary of Slang* media. While significant content is not available to basic users, they may still find the site useful, if not entertaining.—**ARBA Staff Reviewer**

24 Literature

General Works

Dictionaries and Encyclopedias

C, S

327. **Cyclopedia of Literary Places.** 2d ed. Denise Lenchner, ed. Hackensack, N.J., Salem Press, 2016. 3v. index. $395.00/set. ISBN 13: 978-1-61925-884-6.

This new edition adds 101 articles for a total of 1,403, covering over 6,000 literary places. Many of the literary works from which these places are drawn can be found in the publisher's *Masterplots,* 4th ed., or the *Cyclopedia of Literary Characters,* 4th ed., facilitating a review of the three major elements of literary criticism (story, character, and setting) for the titles included. Each of the three volumes includes a complete list of entries which are arranged alphabetically by title, and a pronunciation key. Volume one includes a list of contributors and a lengthy introduction to place and setting in literature which provides the reader with an understanding of the importance of this literary element. Volume three contains the author, title, and place indexes which would facilitate the comparison of the treatment of a particular setting by several authors. Each entry begins with the full title, author's name and vital dates, type of work, type of plot, time of plot, and date of original publication. A brief introductory paragraph explains the setting and themes in use by the author. The more detailed discussion (300-1,000 words) covers the real or imaginary places employed in the work. Bold type indicates places that have their own entries. Literary works covered include novels, plays, and poetry. It should be noted that this is not a gazetteer as the entry to place settings is through the literary works and the places are treated as literary elements rather than geographic points. Owners of the first edition can decide whether its use justifies this updated version; otherwise, libraries that serve high school juniors and seniors and English literature undergraduates may wish to purchase this third related Salem title for beginning literature studies students.

Highly recommended.—**Rosanne M. Cordell**

Handbooks and Yearbooks

C, P, S

328.   **Archive of Recorded Poetry and Literature. http://www.adweek.com/galleycat/ library-of-congress-has-new-audio-archive-of-poets/120673.**   [Website]   Free.   Date reviewed: 2017.

This site offers free digital access to the Library of Congress' recorded poetry and literature collection. Dating back to 1943, the collection maintains recordings originally made on magnetic tape reels of a renowned selection of poets and writers including Robert Frost, Ray Bradbury, Gwendolyn Brooks, Margaret Atwood, and many more. Recordings are extracted from select literary events held at the Capitol Hill campus of the Library of Congress and sessions held at the library's own Recording Laboratory. The website currently features only a sample of the collection but will be updated with new recordings monthly.

Users can access the recordings via the Collection Items tab, where they will encounter recordings such as a 1971 Kurt Vonnegut lecture including excerpts for the not-yet-published *Breakfast of Champions,* Joyce Carol Oates reading from her (also unpublished) *Fabulous Beasts* collection and answering audience questions, Larry McMurtry reading from his novel-in-progress *Somebody's Darling,* and much more. Next to the audio play button, users will find a brief description of the recording, contributor(s) name, and the year the recording was made. A helpful search index on the left side of the page sorts recordings by date, archive location, contributor, subject, and language.

This site is ideal for students and educators across a broad swath of the humanities.—**ARBA Staff Reviewer**

C, S

329.   **Critical Insights: Holocaust Literature.** Dorian Stuber, ed. Hackensack, N.J., Salem Press, 2016. 250p. index. $95.00. ISBN 13: 978-1-61925-527-2.

The idea of Holocaust literature is, for some, controversial. Elie Wiesel felt that it should not exist although he wrote a great deal about it. He was referring to fiction written by those with no immediate connection to the horrific events of the Shoah. This collection of essays by academics examines the literature dedicated to various aspects of the Holocaust. The contributors look at narrative voice in testimonies, how different generations view the historical events, the use of disciplines such as psychoanalysis, sociology, and memory in interpretation, and different types of literature. There are studies of Art Spiegelman's *Maus,* Philip Roth's Jewish identity, Holocaust literature for young people, Holocaust film, Yiddish-language literature, and poetry. This collection will interest students of history and comparative literature. Academic libraries supporting programs in history, Holocaust and Jewish studies, and literature will want to consider this volume.—**Barbara M. Bibel**

Children's and Young Adult Literature

Handbooks and Yearbooks

C, P

330.   **Baldwin Library of Historical Children's Literature. http://ufdc.ufl.edu/juv.** [Website] Free. Date reviewed: 2017.

Housed at the University of Florida, the Baldwin Library of Historical Children's Literature holds a collection of over 130,000 books and periodicals published in the United States and Great Britain from the mid-fifteenth century to the present. This website is home to over 6,000 digitized titles.

The search capabilities are generous as is to be expected with a collection of this size. Users can conduct a general search from the yellow field at the top of the page or an advanced, text, or map search from corresponding tabs. Items in the digital collection include books of many genres, such as adventure stories, poetry, and religious tracts. The collection includes literature from acclaimed writers including Louisa May Alcott, Lewis Carroll, Edward Lear, and many others. The site also links to several library subcollections of note, including The Afterlife of Alice and Her Adventures in Wonderland, Grimm's Fairy Tales, Daniel Defoe's Robinson Crusoe and the Robinsonades, and more. Sharing this collection digitally is ideal considering the fragile nature of these literary treasures, many with unique and lovely illustrations. This impressive collection would be of great interest to educators, writers, students of literature, and others.—**ARBA Staff Reviewer**

C, P

331.   Cart, Michael. **Young Adult Literature: From Romance to Realism.** 3d ed. Chicago, American Library Association, 2017. 328p. index. $68.00pa.; $61.20pa. (ALA members). ISBN 13: 978-0-8389-1462-5.

The third edition of this enjoyably readable work—a high-level, research-based view of the field, rather than criticism of individual works or themes—features a good deal of new and revised content that should be of value to bibliographers as well as patrons. An entertaining prose style combined with plentiful market history and data (including multiple mentions of libraries as a factor in influencing genre and format popularity) lend strength to this account of an ever-evolving field of literature.

Cart begins with five chapters charting the history of young adult (YA) literature by decade up to 2000. The next section of the book focuses on what he terms the "now"—YA literature published in the new millennium. In addition to the expected coverage of genre and industry trends, including emphasis on the returning popularity of realistic fiction, he examines the crucial topics of censorship and diversity (in multiple senses—reader demographics, LGBTQ literature, and more). He also does not fail to explore the field's emerging directions; his last chapters cover the growing impact of film adaptations on the YA industry, research concerning reading on screens vs. in print, the effectiveness and popularity of audio books, and thoughts on the future of the print industry. Also included are helpful title lists, summaries, and notes to guide further reading and research throughout each chapter, as well as a substantial reference section. In all, readers should find this a shrewd and thorough survey of the YA literature landscape.—**Autumn Faulkner**

C, P

332.   **Critical Survey of Young Adult Literature.** Pattee, Amy, ed. Amenia, N.Y., Grey House Publishing, 2016. 677p. illus. index. $185.00. ISBN 13: 978-1-61925-971-3; 978-1-61925-972-0 (e-book).

A basic reference text for the public and college library, Pattee's comprehensive survey of YA titles and authors offers a single source of data on genres, setting, characters, and plot. Most important to the librarian and beginning teacher, overviews of 25 themes suggest adaptation of fiction to curricular needs and additions to book club and free reading lists on the topics of survival, pregnancy, faith, bullying, alienation, and choices. A listing of 68 cinema versions of YA works incorporates films the quality of *Ender's Game* and *Something Wicked This Way Comes,* but overlooks *The Giver.* A commentary on genre summarizes apocalyptic, mythology, epistolary, and dystopian titles. An eight-page timeline spotlights notable works by standard authors—Paulsen, Hinton, Blume, Le Guin (yet slights Hispanic works by Cisneros and Soto)—and recent pop fiction, including *The Hunger Games* and *Harry Potter.* Amply indexed and supplied with corroborative bibliography, this resource is worthy of a place on the professional shelf.—**Mary Ellen Snodgrass**

Fiction

Crime and Mystery

C, P

333.   Brunsdale, Mitzi M. **Encyclopedia of Nordic Crime Fiction: Works and Authors of Denmark, Finland, Iceland, Norway and Sweden since 1967.** Jefferson, N.C., McFarland, 2016. 563p. index. $65.00pa. ISBN 13: 978-0-7864-7536-0; 978-1-4766-2277-4 (e-book).

Brunsdale (Emeritus, English, Mayville St. Univ; *Icons of Mystery and Crime Detection: From Sleuths to Superheroes and Gumshoes, A Dictionary of Fictional Detectives*) has provided an in-depth and scholarly work on an increasingly popular topic: Nordic crime fiction. She provides an account of the historical, cultural, philosophical, social, political, and literary influences that have shaped the individual characters of the crime fiction for each Nordic country. Her essays are thoughtful and well documented, presenting the necessary background for the academic researcher. Each country has a lengthy (60-160 pp.) introduction followed by a list of award-winning crime fiction, a chronology of that country's literature with world events, profiles of authors of its crime fiction, anthologies, and television crime series or other relevant literatures. A works cited section is followed by a general index. Although the layout is acceptable, an expanded table of contents with each country's subsections listed would improve accessibility. Of more concern is the small typeface for all text: it borders on the uncomfortable and is unusual for a reference book. Nonetheless, it is highly recommended for academic libraries supporting comparative literature or Scandinavian or Nordic studies; bibliographic listings may be of interest in public libraries where Nordic literature is popular.—**Rosanne M. Cordell**

P

334.   Kinsman, Margaret. **Sara Paretsky: A Companion to the Mystery Fiction.** Jefferson, N.C., McFarland, 2016. 202p. illus. index. (McFarland Companions to Mystery Fiction). $39.95pa. ISBN 13: 978-0-7864-7187-4; 978-1-4766-2569-0 (e-book).

Sara Paretsky: A Companion to the Mystery Fiction is the first comprehensive reference work about the renowned mystery author, Sara Paretsky. Paretsky is probably most famous for her mystery series about V. I. Warshawski, a Chicago private investigator. The book does emphasize the Warshawski character, but also provides other information relevant and pertinent to Paretsky.

The text begins with a chronological list of Paretsky's works, starting with a piece in a 1959 *American Girl* and ending with "The Detective as Speech" published in *Out of Deadlock* in 2015. For those interested in looking up a specific work, these publications are then provided in alphabetical order. The book continues with a brief eight-page biography and career chronology before delving into the companion section. The companion section provides an alphabetical list of entries related to Paretsky and/or her many works. Some entries contain only a handful of lines, but others sprawl for pages with great insight and detail. An annotated bibliography and index conclude the text.

For anyone even casually interested in Sara Paretsky or any of her works, this companion is wonderfully informational. The entries are dense with interesting and historical information without being overwhelming. The book is organized in a way that allows readers to jump in, out, and around very easily. *Sara Paretsky: A Companion to the Mystery Fiction* would be a great addition to any library that serves an audience familiar with Paretsky and her works.—**Tyler Manolovitz**

National Literature

American Literature

Dictionaries and Encyclopedias

C, P
335. **Dictionary of Midwestern Literature. Volume Two: Dimensions of the Midwestern Literary Imagination.** Philip A. Greasley, ed. Bloomington, Ind., Indiana University Press, 2016. 1057p. illus. maps. index. $59.50. ISBN 13: 978-0-253-02104-5; 978-0-253-02116-8 (e-book).

Unlike volume one of this set, which focused on authors (see ARBA 2002, entry 1091), this volume focuses more on literary style and expression, including such areas as particular works (35 representative titles), literature of particular regions and states, contributions of various ethnic groups, historical and cultural movements (e.g., immigrants, captive narratives, urban and rural life, etc.), social movements (e.g., slave narratives, utopian literature, etc.), literary genres and literary periodicals, methodologies used in writing and in interpretation of literature, and a discussion of misconceptions of Midwestern life, people, and literary approaches. A third volume is planned and all three volumes will offer an extensive, intensive look at Midwestern literature. An introduction explains the arrangement and intention of the presentation. The entries are arranged alphabetically and include a history or overview of the topic, followed by a discussion of the significance of the topic, important editions (of literary works), and suggestions for further reading. The main text is followed by a bibliography, information about contributors, and an index; the entries are enhanced with black-and-white illustrations. Despite the fact that the choice of entries is a little odd, the arrangement is a little disorganized or disjointed (e.g., plot summaries were included for some, but not all of the literary works discussed), and the writing is a bit gossipy, this source is still an excellent discussion and presentation of Midwestern literature.—**Martha Lawler**

Handbooks and Yearbooks

C, S

336.   **Critical Insights: Henry James.** Tom Hubbard, ed. Hackensack, N.J., Salem Press, 2016. 274p. index. $95.00. ISBN 13: 978-1-61925-836-5.

Henry James is no doubt considered to be a literary icon of the nineteenth century: a touchstone by which other writers of his time and beyond are compared. Prolific in many literary forms from novels to criticism, James is naturally an inspiring source of lively discussion. This volume in the Critical Insights series gathers contemporary analysis of James, his era, and his works, offering a variety of fresh and learned insight.

Two opening essays discuss James from a personal perspective. The pieces describe James' "untypical life" as the son of a religious intellectual whose insistence on a European education was a likely source of the prevailing themes in James' fiction. They also make clear James' whole commitment to his art via his constant analysis of it. Like other volumes in the Critical Insights series, the bulk of the essays are collected into two sections. Critical Contexts features a discussion of the general environment in which James wrote, the impact of his personal history, and, in Tom Hubbard's essay titled "'Intensely American,' Henry James and Stephen Crane," the (obligatory) comparison to a contemporary writer. Critical Readings presents 10 essays delving more deeply into James' specific works. Essays are arranged chronologically by the date in which the discussed work was published. Glenda Norquay provides a piece called "The Art of Fiction: Henry James and Robert Louis Stevenson," which describes the respectful relationship between writers of vastly different styles. "A Native Gone Tourist? Henry James, Travel and The American Scene," by Carlo Martinez discusses James' relationship to travel writing. Pieces in this section also discuss James' novels *The Portrait of a Lady, The Princess Casamassima,* and, arguably his most popular novel, *The Turn of the Screw,* in addition to short stories like "Collaboration" and "The Altar of the Dead." Each essay concludes with a list of works cited.

A closing resources section includes a chronology of Henry James' life, works by Henry James (reflecting his many different mediums of choice), a bibliography, notes on the contributors, and an index.—**ARBA Staff Reviewer**

C, S

337.   **Critical Insights: Horton Foote.** Robert W. Haynes, ed. Hackensack, N.J., Salem Press, 2016. 300p. index. $95.00. ISBN 13: 978-1-61925-840-2; 978-1-61925-841-9 (e-book).

Upon his death in 2009, American writer Horton Foote left behind a significant but understated body of work. Beloved for his ability to connect small-town Texas issues with those of many Americans, he is perhaps most famous for his award-winning screenplay adaptation of *To Kill a Mockingbird.* This volume of the Critical Insights series offers new and compelling insights into the unassuming writer and his many stage plays and adaptations.

An opening section, Career, Life and Influence, presents two essays summarizing early critical reception and interest in Foote, and providing salient biographical information.

Critical Contexts offers four essays devoted to examining Foote's work in regards to the social and critical world around him. "All Lives Matter: African Americans in Horton Foote's South," shines his work through the lens of America's contemporary racial divide. And scholar Xueying Wang provides an interesting comparison of Foote's *The Trip to Bountiful* with Chinese writer Lu Xun's short story titled *Blessing,* which reflects the somewhat similar desires of very different protagonists.

Critical Readings then offers nine pieces covering topics such as Foote's relationship to the American South, his artistic sensibilities as conveyed via aged characters, and his overall critical status. A truly engaging essay by Gerald C. Wood tells the story of the somewhat bumpy road to writing and developing the film *Tender Mercies,* for which Foote won the screenwriting Academy Award. And a selection by Cynthia Franco details the archive of Foote's work held at Southern Methodist University.

The volume concludes with a valuable resources section, which includes a chronology of Horton Foote's life, a listing of his works, and a bibliography, followed by an index.—**ARBA Staff Reviewer**

C, S

338.   **Critical Insights: The Hunger Games Trilogy.** Lana Whited, ed. Hackensack, N.J., Salem Press, 2016. 300p. index. $105.00. ISBN 13: 978-1-61925-844-0; 978-1-61925-845-7 (e-book).

In *The Hunger Games* trilogy of books, the Mockingjay pin stands emblematic of the movement to survive and defeat the oppressive government of Panem. In a broader sense, the trilogy stands as the best representative of the Young Adult literary phenomenon that has attracted both young readers and adults by the droves. A dystopian survival story which violently pits children against each other for the entertainment of the elite, the popular books have generated abundant and vibrant discourse among scholars of various backgrounds. *Critical Insights: The Hunger Games Trilogy* presents some of this scholarship in its essays addressing elements as diverse as Machiavelli, Appalachia, gender, PTSD, and horror.

Four essays make up the Critical Context section which provides background discussion of the trilogy's critical reception, literary influences, and more. Lana A. Whited ("Dystopian Copycat or YA Lit on Fire?") ponders the series' fervent critical reception in the wake of a surge of reader interest in dystopian literature after 9/11. And in "Rebelling against the Rebellion: Frustrating Readerly Desire in Suzanne Collins' *Mockingjay,*" Jackie C. Horne contrasts reader hopes with those of reviewers in terms of the final book's narrative arc.

The 10 essays in the Critical Readings section explore diverse topics which confirm the trilogy's relevance to high school and university classroom discussion. Rebecca Sutherland Borah analyzes the most stand-out aspects of the story—fear and terror—in her essay titled "Game Macabre: Fear as an Essential Element in *The Hunger Games.*" Elizabeth Baird Hardy draws a bold line between Appalachian culture and Katniss' home district in "'Where You Can Starve to Death in Safety': Appalachia and *The Hunger Games.*" And "Labyrinthine Challenges and Degenerate Strategies in *The Hunger Games*" delves into a connection between contemporary gaming culture and the seditious strategies employed by the tributes in their quest for survival and, ultimately, revolution.

Additional material includes chapters on Suzanne Collins' background, a chronology of Suzanne Collins' life, a list of her works (including song lyrics and teleplays), a bibliography, and an index. Recommended to high school and academic libraries.—**ARBA Staff Reviewer**

C, S

339.   **Critical Insights: Maya Angelou.** Mildred R. Mickle, ed. Hackensack, N.J., Salem Press, 2016. 296p. index. $105.00. ISBN 13: 978-1-68217-112-7; 978-1-68217-113-4 (e-book).

Maya Angelou certainly carried a wide range of talents beyond her writing, but it is her prolific output as a poet, memoirist, and playwright which makes Angelou the ideal subject for a Critical Insights volume. This book offers a rich contextual exploration of her life and times, in addition to a well-curated selection of textual analyses which give ample attention to her classic *I Know Why the Caged Bird Sings* but also discuss a number of her most beloved poems and other works.

Two opening chapters take a cursory look at Angelou's unconventionally busy trajectory from abuse survivor to Presidential Medal of Freedom recipient. While noting her many accomplishments, these chapters also provide a good sense of how Angelou lived in concert with major events of the twentieth century like the Civil Rights movement. Four Critical Contexts essays follow and touch on the influence of other African American artists and their mediums, censorship, and more. Martin Kich also offers a well-organized chronological review of writings on Angelou, such as obituaries, monographs and magazine articles.

The Critical Readings section separates essays looking at Angelou's prose from those discussing her poetry. Seven essays make up the former section and include "Paradoxical Phrasing in the Later Autobiographies of Maya Angelou," by Robert C. Evans, which looks at the development of her autobiographical writing style. Other pieces offer discussions with Angelou on her work. Of course, *I Know Why the Caged Bird Sings* is a constant reference point. Three essays discuss Angelou's poetry. Notably, "On the Pulse of Peace: Maya Angelou, A Nation's Poet" by Tomeiko Ashford Carter examines how Angelou's poetry speaks to the greater American ideal.

Supplemental material includes a chronology of Maya Angelou's life (compelling in itself), a list of her works, a bibliography, and an index.

Recommended for high school and college libraries.—**ARBA Staff Reviewer**

C, S

340.   **Critical Insights: Short Fiction of Flannery O'Connor.** Robert C. Evans, ed. Hackensack, N.J., Salem Press, 2016. 300p. index. $95.00. ISBN 13: 978-1-61925-874-7; 978-1-61925-875-4 (e-book).

Proficient and profound in both novels and short stories, Flannery O'Connor created works that have attracted diverse and abundant analyses. This volume in the Critical Insights series focuses on the young writer's short stories, which were mainly gathered into two collections published a decade apart.

Flannery O'Connor came of age during the burgeoning post-World War II era. The opening essay in the brief Career, Life and Influence section of this volume shares an illuminating look at the influence of the domestic aftermath of the war upon her stories. This essay is followed by a brief biographical sketch of the writer, who died at the age of 29 due to complications from lupus.

The following four essays, making up the Critical Context section, work to envelop readers' understanding of her stories in the social and political climate of the time, both in regards to her product and the critical response to it. Three of the essays are contributed by this volume's editor, Robert C. Evans, who writes of O'Connor's conservative leanings, provides a meticulous survey of the earliest O'Connor criticism, and analyzes the particular way in which O'Connor presents her stories. The fourth essay in the section offers an interesting comparison between O'Connor's work and that of African American writer Alice Walker.

The Critical Readings section offers essays which look at O'Connor's work in a generally chronological way. "Collards and Consumption in a 'Stroke of Good Fortune'" by David A. Davis relates the placement of food in this early story to broader gender issues of the time. Themes of Christian faith are analyzed through several essays (and through much of O'Connor's work). And Colleen Warren discusses issues of race and more in her piece "Black Doubling in Flannery O'Connor's 'Why Do the Heathen Rage?'"

A helpful Resources section includes a chronology of the writer's life, a listing of her published works, and a bibliography. An index rounds out the work.—**ARBA Staff Reviewer**

C, S

341. Dighe, Ranjit. **The Historian's Mark Twain: Reading Mark Twain's Masterpiece as Social and Economic History.** Santa Barbara, Calif., Praeger/ABC-CLIO, 2016. 352p. $35.00pa. ISBN 13: 978-1-61069-941-9; 978-1-4408-3349-6 (e-book).

Part of The Historian's Annotated Classics series edited by economic historian Ranjit S. Dighe, this title explores the original 1885 text of *The Adventures of Huckleberry Finn,* published by the Charles L. Webster and Company of New York, in the context of pecuniary and social practices.

As introduction, chapter one discusses Samuel Clemens as a historian of nineteenth-century life and also provides biographical detail that coupled with chapter two offer a solid background for Twain the writer and the nineteenth century. Dighe provides inclusive page annotations, giving a full sense of the times. Four themes are predominant in his research: prosperity, expansion, inequality, and commercialism. Annotations are solidly researched from monetary equivalents to social mores to historical references. Obscure terms like tanyard are defined in Dighe's notes. Twain's commentaries reflect his times; slavery, abolition, financial challenges and schemes, class, river commerce, and more are addressed in *The Adventures of Huckleberry Finn.*

Interpretation of Twain's writing coupled with factual documentation gives readers concise understanding of Twain, this classic work, and nineteenth-century American history with significant social and economic overlays. Parallels to current developments are consistent with comments such as "immigrants who stayed in America typically managed to improve their economic lot, but discrimination against them was common and severe" (p. 36). This literature dissection will be of interest to undergraduate students and scholars researching history and literature of the United States. Those studying U.S. economics will also benefit from this examination.

Recommended.—**Janis Minshull**

C, P

342. Martin, Wendy, and Cecelia Tichi. **The Gilded Age and Progressive Era: A Historical Exploration of Literature.** Santa Barbara, Calif., Greenwood Press/ABC-CLIO, 2016. 260p. index. (Historical Explanations of Literature). $61.00. ISBN 13: 978-1-61069-763-7; 978-1-61069-764-4 (e-book).

This volume is one of a series that focuses on classics of American literature. Each title encompasses a specific period of U.S. literary history; in the present case, the period roughly between the end of the Civil War and the outbreak of World War I. While only a relative handful of works are discussed in each of the said volumes, they are treated at length and with significant analysis. This is to be opposed to competing collections of literary synopses, such as the long-running Masterplots by Salem Press, which contain hundreds or even thousands of entries, but with necessarily much more concise treatment.

The Gilded Age and Progressive Era dissects the following four selections from the canon of our country's literary output: *A Connecticut Yankee at King Arthur's Court* by Mark Twain (1889), *The Yellow Wallpaper* by Charlotte Perkins Gilman (1892), *The Jungle* by Upton Sinclair (1906), and *A Lost Lady* by Willa Cather (1924). One chapter covers each work and each follows a standard format. Appropriately, the first segment presents an overview of the work in question. This is followed by a few paragraphs of "Historical Background," which gives the reader a sense of the social and cultural milieu in which the work was first written. Succeeding sections present a thumbnail biography of the specific author, "Why We Read…," which is an examination of those enduring qualities that makes this particular work a classic and still relevant to today's audience, and finally, "Historical Explorations of …," which looks at contemporary themes in American society, bolstered with a generous selection of primary documents that reinforce the ideas described.

Co-author Wendy Martin is Professor of American literature and American Studies at Claremont Graduate University. Her colleague Cecelia Tichi is the Gertrude Conaway Vanderbilt Professor of English and Professor of American Studies at Vanderbilt University. Both are published widely in their respective fields and are well suited for a project such as this.

Overall, *The Gilded Age and Progressive Era* is a well-written, informative, and thought-provoking book. This volume is a useful tool to help readers understand the sometimes perplexing works of the American past, with their unfamiliar language and references to obsolete technologies, such as the telegraph. Therefore, this volume is highly recommended for purchase by all public and academic libraries.—**Michael Francis Bemis**

British Literature

Dictionaries and Encyclopedias

C

343. Brock, D. Heyward, and Maria Palacas. **The Ben Jonson Encyclopedia.** Lanham, Md., Rowman & Littlefield, 2016. 627p. index. $135.00; $134.99 (e-book). ISBN 13: 978-0-8108-9074-9; 978-0-8108-9075-6 (e-book).

Had it not been for a playwright by the name of William Shakespeare, we would always be quoting and offering our adulations and praise for that "other" playwright, Ben Jonson. Jonson gets short shrift—as do many others—whose bright exhalation soared too near the sun of the great bard. While many of those lesser lights deserve their current darkness, the opacity in which Jonson now resides is hardly fair. Granted, he is given better light these days, and Jonson's scholars are now mounting to army size, it cannot be argued they will ever rise to outdo or outshine the eloquence of the one we call Shakespeare.

It's too bad, too, for Jonson has as many memorable lines as his better known rival. Can a better line be found, during this abysmal election cycle, than "ambition makes more trusty slaves than need"? Or, "weigh the meaning and look not at the words"? And who can forget *The Case Is Altered,* a play based on a curmudgeon of an attorney (but I repeat myself), Plowden, who would plead for his clients in half-hearted fashion until a better, higher fee was offered and only then claim that the case had been altered and plead more eloquently and convincingly? But I digress .

What a marvelous tribute this update is to an almost forgotten genius. It's been 35 years since the first edition, the *Companion,* appeared. It is more than time enough for an updated and expanded version, the present *Encyclopedia,* to make its face known.

In alphabetical arrangement, scholars and students alike will find words, phrases, plays, characters, actors, critics, and more as all things Jonson bubble up from every page. Whether the entry is from an actual play or poem, or whether a particular work evokes a philosopher or philosophic work, users will find it here. Although it cannot be said that the work is exhaustive for Jonson, readers will be hard-pressed to find glaring omissions, or even miniscule ones. Particularly useful are the synopses of the plays that appear throughout this handsome tome. A selected bibliography and fulsome index round out this work.

As a quick resource for identifying names, places, or people, or as a companion for refreshing one's memory about a particular play, this volume does tribute to the playwright, poet, actor, critic, and notable friend. It should be on every desk of every Jonson scholar, and all library shelves.—**Mark Y. Herring**

C, P

344.　Burton, Alan. **Historical Dictionary of British Spy Fiction.** Lanham, Md., Rowman & Littlefield, 2016. 494p. $125.00; $124.00 (e-book). ISBN 13: 978-1-4422-5586-9; 978-1-4422-5587-6 (e-book).

This book provides extensive information on the contribution of Great Britain to the genre of spy fiction. The narrative forms of television dramas, films, and novels are covered through various frameworks: a chronology, an introduction, and a dictionary of approximately 300 entries focused on characters, writers, and trends, along with an extensive bibliography. The terms British Secret Intelligence Service (MI6) and British Security Service (MI5) are explained in the reader's notes. The introduction is one of the best, concise explanations of the history of the British spy novel both as a literary and film genre that I know of. This book is an important addition to any public or academic library's reference shelf.—**Bradford Lee Eden**

Drama

C, P, S

345.   **Digital Anthology of Early Modern English Drama. http://folgerpedia.folger. edu/A_Digital_Anthology_of_Early_Modern_English_Drama.** [Website] Free. Date reviewed: 2017.

Part of the renowned Folger Shakespeare Library (see ARBA 2013, entry 936), this site collects an array of single playbook editions of non-Shakespeare plays published between the years of 1576 and 1642. The archive currently offers access to 35 plus plays, authored by Christopher Marlowe, Ben Jonson, Thomas Heywood, and others, but will add to its digital library over the course of the next year.

A User Guide offers a selection of FAQs, a glossary of technical terms, searching and browsing tips, and other information. Users can search via Keyword, Author, and Title with the added filters of Genre, Company, and Theater. The Featured Plays tab will take users to a listing of plays, and clicking on a title leads to a page offering technical data (versions available, bibliography, etc.) and publishing/performance information such as author, printer, publishing date, theater, and more. Depending on the play, users are given a variety of ways to access it, whether reading it online or downloading. A Featured Research tab encourages new and accessible scholarship regarding early modern drama, theater, printing, editing, digital arts, and other fields.—**ARBA Staff Reviewer**

Handbooks and Yearbooks

C, S

346.   **Critical Insights: George Eliot.** Katie R. Peel, ed. Hackensack, N.J., Salem Press, 2016. 300p. index. $95.00. ISBN 13: 978-1-61925-838-9.

This approachable volume offers the reader 16 essays concerning George Eliot's life and work. In addition to the expected essays addressing a variety of specific topics and works, two biographical and four contextual essays are also included at the beginning of the book which help to orient the reader to Eliot's life, her culture, and her contemporaries. Of particular usefulness is the essay "Critical Tipples: Or, A Nip into George Eliot Criticism, Then and Now," which provides a cogent summary of the landscape of Eliot criticism in areas like feminism, Marxism, postcolonialism, and others. Also of interest is the essay concerning Edith Simcox's secret love for George Eliot; her adoring and detailed accounts of her beloved, as recorded in her diary, allow readers a fascinating and unusual view of Eliot's life and work.

Although *Romola, Felix Holt, the Radical,* and *Daniel Deronda* are not addressed specifically by any of the critical essays, Eliot's other major novels do receive individual treatment. *The Lifted Veil,* a novella which famously departs from Eliot's typical realism and instead engages with questions of the mystical and supernatural, is actually addressed by two separate essays. The remaining pieces focus on Eliot's work in journalism and on general themes throughout her work, rounding off a collection that gives satisfying breadth without overwhelming depth. The entire volume would form an ample foundation for beginning scholars of Eliot, but it also has unique content to offer an advanced reader.— **Autumn Faulkner**

C, S

347.   **Critical Insights: The Hobbit.** Stephen W. Potts, ed. Hackensack, N.J., Salem Press, 2016. 300p. index. $105.00. ISBN 13: 978-1-68217-120-2; 978-1-68217-121-9 (e-book).

When it was published in 1937, *The Hobbit* changed the landscape of fantasy literature forever. This collection of critical viewpoints explores some of the reasons why, beginning with two chapters introducing the history and context of the work itself, and the life and times of its author.

The following Critical Contexts section contains four essays, which examine the major influences on Tolkien as an author, the critical reception of *The Hobbit,* and the themes it shares with both medieval Germanic tales and with the Harry Potter series. These viewpoints are meant to orient the reader to the *The Hobbit's* cultural, historical, and literary origins.

Nine essays build upon this foundation by examining more specific motifs in the text of *The Hobbit* itself, notably its juxtaposition of British sensibleness with the lure of magical adventure, its roots in Northern mythologies and heroism traditions, some of the specific fairy stories and fantastical tales whose elements can be detected in Bilbo's journey, the mythopoeic work that formed the foundation of *The Hobbit* and eventually The Lord of the Rings trilogy, and, of course, Tolkien's lifelong passion for philology.

There is too much to say about *The Hobbit* to be contained in one volume, but this collection of perspectives is a good starting place for anyone interested in Tolkien specifically, or high fantasy in general. The Lord of the Rings trilogy sometimes comes in for more than its fair share of analysis, so this critical attention to *The Hobbit* is an important addition to scholarly conversations about Tolkien's work.—**Autumn Faulkner**

C, S

348.   **Critical Insights: Mary Shelley.** Virginia Brackett, ed. Hackensack, N.J., Salem Press, 2016. 280p. index. $105.00. ISBN 13: 978-1-68217-116-5; 978-1-68217-117-2 (e-book).

Salem Press enlisted nineteenth-century literature expert and retired professor, Virginia Brackett, as editor of this 2016 publication. Brackett has written multiple books and her *Mary Shelley: A Literary Reference to Her Life and Work* (Facts on File, 2012) will be a useful companion for those researching Shelley.

Shelley and her works are central to studies of nineteenth-century English literature. Brackett details Shelley's life, influences, and works; contributor essays complement theory with examples of how life experiences prompted themes in Shelley's writing. Shelley is best known for her writing of *Frankenstein: Or the Modern Prometheus,* but this book critiques many of Shelley's works, giving a robust overview of her collective oeuvre.

The opening information is a worthy introduction to Mary Shelley, followed by two sections of discourse, Critical Contexts and Critical Readings. The resources section at the end of the body of work includes six sections that expand research options with the "Chronology of Mary Shelley's Life" and "Works by Mary Shelley" being most useful to those not familiar with the author. The Critical Contexts section situates Shelley as a writer who explored social mores and defied gender expectations. Critical Readings helps establish the legacy of Shelley.

Critical Insights: Mary Shelley is an excellent source for teachers, professors, students, and scholars of nineteenth-century English writers.

Highly recommended.—**Janis Minshull**

C, S

349.   **Critical Insights: Nineteen Eighty-Four.** Horan, Thomas, ed. Hackensack, N.J., Salem Press, 2016. 254p. index. $105.00. ISBN 13: 978-1-68217-118-9; 978-1-68217-119-6 (e-book).

Published near the midpoint of the twentieth century, when an exhausted world looked eagerly to the future, *Nineteen Eighty-Four* perhaps did not offer the most optimistic view of things to come. This volume in the Critical Insights series looks both within and without the novel at its influences, themes, and ultimate relevance as the touchstone of dystopian fiction.

Two opening chapters give a general overview of the novel's literary impact and a brief biographical sketch of its author, George Orwell. The three essays in the Critical Contexts section provide a good foundation for understanding the novel in its time and place. Bradley W. Hart examines the vitriolic political landscape of Britain in the two decades enveloping World War II while Tony Burns writes on the scholarship surrounding the *Nineteen Eighty-Four* in its role as dystopian novel forebear.

The eleven essays in the Critical Readings section build from Gregory Claeys' discussion of *Nineteen Eighty-Four* as its relates to the concept of nationalism to Donald Morris' piece on the role of privacy in both utopian and dystopian societies. In his essay "*Nineteen Eighty-Four* in 1984," Jackson Ayres takes the inevitable but important look at Orwell's views as updated for the late 1970s and early 1980s. And with "Not Death, but Annihilation: Orwell's *Nineteen Eighty-Four* and the Catastrophe of Englishness" Erik Jaccard moves beyond the dystopian label to look at the novel as an English "catastrophe" novel whereby it examines English social decay.

The closing resources section includes a chronology of George Orwell's life, a listing of his major works, a bibliography, notes on contributors, and an index.

Recommended for high school and college libraries.—**ARBA Staff Reviewer**

Russian Literature

Handbooks and Yearbooks

C, S

350.   **Critical Insights: Lolita.** Rachel Stauffer, ed. Hackensack, N.J., Salem Press, 2016. 259p. index. $95.00. ISBN 13: 978-1-61925-846-4; 978-1-61925-847-1 (e-book).

This volume in the Critical Insights series presents varied analyses of Vladimir Nabokov's 1955 novel *Lolita*. In spite of its controversial subject matter and tentative publication, the novel was quickly considered a classic and has attracted a global array of criticism. This volume presents essays expanding on previous threads of analyses while exploring more contemporary ideas.

Two foundational essays offer a general overview of the novel and its main characters (Humbert Humbert and Dolores "Lolita" Haze), as well as a concise biography of Nabokov. The Critical Contexts section then shares four essays providing historical, psychological, and comparative analyses of the novel. Thomas Seifrid, for example, focuses on the influence of Ranier Maria Rilke as manifested throughout Humbert Humbert's story, while Sara Dickinson draws connections to the literary past in her piece "Nineteenth-Century Russian Literature and the Shaping of Lolita."

The nine essays in the Critical Readings section delve further into subtext, style, theme, and more. Priscilla Meyer writes about the novel's use of the doppelganger in her essay "Lolita and the Genre of Literary Doubles: Does Quilty Exist?". Meanwhile, Michael Federspiel points to the distracting effects of Nabokov's literary style, and posits that the use of anagrams, alliteration, and other word play in the work seem to lessen the impact of Humbert's shocking behavior.

Essays in both sections include a clear list of works cited and may also include notes. In addition, a fine resources section includes a chronology of Nabokov's life, a listing of his additional works, and a bibliography. An index rounds out the work.—**ARBA Staff Reviewer**

Poetry

Handbooks and Yearbooks

C

351.   **The Princeton Handbook of Poetic Terms.** 3d ed. Roland Greene and Stephen Cushman, eds. Princeton, N.J., Princeton University Press, 2016. 456p. index. $35.00pa. ISBN 13: 978-0-6911-7043-5; 978-0-6911-7199-9 (e-book).

In this, the third edition of *The Princeton Handbook of Poetic Terms,* users will have at hand a companion piece to the fourth edition of the *Princeton Encyclopedia of Poetry and Poetics.* It stands to reason if that if you have the latter, you may not need this volume, except to say that the latter is likely to be both more costly and more unwieldy for a quick refreshment.

Contained herein are what poets used to think important: conceit, versification, epode, chain rhyme, meter, trope, and—well you get the picture. I said "used to" because modern poetry, save for the few bright exhalations in that firmament, appeal only to other poets by and large. Sad as it is to say, if anyone is still writing poetry, not many are still listening. Like the tree falling in the forest, it's unclear whether anyone is listening any more, whether present or not.

For the time being, however, this handbook will prove somewhat valuable to those still earnestly believing in poetic expression as opposed to political or philosophical expression delivered in makeshift, ham-fisted poetical terms. The good news is that while many if not most of the terms can be "googled," the richness of the explanations found in *The Princeton Handbook* is missing in the virtual elsewhere, unless of course you look for the book itself in an earlier online edition. Accentual meter, for example, can be found online. But its definition, explanation, and illustrative examples (from Hopkins, Eliot, Heaney, and others), as well as its historical beginnings, can only be found in this volume under review.

Contributors to the volume number more than 125 and range from well-known national and international critics, rhetoricians to independent scholars and emeriti faculty. A most expansive index rounds out this poetic offering.—**Mark Y. Herring**

C

352.   **The Princeton Handbook of World Poetries.** Roland Greene and Stephen Cushman, eds. Princeton, N.J., Princeton University Press, 2017. 693p. index. 35.00pa. ISBN 13: 978-0-691-17152-4.

At some point in his quest for adulthood, almost every young man surfaces his thoughts in poetry, or else doggerel, which is the next closest thing. Likewise, every country may be said to have produced its own poets, or poetasters, which may be the next closest thing. Although many of us would be hard pressed to name more than one of two poets outside our own state or township, much less our own country, we rest in the assurance that those versifiers are out there, our own ignorance notwithstanding.

The current volume is an anodyne for international poetry nescience. Drawn from the *Princeton Encyclopedia of Poetry, The Princeton Handbook of World Poetries,* comes just in time to answer the burning question of who is Urdu's most famous poet, or why Rosidi wrote in Sudanese for the Java peoples. Contained herein are more than 150 entries on world poetry, covering more than 100 non-Western literatures and language traditions. Not only are poets identified, but so are their themes, traditions, biographies, and more. In-depth poetries of Tamil, Punjab, Hindi, Marathi. Nepalese, and Thai, as well as indigenous poetries of Guarani, Inuit, and Navajo (and scores more) are provided by signed entries from scholars in these areas. Thankfully, there is an extensive index for greater searching ease.

Anyone wishing to understand the non-Western poetry tradition (though Western culture is also covered) can do no better than to scan through this tome's more than 600 pages. It is indispensable for anyone studying international literatures, and the perfect balm for those libraries wishing to soothe both diversity and global initiative concerns in their collections.—**Mark Y. Herring**

25 Music

General Works

Dictionaries and Encyclopedias

C, P

353. Goldsmith, Melissa U. D., Paige A. Willson, and Anthony J. Fonseca. **The Encyclopedia of Musicians and Bands on Film.** Lanham, Md., Rowman & Littlefield, 2016. 454p. index. $120.00; $119.99 (e-book). ISBN 13: 978-1-4422-6986-6; 978-1-4422-6987-3 (e-book).

Compiled by authors specializing in musicology, film studies, literature, and dance, this impressive volume explores full-length films (not videos or documentaries) that have musicians and bands as narrative subjects. The richly detailed entries seamlessly merge scholarly insight and cultural perceptiveness, honoring both the academic and pop appeal of the films highlighted. Each entry is preceded by a boxed template containing essential information: director, cast, music supervisor, awards, soundtrack availability, etc., followed by a full description of the film's story and plot. What makes this resource so strikingly useful and unique is the interweaving of music and the cinematic narrative arc for each entry. Not a simple listing of songs or artists, this is a comprehensive look at films whose storytelling is of and through music. We find films that are left out of other compendia, and new ways of thinking about films specifically because of their use of music (the larger oeuvres of the lighting and costume designers for *Purple Rain* are presented in depth and in context). The appendixes, making up one-fifth of the book, are extensive and invaluable. Films by country, director's who's-who, genre, and made-for-television films are just a few. Essential for both specialized and general library reference collections.—**Stephen J. Shaw**

Handbooks and Yearbooks

C, P, S

354. Axford, Elizabeth C. **Music Apps for Musicians and Music Teachers.** Lanham, Md., Rowman & Littlefield, 2015. 312p. $58.00; $57.99 (e-book). ISBN 13: 978-1-4422-3277-8; 978-1-4422-3278-5 (e-book).

This book provides a comprehensive guide for anyone with an interest in music. Written in three parts, this resource includes hundreds of apps that will relate to all musicians, songwriters, and music teachers. Part one is Creating Music which includes reading, composing, and recording music. Part two is Performing Music which includes all types of instruments as well as singing. Part three is Responding and Connecting to Music which includes evaluating and listening to music, as well as music appreciation. This title is an excellent resource for all novices, experts, and anyone in between.—**Shelly Lee**

C, P, S
355.   **Music Archive. http://contentdm.ucalgary.ca/cdm/landingpage/collection/emi.** [Website] Free. Date reviewed: 2017.

In March of 2016, Universal Music Canada donated the archive of record label EMI Music, Canada, to the University of Calgary. Home to Canadian artists Anne Murray, Helix, Tom Cochrane, and others, EMI also distributed the music of international musicians including David Bowie, the Rolling Stones, Tina Turner, and others. This digital archive represents over 50 years of contemporary music across a variety of genres. Visitors to this site can watch a five-minute video where both university officials and music executives describe the contents and significance of the archive. A wide range of materials are included in the archive, such as demo tapes, awards, lyrics, promotional materials, correspondence, master recordings, and much more. Users can easily access the digital archive by clicking on the Browse the Collection tab. They can find a brief summary of particular musicians on the Explore Featured Artists tab, and can also redirect to that artist's collection from here. Such specific materials as a 1990 demo tape from the Barenaked Ladies, a 78 rpm audio disc of Jack Kingston the Yodeling Cowboy, and a poster from Pink Floyd's Dark Side of the Moon are included in this impressive collection..

The site is a large and easily navigable resource for students, educators, and music lovers alike.—**ARBA Staff Reviewer**

C, S
356.   Perone, James E. **Smash Hits: The 100 Songs That Defined America.** Santa Barbara, Calif., Greenwood Press/ABC-CLIO, 2016. 335p. illus. index. $89.00. ISBN 13: 978-1-4408-3468-4; 978-1-4408-3469-1 (e-book).

An informative and enjoyable anthology, *Smash Hits: The One Hundred Songs That Defined America* begins with a useful introduction and table of contents. Information is presented in six chronological sections: 1750-1789, 1900-1939, 1940-1959, 1960-1969, 1970-1979, and 1980-2016. The author's song selection includes top hits as well as tunes indicative of a certain time in American history, a new genre in music, a significant transition in culture, or global importance. At junctures, common themes of patriotism, frustration, or tomfoolery speak out. Historical information is powerful here, and the intertwining with popular culture is significant. U. S. history topics of war, socioeconomics, the civil rights movement, and many more are solidly presented. Music genres, lyricists, performers, and collaborators are well represented in *Smash Hits.* Black-and-white photographs enhance the work, and sidebars add fascinating additional facts. This strong reference work, which effectively integrates the history, popular culture, and music that defines America, is highly recommended to high school and undergraduate libraries, as well as teachers looking to incorporate new avenues into their curriculum. Members of the general public will also appreciate this work.—**Janis Minshull**

C, P

357.   Tyler, Don. **Music of the First World War.** Santa Barbara, Calif., Greenwood Press/ABC-CLIO, 2016. (American History through Music). $58.00. ISBN 13: 978-1-4408-3996-2; 978-1-4408-3997-9 (e-book).

The centenary of the First World War has brought project commissions, publications, movies, and other opportunities for public engagement. *Music of the First World War* joins in this commemoration and fills a rather large gap in the reference literature on the music of the War to End all Wars. While there are many scholarly monographs that treat this subject, we lack reference works that provide a starting point to those unfamiliar with the era and its music. To meet this need, author and retired music professor Don Tyler mined the available primary source material on the reception of the war's songs, and also made judicious use of secondary sources like *Variety's* "Hit Parade of a Half-Century." Like other volumes in the series, American History through Music, *Music of the First World War* provides a guidebook to the popular ideas, events, people, technology, and musicology of the period.

Yet one could ask for greater ease of navigation to this wealth of information. We find alphabetical and chronological lists of songs as well as helpful appendixes, notes, bibliographies, an index, and a clear outline. However, the text itself presents some obstacles; one shortcoming of this work is its imprecise organization and lack of transitions in the text. While the table of contents offers high-level document description, it is unclear, when one explores a chapter, how the information is organized, whether by title, date, popularity, or some other standard. Chapter three, for example, "Popular Hits of the War Years," opens with a short introduction explaining the topic and scope before commencing a description of "The Song that Stole my Heart Away." Clearly this was a popular song, and we learn about the cover of the sheet music, its lyrics, the lyricist, and composer. But it is not clear why it is placed first in the chapter, nor is there a discussion of the music itself (apart from a link to Henry Burr's recording). Following a paragraph break, we are introduced to "Rebecca of Sunny-Brook Farm." The logic of ordering here is not altogether clear.

In the next installment of this work, this reviewer would like to see added an introduction to the series as well as an introduction to the volume itself, explaining its organization, scope, and method. This is an informal reference work and does not seem to contextualize its entries with the methods of either historical musicology or the sociology of music. But the short descriptions, links to online resources, and citation data for sheet music provide a needed starting point. Recommended for music, college, and public libraries celebrating the First World War Centenary.—**Amy Koehler**

Musical Forms

Opera

C

358.   McVicker, Mary F. **Women Opera Composers: Biographies from the 1500s to the 21st Century.** Jefferson, N.C., McFarland, 2016. 274p. index. $39.95pa. ISBN 13: 978-0-7864-9513-9; 978-1-4766-2361-0 (e-book).

Even though opera was a field primarily dominated by men, from the 1500s to the twenty-first century, the world has produced remarkable women opera composers. Author Mary F. McVicker has written a comprehensive work of short biographies of noted opera composers from its beginnings in the Renaissance to the present. Included in the book is a table of contents with each section of the book grouped by years. In the introduction, the author notes that several of the composers have successfully had productions of their operas, but there is a lack of a significant discography for many of these operas. Within the biography of each composer, McVicker includes a chronological list of works written by the composer. At the beginning of each section of the book, there is a brief historical look at that time period and composers that were significant during that time. In each section, the composers are grouped by their country of origin. Some composers featured in the book include: Pauline Viardot-Garcia, Nadia and Lili Boulanger, Elsa Respighi, Amy Marcy Cheney Beach, and Meredith Monk. The author has also put together a section on biographies of women librettists (several of the composers included in this book also wrote the librettos for their operas; the Scottish composer Thea Musgrave is an example). The book also includes a bibliography and an index. Readers will find the entries organized and easy to read. This book will be an excellent addition to an academic library music collection for readers interested in learning more about this important topic.—**Holly Skir**

Popular Music

C, P, S

359.   Womack, Kenneth. **The Beatles Encyclopedia: Everything Fab Four.** Santa Barbara, Calif., Greenwood Press/ABC-CLIO, 2017. 624p. illus. index. $30.00pa. ISBN 13: 978-1-4408-4426-3; 978-1-4408-4427-0 (e-book).

The Beatles Encyclopedia: Everything Fab Four is a condensed version of a 2014 publication of the same name (which is a bit confusing without any sort of title note or differentiation). Whereas the 2014 publication encompassed two volumes and over 1,000 entries, this 2017 condensed version is a single volume with about 360 entries. For this condensed version, Womack has decided to narrow the focus on the band's musical accomplishments in the 1960s.

As with any encyclopedia the entries are organized alphabetically, but because the majority of entries are songs or albums, it is a little easier to navigate than the expanded version. The entries vary in length and content, but those entries about specific songs or albums do follow a general template so as to provide similar information. Most entries include some cross-references that are particularly helpful and interesting. The book also contains a chronology, discography, recommended resources, and an index.

As with the 2014 version, this version is dense with information and will be useful to anyone interested in The Beatles. This volume will, of course, be easier to use and more relevant to those focusing on the band's music, whereas the original edition is much more broad in scope and provides much more peripheral information. To those libraries and collectors interested in a dense edition of Beatles musical information, this volume could be a valuable one-stop resource.—**Tyler Manolovitz**

Rock

P

360.   Weiss, Brett. **Encyclopedia of Kiss.** Jefferson, N.C., McFarland, 2016. 227p. illus. index. $39.95pa. ISBN 13: 978-0-7864-9802-4; 978-1-4766-2540-9 (e-book).

In 1973, four musicians in New York City donned costumes and Kabuki-style makeup, chose Kiss as their moniker, and ignited a marketing phenomenon that has continued for over 40 years. Anchored by founding members Paul Stanley and Gene Simmons, Kiss has sold over 100 million albums and has lent its iconic image and logo to action figures, board games, comic books, pinball machines, theme restaurants, and even a coffin, dubbed the Kiss Kasket. In the *Encyclopedia of Kiss,* Brett Weiss, author of *Classic Home Video Games, 1972-1984* and *Retro Pop Culture A to Z,* explores these and other aspects of the Kiss phenomenon while providing a wealth of biographical information on the many individuals who have played in or been associated with the band.

Weiss's enthusiasm for his subject is palpable, and his knowledge of pop culture serves him well in navigating the vast universe of Kiss-themed products. To his further credit, Weiss maintains sufficient distance to acknowledge the less positive aspects of Kiss's legacy (the band's weak creative output in the 1980s, for example) without acting as an apologist. Skimming through the pages one cannot fail to appreciate the extent to which Kiss's success has hinged on perseverance, timing, and the dedication of supporters like manager Bill Aucoin, who personally funded their first tour, and Neil Bogart, who took a chance on signing them to his label, Casablanca Records.

If anything seems lacking, it is the packaging. The generic cover artwork and black-and-white illustrations are hardly in keeping with a band as visually over-the-top as Kiss. This criticism aside, the *Encyclopedia of Kiss* is a comprehensive and detailed guide that is sure to satisfy lifelong fans and curious newcomers alike.—**Craig Mury Keeney**

Sacred

C, P

361.   Swain, Joseph P. **Historical Dictionary of Sacred Music.** 2d ed. Lanham, Md., Rowman & Littlefield, 2016. 379p. (Historical Dictionaries of Literature and the Arts). $95.00; $94.99 (e-book). ISBN 13: 978-1-4422-6462-5; 978-1-4422-6463-2 (e-book).

This second edition contains a limited number of updates and additions from the first edition (see ARBA 2007, entry 1016): some revised datings of certain works, an expansion of the bibliography since 2005, and some updatings of the biographies of living figures. Sacred dance in both Western and non-Western traditions provides a substantial amount of the new material. While this book examines all sacred music from all religious traditions, it is overwhelmingly focused on Christianity, especially Western classical composers and Western sacred music genres. The bibliography section focuses on Western classical composers and includes short sections for music in each of the world's other religions. Some musical examples are interspersed throughout the dictionary, but no pictures are provided. It is extensively cross-referenced with other entries. As part of the Historical Dictionaries of Literature and the Arts series, this book is a good starting point for amateurs and college students wanting short essays on various topics concerning sacred music around the world.—**Bradford Lee Eden**

26 Mythology, Folklore, and Popular Culture

Folklore

C, P

362. **Folktales and Fairy Tales: Traditions and Texts from around the World.** 2d ed. Anne E. Duggan, Donald Haase, and Helen J. Callow, eds. Santa Barbara, Calif., Greenwood Press/ABC-CLIO, 2016. 4v. $415.00/set. ISBN 13: 978-1-61069-253-3; 978-1-61069-254-0 (e-book).

This second edition of *Folktales and Fairy Tales: Traditions and Texts from around the World* is a four-volume encyclopedic set. The first three volumes focus on people (namely authors and characters), themes/topics, related media, and concepts/issues related to folktales and fairy tales drawn from cultures and peoples from around the world. The fourth volume provides a selection of texts of folktales and fairy tales, primarily those best-known stories (including different versions) such as Cinderella or tales from the Brothers Grimm. All four volumes are illustrated, featuring photos, movie stills, and drawings. While these illustrations are appreciated, and no doubt many of them were originally in black and white, some color illustrations would have been welcome. Color representations would reflect the importance of color in the interpretation of such tales as Red Riding Hood. All four volumes also contain a "Guide to Related Topics" which contains subdivisions. These topics include terms, groups (e.g., cultural or ethnic groups), eras, genres, individuals (e.g., important historical scholars or authors), media and other forms, motifs, and titles. The set utilizes established tale-type numbers/names and indexes; motif names and numbers; migratory legend numbers; and ballad numbers. The set presumes familiarity on the part of the user with these systems. However, given the comprehensive approach of this work, it would have been a great idea to have included these systems and indexes in the work itself. After all, the set does include important personages in the study of folktales and fairy tales, including those individuals responsible for such systems and indexes.

Most entries in the set are about a page and a half, or two to two and a half columns of content. They all include further reading and *see also* lists as well as good cross-referencing. Some entries are pages long, but many of these entries focus on cultural types (e.g., Aztec tales). Those cultural/ethnic group entries (e.g., Finish) do not have standardized subdivisions regarding content. This is a good thing—it allows for the exploration of the unique features and development of those tale types. Furthermore, the set contains a good blend of historically significant and modern authors (from Hans Christian Andersen and the Brothers Grimm to Angela Carter and Neil Gaiman). However, pronunciations of names and words would have been useful, especially considering the wide variety of languages explored in this set. The set wraps up with an extensive bibliography and resources section.

Despite the less-polished aspects of this set as well as the aforementioned missing elements which would have enhanced the work, this title is highly recommended, particularly for public libraries and academic libraries, especially those with programs that would study folktales and fairy tales at the undergraduate and graduate level.—**Megan W. Lowe**

C, S

363.   **Folk Heroes and Heroines around the World.** 2d ed. Seal, Graham and Kim Kennedy White, eds. Santa Barbara, Calif., Greenwood Press/ABC-CLIO, 2016. 411p. index. $89.00. ISBN 13: 978-1-4408-3860-6; 978-1-4408-3861-3 (e-book).

Nothing and nobody is perfect and, perhaps, that is why folk heroes and heroines not only elude the restrictions of time but also transcend both continental and cultural barriers. According to introduction of *Folk Heroes and Heroines Around the World,* a one-volume encyclopedia published by Greenwood Press, folk heroes and heroines exhibit some or all the following characteristics: physical strength; cleverness; persistence; luck; magic; wisdom; helping others; righteousness; cunning; prowess; power; lying; and stupidity. But, based upon the examples in this encyclopedia, the human imperfections that help or hinder folk heroes and heroines provide them with the greatest qualities of all: staying power and cultural adaptability. However, like the heroes and heroines it showcases, this encyclopedia, the second edition to 2001's one-volume work, *Encyclopedia of Folk Heroes* (see ARBA 2003, entry 1145) suffers from the same imperfection as its predecessor. Before that imperfection is discussed, a question must be asked: is this second edition a re-imagining of the original work or simply more pages? The first obvious change with this second edition is the new inclusive title of the encyclopedia. The next obvious change is the editorial pairing of Graham Seal, an Australian folklorist and sole author of the first edition, with Kim Kennedy White, an independent folklorist and senior acquisitions editor for race and ethnicity at ABC-CLIO. Once past judging this book by its cover, significant—yet simple—editorial decisions await the reader inside the book. With this second edition, the editors devote a comprehensive section to the explanation of the major types of folk heroes and heroines and the themes of folk tales. In the prior volume, examinations of types such as "Dragon-Slayers" and "Hare" and themes such as "Outlaws" and "Sleepers" were embedded in with the alphabetical listings. With this volume, the editors extracted those elements and placed them in a section, titled "Major Types and Themes," preceding the main listing of folk heroes and heroines, making it clear to the reader the fluid global connections between these major types and themes, how each culture appropriates those types and themes and transforms them into reflections of that culture. The editors also decided to switch from lumping all content into a general alphabetical listing of heroes and heroines and opted, instead, to arrange the heroes and heroines by continent. Each of those continental sections—from Africa to Oceania—are now preceded by detailed introductory essays offering a glimpse into the culture of those continents and how and why these heroes and heroines represent those cultures. Minor layout changes include: moving the "Chronology of Folk Heroes" to the front of the book so that it precedes the entries; updating images; inserting sidebar boxes to highlight well-known heroes or heroines of a certain type (such as Sinbad being an example of "Nautical Heroes"); and, eliminating the main bibliography in favor of embedding bibliographies at the end of each entry and each continental section. Everything else in this second edition, such as indexes and the thorough introductory overview, remain the same as the prior edition (although, in light of the many changes in this edition, the overview was revised to explain the changes). Another similarity the two editions share is the aforementioned imperfection: an incomplete list of folk heroes and heroines around the world. However, the wisdom displayed by the editors with their revisions and their righteous admission of this imperfection in the introductory overview prevents that flaw from hindering the main quality of this encyclopedia: helping others conduct research and offering others the power to embark upon their own quest for heroes and heroines. As for those librarians embarking upon a collection development quest and wondering if this new edition should be added to their library—the answer is yes.—**Brian T. Gallagher**

P

364.   Redfern, Nick. **The Monster Book: Creatures, Beasts and Fiends of Nature.** Canton, Mich., Visible Ink Press, 2016. 432p. illus. index. $19.95pa. ISBN 13: 978-1-57859-575-4; 978-1-57859-629-4 (e-book).

People the world over understand the concept of a monster. It is a word that draws forth powerful emotions and a variety of mental images. It speaks to a being that is utterly inhuman and inhumane, malevolent and cruel, a creature that symbolizes the antithesis of an orderly, natural, safe world. It is an apex beast that epitomizes everything we fear about the unknown, either in nature or within ourselves. Such creatures have taken many forms throughout the world. Most believe that they are figments of our own fears while a few believe that these beasts actually exist in the unexplored and forgotten corners of the world. Whatever your view, *The Monster Book: Creatures, Beasts, and Fiends of Nature* by Nick Redfern, serves as a compilation of these beings. The book contains over 380 pages worth of entries. Entries are organized and divided by common themes such as aquatic, reptilian, or flying creatures. Creatures included primarily represent cryptozoological specimens but some are more representative of legends and folklore. Individual entries are well written and are presented in a colorful storyteller style as opposed to a more clinical descriptive method. Entries themselves do not possess references but there are many photographs and drawings throughout that are credited at the beginning of the work. The book also includes a list for further reading and a detailed index at the end.

Those with interest in the occult or cryptozoology will find this to be a fun resource due to the storyteller mode of the entries. The book contains a large section on cryptic apes such as Bigfoot so this work would serve in place of Redfern's previous work, *The Bigfoot Book* (see ARBA 2016, entry 389), for any reader not specifically interested in that category. While some entries are based on folklore this would not serve as a source for the academic study of such areas due to the lack of references.—**W. Cole Williamson**

Mythology

C, P

365.   Bane, Theresa. **Encyclopedia of Beasts and Monsters in Myth, Legend and Folklore.** Jefferson, N.C., McFarland, 2016. 423p. index. $49.95pa. ISBN 13: 978-0-7864-9505-4; 978-1-4766-2268-2 (e-book).

Every culture has tales passed through time that help bind communities and societies together. Some are meant to be moral lessons, others as warnings to youth about the dangers of the world, and a few are legendary accounts that try to keep ancient events alive for future generations. Such stories often feature appearances by strange and fantastical beasts or monsters as either antagonist or as explanations for a mysterious world. These creatures are often kept alive today by writers of fiction as they recount such beasts in innovative ways. In her longest work to date, the author has compiled a massive list of such beasts featured in folklore from around the world for use by authors and researchers.

All entries in this work focus on creatures with an identifiable cultural history, having been featured in that society's legends and folklore. As such the author avoids modern, purely fictional creations as well as cryptozoological animals and stories of aliens. Care was taken that any tales included with individual entries stay true to their mythological origins with no attempt at theorizing or rationalization on the part of the author. The book contains 330 plus pages of alphabetically arranged entries. Also included is an extensive bibliography of over 30 pages and an index which provides country of origin lists for many of the beasts throughout the text. While there is some overlap of entries from past works, this has been kept at a minimum, and any such entries have been updated for the purpose of this work. Each monster listed also includes all the names they are known by, sources used for their information; any important cross-references within the work are listed in all caps in the description.

As with the author's past works, this encyclopedia serves as an excellent resource for either the novice or expert researcher due to extensive cross-referencing and an exhaustive index. Entries are clearly worded and appear well researched and thus this book would be a good resource for those interested in world folklore, fiction writing, and gaming.—**W. Cole Williamson**

C, P

366.   Bane, Theresa. **Encyclopedia of Giants and Humanoids in Myth, Legend and Folklore.** Jefferson, N.C., McFarland, 2016. 203p. index. $49.95pa. ISBN 13: 978-1-4766-6351-7; 978-1-4766-2338-2 (e-book).

Whether speaking of the giants of Norse mythology or the titans of Greek, humanity has a rich and varied selection of myths about colossal humanoids and their effects on the world. Most any person can name at least one story featuring a giant such as Jack's foe atop the beanstalk or the biblical Goliath. These creatures continue to be featured to this day in science fiction and fantasy genres. In this single volume the author brings together a host of such tales from across the globe to serve as a reference for writers or students of mythology.

The encyclopedia contains over 150 pages of alphabetically listed entries. Entries are cross-referenced and the work itself contains an extensive index. The encyclopedia focuses on what the author identifies as giant "humanoids," defined in the work as "those beings that have the appearance or characteristics of a human..." (pg. 5). Entries are drawn from collected world mythologies and fairy tales. The work does not include specifically fictional creations, cryptohominids such as Bigfoot, or alien human hybrid theories. The book includes a lengthy bibliography for further reading on the subjects included while each entry is also provided with its own specific reference. The author also makes suggestions for resources on topics outside the scope of this work.

The combination of cross-referencing and index provides the reader an excellent reference experience for either casual viewing or more specific research tasks. Entries are both knowledgeable enough to interest the academic and clearly written to appeal to the layman. This encyclopedia would be a welcome addition to the libraries of those interested in folklore or those seeking ideas in the realm of writing and gaming.—**W. Cole Williamson**

C, P

367.   Bane, Theresa. **Encyclopedia of Spirits and Ghosts in World Mythology.** Jefferson, N.C., McFarland, 2016. 169p. index. $39.95pa. ISBN 13: 978-1-4766-6355-5; 978-1-4766-2339-9 (e-book).

Bane, self-titled "professional vampirologist," author of popular fictional and nonfictional books on fantasy and supernatural themes, but also active in the world of role-playing games and a contributor to various TV shows on paranormal subjects, offers in her encyclopedia a more scientific classification of the world of spirits and ghosts, part of a wider project aimed at a systematic taxonomy of mythological creatures. Although apparently a self-educated folklorist and mythologist, Bane provides the reader a sufficiently well-documented and organized quick reference tool to a wide range of mythological figures from different regions and periods. Methodologically, Bane resorts to functional distinctions among various types of spirits and ghosts, being careful to excise both mythological creatures that fall ever so slightly outside this realm but also the purely bizarre phenomena that feed the current popular imagination. She deals exclusively with those spiritual entities that appear in the mythology and folklore of different cultural and ethnic groups that have been studied by professional historians, anthropologists, and folklorists. In this respect, her encyclopedia is different from the better-known one by Rosemary E. Guiley (see ARBA 2008, entry 696), which deals with a vast array of paranormal phenomena. Although Bane organizes her entries alphabetically, she offers handy classifications based on morphological type (such as "nature spirit," "guardian spirit," and "ghost") and used variants (other names designating the same entity). She also offers phonetic transcriptions for some entries, but this feature is not systematic.—**Rares G. Piloiu**

Popular Culture

C, P, S

368.   **Ghosts in Popular Culture and Legend.** June Michele Pulliam and Anthony J. Fonseca, eds. Santa Barbara, Calif., Greenwood Press/ABC-CLIO, 2016. 403p. illus. index. $89.00. ISBN 13: 978-1-4408-3490-5; 978-1-4408-3491-2 (e-book).

This volume focuses on ghosts in English-speaking cultures, with occasional mentions of Japanese and other contexts. Twenty-nine contributors offer 221 articles, some of which are broad, historical topics like gender, folklore, and popular music, to others which discuss individual films (*Ghostbusters*), books (*The Castle of Otranto*), television programs (*Medium*), haunted sites, and individuals. They range in length from less than a page to three pages. Each of the articles provides suggestions for other related entries. An eight-page bibliography provides readers additional resources.

Any library with readers interested in the diverse aspects of the subject, whether literature, contemporary media productions, or the paranormal in general, should consider this volume. School, public, and academic libraries would benefit from its clearly written content.—**Mark Schumacher**

C, P, S

369.   **Know Your Meme: Internet Meme Database. http://knowyourmeme.com/.** [Website] Free. Date reviewed: 2016.

Know Your Meme: The Internet Meme Database launched in 2008 in order to research and document Internet memes and viral phenomena. By 2011 *Know Your Meme* (KYM) had more than 9.5 million monthly visitors when it was acquired by Cheezburger, the organization behind many other popular Internet sites. Registered members can submit memes and other viral phenomenon to KYM and/or can contribute to research. All material is evaluated by an editorial team that ultimately confirms or invalidates submissions. The research and reporting done by KYM has been used in such leading newspapers as *The New York Times* and *The Wall Street Journal,* as well as news magazines like TIME and such radio news outlets as NPR. In 2009, TIME selected KYM as one of the top 50 websites of the year. The American Folklife Center at the U.S. Library of Congress inducted KYM into its web archiving program in 2014.

The site is free and easy to navigate via a series of tabs on the main screen. Featured memes and videos are discoverable under the Home tab. The Memes tab organizes memes according to their status: confirmed, researching, popular, submission, deadpool (rejected), and all. There is also a place to submit a meme to the site. The Images and Videos tabs are further divided into Trending, Most Commented, Most Favorited, Most Liked, Least Liked, and Most Viewed. Like the Memes tab, there is a place for submission. The Forums tab offers a series of discussion threads (there is a link, for example, to serious discussions). Here users will also find links to places for such things as maintenance and suggestions. There are further connections to Interviewers, In the Media, White Papers, Episode Notes, Behind the Scene, and Meme Review under the Blog tab. The Episodes tab links to viral videos. Lastly, users can click on Memes of 2016 to find Outrages of 2016 as well as Election Memes of 2016, Music Memes of 2016, and Sports Memes of 2016. Although the site is riddled with advertising, it is nonetheless highly recommended.— **ARBA Staff Reviewer**

C, P, S

370.   **Pop Culture in Asia and Oceania.** Jeremy A. Murray and Kathleen M. Nadeau, eds. Santa Barbara, Calif., ABC-CLIO, 2016. 444p. illus. index. $97.00. ISBN 13: 978-1-4408-3990-0; 978-1-4408-3991-7 (e-book).

This volume in the Entertainment and Society around the World series begins with an extensive chronology. It then organizes its approximately 100 entries into eight main chapters: "Popular Music," "Books and Contemporary Literature," "Cinema," "Television and Radio," "Internet and Social Media," "Sports," "Video Games," and "Fashion and Couture." Entries cover Asia, South Asia, Central Asia, Southeast Asia, and the Pacific Islands of Oceania, including Australia and New Zealand, an area that includes about half of the world's total population. Whether customs of "Hijabers," influencers like "Han Han," or "Comic Books, India," entries conclude with suggestions for further reading. The appendix, "Top Ten Lists," has enjoyable lists such as "Top Ten All-Time Films of Australia" and fun facts like "Top Ten Asia Pacific Facebook Users by Country." A bibliography and an index round out the work.

Among other things, the book introduces readers to the influence of politics, trends, and other phenomena on popular culture. The book also considers the future trajectory of popular culture in the context of globalization and the dichotomy between tradition and popular culture. For example, Japanese writer Murakami Haruki is very likely the most widely recognized name in Japanese literature today; ironically he is one of the least "Japanese," for he has gone beyond his cultural boundaries, extending both his readership and his themes out into the realm of the universal to become one of Japan's first truly global writers.

This book is recommended for the general public as well as undergraduate students seeking an appealing introduction to contemporary popular culture in Asia and Oceania.—**Janis Minshull**

C

371.   **The Routledge Companion to Comics.** Frank Bramlett, Roy T. Cook, and Aaron Meskin, eds. New York, Routledge/Taylor & Francis Group, 2017. 455p. illus. index. $240.00. ISBN 13: 978-0-415-72900-0; 978-1-315-85133-4 (e-book).

Scholarship on comics is a fairly recent phenomenon, having just begun in the last three decades of the twentieth century. This book is a compilation of 47 essays by numerous experts and amateurs within the comic book industry and popular culture. It is both an introduction as well as a reference work for anyone who is interested in the study of comics and comic books. Divided into four parts (History and Traditions, Comics Genres, Issues and Concepts, and Other Media and Other Disciplines), each part contains essays that are self-contained both in content and bibliography. Some of the interesting topics explored include: the history of manga, Comics Code, art comics, and comix; issues such as comics adaptation, comics ethics, the translation of comics, and the authorship of comics; various links between comics and other artistic media such as film, caricature, drawing, philosophy, and linguistics; and various comics genres such as romance comics, funny animal comics, and war comics. This book is a welcome reference work for those who both enjoy and wish to study the complexities and history of comics.—**Bradford Lee Eden**

27 Performing Arts

General Works

Biography

P
372.   Lentz, Harris M., III. **Obituaries in the Performing Arts, 2015.** Jefferson, N.C., McFarland, 2016. 387p. illus. $49.95pa. ISBN 13: 978-0-7864-7667-1; 978-1-4766-2553-9 (e-book).

The latest in a series published since 1994, this title includes obituaries of what the author refers to as major and minor figures in film, television, cartoons, theater, music, and popular literature throughout the world. The book begins with the author's year-in-review introductory remarks and a reference bibliography, including Internet resources. Among the more than 1,200 entries, users will find obituaries for the cartoonists and writers of *Charlie Hebdo* magazine alongside B.B. King and Leonard Nimoy. Black-and-white photographs accompany the obituaries, which include biographical details, cause of death, and references to such things as film and television appearances and publications. Recommended for public libraries.—**ARBA Staff Reviewer**

Film, Television, and Video

Bibliography

C
373.   **An Annotated Bibliography for Taiwan Film Studies.** Jim Cheng, James Wicks, and Sachie Noguchi, eds. New York, Columbia University Press, 2016. 567p. index. $125.00; $124.99 (e-book). ISBN 13: 978-0-231-17382-7; 978-0-231-54033-9 (e-book).

This annotated bibliography is the second of a three-volume project. The first volume covers Chinese film studies (2004), the second volume concentrates on Taiwan film studies (2016), and the third volume will focus on Hong Kong film studies. Spanning over 100 years from 1895, when Japan occupied Taiwan, until 2013, the current publication links Taiwan cinema historically and politically with that of China, Hong Kong, and Japan. The organization of the book patterns after the arrangement of the first volume that begins with a brief explanatory introduction followed by the main body that includes 10 sections such as reference materials, film history, and film theory and technique. The volume ends with a short bibliography and three indexes of subject, author, and title. The over 2,700 entries consist of monographs, conference proceedings, manuscripts, and theses while journal articles and Chinese translations of publications from other languages are excluded. The majority of the titles are Chinese publications with notes in English to satisfy a wider audience. Each numbered entry provides standard bibliographic information that contains romanizations and original scripts. The comprehensive nature of the compilation makes for a useful resource. Missing titles such as *Historical Dictionary of Taiwan Cinema* (Lee, 2013) could be easily added as the book is published in both print and electronic format. Multiple appearances of the same title could also be eliminated by using *see* or *see also* references. Overall, the bibliography is a resourceful research tool and is recommended for film studies and Asian studies communities.—**Karen T. Wei**

Dictionaries and Encyclopedias

C, P
374.   **The Encyclopedia of Japanese Horror Films.** Salvador Murguia, ed. Lanham, Md., Rowman & Littlefield, 2016. 408p. index. (National Cinema Series). $95.00; $94.99 (e-book). ISBN 13: 978-1-4422-6166-2; 978-1-4422-6167-9 (e-book).

Once opened, *The Encyclopedia of Japanese Horror Films* unleashed wriggly, rubbery tentacles of film analysis and biography and historical context and cultural insight onto the hapless reviewer's initial cursory interest of the topic and infused it with an irradiated concoction of well-written essays, until the reviewer found himself morphing and transforming and mutating into...an ardent appreciator of J-Horror. Who was the mastermind behind the creation of this encyclopedia? Salvador Murguia, associate professor of sociology at Akita International University and Paul Orfalea Center Fellow in Global Studies at the University of California, Santa Barbara, has been identified as the editor, the man who aligned himself with 57 international and multicultural contributors, contributors who range from freelance writers to university professors to graduate PhD students, contributors who, for the most part, are not film reviewers by profession but who, like the editor, oversaw the creation of this one-volume encyclopedia, are passionate about the topic. According to Murguia, in his two-page introduction, *The Encyclopedia of Japanese Horror Films* stands alone as the only encyclopedia in the English-speaking market focusing on J-Horror. Not content with drawing the line there, Murguia chose to mutate the scope of the encyclopedia by including Japanese comedy horror, science fiction horror, hyper-violence, Japanese cyberpunk horror, ero guru (erotic grotesque), tokusatsu horror (live-action special effects), and anime horror. The essays, listed alphabetically by subject, focus on directors and actors and manga artists and series and motifs and influencers (whether individuals or themes or film types) associated with J-Horror. While the essays about the movies provide the reader with the expected summary and analysis of the film or film series, the contributors' expertise add unexpected textures to the content. For example, the review of 2002's *Dark Water* not only sheds just enough light to reveal the movie's theme and plot (but refrains from revealing the ending), it also dissects the cinematic and cultural elements that set J-Horror apart from Western horror movies. Then there are reviews of movies such as 1959's *The Bloody Sword of the 99th Virgin* and 1999's *Junk,* reviews providing the reader not only a complete synopsis of each of those movies but also an examination of the cultural prejudice and controversy clinging to the latter film and the subtle political commentary peeking out from the zombie goo of the former. Then there are essays such as ones on the Ero Guru Nanensu genre (Erotic Gross Nonsense) and the brief history of Pink Films (Pornographic films, for lack of a better term) that set out, not to win over fans, but to illuminate the history of such films, the intersection of Pink Films and horror movies, the implications of censorship, and what those movies expose about Japanese culture and the West's perception (or misperception) of Japanese culture. Some articles offer the reader a bibliography and those sporadic bibliographies range from one entry to twenty. The editor includes the core skeletal framework of an alphabetical table of contents and alphabetical index to hold his creation together. Who aided and abetted Murguia with the publication of this encyclopedia? Rowan & Littlefield Publishing Group published it as the first volume of their new National Cinema Series, a series edited by Cynthia Miller, Liberal Arts & Interdisciplinary Studies, Emerson College. Three questions: Can Murguia improve upon his creation? Only one suggestion: instead of including directors and actors and genres and movies under one big, alphabetical listing, perhaps the encyclopedia could be segmented into separate alphabetical sections: films and genres and directors and actors, for example. Does Godzilla lurk within these pages? Yes. Will your library's patrons—J-Horror connoisseur or curious novice—find themselves ensnared by the content of *The Encyclopedia of Japanese Horror Films*? Place the book on your shelves and walk away.—**Brian T. Gallagher**

C, P

375.   Erickson, Hal. **Television Cartoon Shows: An Illustrated Encyclopedia, 1949 through 2003.** 2d ed. Jefferson, N.C., McFarland, 2016. 2v. illus. index. $49.95pa/set. ISBN 13: 978-1-4766-6599-3; 978-1-4766-0481-7 (e-book).

On September 27, 2014, the CW aired its Vortexx Cartoon Block for the last time, ending an era of Saturday morning cartoons on broadcast television that dated back to 1962. From *Bugs Bunny* to *Dragon Ball Z,* Saturday morning cartoons were a bedrock of American television for five continuous decades. Hal Erickson spent much of his childhood and adult life watching every cartoon that flickered across his television screen. The first edition of this encyclopedia was published in 1995, a golden age of afternoon cartoons on television, like the *Animaniacs* and *Tiny Toon Adventures.* Almost two years after the discontinuation of Saturday morning cartoons on broadcast television, Erickson's second edition has become more of a tribute than an update. In addition to including cartoon shows televised from 1949 to 2003, the second edition includes an expanded list of cartoon voices and production credits. Each entry is extensive, including the original network of broadcast and date of debut for each program. The cross-referencing allows a reader to search by television show or character. For example, the entry for *Doggie Daddy* redirects to the show *Quick Draw McGraw.* Erickson's extensive historical essay on television cartoon shows is almost as admirable as the compilation of the two-volume, illustrated encyclopedia. The bibliography is extensive, consisting of both popular and scholarly sources. One can only hope that a third edition would expand the contemporary range of cartoons at least two decades. Though more children in the twenty-first century have probably seen Bugs Bunny chomping on a carrot for the first time through an iPad screen,

Erickson's updated encyclopedia is a fitting history and homage to the animators, voices, executives, and networks that made televised animation part of the fabric of American society.—**Josh Eugene Finnell**

C

376. Rollberg, Peter. **Historical Dictionary of Russian and Soviet Cinema.** 2d ed. Lanham, Md., Rowman & Littlefield, 2016. 855p. (Historical Dictionaries of Literature and the Arts). $190.00; $189.99 (e-book). ISBN 13: 978-1-4422-6841-8; 978-1-4422-6842-5 (e-book).

This hefty tome, in its second edition, is the definitive work on this topic, as its covers all three major political periods in what is now called Russia (including many liberated and independent countries that once were part of Russia): the Tsarist period, the Communist period, and the post-Communist state. The author grew up in the Communist Soviet Union, and lived near the Gor'kii Studio for Children's and Youth Films in Moscow. He even starred in the 1972 film *Hurray! We Have Holidays!* The dictionary begins with a detailed introduction which divides Russian and Soviet cinema into five eras: bourgeois commercial cinema (1896-1918); the birth of Soviet cinema (1918-30); the transition to sound and implementation of Stalinist values (1931-53); thaw, "stagnation," and final crisis (1954-85); and the end of Soviet cinema and beyond (1986-2015). The dictionary content itself is framed in the front by a substantial chronology, and in the back with an extensive bibliography that follows the five eras of the introduction. Overall, this reference work is a fantastic addition to any college or university library.—**Bradford Lee Eden**

C, P

377. Whitty, Stephen. **The Alfred Hitchcock Encyclopedia.** Lanham, Md., Rowman & Littlefield, 2016. 531p. illus. index. $80.00; $79.99 (e-book). ISBN 13: 978-1-4422-5159-5; 978-1-4422-5160-1 (e-book).

Few filmmakers in the history of cinema loom as large as Alfred Hitchcock. For a certain generation from the late 1950s, the swirling, black-line caricature of the director set to Gounod's "Funeral March of a Marionette" evokes memories of horror and mystery flickering across their black-and-white television. Here, Stephen Whitty undertakes the monumental task of detailing not only the films of this auteur but also the artistic process and people who made each of his films a classic. Surprisingly, but also refreshingly, Whitty forgoes a perfunctory and lengthy introductory essay for a brief and simple orientation to the text. Entries are arranged alphabetically, and intermingle films with people and themes. Though varying in length, each entry is substantial and includes a bibliography for further reading. Moreover, to facilitate searching, each entry is cross-referenced. For example, the entry on long takes will lead the reader to the film *Under Capricorn* and the actress Ingrid Bergman. In addition, functionally breaking up the monotony of text, film stills and photographs are interspersed throughout the work. Supplementing individual references embedded in each entry, a concise bibliography is included highlighting the most foundational scholarship on Hitchcock. Perhaps presuming familiarity with the filmography of this great director, Whitty does not include a list of Hitchcock films. Overall, Whitty manages to capture the breadth, depth, and influence of this great director within a superbly compiled tertiary source. Ever since the publication of Thomas Leitch's

2002 *Encyclopedia of Alfred Hitchcock,* there has been a noticeable gap in the reference literature on this towering figure of cinema. Whitty has produced a book worthy of the wait.—**Josh Eugene Finnell**

Handbooks and Yearbooks

C, P, S

378.   **AdViews. http://library.duke.edu/digitalcollections/adviews/.** [Website] Free. Date reviewed: 2017.

This database of thousands of historic commercials produced during the 1950s-80s by the New York advertising agency D'Arcy Masius Benton & Bowles (DMB &B) is a collective project between the Digital Collections Program, the Hartman Center for Sales, Advertising and Marketing, and other groups at Duke. The home page offers links to copyright and citation information, expert interviews available via YouTube or iTunes U, and a brief description of the collection. Perhaps most valuable is the Research Help link, which takes users to the DMB & B archives, allowing researchers to put the advertisements into context. With the click of a mouse, a user can watch hundreds of commercials for products like Tide, Mr. Clean, Prell, Pampers, Parliament Cigarettes, Pledge, and Bird's Eye. This entertaining database offers something to teachers, students, and researchers in a range of disciplines, from history and gender studies, to health sciences, to sociology, to business and beyond. Highly recommended for school, college, and public libraries.—**ARBA Staff Reviewer**

P

379.   Beck, Simon D. **The Aircraft-Spotter's Film and Television Companion.** Jefferson, N.C., McFarland, 2016. 352p. illus. $45.00pa. ISBN 13: 978-0-4766-3349-4; 978-1-4766-8893-4 (e-book).

This painstakingly researched book begins with a list of abbreviations along with a helpful preface, foreword, and introduction. The book is divided into three sections: Feature Films, Selected Television Series and TV Movies, and Aircraft Manufacturers. Altogether the author investigates aircraft used in 350 movies and television shows in what he describes as an "aircraft identification reference." The length of entries varies depending on the amount of information available, but where possible users will find such things as the cast, directors, studio, running time, whether the film was color or black and white and, of course, the true identity of the aircraft used in the productions. Some entries also have a separate section called "Factual Background." Information is enhanced by the use of figures, black-and-white illustrations, and *see* references. The third section comes in at approximately one hundred pages of aircraft listings by manufacturer, along with cross-references. The book also includes four appendixes: "Aviation Film Pilots and Technicians," "Tallmantz Aviation, Inc.," "Blue Max Aviation, Ltd." and "U.S. Aircraft Carriers on Film." The book ends with references and a bibliography. This informative and detailed title is highly recommended to libraries looking for a work on the aircraft used in aviation film or to individuals who want a reliable guide.—**ARBA Staff Reviewer**

C, S

380.   **Critical Insights Film: Casablanca.** James Plath, ed. Hackensack, N.J., Salem Press, 2016. 280p. index. $95.00. ISBN 13: 978-1-61925-876-1; 978-1-61925-877-8 (e-book).

Undoubtedly one of the most famous Hollywood films ever produced, *Casablanca* is a critic's delight. From its moody visual design to its smart dialogue and stellar cast, the movie invites a lively discourse. This volume in the Critical Insights Film series shares an engaging selection of contemporary scholarship addressing topics such as the film's place in popular culture, approach to gender, global appeal, auteur theory, and much more.

The opening chapters are helpful in establishing the importance of understanding the times in which *Casablanca* was made, and include interesting anecdotes from the film's production. A biography of the film's director, Michael Curtiz, is also included early on.

Three essays make up the Critical Contexts section, which serve to highlight the initial critical and popular reception of the film, as well as its place as an icon of the "noir" genre of film. "Tips of the Hat: The Critical Response to Casablanca" is a good piece which affirms understanding of why so many viewers love the film and perhaps enlightens readers about those who did not.

Critical Readings cover myriad topics, from elements of film art (music, lighting, acting, etc.) to themes such as gender, race, and heroism. "Adlibbing Greatness: Casablanca's Screenplay" by Kirk Honeycutt discusses how because of, or perhaps in spite of, the group approach to writing the film's screenplay, it has become an award-winning classic. Bjorpn Nordfjord, in his piece titled "Rick's Café International: Casablanca as a Film of the World," explains the unique global appreciation of the film, even as it was a strict product of Hollywood's studio system. Nine more essays round out this section.

The volume concludes with a generous resources section, which includes a cast list, awards, a chronology of director Michael Curtiz' life, his filmography, and a bibliography, followed by an index.—**ARBA Staff Reviewer**

C, P, S

381.   **Database of African American Silent film. http://dhbasecamp.humanities.ucla. edu/afamfilm/.** [Website] Free. Date reviewed: 2017.

Stemming from a project out of the University of California, Los Angeles, this database offers information on silent African American cinema or "race films" produced before 1930. This project offers researchers an excellent opportunity to discover works often left out of the American cinematic conversation.

This smartly designed site defines race films as those movies created explicitly for African American audiences. It provides excellent historical context for the films and the difficulties filmmakers encountered. The site also provides background for the project, explaining methodologies behind data collection and presentation, definitions, parameters, and more.

Users can click on several buttons to access the data and learn how to interpret it. They can access a relational data table including entries for People, Films, Companies, and Sources. Another tab helps users process the data via "visualizations," or state-of-the-art tables, diagrams, maps, and other material. And a Tutorial tab provides video assistance in regards to working with the data tools. Some of the films profiled include *The Railroad Porter, A Day at Tuskegee,* and *The Butler.*

A Sources and Further Reading tab offers a generous listing of primary and secondary source materials. This sophisticated website shines a positive light on an obscure but fascinating chapter of the American film story and would appeal to researchers, historians, students, and educators interested in African American culture or film history in general.—**ARBA Staff Reviewer**

C, P

382.   Edwards, Paul M. **World War I on Film: English Language Releases through 2014.** Jefferson, N.C., McFarland, 2016. 256p. index. $39.95pa. ISBN 13: 978-0-7864-9866-6; 978-1-4766-2063-3 (e-book).

Inarguably, World War I was one of the most important events of the twentieth century. As a global military conflict, it destroyed entire empires, saw the rapid emergence of new republics, transformed relationships among nations, and laid the groundwork for the rise of fascism. Death toll estimates have held in the tens of millions for soldiers and civilians alike. In the decades since the war's aftermath, with deeply rooted political lines inexorably drawn, historians continue to cast the war as disastrous and unnecessary. Unsurprisingly, then, a similar assessment of World War I made its way into the film industry and evolved as a distinct genre, i.e. "war film." While few in number compared to other film genres, the timeless endurance of war films makes this book a highly relevant and useful catalog for film historians and consumers alike.

The book profiles numerous films about World War I; an exact number does not seem to be stated, although this is an insignificant detail, given the book's context and plethora of content. Edwards begins by providing a brief but comprehensive preface of how the war film genre evolved; the effect of the genre on American culture; and the ways in which the film industry presented war films as "romantically glorifying." Following the preface is an introduction, the bulk of which is comprised of two essays, with one outlining the history of war films, and the other exploring the genre's major themes and plots. The introduction also includes key facts about the films listed, in terms both general ("Selection," "Time") and unique ("Bloopers," "Warnography"). Next is the main section, entitled "The Films," in which individual films are profiled according to aforementioned key facts. The entries are in alphabetical order by title, and include a corresponding date. On that note, end matter constitutes an appendix of films by date; reference notes; a bibliography; and an exhaustive index.

The book is very well organized, thoroughly explanatory, and an excellent source for anyone interested in gaining ample insight into World War I films. The author fluctuates between mostly objective descriptions in the preface and introduction and subjective comment with each entry, although the latter seems necessary if readers are to keep in mind that the horrific and tragic backdrop of these films was not always about combat, a point which Edwards stresses throughout the book. Lastly, a distinctly notable and useful feature within each entry is a subsection entitled "military correlation," in which Edwards evaluates the extent to which a film in question is correlated to providing an accurate understanding of World War I.—**Sheri Edwards**

C

383.   Hischak, Thomas S. **Musicals in Film: A Guide to the Genre.** Santa Barbara, Calif., Greenwood Press/ABC-CLIO, 2017. 449p. index. $89.00. ISBN 13: 978-1-4408-4422-5; 978-1-4408-4423-2 (e-book).

Thomas S. Hischak truly guides his readers through the film genre of the musical, arguing that it is a genuinely American invention and contribution to the arts and should be placed at the center of any understanding of the history of Hollywood. His deep appreciation for and knowledge of the subject matter is apparent throughout. The entries are written in an enjoyable and accessible, almost conversational style, peppered with tidbits of gossip and vibrant description that could only come from a true aficionado. He does not shy away from expressing his discerning critical opinion, nor in the opinion of this reviewer should he as it contributes significantly to how informative and engagingly the entries read.

The contents of the work are organized into preliminary matter, an opening section listing movie musical genres, and then the largest section of the work detailing the history of the movie musical, followed by a bibliography and an index. The preliminary matter has four sections; a list of biographies of significant players in the genre which are inserted throughout the work next to related entries for a given movie musical. An introduction titled "Who Needs Talking" wherein Hischak lays out his perspective on the subject, pointing out that even when movies were "silent" they were always accompanied by music, and that it was actually Al Jolson performing a song which inaugurated the "talkies," hence music and film have always been inextricably linked and the musical is the foundational genre of modern American cinema. This is followed by a timeline split into three columns; year, notable film musicals, next to concurrent historic and cultural events. The final preliminary matter is a short glossary of movie musical terms.

The work begins with a listing of different genres that the movie musical can fall into, such as frontier musicals or animated musicals, with each entry providing a significantly detailed description including examples. Then the largest section of the book follows providing the history of the movie musical in eight chronological sections by decade starting with "The 1920s: Learning to Sing On-Screen" and concluding with "Musicals since 2000: A Rebirth of Sorts." The individual entries for each film are designed to include studio and release date, producer, who wrote the screenplay, songwriters, director, choreographer, musical director, cinematographer, cast and a complete list of songs that appear in the film. Occasionally a captioned still image from the film accompanies an entry. At the end of each description are citations for suggested further reading and *see also* cross-referencing when appropriate. In a similar vein, at the end of each biographical entry are listed autobiographies, biographies, and memoirs. However, these are limited to author, title, and year of publication.

The scope of the work could be better reflected in the title, as it is strictly limited to musicals in American cinema. Any novice researcher seeking out information on Whoopie Goldberg in *Sarafina!*, Catherine Deneuve in either *The Umbrellas of Cherbourg* or *8 Women,* or any significant information on Bollywood would be misled to seek out this volume although it broadly purports to cover musicals in film. Hischak has conveniently classified all of these and like subject matter under the genre of "foreign musicals" and beyond this they are not included. Overall the entries are written with erudition and infectious enthusiasm for the subject matter creating a book that is not just informative but enjoyable. It would be a useful reference work for any academic institution with a performing arts program or library with an extensive film collection.—**Todd Simpson**

C, P

384.   **Joanie 4 Jackie. http://www.joanie4jackie.com/.** [Website] Free. Date reviewed: 2017.

Miranda July began the Joanie 4 Jackie project in 1995 with a challenge to other female moviemakers to send her their work. The Getty Research Institute and Getty Trust acquired Joanie 4 Jackie, an archive of films by women, in 2016 and much of the material became freely available online in January 2017. Prior to the Getty, Bard College housed the Joanie 4 Jackie project.

The site has an attractive interface and is easy to navigate via links or from tabs across the top of the page: Joanie 4 Jackie, Chainletter Tapes, The Co-Star Tapes, Documents, Events, Where Is She Now?, and Contact + FAQ. There is also a basic search box. The material under each of these tabs is explained on the main page, with links that take you to the same destinations of the tabs. The movies are found by clicking on the Chainletter Tapes and The Co-Star Tapes. Many of these are digitized and can be watched in their entirety by clicking on the thumbnail of the movie. Further links to a filmmaker's website and/or memories (the subject matter under the Where Is She Now? tab) may appear next to the thumbnail of the movie. The Chainletter Tapes series ran from 1995 to 2007. The Co-Star tapes started as a second series in 1998. Bonus materials including thumbnails of posters and announcements of events related to the project are available under the Documents and Events tabs. There is contact information that allows users to ask questions of Miranda July and of Getty staff. The Getty will continue to digitize and post more of the material, but for now no new material is being added to the archive.

The subject matter of many of the films is for mature audiences (a basic search of the terms violence, rape, murder, abortion, and sex returned results), but this would be a treasure trove of primary source material for college students or scholars in film studies, women's studies, and more.—**ARBA Staff Reviewer**

C

385.   Leotta, Alfio. **Peter Jackson.** New York, Bloomsbury Academic, 2015. 304p. $150.00. ISBN 13: 978-1-6235-6653-1.

One in Bloomsbury's Companions to Contemporary Filmmakers series, this book offers a comprehensive but concise profile of New Zealand filmmaker Peter Jackson. Beloved the world over for his The Lord of the Rings and The Hobbit film series, he is also highly regarded for his innovative contributions to global film production. While not an in-depth biography, this book nonetheless does an excellent job of tracing Jackson's career from his youthful experiments with "splatstick" to his large-scale work in epic fantasy and beyond.

Five sections offer easy access to various features of Jackson's film story. Section one tells about the man and his personal relationship to film with a very brief biography, a discussion of the development of his themes and style, and his overall leap from self-funded one-reels to cinema entrepreneur, wherein he founded globally regarded production and special effects companies. Following sections focus on Jackson's most important artistic collaborations, such as with motion-capture actor Andy Serkis or screenwriter Fran Walsh; his impact on New Zealand and its film industry; and his deep connection to New Zealand geography in terms of locating, designing, and marketing his films. A final section offers an A-Z approach to describing his films (which, beyond the Tolkien adaptations include *Heavenly Creatures, King Kong,* and more) as well as relevant concepts (e.g., "splatstick," which refers to a cinematic blend of horror and humor) and themes.

Further reference materials are included in two appendixes: a filmography (listing important dates and detailed cast and crew) and a selected bibliography.

Recommended for academic libraries supporting film studies programs.—**ARBA Staff Reviewer**

P

386.   Leszczak, Bob. **Single Season Sitcoms of the 1980s: A Complete Guide.** Jefferson, N.C., McFarland, 2016. 259p. illus. index. $45.00pa. ISBN 13: 978-0-7864-9958-8; 978-1-4766-2384-9 (e-book).

Carrier Fischer claimed that fame was just obscurity biding its time. Such is the case for many of the forgotten sitcoms mentioned in this book. A follow-up to *Single Season Sitcoms, 1948-1979: A Complete Guide* (see ARBA 2013, entry 1047), this work focuses on the unique decade of the 1980s. And whereas networks were few and programming limited in the decades leading up to the 1980s, cable television and the FOX TV Network dramatically changed the landscape of television. An explosion of sitcoms took to the airwaves of which over 200 never made it past their rookie year. Entries contain basic descriptions of the shows including time slots; duration; network affiliations; production studios; and episode titles. A section dedicated to a small number of shows which returned to the small screen in a much altered format from their freshman season highlights popular shows like *Charles in Charge, Joanie Loves Chachi,* and *Still the Beaver.* What sets this series apart from similar works is the inclusion of behind-the-scenes commentary culled from published and unpublished interviews with cast and crew, which provide revelations or humorous anecdotes about the shows and their production. Descriptions also provide interesting details regarding the background of show and character creations. This book is certainly more than a documented history of short-lived sitcoms.—**Brian J. Sherman**

P

387.   Miller, Thomas Kent. **Mars in the Movies: A History.** Jefferson, N.C., McFarland, 2016. 280p. illus. index. $39.95pa. ISBN 13: 978-0-7864-9914-4; 978-1-4766-2626-0 (e-book).

Miller, a former NASA employee, television crew member, and writer for numerous sci-fi and other publications, has produced one of the more entertaining and informative guides to the genre in some time. Starting with Edison's 1910 short *A Trip to Mars* through Ridley Scott's 2015 *The Martian,* Miller covers 98 well- and lesser-known feature films, direct-to-videos, television films, and miniseries related to the planet Mars. Divided into subgenre chapters (e.g., "Voyages to Mars," "Invaders from Mars"), the guide not only provides a synopsis of each film but also critical assessment, cast, and crew. Black-and-white photos primarily of posters are scattered throughout, along with biographies of many of the behind-the-scenes technicians, directors, and others who gave life to these films. But what really makes this work stand out is Miller's occasionally hilarious commentary on these films—*Mars in the Movies* is part memoir of someone who grew up watching sci-fi, and he even was able to interview some film personnel for additional background. Although the limited scope might not make this work a top choice for most academic libraries, public libraries and fans of the genre should absolutely purchase it. Highly recommended for all sci-fi and film collections.—**Anthony J. Adam**

C, P

388. Romanko, Karen A. **Television's Female Spies and Crimefighters: 600 Characters and Shows, 1950s to the Present.** Jefferson, N.C., McFarland, 2016. 256p. illus. index. $35.00pa. ISBN 13: 978-0-7864-9637-2; 978-1-4766-2415-0 (e-book).

Television's Female Spies and Crimefighters: 600 Characters, Shows, 1950s to the Present is a unique reference work chronicling the memorable women spies, superheroes, detectives, private investigators, and amateur sleuths from live-action television shows airing on U.S. television. The work includes 250 series entries and 350 character entries from shows broadcast from 1950 to 2014. Coverage includes shows in which women are main characters or co-leads and ranges from the obscure (Biff Baker, USA) to the well known (The Bionic Woman). Series entries provide cast and production credits, a detailed synopsis, and critical commentary. Character entries cover supporting and lead roles, with the lead characters garnering more substantial coverage; supporting characters receive a single-sentence description. This user-friendly resource is arranged alphabetically and includes cross-references that allow for the identification of a character by series title or character name. High quality black-and-white photos enhance the book's visual appeal. The introduction offers a brief but thorough overview of the history of women spies and crime fighters on television, placing them in a sociological context and considering them from a feminist perspective. The author highlights the progressive, often groundbreaking, nature of these characters but also acknowledges their contradictions—for example, the reliance on sex appeal typified by Charlie's Angels. A "Note on Sources" outlines the most important resources consulted for this well-researched book. The volume concludes with an appendix of "rewatchable" shows available on DVD and an index of actors featured in the series. Written in accessible language—and with a sense of humor—this book will appeal to pop culture fans and academics alike. This work is recommended for large public libraries and academic libraries.—**Lisa Morgan**

28 Philosophy and Religion

Philosophy

Handbooks and Yearbooks

C

389. **Philosophy: Sex and Love.** Petrik, James and Arthur Zucker, eds. New York, Macmillan Reference USA/Gale Group, 2016. 414p. illus. index. (Macmillan Interdisciplinary Handbooks). $179.00. ISBN 13: 978-0-02-866336-4; 978-0-02-866345-6 (e-book).

The Macmillan Interdisciplinary Handbooks cover various aspects of philosophy using materials from other disciplines to help present relevant ideas. They are useful introductions to philosophy for those who are not familiar with the subject. This volume looks at sex and love.

The articles, all written and signed by academics, examine topics that are central to philosophy and important in daily life. The issues raised are often ethical, involving autonomy, coercion, and consent. They also look at the nature of love, friendship, and pleasure and discuss the role of religion. Prostitution and adultery, pornography, and virtual relationships appear as well. Using material from psychology, anthropology, art, literature, and music to illustrate ideas such as betrayal, the authors discuss all aspects of the topic from many points of view. This gives readers the tools to think about the issue and draw their own conclusions. Since issues such as same-sex marriage, sexual assault, and contraception are often in the news, the material covered here will be very useful for students preparing debates and reports. Each article has a resource list for further research.

This is an excellent source for undergraduate and large public libraries.—**Barbara M. Bibel**

C

390. **Philosophy: Sources, Perspectives, and Methodologies.** Donald M. Borchert, ed. New York, Macmillan Reference USA/Gale Group, 2016. 442p. index. (Philosophy series). $179.00. ISBN 13: 978-0-02-866295-4; 978-0-02-866296-1 (e-book).

Those looking for an introduction to the field of philosophy will appreciate this well-rounded primer to the field. With 27 chapters, divided up into four parts, this volume is unique in its ability to provide enough information to inspire a reader's curiosity, but not so much that it would overwhelm. Edited by Ohio University professor emeritus Donald M. Borchert, this handbook serves as the entry-level volume in the Philosophy Series of the Macmillan Interdisciplinary Handbooks. The four distinct parts of the volume move the reader through different venues in the field of philosophy; the first part introduces the nature of philosophy, the second provides a glimpse into philosophy through interdisciplinary lenses, the third covers some global perspectives, and the last introduces a few of the subfields within philosophy. Each part begins with an introduction that provides an overview of the coming chapters, allowing the reader to easily identify, connect, and relate the material as they move through it. Each of the chapters within the four parts focuses on providing the reader with a nontechnical introduction to the philosophers, theories, terminology, methods, and issues that are most relevant for gaining a base knowledge of the current, historical, and global philosophical landscape. The chapters are written by experts, provide nontechnical overviews of each topic, and all end with a helpful and concise summary. The endnotes, bibliographies, recommended readings, and references at the end of the chapters do an excellent job of providing the reader with extensive resources for further study. Those looking for a basic overview will appreciate the volume's effective scaffolding that allows one to form a base understanding of philosophy; while the reader looking for clarification or an overview of a specific element within the field will appreciate the ease of access, constructed by the clear organization of the parts, chapters, headings, and glossary. This handbook will be most valuable to those institutions serving lower-division college students.—**Kali A. Rippel**

Religion

General Works

Dictionaries and Encyclopedias

C, P
391.   **Melton's Encyclopedia of American Religions.** 9th ed. J. Gordon Melton, James Beverley, Constance Jones, and Pamela S. Nadell, eds. New York, Macmillan Reference USA/Gale Group, 2017. 2v. index. $528.00/set. ISBN 13: 978-1-4144-0687-9; 978-1-4144-6265-3 (e-book).

   J. Gordon Melton, Distinguished Professor of American Religious History at Baylor University, is a prolific scholar who is best known for editing *Melton's Encyclopedia of American Religions*. Now in its ninth edition, this work not only features complete revisions of all the entries found in its predecessor (see ARBA 2010, entry 1094), but also includes coverage of approximately 385 newly identified religious groups. Although the two volumes constitute a set, they can also be utilized independently. Volume one covers the United States, while volume two focuses on Canada. This work continues to deserve its place as one of the standard reference tools found in all public and academic library collections. No other work exists that provides such comprehensive coverage of active and defunct religious groups in North America than this resource.—**John R. Burch Jr.**

Handbooks and Yearbooks

C

392. **Religion: Embodied Religion.** Kent L. Brintnall, ed. New York, Macmillan Reference USA/Gale Group, 2016. 418p. illus. index. (Macmillan Interdisciplinary Handbooks). $179.00. ISBN 13: 978-0-02-866297-8; 978-0-02-866349-4 (e-book).

Editor Kent Brintnall, with expert assistance from an editorial board, has assembled this compendium, bringing together religion, sexuality, and paths for developing scholarly studies. This title is one of 10 in the Macmillan Interdisciplinary Handbooks series on religion.

In the first two chapters, the context of religion and sex are introduced. Chapters 3 through 11 are categorized as "Traditions," while chapters 12 through 22 describe different "Approaches" to the study of sexuality and religion. Chapters have opening ideas leading to case studies, data, methodological approaches, myths, prophecies, religious quotes, and stories. Black-and-white photos are used throughout the chapters. Documentation comes full circle with summaries at the end of chapters followed by bibliographies and filmographies. Back matter includes a practical glossary of terms and acronyms followed by a solid index.

The study of religion and sexuality is given a broad range in *Embodied Religion* with great variance in historical and contemporary time periods, religions, languages and interpretation, social class, and doctrine. Examples of religious interpretation in relation to sexuality are demonstrated with chapters focused on specific religions and how practitioners embody their belief; African American diaspora, Buddhism, Christianity, Judaism, Islam, and Pagan and Indigenous traditions are some of the races and faiths examined in the context of how tradition and belief influence sexual acceptance or dissuasion. Religious aspects of culture, interpretation of texts, ritual, and social mores are described with examples of how practices such as asceticism or tantric traditions find validation. "Tantric traditions have no single origin, but they may be defined as a particular approach to desire evidenced by religious texts and techniques in which practitioners employ the human body as an access point to divine energy, power, and states of awareness" (p. 50).

Contradictory practices and diversity of belief bring forward ideas about abortion, apocolypticism, celibacy, contraception, eroticism, martyrdom, modesty, polygamy, and same sex relations, to name just a few areas of access to this topic. Historical and contemporary thought intertwine as researchers will see the trajectory between traditional thought and modern views such as "the Buddhist encounter with modern and postmodern discourses has resulted in a number of different initiatives regarding Buddhist approaches to desire, sexuality, and embodiment" (p. 67). Culture and evolution of religious thought is well represented here.

The section on different avenues for research, "Approaches," is remarkably useful to scholars as it rich in providing potential areas of study. With chapters of "Ethnography," "Feminism," and "Psychoanalysis," just 3 of the 11 chapters in this section, scholars find pragmatic paths to develop further study in sexuality and religion.

This volume is a very strong entry into the series. Questions and information on religious experience and how gender, desire, and embodiment are interpreted, celebrated, abhorred, and justified are well represented in this compendium of scholarly works. This book is suitable for researchers and scholars of history, sociology, theology, and global studies.

Highly recommended.—**Janis Minshull**

Bible Studies

Dictionaries and Encyclopedias

C, P

393. **Dictionary of Daily Life in Biblical & Post-Biblical Antiquity.** Edwin M. Yamauchi and Marvin R. Wilson, eds. Peabody, Mass., Hendrickson, 2014. 400p. $24.95pa. ISBN 13: 978-1-61970-460-2.

C, P

394. **Dictionary of Daily Life in Biblical & Post-Biblical Antiquity.** Edwin M. Yamauchi and Marvin R. Wilson, eds. Peabody, Mass., Hendrickson, 2015. 480p. illus. $24.95pa. ISBN 13: 978-1-61970-640-8.

C, P

395. **Dictionary of Daily Life in Biblical & Post-Biblical Antiquity.** Edwin M. Yamauchi and Marvin R. Wilson, eds. Peabody, Mass., Hendrickson, 2016. 450p. $24.95pa. ISBN 13: 978-1-61970-727-6.

C, P

396. **Dictionary of Daily Life in Biblical & Post-Biblical Antiquity.** Edwin M. Yamauchi and Marvin R. Wilson, eds. Peabody, Mass., Hendrickson, 2016. 500p. $24.95pa. ISBN 13: 978-1-61970-728-3.

Students of the Hebrew Bible and New Testament as well as historians of the ancient Middle East will benefit from the publication of this four-volume reference set. Unlike other manners and customs reference sources, *Dictionary of Daily Life in Biblical & Post-Biblical Antiquity* has not compiled its list of entries from terms or subjects mentioned in the Bible. Rather, well-respected editors Edwin M. Yamauchi and Marvin R. Wilson used the Human Relations Area Files (HRAF) classification system to illuminate the historical and cultural contexts in which the texts were written. For example, while abortion is not explicitly mentioned in the Bible, it did occur, and the entry here lists the scripture references that may allude to the practice, as well as laws and other writings that treat the subject in more detail. This will provide the reader with an understanding of how abortion was practiced, how it was perceived, and how it was punished according to the laws of the time.

The authors have chosen 120 such HRAF subjects by their importance and their corresponding contextual relevance to the subject of daily life in the ancient world. Six textual source-bases provide the evidence: the Old Testament, New Testament, texts from the Near Eastern World, the Greco-Roman World, the Jewish World, and the Christian World. This gives the essayists a large body of sources, for which even the list of abbreviations is imposing. One difficulty with this framework is the amount of subject knowledge assumed for the reader to locate the appropriate entry. For example, to research the statement in the book of Ezekiel that the Lord will draw his sword against Jerusalem, the reader would have to know something about Nebuchadnezzar's role in this process. The king made use of casting lots (belomancy), asking idols, and examining the liver (heptascopy). These practices fall under the HRAF subject Divination and Sortition, rather than, as one might expect, Magic and Gambling. I found that an additional scripture reference or index would help the reader with navigation.

Volume one covers 39 HRAF subjects in 400 pages, starting with Abortion and ending with Dance. Most of the 33 contributors to the volume write from the United States, with one from China and one from Germany. This is also the first and last volume edited by Allen Emery. For ease of access, one will want to become familiar with the 20-page abbreviations list, the explanation of periods, ages, and dates, and the short introduction. The last two of these seem to be reproduced in subsequent volumes. Each entry begins with a short introduction of the subject followed by discussion under the six headings mentioned above, and ends with cross-references to other essays in the dictionary. Volume one ends with a helpful select bibliography and beautiful colored photograph plates of figures. Additional features that could have proved helpful include indexes by subject, name, and scripture reference.

Volume two includes 25 entries, beginning with Death and the Afterlife and closing with Human Sacrifice. It also features more positive titles like Drama and Theaters, Education, and Hair (which one should cross-reference with Barbers and Beards in volume one). Some of the contributors have changed as well as the sources listed in the abbreviations portion of the front matter. The introduction has been amended to inform the user that a new editor has taken on the project, Jonathan Kline.

Volume three adds an additional 25 entries to the dictionary, from Incense through Nursing & Wet Nurses. Aside from minor changes, the volume provides the same quality of content, bibliography, and figures (photographs). Some of the contributors have changed, as have the abbreviated sources listed in the front matter, and the introduction does not mention a specific editor (although it thanks Andrew Pottorf in its ending paragraph for his scholarly and personal contributions). This particular volume covers many family life topics including infanticide, inheritance, kisses & embraces, laundry, marriage, menstruation, and nursing. Of personal interest, 32 pages are devoted to libraries & books from those mentioned in the Biblical text to the Nag Hammadi.

Volume four finishes the set with 26 entries, covering Oaths & Vows through Wild Animals and Hunting. Similar minor updates have been made to the list of contributors, abbreviations, citations, etc. I was surprised not to see entries for Ritual (Religious) or a similar subject or the Ordering of Time in this volume, although both would prove interesting. The reader should see each volume's "Periods, Ages, and Dates" for the editors' handling of the latter subject. While an expanded edition could include more HRAF subjects, for now this four-volume set provides quality scholarship and is highly recommended for seminaries and libraries with users interested in the Hebrew Bible, the New Testament, and the ancient Middle East.—**Amy Koehler**

Handbooks and Yearbooks

C, P, S

397.   **America's Public Bible. http://americaspublicbible.org/.** [Website] Free. Date reviewed: 2017.

This website traces the presence of biblical quotations throughout newspapers collected in the Library of Congress' (LOC) *Chronicling America* database, which has digitized pages of over 2,000 American newspapers of yore. This site essentially tracks trends of Bible quote usage from the 1840s through the 1920s in order to examine the public dissemination of the words and messages of the Bible (King James) through American journalism. The Explore the Quotations tab allows users to select a specific Bible verse or choose from a series of thematic prompts (e.g., Marriage and Divorce, The Ten Commandments, Children, etc.). The site will then chart the frequency of quote use over time and provide a listing of newspapers using the quote. The listing includes newspaper name, state, date, Bible verse reference, and a link to the applicable LOC's *Chronicling America* database newspaper page. Topics & Verses notes the most-quoted verses by decade and provides a visualization of Bible chapters most frequently quoted together. Sources & Methods describe the technical aspect and scope of the project. While the website plans to expand its scope, it currently offers a good range of scholarship opportunities for those interested in American journalism, social history, religious history, and more.—**ARBA Staff Reviewer**

C, P, S
398. **Bible Odyssey. http://www.bibleodyssey.org/.** [Website] Free. Date reviewed: 2016.

Bible Odyssey, a free database completed in 2014, allows users to study the Bible with expert, academic guidance. The Society of Biblical Literature, the National Endowment for the Humanities, the American Bible Society, Harper Collins, and the Philip G. and Lois F. Roets Endowment for the Bible and the Public partner in this undertaking.

The clean interface makes searching a snap. From the home page users can search using one of three main tabs—People, Places, Passages—all organized in an A to Z format, with the additional option of clicking on illustrations that correspond to the people, places, and passages listed alphabetically. For each person, place, or passage there are lengthy answers to two key questions; interesting facts; links to related publications, Bible passages, and the *Harper Collins Bible Dictionary;* and a place to ask a scholar a question. Two other tabs, Bible and Tools, are positioned on the top right side of the home page. Bible takes users to the searchable and complete text of three Bibles, the *New Revised Standard Version,* the *Contemporary English Version,* and the *King James Version.* The tools link offers access to timelines, a map gallery, an image gallery, a game gallery, a glossary, short biographies of contributors, an extensive bibliography for those who want to pursue a topic in greater depth, a place to ask a scholar, a link to the full Harper Collins Bible Dictionary, the ability to browse the contents of the entire site A to Z, video and audio galleries of scholars explicating Biblical topics, and answers to questions about Bible basics, like "how has the New Testament scholarship changed over time"?

This high-quality site has something to offer students and teachers of all levels. Highly recommended.—**ARBA Staff Reviewer**

C
399. **The Hebrew Bible: A Critical Companion.** John Barton, ed. Princeton, N.J., Princeton University Press, 2016. 613p. maps. index. $45.00. ISBN 13: 978-0-691-15471-8.

Traditional handbooks to the Old Testament provide a chapter-by-chapter analysis of the biblical text. This book is different and bills itself as a critical companion to the Hebrew Bible and views the Old Testament through a variety of thematic treatments that expound on various aspects of the Bible. The book is divided into four main parts: the historical and social context of the Bible; major genres (narrative, prophetic, legal, wisdom, psalms, poems); religious themes (monotheism, creation, human condition, covenants, ethics, space and structure, ritual); "study and reception of the Hebrew Bible. Each part has a number of subessays pertaining to the topic. For example the "religious themes" part is divided into seven subsections: Monotheism, Creation, Human Condition, God's Covenant with Humanity and Israel, Ethics, Religious Space and Structures, and Ritual. Each section is written by a biblical scholar specializing in that topic. The Ritual section written by Seth D. Kunin, Vice Principal for "Internationalisation" at the University of Aberdeen, addresses three issues: diet, purity, and sacrifice. In the essay, Kunin shows how these rituals engage the body to reinterpret the "self, history and covenant" of the Israelites. In another section Dominik Markl, Lecturer at the Pontifical Institute in Rome, expounds on God's Covenant with Israel. He begins the section by writing about the role of treaties in the Ancient Near East, and ends with the use of covenants as God's way of caring for every living creature. The book begins with an opening essay by the editor John Barton on the "Hebrew Bible" vs. the "Old Testament" controversy. Each essay comes with interpretive notes and a bibliographical essay. The bibliographies provide outstanding guides for further study of the topic at hand. Some sections are accompanied by charts and tables. The essay on the use of maps in understanding the Hebrew Bible by Adrian Curtis, Honorary Research Fellow at the University of Manchester, illustrates the topic by a few map examples. Curtis notes that the biblical writers did "have geographic awareness and interests," and concludes that maps help the reader of biblical texts orient toward time and place. Three indexes accompany the books: an index of scripture references found in the text, an index of "Modern Authors," and a general subject index. Overall the book is attractive and an easy read. Written by a group of contemporary scholars, the book will be a great aid to any student of the Old Testament.—**Ralph Lee Scott**

Part IV

SCIENCE AND TECHNOLOGY

29 Science and Technology in General

General Works

Handbooks and Yearbooks

C, P, S

400.   Cabot, Tom. **The Infographic Guide to Science.** New York, Firefly Books, 2017. 256p. illus. maps. index. $24.95pa. ISBN 13: 978-1-77085-791-9.

The global world of the twenty-first century is abundant with information and, correspondingly, visual delivery of content is pervasive. *The Infographic Guide to Science,* a 2017 Firefly Books publication, is an excellent instance of superb graphic quality intertwined with factual scientific data depicting the evolution of our world and life today. Authored by Tom Cabot, a London-based editor and designer, this book is divided into four sections: Universe, Earth, Life, and Human. Each section uses a smaller lens to move toward the science of life as we know it today. Beyond the standard introductory matter, the list of visual contents aligns information in colorful tiles with subject area and pages for another means of access. The book concludes with information for further research, and the index is rich with entry topics and an outstanding tool.

Each of the four primary, sequential sections has an introduction. Science disciplines include, but are not limited to: physics and chemistry, DNA and biology, earth science, and the merging of human technology with human intelligence. Cabot succinctly describes this book as "the journey from pure energy to pure intellect" (p. 15). The trajectory from universe to the evolution of human life is concretely represented here. The two-page spreads, which use different types of graphs, charts, and three-dimensional content, are strongly enhanced with color rich design. Significant information in brief text boxes may spawn further inquiry. At times, terminology may be challenging but definitions work with visuals for greater understanding. Color tabs in the right top corner provide topical entry. The uniqueness of each infographic encourages meaningful browsing.

A stunning visual, *The Infographic Guide to Science* is best suited to public libraries and high school or university libraries where graphic design, science, or evolution studies are taught.

Highly recommended.—**Janis Minshull**

C

401.   **Mixed Methods Research for Improved Scientific Study.** Mette L. Baran and

Janice E. Jones, eds. Hershey, Pa., Information Science Reference/IGI Global, 2016. 336p. index. (Advances in Knowledge Acquisition, Transfer, and Management (AKATM) Book Series). $195.00 (individual chapters available for purchase in electronic format). ISBN 13: 978-1-52250-007-0; 978-1-52250-008-7 (e-book).

Data analysis conjures images of numerical data being analyzed to derive meaning. Statistical methods developed for "hard" data have been successfully applied to data obtained from surveys and other more subjective means to gain deeper perspective in the humanities. Today working with personal reflections as viable data, researchers are building compelling models to explain human behavior. Of course using qualitative or quantitative data depends primarily on the research question that investigators are trying to answer. These different approaches are not necessarily contradictory, but do provide differing perspectives on the same phenomenon, hence painting a more complete picture of the area under investigation.

Paradigms of the various analytical methods are necessarily different. One overarching objective of this work is to show that despite the differing paradigms, it is possible to use various disparate methodologies that ultimately result in a richer and deeper understanding of the inquiry. The 15 chapters are grouped into seven sections that explore the paradigms, historical roots, overarching methodologies, and case studies of using a blend of qualitative and quantitative data analysis. The three chapters in section one explore the historical development and underpinnings of mixed methods research (MMR). Two chapters in section two focus on developing a MMR framework and the most common types of MMR designs. The single chapter in section three addresses sampling, and the single chapter in section four looks at data collection. Both sections focus on common techniques and pitfalls. The four chapters in section five go through data analysis, including descriptive and inferential statistics, data characteristics, hypothesis testing, and correlation. There is a chapter in this section which is a case study. However the three chapters in section six are also case studies. The last section consists of only one chapter that provides a general outline of MMR. Each chapter has a list of references. Some chapters also have references for further reading, a list of key terms and references, and end notes.

The work is not meant to delve into the mechanics of statistical calculations, and hence mathematical formulas are sparse. Its objective is to provide an overview of possible approaches of using MMR for one's study. Readers would find it useful to use this work as a supplement to other statistical works that delve more deeply into statistical theory. Recommended for those working on seminal works that require statistical analysis.—**Muhammed Hassanali**

30 Agricultural Sciences

General Works

Handbooks and Yearbooks

C, P, S

402. **USDA Science Blogs. http://blogs.usda.gov/category/science/.**

The U.S. Department of Agriculture (USDA) blog site is home to numerous posts well organized for easy accessibility. Users can simply scroll through a list of 25 categories from the left sidebar and click to direct to the appropriate page. There is also a "tag cloud" in the sidebar which displays commonly searched topics. Users can then scroll through the category posts, beginning with the most recent. Posts are dated and include tags, photographs, and lists of related posts.

Some of the more popular blog categories include Rural Development, Food & Nutrition, Forestry, Conservation, and Science. The Science category, for example, currently houses 604 posts covering an interesting array of subjects, such as "Honey: A Sweet Topic with New Data This Spring," "Nanostructured Biosensors Detect Pesticide, Help Preserve Environment" "U.S. Agricultural Production Systems of the Future: What Research is Needed Now?" and much more. The USDA reviews all comments before posting them to the blogs. Users can comment on all posts, and blog archives are searchable by month.

This site offers a well-rounded view of the USDA's concerns, and could be a valuable research tool for community agricultural concerns, policy-making, classroom study and much more.—**ARBA Staff Reviewer**

Food Sciences and Technology

Atlases

C, P, S

403. **Food Environment Atlas. https://www.ers.usda.gov/data-products/food-environment-atlas/.** [Website] Free. Date reviewed: 2017.

This simply structured website from the U.S. Department of Agriculture presents data on a variety of "food environment" factors in order to assess a location's ability to incorporate healthy food options into the community diet and lifestyle. Data is assembled into a colored U.S. map or "atlas" which makes it extremely easy to access and place. The atlas considers the food environment against three general categories: Food Choices, which notes data related to grocery stores, restaurants etc.; Health and Well-Being, noting rates of disease and disorder, activity levels, and more; and Community Characteristics, pointing to demographics, amenities, and poverty levels, among other things. Within these categories, the atlas uses 211 targeted indicators, such as price of sodas, farmers markets, crop acreage, and percentage of physically active high school students. From the atlas, users can scroll and click on the particular indicator (listed on the Select Map to Display tab), causing the map to adjust to reflect the information. They can also access the indicator's definition, zoom on a state, or click on a county to narrow their desired data set.

All of the current data (in addition to some prior years) is downloadable into Excel format, and would be of great interest to university students, educators, policy-makers, and many others.—**ARBA Staff Reviewer**

P

404.   Smith, Krisi. **The World Atlas of Tea: From the Leaf to the Cup, the World's Teas Explored and Enjoyed.** New York, Firefly Books, 2016. 240p. illus. maps. index. $35.00. ISBN 13: 978-1-77085-816-9.

Tea is the most widely consumed beverage in the world and there is no shortage of beautiful books on tea. Add one more to your coffee table or library that specializes in the countries of the world that produce tea. Roughly the last half of this picture book is divided into the geographic areas where tea is grown. "Part Four: The World of Tea" is divided into Africa, Indian Subcontinent, Middle East, Far East, and South America. Each country within the region is described in order of production volume with basic facts, colorful maps, and gorgeous photographs.

The first three parts of the book cover 1.) tea basics, 2.) tea brewing and drinking, and 3.) tea blending. There is just the right amount of text to accompany the illustrations to keep the reader's eyes glued to the book. Facts are succinctly explained throughout but especially in the Chemistry of Tea, Health Benefits of Tea, and Question of Tea Sustainability sections. The index and glossary make fact finding easy.

The author describes herself as a tea mixologist who owns a tea company in England. Her love of tea is boldly evident and her recipes in the tea blending section for matcha, chai, and lattes are irresistible. This book will delight tea lovers, history buffs, and travelers. With over half of Americans drinking tea every day, and younger Americans turning from coffee to tea, readers will be interested in where tea comes from and details of processing and blending. Public libraries will find this book a good buy.—**Georgia Briscoe**

Directories

P

405.   **Local Food Directories: National Farmers Market Directory. https://www. ams.usda.gov/local-food-directories/farmersmarkets.** [Website] Free. Date reviewed: 2016.

The USDA Agricultural Marketing Services provides this regularly updated directory to farmers' markets. Farmers' markets are defined as a fixed, regular place where two or more farm vendors sell directly to customers. This free directory is simple to use. Searches can be done by zip code, products available, products accepted, market location, and winter markets. State farmers' market contact information is also easily accessible from a tab on the main page. Searches can be general or specific. A user can find farmers' markets that sell fruits and vegetables nationally or can search for farmers' markets that sell honey in their own zip code. The results are presented in a list; most farmers' markets have exterior links to their own web pages. The results page is also exportable to Excel. Helpfully, users can discover whether a particular farmers' market accepts credit cards of WIC Cash Value Vouchers as well as whether they participate in the Supplemental Nutrition Program, the WIC Farmers Market Nutrition Program, or the Senior Farmers Markets Nutrition Programs. Recommended.—**ARBA Staff Reviewer**

Handbooks and Yearbooks

C, P

406.   **Diet and Nutrition Sourcebook.** 5th ed. Jones, Keith, ed. Detroit, Omnigraphics, 2016. 625p. index. (Health Reference Series). $85.00. ISBN 13: 978-0-7808-1383-0; 978-0-7808-1412-7 (e-book)

Part of the Health Reference Series, this fifth edition of the *Diet and Nutrition Sourcebook* is edited by Keith Jones. A medical review team was used to review the entries for accuracy and currency, ensuring the reliability of the material.

The structure of this volume is comparable with others in this health series. Brief front matter includes a solid table of contents which introduces the eight parts which include one section called Additional Help and Information. Parts are then divided into chapters, for a total of 52, where more specific content is found. For ease of research, chapters are further designated with subtopics. The section areas streamline the process of finding content for consumers. Black-and-white charts, figures, and tables provide more data. The index is significant and is the most pragmatic access point.

Health, food, and nutrition are all in the forefront of personal care and cultural trends in the twenty-first century. The sourcebook updates information such as the new food guidance system and often references the most recent dietary guidelines for Americans. Consumers will find topics that are useful to daily life such as "How to Use Nutrition Labels." Entries focus on healthy and realistic ways to address food challenges through healthy weight loss. The discussion of contemporary food issues not seen in previous generations offers a cogent explanation of why consumers need to take control of food habits. Chapters on medical issues, life stages, and best healthy food practices offer support for those looking for facts and ideas for healthy diet modification.

Health care and nutrition information are critical to a healthy society. This information tool, *Diet and Nutrition Sourcebook,* is a worthy edition to reference collections in libraries whether public, medical, or academic.—**Janis Minshull**

P, S

407.   **Diet Information for Teens: Health Tips about Nutrition Fundamentals and Eating Plans.** 4th ed. Keith Jones, ed. Detroit, Omnigraphics, 2017. 374p. index. (Teen Health Series). $69.00. ISBN 13: 978-0-7808-1386-1; 978-0-7808-1410-3 (e-book).

Diet Information for Teens provides the latest food information for students in their preteen and teen years. This fourth edition is updated in review with medical consultation, and is one volume of the Teen Health Series.

The book's 63 chapters are organized into seven sections. Topics are relevant to teen lives; discussions on eating cafeteria food, body image and self-esteem, dietary supplements, and eating disorders make learning both interesting and germane for tweens and teens. Students seeking research facts will find significant data in this title. Diet challenges are explored, but the emphasis is on educating students about nutritional choices and exercise. Useful tips are found throughout on sensible snacks, getting moving, and less common diet trends such as vegan. The seventh section, chapters 59-63, offers tips for teen girls and boys and is rich with resources for cooking and dietary and fitness information. Highlighted text boxes, black-and-white tables and figures, and plenty of white space divide text well for easy readability. The comprehensive index gives students straight forward access to topics from vitamins and minerals to exercise and fitness.

Diet Information for Teens is best used by middle and high school students. Teachers, librarians, and other educators supporting health, human development, and sociology studies will want to have this book handy.

Recommended.—**Janis Minshull**

C, P, S

408.   **Food and Agriculture Organization of the United Nations. http://www.fao.org/ faostat/en/.** [Website] Free. Date reviewed: 2017.

This freely available database offers an abundance of statistics related to the mission of the Food and Agriculture Organization (FAO) of the United Nations. Specifically, it offers "free access to Food and Agriculture data for over 245 countries and territories" as the organization aims to meet the broader objectives of eradicating poverty and ensuring food security for all.

The site is well designed in offering several ways to access and use data. Clicking on the central Explore Data tab leads users to a variety of specific indicators (crops, pesticides use, energy use, etc.) grouped into broader categories (agricultural emissions, investments, forestry, prices, etc.). Users can also conduct a search via indicators or commodities attuned to particular nations. The site also employs tabs to help group the data in other ways: a Bulk Download allows access to all updated data, Database Updates highlights all recent changes, and the Statistical Yearbook provides data visualizations (graphs, charts, etc.) on selected indicators by country. Users may alternatively choose to access information via a Country Indicator or Rankings tab. Clicking on the former tab will display a nation's map in addition to a sidebar listing of indicators such as Demographics, Food Availability, Land, Economic & Political Stability, and others. The Rankings tab notes export and import data for a country's top commodities such as wheat, milk, vegetables, and meat. Users can also easily access the 2030 Agenda for Sustainable Development which details the most current strategies to advance the FAO's global mission.

A Definitions and Standards tab on the menu bar clarifies abbreviations, national and regional identities, currencies and measurements, and more. There is also a Compare

Data tool which allows users the ability to compare information gathered over more than 50 years, and a sidebar which displays the FAO's latest tweets, which convey snapshot statistics and other food/agriculture news of the day. The site's information is available in six languages. The abundant data would certainly appeal to students, researchers, policy-makers, activists, and many others.—**ARBA Staff Reviewer**

C, P, S

409.   **National Nutrient Database. https://ndb.nal.usda.gov/ndb/.** [Website] Free. Date reviewed: 2016.

The *National Nutrient Database* is a project run by the USDA's Nutrient Data Laboratory. There are several ways to search this comprehensive, free, and regularly updated database: Food Type, Nutrients List, and Ground Beef Calculator. To search by food type, a user can enter a basic search term like flour tortillas. This search can be further refined by manufacturer name and/or source (Branded Food Products or Standard Reference). The list produced by this search will allow direct comparisons of the nutrients and ingredients in, for example, the organic flour tortillas from Buenatural and the regular flour tortillas from La Tortilla Factory (the latter has fewer grams of carbohydrates per 100 grams). Those who want to search by nutrients rather than type of food can search up to three ingredients in an individual search and further refine the search by food type group (baby food, baked products, beef products, beverages, and breakfast cereals), food name, or measurement (household or 100 grams). The inclusion of the Ground Beef Calculator as a major search screen makes sense because ground beef is the most commonly consumed beef product in the United States (according to information at www.ars.usda. gov). The calculator allows users to generate nutrient profiles for ground beef products containing any level of fat between three and thirty percent. The site also includes a tab for Documentation and Help as well as a Contact Us tab. Under the latter, researchers will find a sample citation, links to articles by Nutrient Data Laboratory staff; Food Composition and Nutrition Links; instructions for submitting data to USDA Nutrient Databases; and a list of FAQs that includes answers to questions on copyright, the difference between calories and kilocalories, and much more. Results are all printable and downloadable and all data is in the public domain. Data is regularly updated (a list of updates appears on the site) so users can keep their own information current.

Highly recommended.—**ARBA Staff Reviewer**

P

410.   **Organic Integrity Database. https://organic.ams.usda.gov/Integrity/.** [Website] Free. Date reviewed: 2017.

This database is provided as a service of the United States Department of Agriculture (USDA) and allows users to locate a certified organic farm or business worldwide. There are several ways to search the database from the home page: by name of operation, by certifier, by status (certified, surrendered, or revoked), by city, state/province, or country, or by certified product. There is also an advanced search button, which is revealed when clicking on the Search tab at the top of the page. Next to this is a Reports tab, which provides current counts of USDA certified organic operations by country, U.S. state or province, or by certifier. A map also shows the location of certified organic operations in the United States. This section of the database also has a link to data history from 2010-2015. Data is posted regularly, but there is a lag. The site cautions users to check directly with certifiers for the most up-to-date information. Additionally, researchers should consult the Canadian Food Inspection Agency for information because Canadian operations no longer need to maintain certification by the USDA to sell in the United States. Additionally, operations certified under international trade agreements do not need to appear on the list.—**ARBA Staff Reviewer**

P

411.   Philpott, Don. **The World of Wine and Food: A Guide to Varieties, Tastes, History, and Pairings.** Lanham, Md., Rowman & Littlefield, 2017. 490p. illus. index. $100.00; $99.99 (e-book). ISBN 13: 978-1-4422-6803-6; 8-1-4422-6804-3 (e-book).

This volume presents detailed information on wine and its production in 63 countries, from major entries about France, Italy, and the United States to brief discussions of countries like Zimbabwe, Kyrgyzstan, Madagascar, and Brazil. Discussion includes the regions of the countries that produce wine, the grapes that are grown there, the climates that permit successful viniculture, and the styles of wines produced in each area—crisp whites, bold reds, etc. Despite the detail provided, individual vintners, even the legendary ones, are not mentioned, the author preferring to focus on types of wine and their particular characteristics. One minor disappointment: almost 200 pages simply list food dishes from scores of countries, with no obvious connection to appropriate wines, and only brief descriptions. Following that is a 14-page section that matches wines with food. Amusingly, the history section of his "Wine and Food" section begins about two million years ago, moving quickly to more recent times.

This book provides a fine introduction to the wines of the world and, to a lesser extent, their interplay with food. Public libraries will best benefit from its content, although academic libraries may find it useful for programs of nutrition, culinary arts, or hospitality.—**Mark Schumacher**

C, S

412.   Redman, Nina E., and Michele Morrone. **Food Safety: A Reference Handbook.** 3d ed. Santa Barbara, Calif., ABC-CLIO, 2017. 329p. illus. index. (Contemporary World Issues). $60.00. ISBN 13: 978-1-4408-5262-6; 978-1-4408-5263-3 (e-book).

A central focus to healthy living in the twenty-first century is the food we eat. Written by Nina E. Redman and Michele Morrone, this third edition (see ARBA 2007, entry 1132) provides revised information with the latest in food safety trends, opportunities, and threats. This 2017 volume is part of the Contemporary World Issues series.

Like the other volumes in the series, this one is organized in seven sections that include background and history, profiles, data and documents, resources, and more. Each chapter has subsections, which are clearly listed for ease of access. Additionally, the glossary and index are valuable aids to the reader.

From the initial overview of legislative and regulatory development to current health, nutrition, and food safety concerns, *Food Safety* is a robust compilation of government guidance, food industry and trade, and consumer thought. For example, Genetically Modified Organisms (GMOs) are a hotly debated, modern-day food controversy. The book provides multiple perspectives on the debate and gives readers important information, such as the fact that "in the United States, genetically engineered crops have grown from below 25 percent of all acreage in 1996 to 94 percent of acreage in 2016 for some crops such as herbicide-resistant soybeans" (p. 811). This book is particularly effective because of the representation of multiple perspectives and section three has a collection of essays from food industry experts, social and scientific scholars, and practitioners in the fields of health and environmental health. From Rachel Carson to Joel Salatin, an organic farmer and author, biographies of leaders are found in section four. The Food and Drug Administration (FDA), Food Safety Modernization Act (FSMA), and other agencies, regulations, and acts are clearly defined and mentioned. Visual data is solid in all sections. Avenues for extended research are plentiful due to the extensive section on resources.

Food Safety is a strong reference guide with the latest updates, and will be best suited for researchers, scholars, scientists, and practitioners in the food and trade industry.

Highly recommended.—**Janis Minshull**

Horticulture

Dictionaries and Encyclopedias

P

413.   Biggs, Matthew, Jekka McVicar, and Bob Flowerdew. **The New Vegetables, Herbs & Fruits: An Illustrated Encyclopedia.** New York, Firefly Books, 2016. 704p. illus. index. $45.00. ISBN 13: 978-1-77085-798-8.

This beautifully illustrated encyclopedia of vegetables, herbs, and fruits guides readers in choosing which plants to grow and how to grow them successfully.

The encyclopedia is roughly divided into three major parts. First, vegetables are arranged alphabetically by their scientific names. Second, herbs are arranged similarly. Third, fruits are divided into groupings by type: 1) orchard fruits, 2) soft bush and cane fruits, 3) tender fruits, 4) tropical fruits, 5) shrub and flower garden fruits, and 6) nuts. There is a smaller fourth part titled Practical Gardening that discusses planning, soil preparation, maintenance, pests, natural dyes, etc. A glossary, list of seed sources, bibliography, and list of planting zones all add value.

Each entry is listed by their genus and species in small print. However, the common name is listed in large print so it is easy to flip through the book and find what you want. For example, the first vegetable entry is Agaricus (Mushroom) and the last vegetable entry is Zea (Corn). Herbs begin with Achillea (Maces) and end with Zingiber (Ginger). There is a very good index which this reviewer used frequently. Each plant entry has an introduction that covers the origins and history of the plant, recommended varieties, details of cultivation with calendars, pruning, harvesting, and storing recommendations, companion planting guidelines, container growing recommendations, medicinal uses, and usually a sidebar or full page of culinary suggestions with recipes.

Many unusual plants are included such as burdock, cherimoyas, eddoe, dasheen, sea kale, samphire, cardoon, betony henbane, and viper's bugloss. This book is very practical and fun. There are lovely color photographs on every page. A reader will be anxious to become a gardener, try out a new herb, or become hungry just paging through the encyclopedia. Since plants are the basis of the food chain most libraries would find the book well used.—**Georgia Briscoe**

Handbooks and Yearbooks

P
414.   Adam, Judith. **Your First Garden: A Landscape Primer for New Home Owners.**
New York, Firefly Books, 2016. 120p. illus. maps. index. $19.95pa. ISBN 13: 978-1-
77085-708-7.

This compact guide provides new homeowners with a wealth of information about
creating a garden from the initial drawing stage to planting. The lively writing style, color
photographs, and text boxes make the book an enjoyable read. The beginning of the book
explains how much value a well-done garden can add to a new home and lays down the
steps new homeowners should take. A concise ten-point assessment survey encourages
readers to take into consideration such things as the size and shape of the yard, irrigation
needs, trees and shade, and the location and materials used for the garage and driveway. A
checklist outlines steps to be taken before beginning a project. This is particularly useful
for new homeowners who might not otherwise know to call the utility company about the
location of power lines or to call local authorities about permits. The extensive chapter on
soil composition and soil preparation provides essential, straightforward information on
what to do about clay or sandy soil, in particular, and any soil in general. Another chapter
addresses the best ways to create garden beds while another suggests best practices for
achieving high performance in a low-maintenance garden. This chapter discusses fertilizer,
watering needs, ground cover, mulch, weeding, and more. The fifth chapter "Growing
Annuals & Perennials," is followed by "Trees & Shrubs." Here readers will find planting
guidance, among other tips. The book concludes with what to look for in an initial trip to
the garden center. A one-page index rounds out the work. This book is a real bargain and
a great resource for new homeowners. Recommended for public libraries.—**ARBA Staff
Reviewer**

P
415.   Garrett, Howard, comp. **Texas Gardening the Natural Way: The Complete
Handbook.** Reprint ed. Austin, Tex., University of Texas at Austin, 2016. 386p. illus.
maps. index. $39.95. ISBN 13: 978-1-4773-1023-6.

Howard Garrett, (a.k.a. The Dirt Doctor), is a prolific author, speaker, and the host
of a Website titled www.TheDirtDoctor.com. He has extensive experience in landscaping,
natural organic gardening, and many other related areas. This knowledge is showcased in
Texas Gardening the Natural Way: The Complete Handbook.

Since there is no mention that the original 2004 version has been updated, it would
appear that this is a reprint. Fortunately, the information that has been included is basically
timeless (i.e., descriptions of plants, growing conditions, etc.). The author was apparently
careful not to include any online resources or other information that would have become
dated.

The book consists of eight chapters, an appendix, and an index. The opening chapter,
titled "Texas Garden Fundamentals," includes an overview of all of the components of
gardens and landscapes with a focus on the advantages on organic gardening and the

difference between toxic chemicals and organic approaches. Chapters two through eight contain detailed information on trees, shrubs, specialty plants, ground covers and vines, annuals and perennials, lawns, fruits and vegetables, herbs, and pest management. This text is liberally supplemented with over 800 colored photographs. Even those readers who do not live in Texas will find useful tips and explanations.

The appendix includes lists of formulas, freeze dates, organic fertilizer and soil amendments, pest control products, house plants, poisonous plants, and the Texas Organic Research Center's list of acceptable and unacceptable products for organic production. Also contained here is a small section on night gardening.

Recommended for Texas and southwestern libraries that do not already own the 2004 original.—**January Adams**

P

416. Morrow, Baker H. **Best Plants for New Mexico Gardens and Landscapes.** Albuquerque, N.Mex., University of New Mexico Press, 2016. 286p. illus. maps. index. $34.95pa. ISBN 13: 978-0-8263-5636-9; 8-0-8263-5637-6 (e-book).

Baker H. Morrow, the author or editor of many books and professor at the School of Architecture and Planning at the University of New Mexico, has over 40 years experience as a practicing landscape architect in Albuquerque. The knowledge that he has accumulated is beautifully and artfully displayed in *Best Plants for New Mexico Gardens and Landscapes.* This revised and expanded edition includes new plants that are now available in New Mexico and the Southwest, updated botanical names, and many new photos and sketches. The book is divided into four sections. In section one, Background, Baker covers the nature of the New Mexican landscape, life zones, cultivation requirements, native plants, and the legacy of trees and stone, which includes notes on New Mexico's historic man-made landscapes. The second section delves into tips for gardening and landscaping. It includes detailed information on plant selection, the 11 precepts of landscape design, and information on the "best" of every imaginable type of plant or tree. The author follows this with section three, which is a comprehensive list of trees, shrubs, ground covers, grasses, vines, and flowers that grow well in New Mexico. The fourth and final section, which is the centerpiece of the book, gives specific and comprehensive recommendations and advice for plantings in 36 New Mexican cities. The work concludes with an appendix, additional sources of information, a bibliography, suggestions for further reading, and an index. All libraries should purchase this extraordinary work and every gardener in New Mexico should also have a copy.—**January Adams**

Soil Science

Handbooks and Yearbooks

C, P

417. **Web Soil Survey. http://websoilsurvey.sc.egov.usda.gov/App/HomePage.htm.** [Website] Free. Date reviewed: 2017.

This site from the U.S. Department of Agriculture Natural Resources Conservation Service offers users a unique way to discover information related to soils covering mostly all lands of the United States. Its main appeal lies with the easy to use Soil Survey, which allows users to pinpoint a geographical Area of Interest, access its map and general soil description, then peruse its unique data profile. Users are also able to customize a downloadable Soil Survey report (note: users will be asked to insert desired data into the "shopping cart," but there is no fee for the customized report). Users can walk through the home page schematic in order to understand how to work with the Soil Survey, then simply click on the green Start WSS button to begin. Supplemental material such as a glossary, archived surveys, and more, are available to further assist users within the survey. From the main page, users can also conduct a search or browse through related links regarding such topics as soil geography, soil health, tools, and maps. This site would appeal to a good range of researchers, biologists, farmers, landscapers, land use planners, and others.— **ARBA Staff Reviewer**

Veterinary Science

Handbooks and Yearbooks

C
418.   **Veterinary History Archive. http://www.rcvsarchives.org/.** [Website] Free. Date reviewed: 2017.

Managed by the Royal College of Veterinary Surgeons, this website catalogs nonpublished documents such as letters, diary entries, research data, and photographs related to the field of veterinary science in Britain. As this website is a work in progress, no actual images are currently found on the site. Rather, a search will lead to descriptions of items in the two collections consolidated so far: the Frederick Smith Papers and the watercolors of nineteenth century vet Edward Mayhew. The site notes that other collections are forthcoming. Users can click on a variety of tabs on the vertical menu for orienting information, such as FAQs, Useful Links, and Help questions. This is also where users can begin an advanced search through the catalog or for particular people. Each cataloged item has a reference number, level, title, date, extent, detailed description, format, and collection title. While not displaying actual materials—only descriptions—the site could nonetheless be a starting point for researchers interested in British veterinary history.— **ARBA Staff Reviewer**

31 Biological Sciences

General Works

Handbooks and Yearbooks

C, P

419. Roossinck, Marilyn J. **Virus: An Illustrated Guide to 101 Incredible Microbes.** Princeton, N.J., Princeton University Press, 2016. 256p. illus. maps. index. $35.00. ISBN 13: 978-0-691-16696-4.

An illustrated guide to the viruses. All the familiar viruses are here: Zika, West Nile, polio, mumps, measles, Ebola, etc., as well as many viruses most of us have never heard of. Each virus receives one page of text and a full-page color illustration. The descriptions are arranged in sections: human, plant, vertebrate animal, invertebrate animal, fungal, and bacterial. A text of some 50 pages precedes the listings, containing the definition of a virus, a history of virology, transmission, controversies about viruses, etc. A diagram accompanies each entry. Included are a four-page glossary, a list of 43 resources (books and websites), and an index. The author, Marilyn J. Roossinck, is professor of virus ecology at Pennsylvania State University.

This is a handsome book with readable text and a reasonable price. Public and academic librarians with up-to-date medical dictionaries, such as *Mosby's Medical Dictionary,* 10th edition (Elsevier, 2017), and a limited budget may not need this volume, but it could be used for reference or circulation purposes. There is at least one other recent book on viruses: Carl Zimmer's *A Planet of Viruses,* (Chicago, 2013), by the author of the foreword of this volume.—**Jonathan F. Husband**

Botany

Handbooks and Yearbooks

C, P, S

420. **Invasive Species: Plants. https://www.invasivespeciesinfo.gov/plants/main. shtml.** [Website] Free. Date reviewed: 2017.

A page from the National Agricultural Library of the U.S, Department of Agriculture, this site offers free access to abundant information on invasive plant species. Users can browse a list of 50 invasive plants. Selecting one brings up the particular Species Profile showing its visual image as well as a variety of characteristics: Means of Introduction, Impact, Scientific and Common name(s), and more. The profile also includes links to more images, videos, and reference material.

Users can also pursue a number of avenues of information beyond the custom search or browse. Links on the sidebar allow users to join Discussion Groups, browse Image Galleries, and engage in other activities. The site also links to a number of off-site databases in addition to research on topics such as the Economic Impact or Management of Invasive Species, plus a host of multimedia work. The information on this hub of invasive plant species can be translated into many languages and will be a welcome resource for landscape designers, botanists, educators, and others.—**ARBA Staff Reviewer**

Natural History

Handbooks and Yearbooks

C, P, S
421.   **CalPhotos.   http://calphotos.berkeley.edu/about.shtml.** [Website] Free. Date reviewed: 2017.

CalPhotos is a visual image database dedicated to natural history. The site houses over a half million photographs sorted into the categories of Plants, Fungi, Animals, Landscapes; and People and Cultures. Users can easily select a subject category to retrieve a form which they can fill out to narrow their search. In addition, the site incorporates common and scientific name browse lists of particular use in regards to plants and animals. Users can click on displayed thumbnail photos to enlarge images, and will find descriptive information accompanying each one, such as location of photo, date taken, notes, contributor identification numbers, and usage information. A side bar on the home page lists helpful links such as FAQs, Contributing Organizations, Photographers, and more. The site manages its collection with care, having a strict annotation system whereby reviewers can correct or update photographs and their accompanying details. The site updates monthly with new photos. With the emphasis on the photos, the site is easy to navigate and would be highly appealing to students of many grade levels, researchers, educators, and others with an interest in natural history or photography.—**ARBA Staff Reviewer**

C, P, S
422.   Weber, Edward P. **Endangered Species: A Documentary and Reference Guide.** Santa Barbara, Calif., Greenwood Press/ABC-CLIO, 2016. 370p. index. (Documentary and Reference Guides). $108.00. ISBN 13: 978-1-4408-3656-5; 978-1-4408-3657-2 (e-book).

This volume explores multiple dimensions—social, political, biological, and philosophical—of the dangers of, and possible solutions for, the loss of species, both fauna and flora. While the focus is on the evolution of the situation in the United States over the last 200 years, broader perspectives are also explored. The author's introduction explains the purpose and the organization of the volume, which consists of several dozen documents, from John Locke and John Stuart Mill to the present, each with an analysis of the place of the document in the discussion of endangered species and, more broadly, the environmental issues facing us today. Each analysis contains "further reading," which is gathered together in a bibliography at the back of the volume.

This is an important topic, broadly presented here in a historical setting. The language is clear and accessible to a wide range of readers. Many kinds of libraries will benefit from having this volume in their collections, from middle schools and public libraries to colleges and universities.—**Mark Schumacher**

Zoology

General Works

Handbooks and Yearbooks

C, P, S

423. **EcoReader. http://ecoreader.berkeley.edu/about.jsp.** [Website] Free. Date reviewed: 2017.

This site from the University of California, Berkeley, allows free access to its Museum of Vertebrate Zoology's (MVZ) digitized field notebooks in addition to a catalog of yet-to-be digitized work (the project is ongoing). Users can search via a small selection of parameters, including author name, year, volume identification, geographic location, and section title. The best way for users to browse is through the alphabetical list of 257 authors/field journalists. Selecting one will direct to a page listing all archived field journals, correspondence, etc., and provide links to those that have been digitized. Examining these artifacts gives users a great sense of the painstaking and detailed worldwide scientific work in the field. Selecting the MVZ Archives tab from the home page leads to five years of posts from the archive blog. The blog follows progress of the digitization project (a partnership with the Smithsonian and the Internet Archive began in 2017) in addition to sharing stories of the many scientists, collectors, and benefactors whose interests and work fill the archive.—**ARBA Staff Reviewer**

P

424. Fitter, Julian, Daniel Fitter, and David Hosking. **Wildlife of the Galapagos.** 2d ed. Princeton, N.J., Princeton University Press, 2016. 287p. illus. maps. index. $19.95pa. ISBN 13: 978-0-691-17042-8.

This small, striking volume presents 400 species of animal life in the Galapagos Islands. The title is slightly misleading, as the second half of the book explores other realms of the islands' ecology, mainly plants, and provides 92 maps of the various visitor sites. From the Nazca booby and the lava heron to the pink iguana and the pelican barracuda, the reader is given a physical description of each animal, its behaviors, and the best locations to view the species. Striking photos of animals, plants, and even mineral formations enhance the work throughout.

Although a narrowly focused work, it will attract anyone interested in the ecology of the Galapagos, and potential visitors to the islands. Its reasonable price should make it a choice for a wide range of libraries.—**Mark Schumacher**

Birds

C, P

425. Armistead, George L., and Brian L. Sullivan. **Better Birding: Tips, Tools & Concepts for the Field.** Princeton, N.J., Princeton University Press, 2015. 318p. illus. maps. index. $29.95pa. ISBN 13: 978-0-691-12966-2.

This richly illustrated volume provides numerous insights into enhancing one's experience of birding, while presenting scores of birds: their various appearances (juvenile, breeding, molting, adult), their behaviors and motions, their habitats, and the often subtle differences between related species. Swans, herons, ducks and other water birds along with forest birds, "night birds," and "open-country birds" populate this work, with clear, detailed descriptions and stunning color photographs. While not a guide to all the birds of North America, this guide will give all but the most experienced and adept birders valuable information to enhance the time bird watchers spend with their avian friends.

Any library with readers interested in birds and birding should certainly acquire this volume, priced incredibly low for a work full of color photography. Academic libraries supporting programs in zoology or ornithology should also consider it.—**Mark Schumacher**

C, P

426. Elphick, Jonathan. **Birds: A Complete Guide to Their Biology and Behavior.** New York, Firefly Books, 2016. 272p. illus. index. $29.95pa. ISBN 13: 978-1-77085-762-9.

Birds: A Complete Guide to Their Biology and Behavior is a narrative description of all aspects of bird life internationally. There are chapters on the evolution of birds, anatomy and physiology, flight, food, bird society and populations, breeding, habitats, migration, and the impact of birds and humans upon each other. There is an index to subjects, hundreds of color photographs, and charts and diagrams. The English author is a wildlife writer, editor, consultant, lecturer, and broadcaster, specializing in ornithology. He is the author of several books, including *The World of Birds* (see ARBA 2016, entry 442), which is oriented more toward taxonomy.

This is a splendidly illustrated book with a text which is readable but fairly technical, which might discourage casual readers. Although the author is English, many American examples are included with, usually, American common names. This is not a field guide, and readers interested in a particular bird or bird family will have to go elsewhere. The information included is more up-to-date than the information in the latest encyclopedias of birds such as *The Princeton Encyclopedia of Birds* (2004), *The Cambridge Encyclopedia of Ornithology* (1991), the *Firefly Encyclopedia of Birds* (see ARBA 2004, entry 1363), or *The Illustrated Encyclopedia of Birds* (Prentice-Hall, 1990). Most public or academic libraries will want to purchase this book for circulation and/or reference. The price is right for such a handsomely illustrated book.—**Jonathan F. Husband**

C, P

427.   **Handbook of the Birds of the World. http://www.hbw.com/.** [Website] Barcelona, Spain, Lynx Edicions, 2017. Price negotiated by site. Date reviewed: 2017

The Handbook of the Birds of the World Alive is the comprehensive online version of the 17-volume eponymous book series produced by Lynx Editions in association with such scientific partners as the American Museum of Natural History and BirdLife Interational. While some of the content is free to all users, most of it is available only by annual subscription (roughly $31 U.S. dollars at time of this writing).

Nonpaying users are limited to a rotating sample of species accounts and bird family descriptions. They also have access to Latest Ornithological Notes, a moderated forum sharing recent reports of bird sightings.

Subscribers, on the other hand, have access to thousands of species accounts, which generally include information on taxonomy, breeding, habitat, voice, food, status, and more. Other features include color illustrations, photographs, distribution maps, and video and audio vignettes. In addition, the site holds over 1,000 detailed color plates. The information is easily accessed by clicking on the Families, Species, or Plates tab on the menu bar. Users can additionally scroll through a Taxonomic Tree to find what they are looking for, or conduct a general search.

Subscribers are able to customize the site as well, by adding geographic filters, personal notes, and more. Bibliographical information is extensive. The site can be translated into over 70 languages and would greatly to appeal to professionals, researchers, and genuine bird lovers willing to pay the nominal subscription fee.—**ARBA Staff Reviewer**

P

428.   Howell, Steve N.G., and Brian L. Sullivan. **Offshore Sea Life ID Guide: East Coast.** Princeton, N.J., Princeton University Press, 2015. 56p. illus. maps. index. $14.95pa. ISBN 13: 978-0-691-16613-1.

This handy guide provides an easy reference to sea life on the East Coast of North America. The guide is arranged by type of sea life: mammals, birds, turtles, fish, seaweed, and jellyfish. Some 100 color photos on composite plates show pictorially exactly how the reader would encounter marine life. Each animal depicted is described in a brief annotation along with field identification notes. The photos provided are extremely well reproduced and accurate. The book begins with a brief introduction to sea life viewing, and tips for having a safe offshore or birding trip. There is an index of species codes and scientific names. The end-leaves contain two handy illustrations: a quick species page finder and East Coast map of selection sea ports that feature offshore trips. This small compact guide is essential to those who wish to observe birds and sea life off the East Coast.—**Ralph Lee Scott**

P

429.   Howell, Steve N.G., and Brian L. Sullivan. **Offshore Sea Life ID Guide: West Coast.** Princeton, N.J., Princeton University Press, 2015. 64p. illus. maps. index. $14.95pa. ISBN 13: 978-0-691-16621-6.

Observers of sea life on the West Coast of the United States will find this a handy guide to marine life in their area. The guide is arranged by type of sea life: mammals, birds, turtles, seaweed (kelp,) and jellyfish. Over 300 photographs of sea life are shown in composite plates in typical marine settings. Each animal is described under its photograph in a brief annotation at the foot of the page. The annotations include excellent field identification notes and tips for encountering the animal. The photos are very well done and give the reader an accurate account of the conditions they might encounter in the field. The book begins with a brief introduction to the hobby and gives tips for having a safe offshore or land birding trip. There is an index of species codes and scientific names. The end-leaves contain two handy illustrations: a quick page finder by species and a map of selected sea ports that feature offshore trips. The ports are color coded on the map, but the publisher forgot to include the legend for the color coding on the map! The authors have a keen sense of humor and include one photo of a Brown-headed Cowbird "experiencing a marine toilet" (i.e., perched on a toilet seat). While hardly the typical environment one would expect to encounter this bird in, it nevertheless adds to the enjoyment of the book. This small compact guide will be essential for those observing birds and sea life off the West Coast.—**Ralph Lee Scott**

C, P, S

430.   **New Zealand Birds Online. http://nzbirdsonline.org.nz/.** [Website] Free. Date reviewed: 2016.

Launched in mid-2013, *New Zealand Birds Online* provides detailed information on 467 New Zealand bird species—living, extinct, fossil, vagrant, and introduced. The site provides users (from novices to professionals) with expert-written text, more than 8,700 photographs, and sound files of bird calls. The site is comanaged by the Department of Conservation, Te Papa (New Zealand's national museum), and Birds New Zealand.

The easy-to-use site offers searches by name, conservation status, bird group, and geographical distribution. The Identify that Bird tab even allows users to find a bird without knowing the species name. Once a bird like the great spotted kiwi is selected, for instance, the website provides basic information about order, family, New Zealand status, conservation status, other names, and geographical variation. This is followed by more detailed species information on identification, food, behavior and ecology, and more. The information concludes with references, a recommended citation, and a related website link. Photographs and sound recordings of bird calls are also included.—**ARBA Staff Reviewer**

P

431.   Reeber, Sébastien, comp. **Waterfowl of North America, Europe & Asia.** Princeton, N.J., Princeton University Press, 2015. 656p. illus. maps. index. $45.00. ISBN 13: 978-0-691-16266-9.

This identification guide to ducks, geese, and swans is a handsome hardcover volume designed for the serious birder. Eighty-three breeding species are included, grouped under one of nine tribes (whistling, comb, dabbling, diving, sea, and stifftail ducks; shelducks and sheldgeese; swans; and geese). The order in which each species is listed under its tribe follows no discernible order, so the reader looking to identify a bird will first need to find it in the section of 72 plates near the front of the book. Each plate contains labeled artistic color renderings of the birds at rest and in flight, faced by a page of brief descriptive captions and small map(s) of their range color-coded for breeding, overwintering, and year-round presence.

The bulk of the volume is made up of the species accounts. Each account includes common and scientific names, notes on taxonomy and identification, plumages, geographic variation(s), measurements and mass (using metric units), voice, molt(s), hybridization, habitat and life-cycle, range and population, captivity (for those outside their usual range), and a list of numbered references (to be found at the end of the book) for further information. Each account concludes with one or more pages of color photos of the birds in the wild, usually five or six per page. Image quality is excellent, displaying physical features sharply. Plates and species accounts are cross-referenced to each other.

For the reader with knowledge of a bird's scientific or common name, either the table of contents or one of the indexes (hybrid or species/common name) is the first point of access. Boldfaced numbers in the indexes refer to plates; italicized numbers refer to the first page of the species account. Introductory matter consists of directions for using the guide and general text on topography, molt and plumage, aging and sexing, and hybridization.—**Lori D. Kranz**

P

432.   van Perlo, Ber. **Birds of South America: Passerines.** Princeton, N.J., Princeton University Press, 2015. 464p. illus. maps. index. (Princeton Illustrated Checklists series). $29.95pa. ISBN 13: 978-0-691-16796-1.

This volume in the respected Princeton Illustrated Checklists series presents over 1,900 avian species from across South America, described and illustrated by the author. The passerines included here are basically perching birds, so that others—penguins, shore birds, etc.—are not included. Maps indicate the habitats for each of the birds, and whether they are resident or migratory species. Color variations based on age and gender are pointed out in text and illustration; bird calls are described for many of the birds. An introduction outlines the 32 families of birds found on the continent. The illustrations on a given page also reflect accurate comparative sizes of the birds portrayed.

A compact work quite appropriate for birders on location, it also serves as an excellent introduction for anyone interested in the birds of South America. Various kinds of libraries should consider purchase of this handsome, informative, and reasonably priced volume.— **Mark Schumacher**

P

433.   **Wildlife Conservation Society Birds of Brazil: The Atlantic Forest of Southeast Brazil, including São Paulo and Rio de Janeiro.** Ridgely, Robert S., John A. Gwynne, and Guy Tudor. Ithaca, N.Y., Cornell University Press, 2016. 417p. illus. maps. index. (Birds of Brazil series). $35.00pa. ISBN 13: 978-1-5017-0453-6.

This volume of the *Birds of Brazil* field guide series focuses on the Southeastern Atlantic Forest region surrounding São Paulo and Rio de Janeiro. Presenting accounts for over 900 bird species, 863 of which are illustrated, the volume is particularly valuable due to the accessibility of the Atlantic Forest region to the global birdwatching community. A generous introductory section presents several beautifully photographed essays discussing the variety of the region's habitats, from the lush lowland forests to the sandy

Restingas. Essays also address shrinking habitats, declining bird populations, and ideas related to habitat rehabilitation efforts, such as private nature reserves. Readers can also find helpful maps and a key for symbols used throughout the accounts in this section. The accounts themselves organize birds via their family classifications down through the specific species. All accounts are accompanied by range maps, while most include color illustrations (which, according to the book, provide better species contrast than photography). Accounts also provide common and scientific name, measurements, general population information, physical descriptions, behavior, diet, reproductive information, and more. Symbols alert readers to the species status: vulnerable, endangered, or critically endangered. Readers will note the vast array of hummingbirds, the interesting variety of endemic (found only in Brazil) species, the many rarely sighted birds such as the Fasciated Tiger Heron, and much more. End pages include a list of references, separate indexes for English, Portuguese, and scientific names, and a regional map highlighting the specific biomes of the region. Published by the Wildlife Conservation Society, the volume is an exceptionally researched tool for use in bringing attention to the many endangered bird species in this region of Brazil that could benefit from increased conservation and educational efforts. Recommended.—**ARBA Staff Reviewer**

Domestic Animals

P
434.   Hajeski, Nancy. **Every Dog: A Book of Over 450 Breeds.** New York, Firefly Books, 2016. 536p. illus. index. $24.95pa. ISBN 13: 978-1-77085-825-1.

This handy title provides reference information on more than 450 dog breeds worldwide. Some are familiar—St. Bernard's, Boxers, and Bloodhounds—but many are less well known like the Schapendoes (from the Netherlands), the Phu Quoc Ridgeback (from Vietnam), the Chien Français Blanc et Noir, and the Cesky Terrier from the Czech Republic.

The book begins with a brief introduction that touches on dog evolution before jumping into its nine sections, broken down into dog type: Sighthounds and Pariahs, Scent Hounds, Herding Dogs, Guarding Dogs, Sporting Dogs, Spitz-Type Dogs, Terriers, Companion Dogs, and Designer Dogs. The information provided is compact but thorough thanks in part to useful photographs, graphics, and text boxes. For example, readers interested in Newfoundland dogs will see a color photograph of an adult dog and a smaller color photograph of a Newfoundland puppy. The page also indicates common coat colors, average height, weight, and life expectancy, general health information, the history of the breed, and main characteristics. All dog descriptions also include basic health information and At a Glance text boxes that rank the breed on a one-to-five scale in six categories: ease of training, affection, playfulness, good with children, good with other dogs, and grooming. The introduction indicates that the information used in the At a Glance boxes is based on kennel club guidelines, breeder's recommendations, and studies of various breeds.

One wishes the author had utilized a bibliography and included sources for further reading. Nevertheless this book is modestly priced and would be a fine addition to a public library or to personal collections.—**ARBA Staff Reviewer**

Fishes

C, P

435.   Kells, Val, Luiz A. Rocha, and Larry G. Allen. **A Field Guide to Coastal Fishes: From Alaska to California.** Baltimore, Md., Johns Hopkins University Press, 2016. 368p. illus. maps. index. $25.00pa. ISBN 13: 978-1-4214-1832-2.

This beautifully illustrated guide to the marine fishes of the Pacific Coast of North America (the illustrator is listed as the first author) provides information about nearly 700 species. Each entry includes features and habitat, while many also include a section on biology. The illustrations clearly point out often minute differences between related species. The dates of their identification, ranging from 1758 by Linnaeus to the early twenty-first century, are also provided. The fishes range from 2.5 inches (sharpnose sculpin) to 40 feet (whale shark—"approachable by divers")!

Clearly this volume will be most useful to libraries, both public and academic, on the Pacific Coast. However, other libraries dealing with marine biology and ichthyology should consider it as well.—**Mark Schumacher**

C, P

436.   Snyder, David B., and George H. Burgess. **Marine Fishes of Florida.** Baltimore, Md., Johns Hopkins University Press, 2016. 373p. illus. maps. index. $39.95pa. ISBN 13: 978-1-4214-1872-8.

This beautiful volume, which seeks to be more than a "field guide," presents 133 fish families (hundreds of species) with over 500 photographs and clear, often fascinating, texts about the lives of these creatures. (Did you know that there were 16 species of searobins, and 19 kinds of moray eels, in Florida waters?) From the physical appearance and habitats of each fish in a family, to their mating habits and specific behaviors, the information is presented in a clear and engaging manner. The photos, taken in large part by the authors, are clear and often stunning.

This book has a clear geographical focus, but will be fascinating for anyone wishing to learn about these intriguing animals. Libraries in the southeast United States, and any institution, including colleges and universities, with patrons interested in the lives of fish will find the reasonably priced volume worth having.—**Mark Schumacher**

Insects

C, P, S

437.   **Butterflies and Moths of North America http://www.butterfliesandmoths.org/.** [Website] Free. Date reviewed: 2017.

For anyone interested in viewing photographs and other information about moths and butterflies in North America (Panama to Canada), this extensive database is an authoritative place to start. Data is discoverable via a series of tabs from the home page: Home, About, Identify, Get Involved, Learn, Regional Checklists, Image Gallery, and What's New. Information under the About tab explains the history of the project and how information is curated to ensure high quality and accuracy. The Identify tab offers online tools for butterfly and moth identification as well as a bibliography of print resources. For those who want to submit sightings or photos or partner with BAMONA in some capacity, information is available by clicking on Get Involved. The Learn tab offers a glossary, related links, a species search function, and a taxonomy, while the Images tab has hundreds of clickable photos that reveal the name of the moth or butterfly and the location where it was photographed. The What's New tab leads to a blog as well as information about new sightings. This is updated regularly. The Regional Checklists tab takes users to the heart of the site. Here one can search by butterfly or moth by country and state. Users can search for butterflies in the Mexican state of Oaxaca or for moths sighted in California. A search produces a list of butterflies or moths; each is linked to a color photograph and a map. There is information (this varies) on caterpillar host plants, adult food, range, family and subfamily, and more.—**ARBA Staff Reviewer**

C, P, S
438.   Wilson, Joseph S., and Olivia Messinger Carril. **The Bees in Your Backyard: A Guide to North America's Bees.** Princeton, N.J., Princeton University Press, 2015. 288p. illus. maps. index. $29.95pa. ISBN 13: 978-0-691-16077-1.

About 4,000 species of bees live in North America (compared to 400 species of mammals). This richly illustrated volume provides a detailed introduction to the lives of bees, then presents the six families of bees found here. Charts and detailed maps show their size, their range, and their active times of the year within different regions of the continent. Hundreds of close-up photos present fascinating details of many of the different kinds of bees. An interesting chapter discusses supporting bees in one's neighborhood; another feature is an "identification tips" section for each bee family, which points out their common characteristics.

This reasonably priced book will appeal to both those who study bees professionally (biologists, zoologists) and others interested in bees more generally. Public and academic libraries should find it useful, and high school libraries could also benefit, given its cost.—**Mark Schumacher**

Mammals

C, P
439.   Schmidly, David J., and Robert D. Bradley. **The Mammals of Texas, Seventh Edition.** 7th ed. Austin, Tex., University of Texas at Austin, 2016. 608p. illus. maps. index. $39.95pa. ISBN 13: 978-1-4773-0886-8; 978-1-4773-1003-8 (e-book).

This volume represents the latest version of a work first published in 1947 by the Texas Parks and Wildlife Department. For each of the 180+ species, the authors provide a physical description, the animal's distribution within the state, its habits, and its population and conservation status. Included are 68 rodents (pocket gophers, mice, and rats), 32 bats, and 28 carnivores, each with a black-and-white photograph. There are also 14 pages of color plates included. Maps are provided for each animal, showing which counties in Texas have recorded the creature's presence. The information is presented in a clear way, accessible to a wide reading public. The authors, longtime scholars in the field, thank many colleagues who helped to bring this large volume to fruition.

This book will clearly interest readers in Texas, but many other libraries will be interested in this information. Many academic libraries across the United States have purchased earlier editions, supporting programs in biology, ecology, and zoology, and may well wish to acquire the latest version. Natural history institutions will find this of use as well.—**Mark Schumacher**

C, P, S

440. **Watkins Marine Mammal Sound Database. http://cis.whoi.edu/science/B/ whalesounds/index.cfm.** [Website] Free. Date reviewed: 2017.

This site has collected roughly 70 years of marine mammal recordings into a unique database. Vocalizations of over 60 species of marine creatures have been carefully categorized, digitized, and annotated for use in a variety of research.

Navigation through the site is simple. Users can select from one of three tabs or can conduct a search by name (common or scientific) or in some cases by animal photo. Choosing the Best Of tab takes users to the highest quality recordings which includes over 1,600 individual "cuts" or taped vocalizations. The recordings in this section include vocalizations of Humpback Whales, Common Dolphins, Harp Seals, Killer Whales, Walruses, and more. The All Cuts tab includes every sound in the inventory (close to 15,000 cuts) and is searchable by name only. Master Tapes contains nearly 1,600 complete unedited recordings searchable by name or year made.

Sound files are free to download for noncommercial use. Information accompanying each file includes location where recording was made, observation date, and metadata. This unique database would appeal to students and educators in a number of life science fields.—**ARBA Staff Reviewer**

Marine Animals

C

441. **Rays of the World.** Peter R. Last and others. Illustrated by Lindsay Marshall. Ithaca, N.Y., Cornell University Press, 2016. 790p. illus. maps. index. $149.95. ISBN 13: 978-0-6431-0913-1; 978-0-6431-0915-5 (e-book).

This massive volume provides detailed information on 633 species of rays, divided into 26 families. Each of the fishes is illustrated in color (wonderfully done by Lindsay Marshall), its habitat on a world map is clearly shown, and information about its behaviors and life cycle, identifying marks, and related species is provided. Some species are known by a handful of specimens, and some live in microhabitats, such as a small group of islands. An 18-page glossary does assist the less knowledgeable reader to navigate the fascinating world(s) of these creatures. A checklist of all species indicates both which regions of the oceans they are found in, and the depths at which they live in each area.

Given the scientific language used through this book and its detail, libraries serving ecologists, zoologists, biologists, or ichthyologists will be most interested in this work. Other libraries will want to look for a simpler introduction to these creatures.—**Mark Schumacher**

32 Engineering

Civil Engineering

Handbooks and Yearbooks

C

442. **Civil and Environmental Engineering: Concepts, Methodologies, Tools, and Applications.** Mehdi Khosrow-Pour, ed. Hershey, Pa., IGI Global, 2016. 3v. index. $2,250.00/set (individual chapters available for purchase in electronic format). ISBN 13: 978-1-4666-9619-8; 978-1-4666-9620-4 (e-book).

The impact of built environment is felt generations after its creation. These influences go beyond providing a structure and influence human behavior, perception, and even cultures. This three-volume work broadly brushes the various contemporary methodologies and techniques used in civil engineering—focusing on public works projects. No engineering discipline can exist without interacting with other engineering disciplines. Civil engineering projects leverage advances in material science (smart structures), sustainability (environmentally friendly and energy efficiency), mathematics (simulation and optimization), and communications (data acquisition and synthesis). This work emphasizes advances in the digital sciences that are integrated in civil engineering. This volume also touches on the cultural aspects of civil engineering, specifically organizational and human behavior, ethics, and political science.

The work's broad scope is organized into five sections. Section one provides a background on public works projects. This section serves as an overview of current civil engineering practices. Section two explores some novel methodologies and applications in primarily public works projects. It also addresses other nonengineering factors (such as human behavior) that are currently integrated in project design and layout. Section three is primarily a collection of case studies showcasing the marriage of contemporary engineering practice and novel approaches in public works projects. Section four critically analyzes our approach to civil engineering issues. While some chapters suggest other approaches, the focus is on outlining the issues, and asking relevant questions. Section five looks at the possible trajectories civil engineering could take. Some of the issues are universal (such as sustainability and efficiency), others are more unique to developments in the twenty-first century (such as real-time data acquisition and decision-making, and mobile communication).

The broad scope of this work necessitates omissions. The articles do not delve too deeply in the technical aspects of engineering, and hence are appropriate for project managers and nonengineering but technical specialists. The broader and more social-political essays can be appreciated by nontechnical readers. Each essay has an extensive list of references, making this work an excellent starting point for those interested in contemporary civil engineering. Recommended for not only civil engineers, but also for managers of civil engineering projects.—**Muhammed Hassanali**

C

443. **Environmental Impacts on Underground Power Distribution.** Osama El-Sayed Gouda, ed. Hershey, Pa., IGI Global, 2016. 405p. index. (Advances in Computer and Electrical Engineering (ACEE) Book Series). $225.00 (individual chapters available for purchase in electronic format). ISBN 13: 978-1-4666-6509-5; 978-1-4666-6510-1 (e-book).

Environmental Impacts on Underground Power Distribution begins to explore the impact that an environment can have on distribution of power. The book observes the factors that affect the maximum rating of subterranean power cables as well as various methods to maximize electrical current transmission. The book begins to explore ways that the environment can impact power distribution, and shares the latest research into the aforementioned. Topics covered include artificial backfill materials, cable losses, cross-bonding systems, dry zones, electric power transmission, heat flux density, and thermal resistivity.

This book is another entry in IGI's Engineering Science Reference series, which aims to provide a reference material for students, academics, and practitioners for the best practices in engineering science.

While the topic of underground power distribution may seem convoluted at first blush, the aims behind using underground cables are simple. A cable, if underground, is less susceptible to severe weather such as high wind or damaging ice and rain storms. Additionally, from an aesthetic perspective, many communities prefer their power distributions underground as such a method of distribution is more aesthetically pleasing. No matter the community's motivation for underground power distribution, the fact remains that distributing power underground is much more expensive on the front end (the installation period) than it is on the back end (maintenance). As such, a community would do well to ensure that power lines installed underground is done properly the first time.

This book begins to discuss getting the installation right the first time. Containing pages on the latest research, graphs, and formulas for installing underground power distribution correctly, this book can hardly be described as light reading. The book will likely be of most use to practitioners, academics, and advanced students. Additionally, the book can almost certainly serve as a reference point for practitioners. While the book does offer an introduction to underground power distribution in its early chapters, it also offers an easy reference for practitioners to refer to in particular situations that arise over the course of engineering practice.

Overall, the book will nestle well on the shelves of practitioners. While it may not be a daily reference, it will be a useful reference in specific situations. This book is recommended for academic libraries.—**Sara Mofford**

C, P

444.   **LTBP Bridge Portal. https://ltbp6.rutgers.edu/.** [Website] Free. Date reviewed: 2017.

Developed in conjunction with the Rutgers Center of Advanced Infrastructure and Transportation, this site from the U.S. Department of Transportation's Federal Highway Administration offers users a flexible way to analyze data about bridges across the United States.

All users can scroll down through the site for tutorial information, or click from a selection on the right sidebar. From here, users must provide basic information to register with the site to access its search and data capabilities. The site offers a number of state-of-the-art viewing options for its registered users via a Google Maps interface when locating bridges. Users can conduct a basic or advanced search of particular bridges, state bridge systems, or bridge specifications such as location, number of lanes, owner, structure number, material, and design style. Users can view/generate data in a variety of formats, such as pie charts, bar charts, and tables and can also create exportable and workable spreadsheet reports. Additionally, the site allows users to save and edit their selected data searches across repeat site visits.

The specialized focus of this site would appeal to transportation and engineering researchers, educators, and professionals.—**ARBA Staff Reviewer**

33 Health Sciences

General Works

Handbooks and Yearbooks

C, P, S

445. Goldstein, Myrna Chandler, and Mark A. Goldstein. **The 50 Healthiest Habits and Lifestyle Changes.** Santa Barbara, Calif., Greenwood Press/ABC-CLIO, 2016. 303p. index. $58.00. ISBN 13: 978-1-4408-3471-4; 978-1-4408-3472-1 (e-book).

The 50 Healthiest Habits and Lifestyle Changes is founded on scientific research that healthy lifestyle habits established and entrenched at a young age will benefit people as they age. This book talks about 50 different healthy habits. The topics are geared towards teens and young adults. The first topic is about habits, making something a habit, and reforming habits. This is essentially a learning process that will help people of all ages become healthier and sets the tone for the book. The broad topics in this book include: Healthy Foods, Exercise, Medical Care, Safety, Mental and Social Health, Sex and Dating, and Other Lifestyle Choices. Within those topics are detailed sections on issues such as texting while driving, STDs, avoiding electronic cigarettes, avoiding tanning beds, limiting processed food, and more. Each topic includes an overview, explanations from experts including scientific authoritative sources, noted citations, and sources for further research. The book also includes an index and a glossary of terms. The chapters are designed to be a starting point to discuss and explore these topics. This book would be a welcome addition to a health curriculum collection for middle and high school libraries as well as public and academic libraries.—**Amy B. Parsons**

C

446. **Handbook on Gender and Health.** Gideon, Jasmine, ed. Northampton, Mass., Edward Elgar, 2016. 650p. index. (International Handbooks on Gender series). $295.00. ISBN 13: 978-1-78471-085-9.

The new *Handbook on Gender and Health,* edited by Jasmine Gideon of the University of London, attempts to dive into the complexity of gender and health and promote a greater understanding of the myriad issues that interplay with gender and health. By all measures, Gideon succeeds in this task. Gideon has compiled an extensive and thorough collection of essays on gender and health, including public policy, work and health, migration and health, health systems, households, sexuality, and health care. The book is a nearly 650-page volume that fearlessly addresses many of the pressing topics on gender and health in a progressive manner.

One welcome addition to the handbook is a discussion on public health discourses on men's health. James Smith, Noel Richardson, and Steve Robinson discuss issues of public policy that are often disguised to individuals in the West, including the relatively short life span of men worldwide today. The authors also discuss the controversy behind gender-specific health policies, but fiercely defend the need for said policies as a path forward for developing public health. The authors explore gender-specific health policies in Australia and Ireland, and detail these policies from development to implementation to measurement of results.

Gideon also devoted an entire chapter of her handbook to gender, health, and migration. This is a welcome addition, considering the current worldwide migrant crisis. Gideon includes an article by Denise Spitzer that details Spitzer's research on migration and gender and health. Spitzer studied migrants in Canada, Southeast Asia, and Ethiopia and includes personal recollections from migrants on issues as diverse as gender roles, racial differences, and immigration policies. What emerges from Spitzer's research is an intimate, intensely humanized portrait of migration, gender, and the often complex and sometimes conflicting points of view that accompany contemporary migration.

The handbook is a useful tool for those interested in gender and health. It is wide in its reach, covering a diverse and extensive range of topics, and deep in its coverage of specific topics. It is termed a "handbook," but could more accurately be described as a "survey." The book is a useful reference for students, academics, and practitioners alike. Doubtlessly, this book is a good jumping off point for additional reference. The book is easy to navigate and contains an easily searchable index. The timeliness of this book will make it useful for years to come.

Highly recommended for academic libraries.—**Sara Mofford**

C

447. **Healthcare Community Synergism between Patients, Practitioners, and Researchers.** Valerie Bryan and Jennifer Bird, eds. Hershey, Pa., Medical Information Science Reference/IGI Global, 2017. 348p. index. (Advances in Medical Diagnosis, Treatment, and Care (AMDTC) Book Series). $210.00 (individual chapters available for purchase in electronic format). ISBN 13: 978-1-52250-640-9; 978-1-52250-641-6 (e-book).

This resource is part of a book series that "seeks to highlight publications on innovative treatment methodologies, diagnosis tools and techniques, and best practices for patient care." *Healthcare Community Synergism between Patients, Practitioners, and Researchers* "has the overall objective of connecting the fields of education and medicine to demonstrate effective collaborations among, patients, practitioners, and researchers." It is comprised of chapters written by experts in the field and its coverage includes: "Writing Healing Narratives"; "Synergism through Therapeutic Visual Arts"; "Heartmath: A University Initiative"; "A Need for Greater Collaboration: Initiatives to Improve Transitions of Care"; "Humane Education: A Call to Action for Elementary School Students"; "Preparing Future Physicians to Adapt to the Changing Health Care System: Promoting Humanism through Curricular Design"; "Mental Illness, Youth, and Applicable Lessons from Residential Treatment Centers"; "Culture of Learning Cities: Connecting

Leisure and Health for Lifelong Learning Communities"; "The Role of Self-Efficiency and Aging in Managing Disease"; "Stress and Its Relationship to Leadership and a Healthy Workplace Culture"; "Framework of Indian Healthcare Systems and its Challenges: An Insight"; and "Incognito: The Neuroscience of Grief and Grieving." Chapter contributors include those representing universities and organizations including: Florida Atlantic University, University of Illinois at Chicago, Southern New Hampshire University, Nova Southeastern University, and Columbia University Teachers College. Also included are an index and a compilation of references.

Recommended to practitioners and students and faculty of universities with curriculum in health care.—**Lucy Heckman**

C, P, S

448. Klosek, Jacqueline. **Wellness by the Numbers: Understanding and Interpreting American Health Statistics.** Santa Barbara, Calif., Greenwood Press/ABC-CLIO, 2016. 341p. index. $37.00. ISBN 13: 978-1-61069-963-1; 978-1-61069-964-8 (e-book).

With the Internet, health reports and statistics from the media are everywhere. The public is inundated with reports and news about the latest health trends whether it's validation for a health supplement or a warning about taking a specific medication. Accurate reports rely on and are built around authoritative facts to share the information out to the public. *Wellness by the Numbers* functions as an almanac of sorts for various topics in health and wellness. This book includes 50 popular health topics; including physical health topics such as allergies and thyroid cancer, and mental health issues such as depression, suicide, teenage pregnancy, and many more. Each entry is easy to read, and is organized in an orderly fashion including an introduction, risk factors, signs and symptoms, tables, data, and analysis. Each entry includes citations from credible sources that include the Center for Disease Control, World Health Organization and National Library of Medicine, and more. At the end of each entry are several detailed discussion questions for each topic. These discussion questions allow the reader to use this book in creative ways other than just as a handbook for facts. This book could be used as a foundation for a group discussion on a health topic, a class debate, or any type of research that needs to include facts and critical thinking. A nice index of resources for further research is included at the end. Recommended for all ages of researchers, for consumer health libraries, a public reference library collection, or an academic library health collection.—**Amy B. Parsons**

Medicine

General Works

Dictionaries and Encyclopedias

C, P, S

449. **Chronic Diseases: An Encyclopedia of Causes, Effects, and Treatments.** Jean Kapaln Teichroew, ed. Santa Barbara, Calif., Greenwood Press/ABC-CLIO, 2017. 2v. index. $189.00/set. ISBN 13: 978-1-4408-0103-7; 978-1-4408-0104-4 (e-book).

This two-volume set of over 300 entries catalogs chronic diseases and disorders, general health topics, treatment, and social issues. Alphabetical ordering is preceded by common introductory matter. Additionally, each volume begins with the "Guide to Related Topics." Black-and-white tables such as "Asthma Severity Classifications" provide supplementary data within entries. Entries end with cross-references and "Further Reading" provides authoritative sources. Website links provide access to organizations with the very latest information for patient or researcher. The comprehensive index provides a plethora of subjects and assists in navigation to specific listings. "Recommended Resources" will be quite useful to users.

The majority of entries address diseases and disorders. Diseases may have individual entries such as the cancer Kaposi's Sarcoma or a cluster of related diseases may be found under headers like Ear Diseases or Lung Diseases. Strong cross-referencing will provide easy search progression. Disorders such as Attention Deficit Hyperactivity Disorder and Metabolic Disorders provide symptom information (a strong component of disorder investigation) in addition to an overview, diagnosis, and prognosis. Procedures, testing, and long-term options are represented. Furthermore, entries about positive wellness tactics of Physical Therapy and Self-Management describe avenues for improved health.

As a resource tool, *Chronic Diseases* delineates disease and disorder, health options, support organizations, and long-term projections for those living with chronic illness. This book is suitable for high school and undergraduate students seeking introduction to subjects of chronic conditions. Librarians working with the general public, patients, and caregivers will want to have this reference available to all.

Recommended.—**Janis Minshull**

Handbooks and Yearbooks

P, S

450.   Brill, Marlene Targ. **Chronic Illnesses, Syndromes, and Rare Disorders: The Ultimate Teen Guide.** Lanham, Md., Rowman & Littlefield, 2016. 233p. illus. index. $45.99; $44.99 (e-book). ISBN 13: 978-1-4422-5161-8; 978-1-4422-5162-5 (e-book).

Chronic Illnesses, Syndromes, and Rare Disorders: The Ultimate Teen Guide is a single-volume title and is part of the It Happened To Me series (Book No. 49). The introduction defines books published in this series as "designed for inquisitive teens digging for answers about certain illnesses, social issues, or lifestyle interests." Past books in the series have addressed topics such as adoption, body image, substance abuse, depression, divorce, food allergies, finances, and money and bullying. *Chronic Illnesses, Syndromes, and Rare Disorders* offers specific chapters on celiac, Crohn's, Down Syndrome, hemophilia, melanoma and other skin cancers, multiple sclerosis, phenylketonuria, sickle cell disease, and Tourette Syndrome. The book opens with a chapter defining syndrome, chronic illness, and what's rare and concludes with a chapter of information on managing daily activities and well-being.

Chapters include facts and a basic medical explanation about each topic. There are accompanying boxes of text with individual teen stories about living or managing the specific illness, syndrome, or disorder. There are also simple black-and-white diagrams, drawings, and photos that illustrate the text. Symptoms, screening, diagnosis, treatment and living with the illness, syndrome, or disorder is also included. Chapters end with resources for further information, which may include organizations, books, and websites. The book concludes with a simple glossary of terms, cited source notes from individual chapters, and an index.

Chronic Illnesses, Syndromes, and Rare Disorders provides a basic introduction to the topics addressed; like any medical source, one should consult with a physician for complete medical advice and information. A good source for the circulating collection of a high school or public library collection.—**Caroline L. Gilson**

C, S

451. **Contagious Diseases Sourcebook.** 3d ed. Keith Jones, ed. Detroit, Omnigraphics, 2016. 666p. index. (Health Reference Series). $95.00. ISBN 13: 978-0-7808-1488-2.

Contagious Disease Sourcebook is constructed for the general individual who would like more information on contagious diseases. It is intentionally not an in-depth textbook and is intended to rest on the bookshelves of laymen for information on contagious diseases. The book is a continuation of the well-respected Health Reference Series and is the third edition of said book.

The sourcebook covers diseases spread from person to person through direct physical contact, airborne transmissions, sexual contact, or contact with blood and other bodily fluids. Further, the book contains common remedies to rectify these diseases, including home remedies and over-the-counter medication. While the book does not claim to be a substitute for a competent physician, it does somewhat alleviate the information void that may exist between medical professionals and patients.

The book provides an educational experience for the reader. While books of this stripe are useful for reference purposes, it is a common temptation for books like this to be overinterpreted by the nervous reader. This book, when used properly, provides a good background for what a contagious disease is, and then begins to explore the specifics of each contagious disease.

The book is broken down into six parts: What You Need to Know about Germs, Types of Contagious Diseases, Self-Treatment for Contagious Diseases, Medical Diagnosis and Treatment of Contagious Diseases, Preventing Contagious Diseases, and Additional Help and Information. Within these sections, there are 85 chapters within the book's 641 (preindex) pages. Of note, the book also contains chapters on emerging issues that may not have been included in a similar book a generation before, including issues that deal with the morbid reality of a bioterrorism threat.

While all of the information in the book is useful, the book shines in its presentation of a chapter on each disease. Each chapter contains a quick introduction, the symptoms of the disease, the seriousness of the disease, whether the disease is contagious, the individuals at risk for the disease, whether the disease can be treated, and whether the disease can be prevented.

The book is of great use to all individuals who are concerned about their health and want a bit more information about symptoms, treatment, or diagnosis of a contagious disease. It is useful for layman and students, as well as medical professionals. This book is recommended for academic and high school libraries.—**Sara Mofford**

C, P, S

452. **Images from the History of Medicine. https://ihm.nlm.nih.gov/luna/servlet/ view/all.** [Website] Free. Date reviewed: 2017.

This database offers no bells and whistles but contains a vast and varied collection of images reflecting the global history of medicine. The U.S. National Library of Medicine has amassed nearly 70,000 images, including postcards, photographs, posters, maps, and much more that contribute to telling the story of medicine. The collection goes back centuries to include the most basic anatomical sketches but also has considerable holdings from the modern era, such as x-rays and eye charts.

Search capabilities encompass a vast array of subject parameters, such as nurses, military hospitals, facial injuries, first aid, and craniocerebral trauma. Users can additionally narrow their search by collection date, author, title, format, language, and other qualifiers.

Selecting an item to view allows users to view an enlarged image or download it. General information accompanies each image, such as publication date, genre, description, NLM identification number, and medium. This database would appeal to a variety of students, educators, and researchers.—**ARBA Staff Reviewer**

C, S

453.   LeMay, Michael C. **Global Pandemic Threats: A Reference Handbook.** Santa Barbara, Calif., ABC-CLIO, 2016. 366p. index. (Contemporary World Issues). $60.00. ISBN 13: 978-1-4408-4282-5; 978-1-4408-4283-2 (e-book).

From the earliest documented Plagues of Egypt (13th century B.C.E.), disease and health epidemics have threatened populations around the world. *Global Pandemic Threats,* part of the Contemporary World Issues series, describes the history of epidemics, medical successes and failures, the establishment of national and global efforts to combat disease, and much more in four chapters: "Background and History," "Problems, Controversies, and Solutions," "Perspectives," and "Profiles." Chapter five, "Data and Documents," also includes black-and-white maps, figures, and tables including one that lists nine of the deadliest viruses that cause pandemic outbreaks, such as smallpox, HIV, influenza, yellow fever, and Ebola. As a springboard for research, the last two chapters, "Resources" and "Chronology," will provide strong engagement and incentive to delve deeper.

As a robust source for disease information, *Global Pandemic Threats* will be extremely useful to high school students, undergraduates, medical students and professionals, and researchers seeking data and reference access to health threats in the twenty-first century with historical background.

Highly recommended.—**Janis Minshull**

P, S

454.   **Men's Health Concerns Sourcebook.** 5th ed. Keith Jones, ed. Detroit, Omnigraphics, 2016. 600p. index. (Health Reference Series). $95.00. ISBN 13: 978-0-7808-1482-0.

A volume of the notable Health Reference Series, this book is an invaluable reference offering basic, comprehensive information covering a series of issues affecting men's health. The book is designed to assist nonmedical professionals, patients, caregivers, and others who seek straightforward, educational information about the latest trends and concerns affecting the health of the male population, from genetic disorders to mental health and much more.

Five parts organize the material, beginning with a general overview of Men's Health Basics. Following parts address Leading Causes of Death in Men, Sexual and Reproductive

Concerns, and Other Medical Issues of Concern to Men. A final part contributes a Glossary of Men's Health Terms and a useful directory of organizations offering men's health information.

Each part is further divided into detailed chapters addressing the particulars of its subject. Part one includes chapters on recommended self-examinations, screening tests, vaccinations, risk factor management, and much more. Part two's chapters look at the way many common diseases, such as diabetes, Alzheimer Disease, or cancer manifest in men, in addition to examining less frequently discussed manners of death such as homicides, suicides, or accidents. Part three covers topics ranging from urological and reproductive disorders to sexually transmitted diseases. And part four examines issues ranging from male pattern baldness to mental health and body image.

While the amount of information can seem overwhelming, the book does an excellent job of presenting it clearly and concisely with short sections and many headings and subheadings. The book may employ a question-and-answer format (e.g., How Do Anabolic Steroids Affect the Brain?), along with diagrams, bullet points, and tables.

This fifth edition conveys the most up-to-date information in regards to men's health issues relative to the rapid advancements in research happening as we write this. Recommended.—**ARBA Staff Reviewer**

P

455.　Paul, Gill. **A History of Medicine in 50 Objects.** New York, Firefly Books, 2016. 224p. illus. index. $29.95. ISBN 13: 978-1-77085-718-6.

Like many history through object books this one selects from among many options to give a general sense of a subject. In the case of this book, the timeline is long—10,000 B.C.E. to 2015, starting with the practice of trepanning used worldwide by Neolithic people to treat injuries. From there the book moves on to the Edwin Smith Papyrus produced in Egypt in 3,000 B.C.E., which lists 48 ailments and care suggestions (showing a remarkable understanding of such things as brain function and the heart's role in circulation). The last object covered is the Ebola suit created for health care workers in West Africa during the Ebola epidemic, which reached its height in 2014-15. Along the way readers are treated to larger discussions of medicine surrounding such objects as the tree under which Hippocrates taught, the herbal remedy book written by Greek doctor to the Roman army, Dedanius Dioscorides, the plague mask worn by doctors in the fourteenth-seventeenth centuries, John Snow's 1854 cholera map of the Soho neighborhood of London, Sigmund Freud's couch, and the health warning first printed on cigarette packages in the United States in 1965.

The entries vary in length from two to eight pages. Each discussion includes general historical information, interesting facts, illustrations, and contextualization within the history of medicine. The book ends with a short bibliography of books, journals, and websites followed by an index.

The material is fascinating and the writing style is engaging. Though the table of contents and the index make it possible to read about an object in isolation, most will want to read this book from cover to cover. It is a good place for basic information or for beginning a research project. Overall, the book achieves its objective of conveying the history of medicine through the 50 objects examined. Recommended for public libraries.—**ARBA Staff Reviewer**

C

456.   **Philosophy: Medical Ethics.** Craig M. Klugman, ed. New York, Macmillan Reference USA/Gale Group, 2016. 418p. index. (Macmillan Interdisciplinary Handbooks). $179.00. ISBN 13: 978-0-02-866333-3.

Biomedical ethics comprises a tremendous range of topics, so any introductory reference work will necessarily reflect difficult editorial choices about which issues to cover. This work aims to provide an overview of the field while primarily discussing fiduciary relationships and ethical challenges related to financial aspects of medical procedures, including payment for surrogacy and eggs, payments to doctors to promote medications, conflicts of interest, and costs related to organ transplants and public health. Every chapter includes examples drawn from movies or television series in an effort to make the text interesting to an undergraduate audience. The introductory essay outlining the history of the development of biomedical ethics is excellent. Since the chapters have different authors, some focus much more carefully on historical or contemporary examples while others focus on fiction and even science fiction. Each chapter includes a summary and bibliography; a glossary and index are found at the end. Recommended for an undergraduate audience.—**Delilah R. Caldwell**

C, P, S

457.   **ProMED-mail. http://www.promedmail.org/.** [Website] Free. Date reviewed: 2017.

With the goal of enhanced communication within members of the global health community, this website meets the modern need of rapid news dissemination as it reports information related to global disease outbreaks and toxin exposures.

Simply structured, *ProMED-mail* supplies a listing of moderated posts contributed by media reports, local observers, and others throughout the world. Posts name individual incidents of disease outbreak, and provide any reported data such as location and numbers of outbreak, source of report, nature of diagnosis, affected population, and more.

Users can search for *ProMED-mail* posts via country, date, keyword, or archive number. Users will find posts relating to myriad types of incidents, from pertussis outbreaks in California to Lassa fever in West Africa. Foodborne Illnesses, Avian Influenza, Ebola, Hantavirus, Mumps, and even the recent mysterious chemical weapon fatality in Malaysia are only some of the noteworthy submissions.

All posts are included under the Latest tab, or users can also browse posts particular to Plants, Hot Topics or Errata, which notes recently corrected posts. Access to *ProMED-mail* is free, and it is designed for use by both researchers and those who would submit a report of outbreak information (easy to do via a tab at the top). Users can also choose to subscribe to email reports related to particular topic interests. This site would be of great interest to policy-makers, health care workers, and many others.—**ARBA Staff Reviewer**

C, P, S

458.   **U.S. National Library of Medicine. https://learn.nlm.nih.gov/.** [Website] Free. Date reviewed: 2017.

Known as the Learning Resources Database, this website managed by the National Institute of Health offers a no-frills guide for users looking to access educational materials related to a number of specialized medical topics and National Library of Medicine (NLM) products and services. The site offers no bells or whistles, but rather a straightforward directory that looks to assist with the merger of medical research and web-based technology. The home page is organized into two vertical halves. The left side offers a search bar in addition to a Subject/Product directory of roughly 50 search terms, from the more general Agriculture, K-12 Education, and Minority Health, to the highly specialized SNOMEDCT, VSAC, and more. The right side of the page displays numbered listings associated with the search terms. Arranged chronologically by latest revision date, the listings link to educational resources related to the submission, access, management and interpretation of particular data. Each listing offers a brief description of the material, its format (e.g., webinar, tutorial, etc.), subjects, archival information, and last revision date. Listings range from the simple web tutorial on Understanding Medical Words to the more technical BioProject NCBI Minute which conveys "how to search for genomic studies and quickly identify related PubMed articles and experimental data."

This website will be useful for advanced students, researchers, and others.—**ARBA Staff Reviewer**

Alternative Medicine

Handbooks and Yearbooks

P, S

459.　Milosavljevic, Nada. **Holistic Health for Adolescents: How Yoga, Aromatherapy, Teas, and More Can Help You Get and Stay Healthy.** New York, W. W. Norton, 2016. 258p. index. $21.95pa. ISBN 13: 978-0-393-71114-1.

Fatigue, stress, substance abuse, and depression impact a great segment of adult society. It is perhaps more alarming that these issues and others like them can be so prevalent throughout the teen population. Furthering our concern are the potential risks of traditional medications such as their overuse and their possible impact on still-developing brains. So what can we do?

Holistic Health for Adolescents draws on its author's extensive and diverse background in law, psychiatry, and alternative medicine, as well as her own family story to propose solutions encompassing nonconventional therapies that can work alongside more common and traditional medical approaches.

Seven chapters target specific issues and their particular effects on teenagers: stress, fatigue, low mood, sleep difficulty, focus and concentration, and headache and substance abuse. Within each chapter, the author uses real patient examples of therapies based on the five senses, such as acupuncture, aromatherapy, yoga, and more. The chapters are well organized and define each condition, discuss its particular impact on adolescents, present signs and symptoms, and provide general information on alternative therapies which can work for this problem. Chapters also include large line illustrations of potential therapies, such as acupressure points, herbs, and yoga poses.

Other chapters provide enlightening background behind many alternative therapies and emphasize the importance of integrating these therapies into more traditional medical discussion and the latest research on them.

The book also includes a Sensory Treatment Protocol Information and Resource Guide, extensive references, and an index. Recommended.—**ARBA Staff Reviewer**

Psychiatry

Handbooks and Yearbooks

C, P, S

460.   **Ask Hopkins Psychiatry. http://www.askhopkinspsychiatry.org/.** [Website] Free. Date reviewed: 2017.

Created and managed by Johns Hopkins Medicine (JHM) Department of Psychiatry and Behavioral Sciences—long a highly regarded leader in medical treatment and research, this website offers a simply structured resource for people interested in learning more about mental health. Users are encouraged to type in a question related to mental health, and there are several places throughout the site where they can do so. A Q & A tab then leads to a series of these questions answered via video response. Questions such as "What are symptoms of bipolar disorder?", "How do I help a teenage family member of mine who is addicted to drugs?", "If I start taking lithium what medical monitoring am I supposed to have?", and more are answered by a range of experts in the field of mental health, including social workers, researchers, physicians, psychologists, and others. The Q & A page highlights the most recent question/video response but displays many others which users can easily scroll through. The site updates with one new question/video response per week. Other tabs include Resources, which leads to contact information for several other mental health associations/organizations; Ask A Question where users can discreetly submit their question; and About Us, which provides information about JHM Department of Psychiatry and Behavioral Sciences and links to the larger site. The site also includes contact information for the National Suicide Prevention lifeline. With its clean design and straightforward organization, the site exudes a professional and reassuring air.—**ARBA Staff Reviewer**

Specific Diseases and Conditions

AIDS

C, P, S

461.   **AIDSInfo. http://aidsinfo.nih.gov/.** [Website] Free. Date reviewed: 2017.

This site is a well conceived accessible and freely available gathering spot for information on the HIV virus and AIDS treatment, prevention, and research. Material can be easily accessed from the menu bar at the top or from the display below. Categories include Guidelines, Clinical Trials, Drugs, HIV/AIDS Health Topics, Education Materials, and Mobile Resources & Tools (which makes the site even more accessible in this fast-moving world). A news banner highlights recently updated information, such as guideline corrections, drug label changes, and more. Clicking on a category opens more specific materials. HIV/AIDS Health Topics, for example, brings up Fact Sheets, Infographics for visual data, and a Searchable Index of many specific topics. Simple construction makes the vast amount of information easy to navigate and makes the site ideal for both the basic researcher and the layperson.—**ARBA Staff Reviewer**

Alzheimer's Disease

P

462.　**Alzheimer Disease Sourcebook.** 6th ed. Keith Jones, ed. Detroit, Omnigraphics, 2016. 552p. index. (Health Reference Series). $85.00. ISBN 13: 978-0-7808-1470-7; 978-0-7808-1469-1 (e-book).

As more is learned about Alzheimer disease and other forms of dementia, it is imperative that the public has access to basic information. *Alzheimer Disease Sourcebook,* a 2016 Omnigraphics publication, is available in a hardcover book and as a digital source. This updated volume is part of the Health Reference Series which provides general information for supporting a specific health area and how to create the most proactive lifestyle.

As with all books in this health series, the contents page demonstrates the logical organization. Information on Alzheimer and other brain diseases is divided into 55 chapters and six parts: Facts about the Brain and Cognitive Development; Alzheimer Disease (AD): The Most Common Type of Dementia; Other Dementia Disorders; Recognizing, Diagnosing, and Treating Symptoms of Alzheimer Disease and Dementias; Living with Alzheimer Disease and Dementias; and Caregiver Concerns. Chapters are divided into easy subtopics for greater specification of information. Black-and-white visuals deliver statistics via charts, figures, and tables. Perhaps the most useful chapter for those seeking help is the final chapter, "Directory of Resources for People with Alzheimer Disease" which lists contact information for public and private organizations that offer the latest information, support, and options. The index is solid and affords the simplest access to material.

Part one introduces the workings of the brain and leads to brain impairment information. This is a good foundation though this reference source is more likely to be used for specifics like "Identifying the Genetics of Alzheimer Disease" in chapter 26 where testing guidelines for AD are explained. While the preface states "more than 5.3 million Americans experience AD," this text does differentiate between this brain disorder and other forms of dementia that are also described here. Disease structure, cognitive symptoms and decline, stages of degeneration, and options for care will be useful to caregivers looking for answers. Information on what to expect, while not a template for all patients, promotes awareness and real-life suggestions for best life experience for AD and dementia patients.

This compilation of brain disease information, *Alzheimer Disease Sourcebook,* brings together the most recent content on AD and other brain disorders. As a starting point or for general information, this book will be useful for patients, caregivers, and medical personnel seeking basic information. Public, medical, community, and clinic libraries will find this a useful primary tool.

Recommended.—**Janis Minshull**

Cancer

P

463.   **Breast Cancer Sourcebook.** 5th ed. Keith Jones, ed. Detroit, Omnigraphics, 2016. 662p. index. (Health Reference Series). $95.00. ISBN 13: 978-0-7808-1462-2; 978-0-7808-1461-5 (e-book).

Breast cancer is one of the most common cancers in women. One woman in eight may receive a diagnosis of this disease. Current, accurate information is vital to understand the disease and its treatment options. This new edition of the *Breast Cancer Sourcebook* offers the latest information from federal government agencies such as the Centers for Disease Control and Prevention (CDC), the National Cancer Institute (NCI), and the National Center for Complementary and Integrative Health (NCCIH). All articles are reviewed by medical consultants.

The book contains five parts divided into chapters. These cover an overview of the disease and its anatomy; the types of breast cancer; risk factors, symptoms, and preventive measures; screening, diagnosis, and staging; treatments; managing side effects and complications; living with breast cancer; research and clinical trials; and a glossary and resource list. The book includes information about male breast cancer and useful information about alternative therapies, spirituality, nutrition, and sexuality. The resource list includes information for people without health insurance and those who have low income. It is a useful resource for an overview and introduction to the disease. Public and consumer health libraries will want to consider it if they need a concise print resource. All of the information here is readily available online.—**Barbara M. Bibel**

C, P, S

464.   **Cancer Statistics Center. https://cancerstatisticscenter.cancer.org/#/.** [Website] Free. Date reviewed: 2017.

The home page of this website will definitely capture your attention, conveying in large print the fact that every day there are roughly 4,630 new diagnosed cases of the disease and 1,650 deaths. Produced by the American Cancer Society, the site gives users the important numbers behind the deadly disease in the hopes of enhancing public and governmental awareness and support. The site is all about the data, which is presented with large, brightly colored, and easy-to-read graphics. Tables illustrate both general and specific points, such as 2017 estimates of new cases or deaths by cancer type, death, and incidence rates measured over time, death rate trends per gender and type of cancer, survival rates, and much more. Users can target data by state or by cancer type. Clicking on the analysis tool makes data comparisons easy. The site benefits from streamlining its mission, and is an excellent complement to the work of the American Cancer Society and other cancer education advocates.—**ARBA Staff Reviewer**

Eating Disorders

C, P, S

465.   **Eating Disorders Sourcebook.** 4th ed. Keith Jones, ed. Detroit, Omnigraphics, 2016. 510p. index. (Health Reference Series). $95.00. ISBN 13: 978-0-7808-1466-0.

Eating Disorders Sourcebook, 4th edition, provides information about anorexia nervosa, bulimia nervosa, binge eating disorder, and other related eating disorder concerns, timely prevention, and interventions. This sourcebook explains factors that put people at risk for developing eating disorders, and it discusses the adverse effects and therapeutic modalities used to diagnose and treat related disorders. A meaningful contribution to Omnigraphics' Health Reference Series, this volume provides librarians and users with a unique, useful, thoughtfully crafted, and trustworthy resource.

The physical and psychological toll of eating disorders is high. Suicide, depression, and severe anxiety are common. Eating disorders can lead to complications such as cardiac arrhythmia, cognitive impairment, osteoporosis, infertility, or even death. Furthermore, estimates suggest that only one in ten people with an eating disorder receives appropriate management, even though practitioners can treat these diseases with some success. Shame and denial often thwart efforts to acknowledge the need to initiate professional help. This book may serve as an impetus to help those who suffer and observe in silence.

In reviewing this book, the principal criteria included content, organization, and reference sources. The book's outstanding format and organization allows readers to comprehend and follow relevant content and terms. The construction of the book meshes well with its organization and lends itself successfully to the study of eating disorders. The author supplies an in-depth analysis of various topics of interest often glossed over in basic health textbook chapters, pamphlets, and brochures. The orderliness of the book conforms to an academic curriculum. The author provides excellent material and content, enhanced by well-defined organization. Tables, graphs, and illustrations supplement the volume, along with a helpful glossary, professional resource directories, and a professionally prepared index.

The book is divided into seven parts: What Are Eating Disorders; Risk Factors for Eating Disorders; Causes of Eating Disorders; Medical Complications of Eating Disorders; Recognizing and Treating Disorders; Preventing Eating Disorders and Achieving a Healthy Weight; and Additional Help and Information. Each chapter is broken down into sections, which typically fit logically into the topic of the chapter. All chapters contain several defining parts that maintain a sense of continuity throughout the volume. Overall, the content is written in readable and interactive style. The author uses a question-and-answer format in several passages that serves as a teaching tool. Visual hooks enhance retention and encourage readers to move forward in their inquiry for additional knowledge and understanding.

This book is designed for undergraduates, high school students, and general nonspecialists. Middle schools, high schools, community colleges, and universities will value this book as an essential addition to their library reference shelves. Health organizations and school counselors will benefit from purchasing this timely publication as a reference book.—**Thomas E. Baker**

Sleep Disorders

C, P, S

466. **Sleep Disorders Sourcebook.** 4th ed. Jones, Keith, ed. Detroit, Omnigraphics, 2016. 482p. index. (Health Reference Series). $95.00. ISBN 13: 978-0-7808-1474-5.

According to the National Sleep Foundation, nearly 50 million Americans suffer from sleep problems that can affect their careers, health, personal relationships, and safety.

For example, individuals who experience sleep deprivation are more likely to suffer chronic diseases such as hypertension, diabetes, depression, and obesity. *Sleep Disorders Sourcebook* provides consumer health information that addresses common sleep disorders and related issues.

This Health Reference Series contribution explains the basic physiological and psychological need for sleep, as well as the causes and consequences of sleep deprivation. In addition, discussions explore methods applied to prevent, diagnose, and treat sleep disorders. The text is easy to read, enjoyable, and maintains definitive attention. Keith Jones, author and editor, achieves the publisher's goals and makes an important contribution. *Sleep Disorders Sourcebook* has the capacity to reach multiple audiences because of its simplicity and reasonable presentation of essential information regarding the topic. Designed for undergraduates, high school students, and general nonspecialists, this excellent book presents a current, balanced, and reliable collection of material. The information presented is supplemented by tables, charts, and illustrations; a helpful glossary; a directory of sleep-related resources; and a professionally prepared index.

Sleep Disorders Sourcebook is divided into seven parts. Part one, Sleep Basics, includes an explanation of the circadian rhythms, stages, and physical characteristics of sleep, the benefits of napping, and known information about dreaming. The Causes and Consequences of Sleep Deprivation, part two, defines sleep deprivation and discusses its negative physical effects. The third part, Sleep Disorders, describes disorders that directly affect the ability to get a good night's sleep. These include breathing disorders, insomnia, circadian rhythm disorders, and parasomnias. This part also discusses Kleine-Levin syndrome, periodic limb movement disorder, and restless leg syndrome. Narcolepsy and disorders associated with excessive sleeping are included in the discussion. Part four, Other Health Problems That Often Affect Sleep, provides information about Alzheimer disease, cancer, fibromyalgia, gastroesophageal reflux disease, Parkinson's disease, respiratory disorders, and mental health concerns. Preventing, Diagnosing, and Treating Sleep Disorders, part five, identifies common sleep disruptors and explains the importance of proper sleep environments. The content describes how sleep studies work and details treatment options, including medications, dietary supplements, cognitive behavioral therapy, bright light therapy, continuous positive airway pressure and other devices, and surgery. Part six, A Special Look at Pediatric Sleep Issues, discusses safe sleeping environments for infants and explains sudden infant death syndrome. It provides suggestions for getting children into bed and offers information about bedwetting, sleepwalking, and teeth grinding. Furthermore, this section discusses problems associated with sleep deprivation in teenagers including school difficulties, drowsy driving, and mental health concerns. The last part, Clinical Trials on Sleep Disorders, defines the term "clinical trial" and provides information on some recent clinical trials related to sleep disorders.

Middle school, high school, community college, and university librarians will value this book as an essential addition to their library reference shelves. Health organizations and school counselors will also benefit from purchasing this timely reference book.——
Thomas E. Baker

Pharmacy and Pharmaceutical Sciences

Handbooks and Yearbooks

467.   **AERSMine. https://research.cchmc.org/aers/.** [Website] Free. Date reviewed: 2017.

This freely available data mining system, developed by the Division of Biomedical Informatics and the Center for Clinical & Transitional Science Training at Cincinnati Children's Hospital Medical Center, allows users to mine the massive amount of data available from the U.S. Federal Drug Administration Adverse Reporting System http://www.fda.gov/Drugs/GuidanceComplianceRegulatoryInformation/Surveillance/AdverseDrugEffects/. AERSMine allows users to not just identify adverse reactions to drugs but to also indicate potential benefits and alternative treatments for patients. The AERSMine interface is simple. There are four tabs on the main page: Home, Explore, About, and Help. The information included under the Help tab (including three example searches) is best consulted before heading to the main search screen under the Explore tab where frameworks are used to build searches by Drugs, Indications, Adverse Events, Demographics, and Layout Options. An analysis can then be run, cleared, saved, or loaded. AERSMine may be most useful to physicians and/or medical researchers, but with a bit or patience and trial and error, this is also a tool useful for the general public. Recommended for public, school, and academic libraries.—**ARBA Staff Reviewer**

34 Technology

General Works

Handbooks and Yearbooks

C

468. **Effective Big Data Management and Opportunities for Implementation.** Manoj Kumar Singh and Dileep Kumar G., eds. Hershey, Pa., Information Science Reference/ IGI Global, 2016. 324p. index. (Advances in Data Mining and Database Management (ADMDM) Book Series). $195.00 (individual chapters available for purchase in electronic format). ISBN 13: 978-1-52250-182-4; 978-1-52250-183-1(e-book).

Effective Big Data Management and Opportunities for Implementation is a useful resource for researchers and students seeking to interpret and analyze the implications of big data. The recent trend in big data for researchers and students has amassed a tremendous amount of data, but interpreting and analyzing that data has proven troublesome. The book is written for a wide variety of people, including data analysts, IT professionals, researchers, and graduate-level students who wish to learn more about big data. The book covers eight broad topics: applied big data, complex data, data analytics, data management, data visualization, information retrieval, large-scale recommendation systems, and open data sets.

The book is made up of 15 chapters with titles such as "Big Data: Challenges, Opportunities, and Realities," "Big Data Analysis," and "Using Big Data to Improve the Educational Infrastructure and Learning Paradigm." Each of the chapters contains an abstract, significant discussion, helpful tables and figures for illustrative purposes, a conclusion, and a reference list. Each entry also contains a key terms and definitions list, which is useful for the reader to consult if confusion arises over the meaning or origin of a word in the context of the article.

Chapter 11, "Using Big Data to Improve the Educational Infrastructure and Learning Paradigm" discusses the advances in learning technology as they relate to big data. As education is deliverable in new and varied ways, more data is generated from the delivery of that education. As such, more data is generated by users who receive education from a distance. Data generated from the education sector can be broken down into four categories: descriptive data, behavior data, interaction data, and attitudinal data. Out of these four categories, myriad possibilities present themselves. Of course, there are limitations to this tremendously large amount of data—namely, the ability for student assessment.

The authors caution away from instructors who are too "data driven" at the expense of cultivating and embracing real connections with their students. The macro trends gathered from data should not replace the micro trends, but can provide a useful roadmap on a path forward for future growth.

Overall, the book is a useful resource for understanding the role that big data plays in our society. While sometimes the reading is dense that can likely be attributed to the nature of the material rather than the fault of the author. This book is strongly recommended for researchers and students alike as they begin to grapple with the implications of a data-driven world. This book is recommended for academic libraries.—**Sara Mofford**

C

469.   **Managing and Processing Big Data in Cloud Computing.** Kannan, Rajkumar, Raihan Rasool, Hai Jin, and S. R. Balasundaram, eds. Hershey, Pa., Information Science Reference/IGI Global, 2016. 307p. index. (Advances in Data Mining and Database Management (ADMDM) Book Series). $200.00 (individual chapters available for purchase in electronic format). ISBN 13: 978-1-46669-767-6; 978-1-46669-768-3 (e-book).

Managing and Processing Big Data in Cloud Computing is the newest IGI Global (Information Science Reference) publication from the Advances in Data Mining and Database Management Book Series. As big data becomes more and more prevalent across a multitude of industries, and as these data sets become more cumbersome, analysts face very real challenges in how to handle, analyze, and store such information. This volume tackles that issue and focuses on cloud computing as a potential solution.

The 15 "chapters" in this book represent a collection of 15 essays from authoritative authors all across the world focusing on different aspects of cloud computing. These topics include the dynamic shifting of MapReduce timeout, ceaseless virtual appliance streaming, mobile cloud computing, big data virtualization, etc. As one may expect, the writing and presentation is very academic, detailed, and jargon-heavy. This is by no means an indictment, but the book does lend itself to an audience already familiar with the concepts being discussed.

This is a very research-heavy volume and dense with original research, analyses, and a lot of additional reading references. Although the topics are sometimes fairly narrow, some chapters contain pages and pages of references for additional reading and research that can be incredibly valuable. For researchers or those trying to better utilize big data and cloud computing, this volume should prove to be a very valuable resource.—**Tyler Manolovitz**

C

470.   **Privacy Rights in the Digital Age.** Christopher T. Anglim and Jane E. Kirtley, eds. Amenia, N.Y., Grey House Publishing, 2016. 712p. index. $165.00. ISBN 13: 978-1-61925-747-4; 978-1-61925-748-1 (e-book).

Privacy Rights in the Digital Age may serve as the definitive reference work on the subject of contemporary privacy rights. The general editor aspires to assist scholars in researching broad academic issues, students in seeking introductory material, and practitioners in searching for the origins of particular legal doctrines. The editor is Christopher T. Anglim, Associate Professor/Archivist/Reference Librarian at University of the District of Columbia, and the advisory editor for the book is Professor Jane E. Kirtley,

JD, Director of the Silha Center for the Study of Media Ethics and Law at the University of Minnesota's School of Journalism. Together, along with over 60 distinguished contributors, they have made a substantial contribution to the understanding of a significant current issue that influences our daily living and quality of life.

This volume discusses the practical, political, psychological, and philosophical challenges individuals face as technological advances transform the landscape of traditional concepts of privacy during the digital age. Scholars define the digital age, also called the information age, as the time period starting in the 1970s with the introduction of the personal computer.

Data collection applications saturate our social and civic lives: government surveillance in the name of national security, Supreme Court-sanctioned collection of DNA fingerprints of criminal suspects, targeted online ads tailored to our interests based on personal search histories, wearable computers with camera and recording devices, and cell phone GPS capabilities to track our every movement. As Kirtley points out, there is a paradox of privacy. "On one hand, we benefit from the easy exchange of personal information through digital communications. On the other, we give up some degree of control about what happens to that information." This volume explores issues related to this paradox.

Enlightening entries vary in length depending on the subject matter. The writing style is concise and the editor's topic selection offers readers a noteworthy collection of pertinent information. The book has 712 A-Z entries, an informative introduction, and appropriate font size and line spacing. It also contains bullet point information, bold font titles, primary source documents, a glossary, a bibliography, a subject index, a table of statutes, and a chronology of privacy rights. In addition, over 150 original articles cover laws, legal cases, events, organizations, individuals, technology, and important terms. Moreover, coverage is international in scope with an emphasis on U.S. legal, technological, educational, corporate, and social contexts.

Privacy Rights in the Digital Age mirrors the editor's expertise and dedication to excellence. This encyclopedia reflects a sincere effort to meet the needs of students, scholars, and inquiring minds. Readers will likely feel motivated to peruse topics unrelated to a specific inquiry because the topic selection and writing style encourages further investigation. Library acquisition decision-makers will consider this book a welcome addition to their research collection.—**Thomas E. Baker**

Computers

Handbooks and Yearbooks

C, P, S

471. Schell, Bernadette H. **Online Health and Safety: From Cyberbullying to Internet Addiction.** Santa Barbara, Calif., Greenwood Press/ABC-CLIO, 2016. 345p. index. $89.00. ISBN 13: 978-1-4408-3896-5; 978-1-4408-3897-2 (e-book).

Online Health and Safety acknowledges that the Internet represents an essential and fundamental influence on today's world. The Internet enhances communication, but risks accompany endeavors to share information in a seemingly immeasurable and potentially hazardous cyberspace. Instantaneous worldwide communication is possible across time zones just by clicking on a wireless mouse. It's that easy. Individuals of all ages benefit from limitless opportunities for entertainment and learning. However, threats from those who lurk behind screen names should cause surfers to pause and consider safety concerns. This is especially true for novice Internet users, and vulnerable population targets often include students and teenagers.

Author Bernadette H. Schell is Vice Provost at Laurentian University in Barrie, Ontario, Canada. Previously, she was the founding Dean of Business and IT at the University Of Ontario Institute Of Technology in Oshawa, Ontario. The author has written several books on topics that range from stress management and stalking to cybercrime and hacking.

Online Health and Safety highlights the importance of carefully examining online issues involving harm to persons and policies that influence online health and safety issues. This book addresses worrisome concerns that include cyberbullying, cyberstalking, and online predation. The consequences of online addiction also receive considerable attention. This noteworthy contribution explores 10 unique facets of Internet health and safety, including physical safety, information security, and the responsible use of technology. In addition, Schell offers interviews with field experts and recommends suggestions that encourage a proactive approach to improving Internet safety for users. Schell also uses Q & A sections with experts in the field as well as bullet points, bold face type, a directory of resources for further investigation, extensive footnotes, and a helpful index.

Designed for undergraduates, high school students, and general nonspecialists, *Online Health and Safety* presents a current, balanced, and reliable collection of material to map Internet misuses in an easy-to-understand, thought-provoking manner. The digital age has changed global society in unimaginable ways, and this is only the beginning of a new and sometimes uncertain frontier. This book is an essential title for anyone who uses a computer. High schools, community colleges, and universities would welcome the addition of this book. Health organizations assuredly would benefit from acquiring this timely Greenwood publication as a reference book.—**Thomas E. Baker**

Medical Technology

Handbooks and Yearbooks

C

472. **Advancing Medicine through Nanotechnology and Nanomechanics Applications.** Keka Talukdar, Mayank Bhushan, and Anil Malipatil, eds. Hershey, Pa., Medical Information Science Reference/IGI Global, 2017. 359p. index. (Advances in Medical Technologies and Clinical Practice (AMTCP) Book Series). $195.00 (individual chapters available for purchase in electronic format). ISBN 13: 978-1-52251-043-7; 978-1-52251-044-4 (e-book).

Advancing Medicine through Nanotechnology and Nanomechanics Applications begins to explore the tremendous potential that nanotechnology and nanomechanics represents for medicine and healing. The book begins to explore nanotechnology out of the theoretical and into the practical, and discusses the impact this technology has made on the treatment of diseases, regenerative medicines, and drug delivery systems.

The book is an entry in IGI's Advances in Medical Technologies and Clinical Practices series, which brings together the newest advancements to provide up-to-date medical information to practitioners and researchers alike. Numbering 358 pages and broken down into 11 chapters, the essays in the book are authored by experts in the field and explore the latest developments.

The book starts with the simple premise "What is nanotechnology?" This is a useful contribution for those who may be unfamiliar with the idea of nanotechnology. The book dives further into the issues at hand by exploring chapters with seemingly complicated titles such as "Ion Channels, Nanomechanics, and Nanomedicine." While this chapter title is undoubtedly complicated, a deeper reading of the chapter establishes that the chapter, despite its complicated title, has a practical purpose. Ion channels, for example, are a naturally occurring pore that is found in all living organisms, and allow some ions through them and block others. In doing so, the ions block some helpful healing functions. However, researchers have discovered mechanisms to use nanotechnology to open these ions to advance and hasten healing.

The book, like lots of books on similar subjects, is not easy reading. However, this is not a fatal flaw in the substance of the book: the book is not intended to be easy reading. The material contained in the book is complex by design, but so is the subject matter. The individuals who are likely to be receptive to this work, including researchers, students, and practitioners, are almost certainly familiar with the subject matter at hand. The book is by no means an elementary introduction to the subject matter, but will be a useful resource for medical professionals who are seeking to expand their knowledge of what will be a game changing technology. This book is recommended for academic and medical libraries.—
Sara Mofford

35 Physical Sciences and Mathematics

General Works

Handbooks and Yearbooks

P, S

473.   Cochrane, Rich. **The Secret Life of Equations: The 50 Greatest Equations and How They Work.** New York, Firefly Books, 2016. 192p. illus. maps. index. $24.95pa. ISBN 13: 978-1-77085-808-4.

The introduction sets the tone for this book dedicated to explaining 50 of the greatest equations to nonspecialists and those who might wonder why the equations matter. The introduction includes a table of symbols commonly used in equations and assures readers that this language can be more easily mastered than the English language. The book is divided into four sections: The Shape of Space: Geometry and Number; A Mirror Up to Nature: Science; What Have You Done for Me Lately? Technology; and Known Unknowns: Chance and Uncertainty. These sections include equations that are most likely familiar like Pythagoras's Theorem and others that are less well known to the general public like the Quaternion Rotation and the Navier-Stokes Equation. The author explains each equation in an accessible manner and takes great pains to note an equation's importance. Photographs, illustrations, and other visuals help maintain reader interest. There are also a number of cross-references that allow readers to move quickly between related ideas. This highly recommended book closes with a short, but complete, index.—**ARBA Staff Reviewer**

S

474.   **Gale Interactive: Science. http://www.gale.com/c/interactive-science.** [Website] Farmington Hills, Mich., Gale/Cengage Learning, 2016. Price negotiated by site. Date reviewed: 2016.

Interactive online testing has recently increased the demand for science educators to offer more interactive and virtual science resources, and this database meets this demand and more. Featuring what is termed a 3D Viewer, students are able to see and manipulate models and interactive lessons on a variety of concepts. Students can zoom, rotate, and explore the 3D models, as well as view informational articles on the same topic. The main guided activity areas are divided into topic sections on Biology, Earth Science, and Chemistry, as well as Common Core State and Next Generation Science Standards. Also included is the ability to share lessons directly to teachers' Google Classroom, allowing for ease of access for students. As with all Gale online resources, there are citation tools and downloading options for each activity, as well as the option to download 3D printable models for those schools with access to a 3D printer. Teachers can provide students a link to any activity or individual slide within each interactive lesson, easing the sharing of specific activities especially in blended or flipped classroom environments. Highly recommended, grades 9 and up.—**Angela Wojtecki**

Physical Sciences

Chemistry

Handbooks and Yearbooks

S
475.   Mooney, Carla. Illustrated by Sam Carbaugh. **Chemistry: Investigate the Matter that Makes Up Your World.** White River Junction, Vt., Nomad Press, 2016. 128p. illus. index. $17.95pa. ISBN 13: 978-1-61930-365-2.

    This book, one of the five titles in the "Inquire and Investigate" series from Nomad Press, is a comprehensive introduction to chemistry. Chapter headings include an introduction, atoms and the periodic table, states of matter, compounds, mixtures and solutions, chemical reactions, acids and bases, nucleus and radioactivity, and other branches of chemistry. It also includes QR codes to discover more on the subject and for pertinent additional information including primary sources and videos, which will appeal to the intended audience. Included are simple experiments with supply lists, comic strips, and cartoon illustrations in side bars, but no actual photographs. This is a unique reference resource for upper elementary through high school students that want to learn more about the subject. The book also includes a glossary, index, and timeline. Recommended.—**Kay E. Evey**

C, P, S
476.   **Periodic Table of Elements: LANL. http://periodic.lanl.gov/chem.shtml.** [Website] Free. Date reviewed: 2017.

    The Los Alamos National Laboratory developed this freely available database as a service to the public. The simply designed home page offers several main links: About the Resource, About the Periodic Table, How to Use, Characterizing the Elements, Chemical Properties, Elements List, and Periodic Table Downloads. The information discoverable by clicking on these tabs is geared toward those unfamiliar with the periodic table. So, for example, when the information under How to Use is accessed, users will find straightforward explanations of atomic number, atomic symbol, standard atomic weight, electron configuration, and atomic radius (this last term has external links for those wanting more information). Characterizing the Elements provides a basic explanation for how elements are classified as metals or nonmetals, while Chemical Properties provides basic definitions for an atom, subatomic particle, nucleus, electron, and chemical bonding. The

Elements link takes users to the heart of the site. Here each element is listed in alphabetic order; a click on the element name pops up basic information like atomic number, boiling point, atomic radius, etc., along with a history of the element's discovery, the production and properties of the element, isotopes, uses, and handling instructions where necessary (as in the case of Polonium). Some of these element descriptions are enhanced by illustrations. Radium, for instance, features a black-and-white picture of Madame Currie, the scientist who first discovered it.

In addition to the periodic table, the site provides links to outside resources like the American Chemical Society and the *CRC Handbook of Chemistry and Physics* (subscription required) along with links to current chemistry news.

Highly recommended to school and public libraries.—**ARBA Staff Reviewer**

C

477.   **Principles of Chemistry.** Donald R. Franceschetti, ed. Hackensack, N.J., Salem Press, 2016. 462p. illus. index. (Principles of Science series). $165.00. ISBN 13: 978-1-61925-501-2; 978-1-61925-502-9 (e-book).

The American Chemical Society (ACS) has referred to chemistry as "central science" due to its focal role in bridging the physical and life sciences. This resource introduces students and researchers to the fundamentals of chemistry using plain languages, illustrations, equations, and sample problems. This reference book is recommended to audiences from lower-level undergraduate students to professors. There are 128 entries in an A to Z order that is easy to browse by the topic of interest. The topics cover a broad range of chemistry including biochemistry, organic and inorganic chemistry, physical chemistry, and geochemistry. Each entry includes a brief summary of the topic, principle terms that are crucial to understanding the concepts presented, illustrations such as diagrams and charts for chemical structures or reactions, equations, sample problems, and an up-to-date bibliography at the end. These entries are written by experts in each field and their names and affiliations are noted at the end of each entry. In addition to the entries, the book's appendixes are valuable resources too. They include the periodic table with an introduction to the history of the table and information on atomic weights, an introduction to the Nobel Prize and its winners in chemistry, a glossary, a general bibliography, and a subject index. This reference book is part of the Principles of series from Salem Press, which also includes titles on physics, astronomy, and computer science.—**Tina Qin**

P, S

478.   Still, Ben. **The Secret Life of the Periodic Table: Unlocking the Mysteries of All 118 Elements.** New York, Firefly Books, 2016. 192p. illus. index. $24.95pa. ISBN 13: 978-1-77085-810-7.

The book starts with a brief but informative look at the discovery of elements and the development of the periodic table from the alchemists, to seventeenth- and eighteenth-century scientists, to Dimitri Mendeleev's ordering and classifying of the elements in the periodic table. This is followed by short chapters on atomic physics, the quantum atom, trends and patterns in the periodic table, and a two-page Trends Table. The majority of the book is devoted to the elements themselves, starting with Hydrogen and ending with the last element (as of 2016), Ununoctium, element number 118. Most elements have one or two pages of text, and a shaded text box that includes: atomic number, atomic weight, abundance, radius, melting point, boiling, configuration, and discovery information. Starting with element 98, Californium, descriptions do not include the text box. Other descriptions can include information about uses for individual elements, special characteristics of the elements, and/or historical tales about an element's discovery. These descriptions are enhanced by color photos, figures, or more.

This readable and informative book, which is modestly priced, is recommended to school and public libraries.—**ARBA Staff Reviewer**

C, P, S
479.   **WebElements Periodic Table of the Elements. https://www.webelements.com/.** [Website] Free. Date reviewed: 2017.

Hosted by Professor Mark Winter, University of Sheffield, United Kingdom, *WebElements* offers free and easy access to the periodic table of elements, a visualized organization of all known chemical elements such as oxygen, uranium, or aluminum. The home page is, in fact, the periodic table, by which elements are arranged by group and period. Users can access more detail by either clicking on an element within the table or by clicking on a topic (such as History or Atoms) from the menu above the table. Clicking on the element itself leads to a generous description of the element, including historical information, element properties, and more. Particular points are bulleted, such as atomic number, symbol, color, classification, and other technical information. Users who choose to click on the menu bar will go directly to their chosen topic within the element's broader description (e.g., the Physics tab leads users to information regarding the physical attributes of an element based on several scientific scales). Supplementary features include photographs, audio recordings (pronunciation and facts), and more. The site's navigable structure makes it ideal for secondary school students but the depth and detail of the content make it suitable for more advanced students as well.—**ARBA Staff Reviewer**

Earth and Planetary Sciences

Climatology and Meteorology

C
480.   **Examining the Role of Environmental Change on Emerging Infectious Diseases and Pandemics.** Maha Bouzid, ed. Hershey, Pa., Information Science Reference/IGI Global, 2017. 327p. index. (Advances in Human Services and Public Health (AHSPH) Book Series). $200.00 (individual chapters available for purchase in electronic format). ISBN 13: 978-1-52250-553-2; 978-1-52250-554-9 (e-book).

The Advances in Human Services and Public Health (AHSPH) book series provides up-to-the-minute discussion and analysis of the most pressing social and health-related issues of the day. This volume targets its discussion on the hot-button issue of environmental change and its relation to the global development of infectious diseases and how we approach them.

Ten chapters gather the work of a number of scholars and professionals from a variety of fields for a multifaceted approach to the broader topic. Specifically, essays work to connect climate change and its many impacts to the emergence and resurgence of diseases such as malaria, ebola, and zika in addition to the expanding menu of waterborne pathogens and other diseases. The chapter titled "Climate Change-Associated Conflict and Infectious Disease," for example, examines the violent conflict that arises when natural resources diminish (due to climate change) and how this conflict creates conditions (such as forced migration, starvation, sexual assault, etc.) ripe for the spread of disease. Chapters also look at specific regions (South America, Morocco, etc.), policy, community response, specific health impacts, and much more.

Chapters are clearly organized and provide solid background and thorough analysis. Several essays in this volume present case studies, such as "Rift Valley Fever and the Changing Environment: A Case Study in East Africa." Many also offer definitions, summaries, tables, and maps. End pages compile each chapter's references, offer brief contributor biographies, and include an index.

This timely volume would be very useful for medical professionals, policy-makers, environmentalists, researchers, and many others.

Recommended for academic libraries.—**ARBA Staff Reviewer**

C, P, S

481. **Global Climate Change. http://climate.nasa.gov/.** [Website] Free. Date reviewed: 2017.

This site aims to facilitate the global climate change discussion via eye-opening statistics, compelling narrative, and striking visuals. Both the information and the design of the site truly extol the work of the National Aeronautics and Space Agency, whose extensive climate research and cutting-edge technology is made accessible throughout this easily navigable database.

From the bottom of the homepage, users can scroll through a number of significant (and somewhat alarming) statistics regarding land ice reduction, sea level, global temperature, and much more. They can then simply click on a selection of tabs at the top to discover the site's contents. Facts leads to a number of pages showcasing the basic realities about climate change, how evidence is gathered, causes, effects, and scientific consensus, among other topics. This section includes a generous use of graphs, charts, videos, and other information. Articles hosts archived and current news and feature stories on NASA and climate, topical blog posts, links to other climate science sites, and more. Solutions describe current approaches to dealing with the effects of climate change, like technological innovations, public education, and government policies. And Explore allows users to access interactives such as quizzes or maps, galleries of stunning photographs, climate related apps, and videos.

This website would be highly valuable to a classroom, and is a must stop for a range of users interested in earth science, from young students to seasoned environmentalists and many in between.—**ARBA Staff Reviewer**

Oceanography

C

482. **Oceanographic and Marine Cross-Domain Data Management for Sustainable Development.** Paolo Diviacco, Adam Leadbetter, and Helen Glaves, eds. Hershey,

Pa., Information Science Reference/IGI Global, 2017. 425p. index. (Advances in Environmental Engineering and Green Technologies (AEEGT) Book Series). $205.00 (individual chapters available for purchase in electronic format). ISBN 13: 978-1-52250-700-0; 978-1-52250-701-7 (e-book).

This volume from the Advances in Environmental Engineering and Green Technologies Book Series addresses best practices for managing oceanographic and marine cross-domain data with the goal of supporting sustainable development. The theoretical first section contains such chapters as "Developing a Common Global Framework for Marine Data Management" and "Documenting Provenance for Reproducible Marine Ecosystem Assessment in Open Science." The second section, Technologies, presents such chapters as "Repositioning Data Management Near Data Acquisition" and "Interoperability in Marine Sensor Networks through SWE Services: The RITMARE Experience." The last section of the book presents case studies in chapters like "Data and Operational Oceanography: A Review in Support of Responsible Fisheries and Aquaculture."

A table of contents and a detailed table of contents are included in the front matter along with an extensive preface that contextualizes the research and makes clear the aims of the book. Chapters include abstracts, subheadings, extensive references, and key terms and definitions. The book concludes with a compilation of references, information about the contributors (who are mostly from Europe and North America), and an index. Black-and-white figures are used throughout the text. The book's structure makes it possible to find a particular topic, and it is possible to purchase individual chapters electronically. Despite its technical nature, the book is quite readable.

Recommended for academic libraries.—**ARBA Staff Reviewer**

Paleontology

P, S
483.   Parker, Steve. **Dinosaurs: The Complete Guide to Dinosaurs.** 2d ed. New York, Firefly Books, 2016. 320p. illus. maps. index. $29.95pa. ISBN 13: 978-1-77085-776-6.

Dinosaur information is fascinating to all, no matter the age. This second edition reflects the changes in dinosaur knowledge in the past 13 years. The introduction of this engaging book includes a timeline from the Cambrian to the Quaternary periods. Clear chapter titles include the following topic areas: land conquerors, early dinosaurs, small meat-eaters, great predators, ostrich dinosaurs, large dinosaurs, bird-footed dinosaurs, duckbills, boneheads, other creatures, and armored, plated, and horned dinosaurs. Chapter fourteen, the final chapter, explores life after dinosaur extinction. An index provides ease of access to Greek and Latin dinosaur names while the glossary proves extremely useful. The book's concluding picture credits and acknowledgements may be useful to those who are curious about the plethora of visual content. Each chapter is introduced with color coding that will be found in each animal or dinosaur "Factfile." Color-coded "Factfiles" include: name meaning, pronunciation, period, main group, length, weight, diet, and location of finds. Each creature has at least one page of content and cutting-edge information in this fast-paced field makes this book extremely relevant. Controversy and conjecture is rooted in ongoing discoveries. Having the latest information on this evolving piece of earth science coupled with exceptional design make this book essential for all ages. Each discovery described here is one more piece in understanding the evolution of earth events and prehistoric creatures.

Terminology will be over the heads of emergent and early readers, but fantastic full-color images, photographs, maps, and other relevant images will engage the youngest of students. The quest for information continues as author Steve Parker reminds readers of the continuing need for more research and that the reasons for the total extinction of dinosaurs are hotly debated. Such open-ended conversation encourages future scientists and other dinosaur aficionados to dig deeper.

This is an excellent catalog of current dinosaur knowledge with engaging visuals. Public, school, and special librarians will want to have this in their collection, both for pleasure and for research purposes. This is a worthy addition to personal libraries as well.

Highly recommended.—**Janis Minshull**

C, P

484. Paul, Gregory S. **The Princeton Field Guide to Dinosaurs.** Princeton, N.J., Princeton University Press, 2016. 361p. illus. index. (Princeton Field Guides). $35.00. ISBN 13: 978-0-691-16766-4; 978-1-400-88314-1 (e-book).

This wonderfully priced volume updates and expands the first edition published in 2010 (see ARBA 2011, entry 1373). About 100 new species are included, as are almost 200 new or reworked illustrations, many of which depict skeletons of the animals in great detail. The 60-page introduction discusses many useful topics, including biology, behavior, growth, and where dinosaurs have been found. In the main section of the book, dinosaurs are presented in three major groups—theropods, sauropodomorphs, and ornithischians—then arranged down to the genus and species level. Information on each dinosaur includes length, weight, the nature of their habitat, fossil remains, and where they have been found.

This book is clearly aimed at an advanced readership. Young fans of dinosaurs will find the language here too complex for easy understanding; terms like "gastralia" and "lunate carpal" escaped this reviewer! Libraries with adult patrons interested in the topic will find this volume useful; public and academic libraries should certainly consider adding it to their collections.—**Mark Schumacher**

36 Resource Sciences

Energy

Biography

C, P

485.   Desmond, Kevin. **Innovators in Battery Technology: Profiles of 93 Influential Electrochemists.** Jefferson, N.C., McFarland, 2016. 271p. illus. index. $45.00pa. ISBN 13: 978-0-7864-9933-5; 978-1-4766-2278-1 (e-book).

This specialized volume explores the development of batteries over the last 270 years through biographies of the scientists who made the advances in this field. From Benjamin Franklin, born in 1706, to Ann Marie Sastry, born in 1967, these one-to-eight-page sketches present a holistic view of these lives, incorporating personal elements such as family relations and hobbies, as well as scientific achievements. While several figures in this collection are fairly well known, such as Franklin, Thomas Edison, Alessandro Volta, and Humphry Davy, most will be familiar to a small audience in the electrochemistry field.

For students and scholars of the history of battery technology, this will be a useful resource to consult. Academic and special libraries with patrons working in this area should consider adding this volume to their collections.—**Mark Schumacher**

Handbooks and Yearbooks

C, P, S

486.   **Energy In Context.** Brenda Wilmoth Lerner, K. Lee Lerner, and Thomas Riggs, eds. Farmington Hills, Mich., Gale/Cengage Learning, 2016. 2v. illus. maps. index. $344.00/set. ISBN 13: 978-1-4103-1748-3; 978-1-4103-1751-3 (e-book).

Energy In Context is a well-organized and well-written resource that provides a good overview of energy topics. Part of the In Context series from Gale, the 224 articles in this two-volume set cover a wide variety of topics from the science of energy, to the different types of traditional energy resources, to alternative/renewable energy resources. The coverage does not stop there, as major regulations, major corporate players, government agencies, and more are also discussed.

Articles are well written without being overly technical; thus, this resource can serve as a starting point for someone wanting to learn more about energy science or a specific energy source like biofuels. The article style is consistent; each article has the same basic format including an introduction to the topic, background information, and a discussion of the impacts and issues for the topic. Articles also include a "Words to Know" box, defining key terms, and a bibliography. Depending on the topic, articles may also include citations to important primary sources and an "In Context" sidebar providing more explanation. *Energy In Context* is richly illustrated with numerous color photos, figures, and illustrations.

The overall structure of this resource makes it very easy for users to find what they need. A table of contents for the whole set is found in each volume and articles are arranged alphabetically. Each volume contains a glossary of important energy-related terms, as well as an historical chronology of important events related to energy. Volume two contains a very detailed index making it easy to find any mention of a specific concept in either volume. Lists of sources consulted and selected organizations and advocacy groups are also included in volume two, providing researchers with additional avenues to explore.

Energy In Context is an excellent resource for high school students, community college students, and public library patrons wishing to learn more about different forms of energy, use and regulation, environmental impact, and more.—**Theresa Calcagno**

Environmental Science

Dictionaries and Encyclopedias

C, P, S
487.   Dauvergne, Peter. **Historical Dictionary of Environmentalism.** 2d ed. Lanham, Md., Rowman & Littlefield, 2016. 317p. (Historical Dictionaries of Religions, Philosophies, and Movements). $100.00; $99.99 (e-book). ISBN 13: 978-1-4422-6960-6; 978-1-4422-6961-3 (e-book).

The second edition of this book provides details on the history and current directions of the environmental movement and environmentalism. The dictionary itself takes up about two-thirds of the content, and encompasses people, places, concepts, topics, and important events and conferences. Extensive cross-referencing is indicated by bold face to other entries and related terms. The other one-third of the content is comprised of a large and detailed bibliography divided into over 60 subtopics of specificity, along with a number of Internet resources; a preface discusses three trends on this topic in the last decade (climate change, a proactive assertive shift by multinational corporations regarding environmentalism, and the embrace by businesses and markets as a "solution" for global environmental challenges); a section on numerous acronyms and abbreviations used throughout the book; a historical chronology on the topic from 1601 to the present; and an introduction that provides background information on subtopics such as scholarly environmentalism, governmental environmentalism, nongovernmental environmentalism, corporate environmentalism, and the future of environmentalism. Overall, this is an excellent reference and resource guide on this topic, and I highly recommend it as part of the Historical Dictionaries of Religions, Philosophies, and Movements series.—**Bradford Lee Eden**

Handbooks and Yearbooks

C

488.   **Applying Nanotechnology for Environmental Sustainability.** Sung Hee Joo, ed. Hershey, Pa., Information Science Reference/IGI Global, 2017. 558p. index. (Advances in Environmental Engineering and Green Technologies (AEEGT) Book Series). $225.00 (individual chapters available for purchase in electronic format). ISBN 13: 978-1-52250-585-3; 978-1-52250-586-0 (e-book).

Applying Nanotechnology for Environmental Sustainability is the latest entry in IGI Global's series on Advances in Environmental and Green Technologies. The aim of the series is to use advances in technology as a conduit for positive change to promote sustainable green initiatives.

Nanomaterials have emerged as a key ingredient in consumer products, textile production, and biomedicine. These materials, while widely embraced by industry as an efficient and cost effective material for use as a material component, have not been appropriately vetted for safety, toxicity, transportation, and removal concerns. To ensure that the materials are being handled safely, it is important that the materials are properly vetted and researched through a uniquely environmental, rather than a for-profit, lens. This unique worldview to exploring an emerging field is one that is explored in the book, and is profoundly useful for two reasons: the research explored in the book is exemplary, and the research represents a precious small amount of scholarly research on an important topic.

The book numbers over 550 pages, and is broken down into 17 chapters. The chapters, written by scholars in the field, include entries from the basic ("What is Nanotechnology?") entries to the more complex "Assessment of Advanced Biological Solid Waste Treatment Technologies for Sustainability."

There is no doubt that this book is written at a high level and requires a certain amount of complex understanding to tackle. It goes without saying that this work is not light reading; however, its target audience is not the individual seeking light reading. The book may most properly be viewed as a response to a problem: nanotechnologies are an emerging and underexplored area of study, especially as it relates to their impact on our environment. While nanotechnologies may represent an exciting advancement for both industry and end consumers, they must be explored through an environmental lens to ensure that the environment is protected and properly preserved. This book begins to start that conversation, and should be viewed as a welcome addition to communal learning and knowledge. This book is recommended for academic libraries.—**Sara Mofford**

C, P, S

489.   **EcoWest. http://ecowest.org/.** [Website] Free. Date reviewed: 2017.

This free website is dedicated to sharing environmental issue and trend data particularly attuned to the Western region of the United States, including Arizona, California, Colorado, Idaho, Montana, Nevada, Oregon, Utah, Washington, and Wyoming. Users can access data and commentary related to issues such as drought, wildfires, and water supply.

Users can also search broad categories such as Biodiversity, Climate, or Land from the menu bar at the top of the page, and can access these and additional subcategories (Ozone, Wilderness, Conservation, etc.) by scrolling down through a listing on the right side of the page. Clicking on the categories leads to textual summaries and visualizations (charts, graphs, etc.) of applicable data trends. For example, clicking on Greenhouse Gases (GHG) leads to charts noting state-by-state origins of GHG, Carbon Flow diagrams, and more in addition to summary interpretation of the data. Users are able to download slides, notes, and data, and will see bulleted summaries of the various topics as well.

Users can connect with the information on this site through a good variety of social media platforms, such as Facebook, Twitter, and Pinterest. The focus of this site, enhanced by straightforward navigation, makes it highly appealing to secondary and advanced students, educators, researchers, public agencies, and many others.—**ARBA Staff Reviewer**

C, P, S

490.   **John Muir Exhibit. http://vault.sierraclub.org/john_muir_exhibit/.** [Website] Free. Date reviewed: 2017.

This page of the greater Sierra Club site is focused entirely on its founder, John Muir, whose devotion to the wilderness of the Sierra Nevada earned him the sobriquet "Father of the National Parks."

The abundance of material on this site truly reflects the achievement of the man. From this page, users can choose from an ample variety of links, such as a Chronology of the Life and Legacy of John Muir, Current and Upcoming Events celebrating Muir (note: the calendar has not been updated for the current year 2017), Tributes, or a Geography of John Muir. The Writings link will appeal to researchers looking for core Muir material such as his many articles, letters, downloadable (HTML) text of his books, and much more. Some of this information is also accessible via the menu tabs at the top of the page.

Users will find many resources specifically designed for educators and students of many ages, such as puzzles, activities, audio, and video. Users can even volunteer to assist with the transcription of Muir's many journals.

Additional touches, like photographs, and the John Muir Quote of the Day contribute to the appeal of the site, which would interest nature lovers and conservationists, among many others.—**ARBA Staff Reviewer**

C, P, S

491.   **Mapping Ocean Wealth. http://oceanwealth.org/resources/atlas-of-ocean-wealth/.** [Website] Free. Date reviewed: 2016.

This is a freely available database under the direction of The Nature Conservancy with the collaboration of scientists, policy practitioners, and financial experts. *Mapping Ocean Wealth* strives to provide scientific and mapping data about the health and wealth of the world's oceans in order for stakeholders to make better-informed decisions.

The site provides extensive information organized under several tabs on the home page: About, Ecosystem Services, Our Work, Resources, Tools, and Mapping Portal. There are several avenues for further information under each tab. Under the Ecosystem Services umbrella, for instance, one can choose from a variety of further such topics as coastal protection, fisheries, and recreation and tourism. The Resources tab takes users to links for the *Atlas of Ocean Wealth,* with expert essays, color photographs, and dozens of color maps. The Resources tab also links to infographics, a spotlight section (updated regularly) with interesting articles, and materials in the research library.

Highly recommended for students, teachers, policy-makers, and anyone interested in the wealth and health of the oceans.—**ARBA Staff Reviewer**

C, P, S

492.   **State of Global Air. https://www.stateofglobalair.org/.** [Website] Free. Date reviewed: 2017.

This project from the Health Effects Institute, the Institute for Health Metrics and Evaluation, and the University of British Columbia acts as an interactive and educational hub for current data on air quality and its effects on health across the globe. The site offers access to downloadable data and a report regarding a number of air quality measures, provides explanations of common air quality terminology and processes, and links air quality to the health and well-being of the global population. Users can select one of four tabs from the header bar. How Clean is Your Air? uses maps, graphs, and brief essays to establish the state of global air quality related to ozone and fine particulate matter levels. Impact on Your Health uses a similar structure to explain the connection between air quality and specific health concerns and trends throughout the world, such as the growing number of COPD (Chronic Obstructive Pulmonary Disease) deaths. Explore the Data allows users to customize air quality data in a number of ways, such as creating health impact maps or country-specific, population-weighted ozone measurements. Read the Report melds air quality and health data (from 2015) to provide a detailed overview of recent trends and issues. The site's mix of straightforward narrative and comprehensible data make it valuable to a broad range of academic (high school +) users and to educators, policy-makers, and advocates, among many others.—**ARBA Staff Reviewer**

C

493.   **Toxicity and Waste Management Using Bioremediation.** Ashok K. Rathoure and Vinod K. Dhatwalia, eds. Hershey, Pa., IGI Global, 2016. 421p. index. (Advances in Environmental Engineering and Green Technologies (AEEGT) Book Series). $205.00 (individual chapters available for purchase in electronic format). ISBN 13: 978-1-4666-9734-8; 978-1-4666-9735-5 (e-book).

We have known about bioremediation for three decades, but serious attempts to implement it are more recent, and generally only considered as viable options under extreme conditions. As pressures to keep our environment clean increase, so will the need to turn to bioremediation to aid in this effort. The promise of this technology is that it is low cost and more benign than some of the other techniques used today. However, bioremediation is not without significant challenges—not just technical ones, but social and cultural ones too. This work does address some of the major technical challenges when comparing the various methodologies (including conventional ones) available to keep our environment clean.

This work is a collection of 15 papers outlining specific areas where bioremediation can be used. Three chapters concentrate on using these techniques to combat heavy metal pollution. Sources of heavy metal contamination, methods to chelate and dispose of heavy metals, and challenges with the various proposed processes are discussed. A chapter is devoted to microbial response to heavy metal toxicity. Similarly, another three chapters are devoted to removing dye molecules. Other chapters discuss specialized methods of treating waste. These include genetically engineered microbes and plants, using spent mushroom substrates, and others. The remaining chapters address topics of interest such as biodegradation of phenol, novel bioremediation techniques, treatment of wastewater, and biotech networks.

Bioremediation is a multidiscipline field, and this work addresses all of the most important scientific disciplines that contribute to successful bioremedial efforts. The social and economic aspects are mentioned, but an in-depth discussion in the nontechnical aspects of bioremediation is beyond the scope of this work. A strength of this work is that virtually every chapter provides a case study along with its specific nuances to illustrate the topic under discussion. When applying similar methods to other applications, the practitioner's challenge would be decoupling those aspects of bioremediation specific to the case study and recognizing the nuances inherent to his/her situation. The book is useful for technical people either considering or working on bioremediation projects.—**Muhammed Hassanali**

Water

Handbooks and Yearbooks

C, P

494. **Water Planet: The Culture, Politics, Economics, and Sustainability of Water on Earth.** Camille Gaskin-Reyes, ed. Santa Barbara, Calif., ABC-CLIO, 2016. 450p. illus. index. $89.00. ISBN 13: 978-1-4408-3816-3; 978-1-4408-3817-0 (e-book).

This volume provides an excellent starting point for discussion of, and research into, issues around water. It looks at water's function as sustenance, an agricultural necessity, and a transportation tool, along with its integral role in exploration, ecological change, human settlement, and conflict. Through additional themes related to gender, culture, and energy, it does its best to emphasize "the role of water in everyday existence." The volume's focus is impressively broad, in time, location, and topic; it is not overly U.S.-centric. The bibliographies that follow each section are particularly worth note, as they provide an excellent range of documents, including journal articles, monographs, governmental and NGO reports, and more. Documents, References, and Case Studies sections present facts and background as a basis for encouraging more research, while Perspectives sections offer opposing views on relevant topics.

While this title may not have a vital role as a reference tool, it is clearly valuable, particularly for high school and undergraduate libraries. Students will discover new topics regarding water on every page, and this volume will be useful in helping researchers get an excellent start on projects associated with water, its policies, and its impacts.—**Peter H. McCracken**

37 Transportation

General Works

Handbooks and Yearbooks

C, P, S

495. Graham, Ian. **Fifty Ships That Changed the Course of History: A Nautical History of the World.** New York, Firefly Books, 2016. 224p. illus. maps. index. $29.95. ISBN 13: 978-1-77085-719-3.

These are great ship histories: the vessel and its technology may be fascinating, but how people use the ship, and how their actions impact the rest of the world, is far more important. In choosing 50 ships to tell the "nautical history of the world," Ian Graham made some tough choices. From a 4,600-year-old Egyptian barge to the latest massive cruise ship, Graham presents a bit about the ship and its impact on humanity over each four-page spread (five ships get six pages each). Graham's additional stories, like those about the *USS Missouri* just barely squeezing through the Panama Canal in 1945, or the earliest circumnavigators being confused by their lost day in transit, are genuine treats. Many brief entries on related ships ensure the volume describes more than 100 vessels.

Of the fifty main entries, 17 are American, 15 are British, 13 are other European, and five are from the rest of the world. One can argue about missing vessels, but choosing the ones to be replaced would be difficult indeed. You may not know of *Ideal X,* for example, but its role as the first practical container ship certainly guarantees it a spot here.

This is a great volume to introduce readers to ships. Reference may not be its proper home, but general stacks in middle school through undergraduate, plus public libraries, will certainly find it appropriate.—**Peter H. McCracken**

P

496. Grey, Paula. **A History of Travel in 50 Vehicles.** Thomaston, Maine, Tilbury House Publishers, 2016. 269p. index. $24.95. ISBN 13: 978-0-88448-399-1; 978-088448-491-2 (e-book).

This book offers an engaging examination of human travel through the ages. The book is one in the clever History in 50 series which concisely connects centuries of civilization via a particular theme.

Each chapter in this book represents a point on the timeline of travel, opening with the story of basic foot travel and culminating 49 chapters later with the story of the Segway. Chapters are relatively brief, but contain a host of interesting details and facts. The chapter on dogsleds, for example, explains why dogs were so well suited to this mode of transportation, where dogsleds were historically used, how dogsleds are designed, and much more. Topics within the book range from the common bicycle to the more unexpected aerial lift.

Chapters are arranged in a chronological fashion, although the timeline is general. The consistent use of color illustrations and shaded text boxes holding further topical detail enhance each chapter. Supplementary material at the book's close includes a glossary, a chapter-by-chapter list of sources and additional resources, extensive endnotes, and an index.

While not delving too deeply into its topics, the book manages to both inform and entertain readers and can certainly pique their interest in further research.—**ARBA Staff Reviewer**

C, P, S

497.   **National Transportation Statistics. https://www.rita.dot.gov/bts/sites/rita.dot. gov.bts/files/publications/national_transportation_statistics/index.html.**   [Website] Free. Date reviewed: 2017.

This page from the Bureau of Transportation Statistics provides online access to a report (updated quarterly) detailing wide-ranging information on the U.S. transportation system. Simply structured, the page displays the report's table of contents, wherein each chapter's data tables may be accessed and downloaded in a variety of formats. The full report, last updated in October of 2016, may also be downloaded as a PDF. Chapters are as follows: "The Transportation System," "Transportation Safety," "Transportation and the Economy," and "Transportation, Energy and the Environment." Data within these chapters includes number of U.S. airports, condition of rail transit infrastructure, worldwide commercial space launches, price trends of gasoline versus other consumer goods and services, and much, much more. Five appendixes offer such aids as metric conversion tables, a glossary, and a list of acronyms and initialisms. For users looking for the numbers and trends regarding transportation in the United States, this site is the place to visit.—**ARBA Staff Reviewer**

C, P, S

498.   **World Shipping Council. http://www.worldshipping.org/.** [Website] Free. Date reviewed: 2017.

This site is freely accessible and sponsored by World Shipping Council (WSC) members whose companies account for 90% of the global liner ship capacity and 60% of the value of global seaborne trade.

Though designed to provide a coordinated voice for the shipping liner industry, there is nevertheless much valuable free information. From the home page, users can choose from a variety of links: About the Industry, Benefits of Liner Shipping, Industry Issues, Public Statements, Additional Resources, and About the Council. The top of the page also links users to the Press Room (media contacts and inquiries), Contact Us, and the Image Gallery, which offers dozens of downloadable photos of ships, containers, ports and terminals, and trucks and trains. Under Additional Resources, users can learn more about the international organizations with which the WSC works (these include the EU and U.S. government organizations). There is also a link to Educational Resources developed by the

WSC and shipping industry for use with kids. One link is to the BBC project, "The Box." "The Box" followed a shipping container for year to tell the story of globalization and the world economy. There are also sophisticated presentations on the Suez and Panama canals, which users can download. Though told from the perspective of the shipping industry, researchers can get a least one side of debates over environmental, security, and safety concerns under the Industry Issues tab. There is also plenty of raw data under Public Statement; for example, there are links to speeches made by WSC members, WSC testimony before the U.S. Congress, and a 2014 update to the WSC survey of containers lost overboard. Under About the Council, users will find further links to the history of the WSC, member companies, board members, and council management.—**ARBA Staff Reviewer**

Author/Title Index

Reference is to entry number.

Subject Index

Reference is to entry number.